I0818479

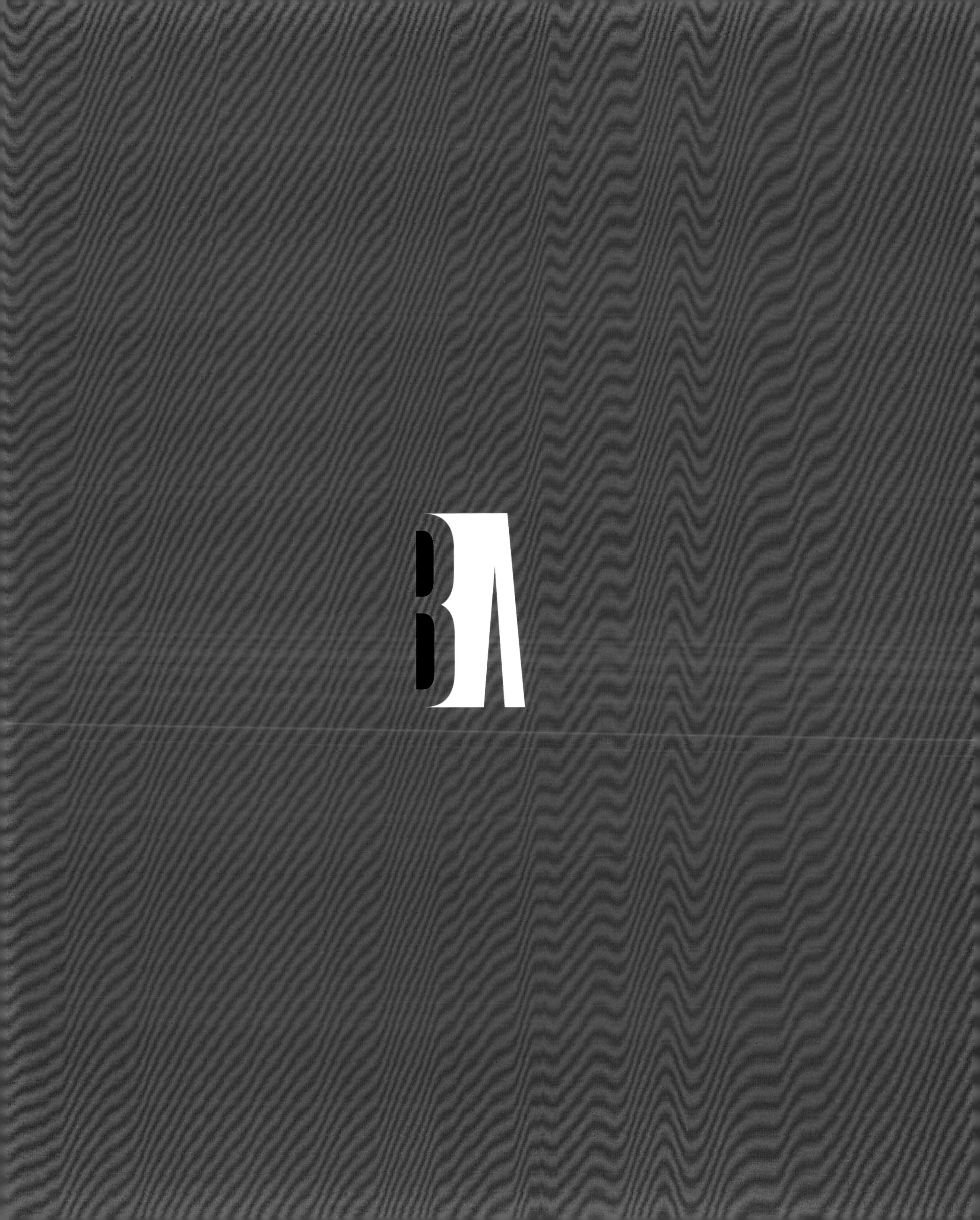

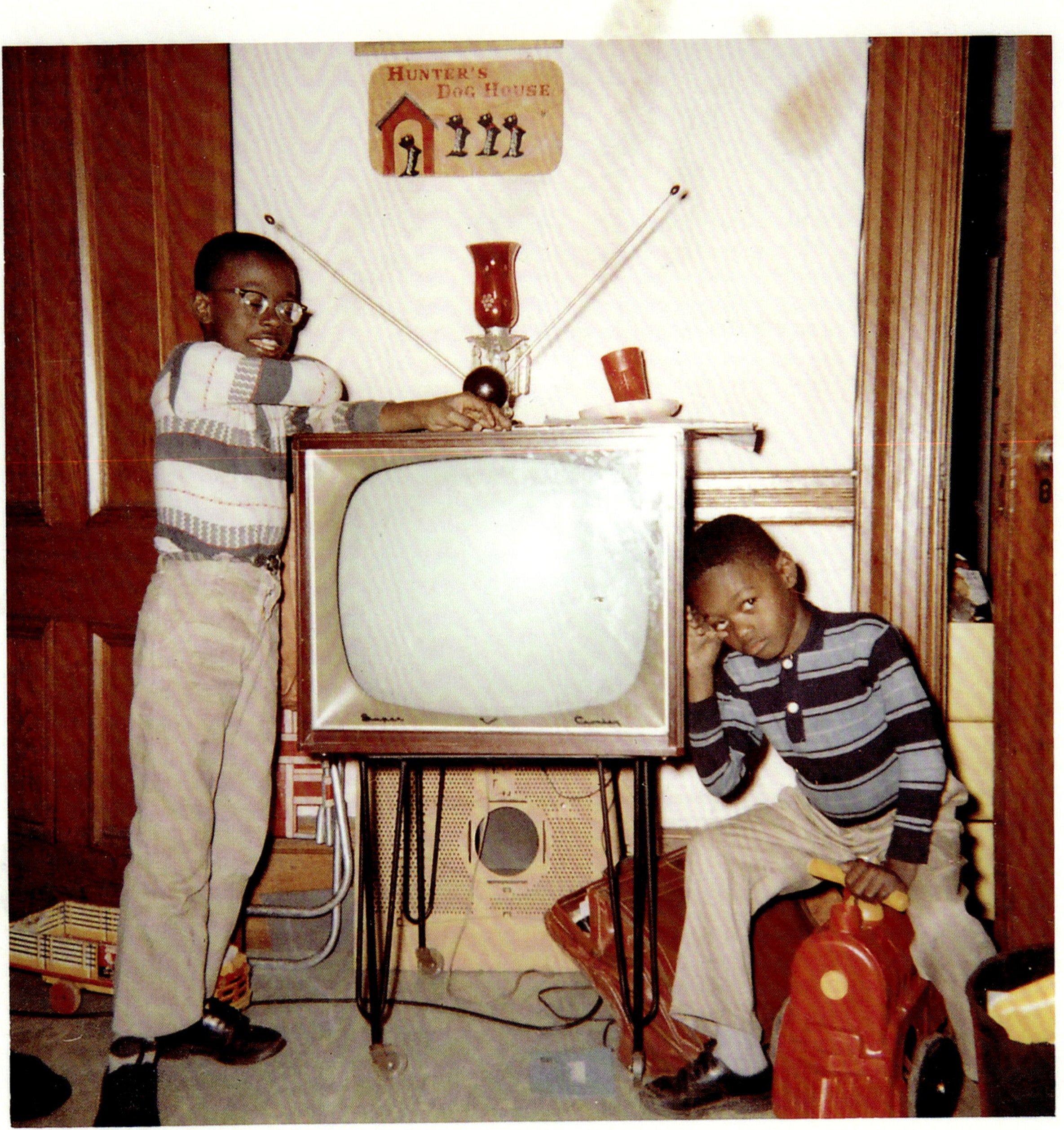
HUNTER'S
DOG HOUSE

BLACK ARCHIVES

A PHOTOGRAPHIC CELEBRATION OF BLACK LIFE

RENATA CHERLISE

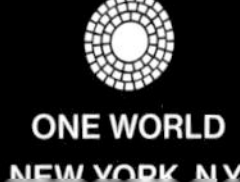
ONE WORLD
NEW YORK, NY

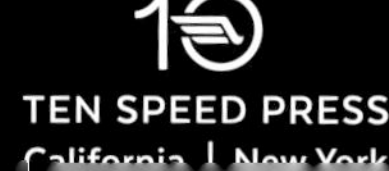
TEN SPEED PRESS
California | New York

PART I

THE FOUNDATION: KEEPER OF STORIES

PART II

INTERIORS: HOLDING SPACE AND KEEPING TIME

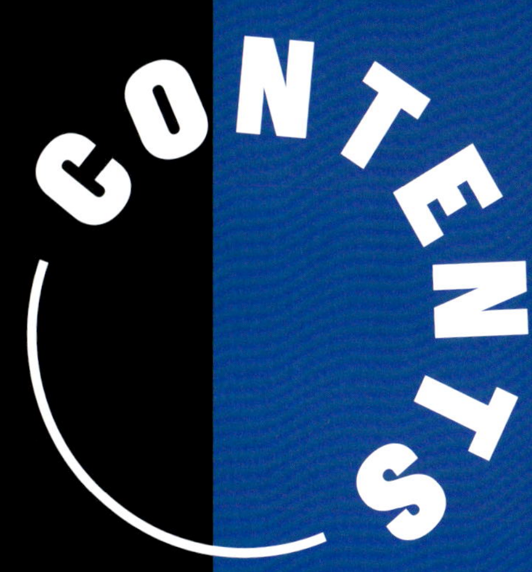

PART III

EXTERIORS: TO BE WITNESSED

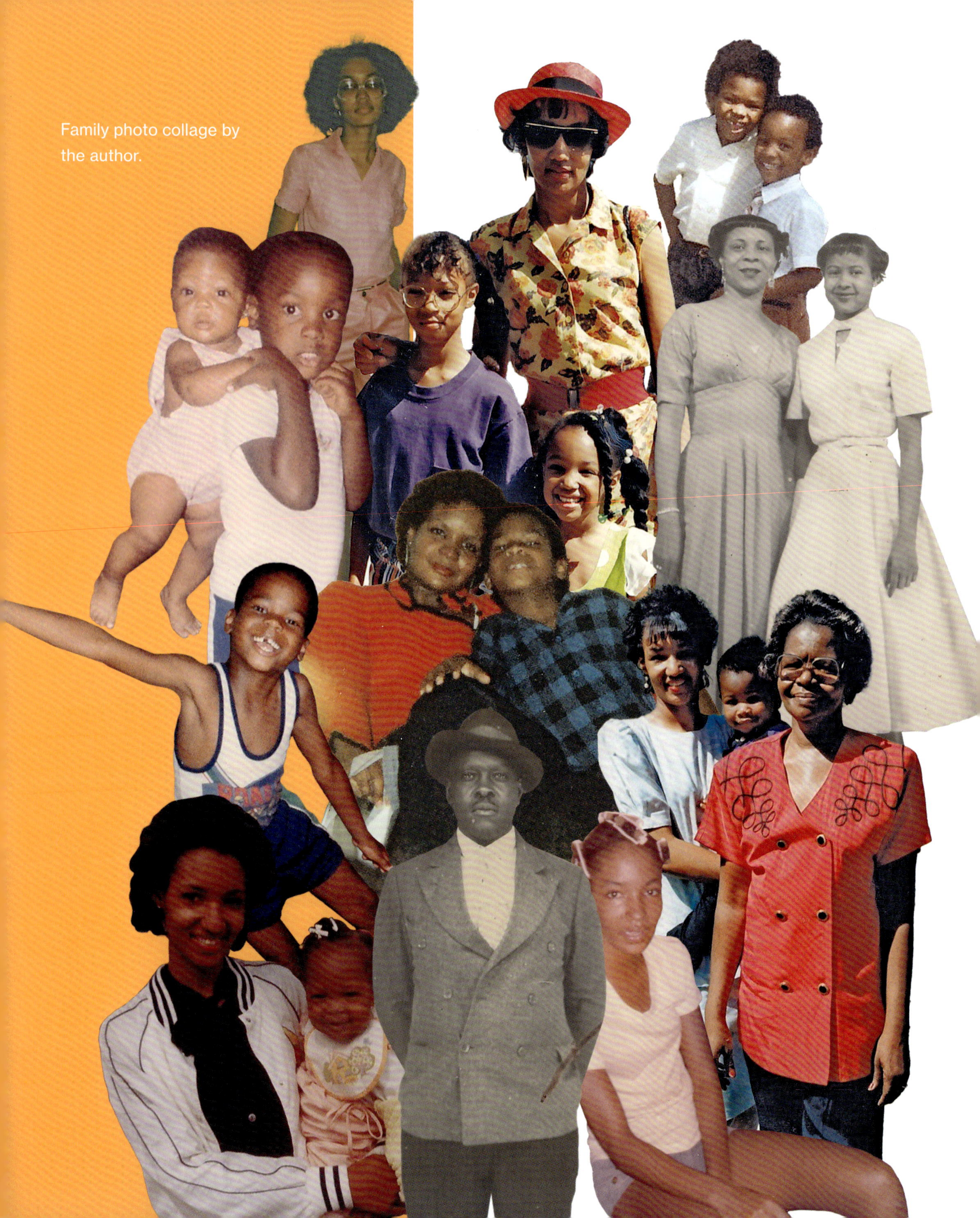

Family photo collage by the author.

INTRODUCTION

To meditate on a name, a face, or the sound of someone's laughter is an intentional act of remembering, or an attempt to resist forgetting. Remembering, or being reminded of, helps to rework our understanding of our identity by giving us insight into the people and places that shape us. Through photography, particularly family pictures and snapshots, we get a better sense of our people, our histories, and our stories – we are able to add to, or cultivate, a language for the parts of our lives that cannot be fully known, even if felt.

A series of snapshots helps illuminate the stories we tell – and are told – about our lives. The intimacy held within these types of pictures gives us the agency as Black people to show up and to be witnessed as our full selves through our mannerisms and body language, often without an outside influence, gaze, or imposed restriction. With snapshots, anything goes, and historically they have served as a quick and affordable way to document the celebratory (and the mundane) moments in one's life. I consider snapshots the most authentic storytelling medium in the written and visual language – they require very little technical skill yet can render some of the richest and most beautiful stories. It's no wonder that snapshots are memorialized in family photo albums and passed down as evidence of lives, fully lived, throughout generations.

In many families, each generation has a designated member that curates their family photos. The work of this curation is a labor of love, and an impressive skill not to be taken lightly. Family photo albums are magical, yet familiar. For many, they are home. They are spaces to find comfort, strength, and even escape. An album is a place where you are met with faces you know, and perhaps some you come to know – faces that reveal and inspire stories and confessionals. They force us to reflect on the various ways that we have appeared – and faded away – throughout the years.

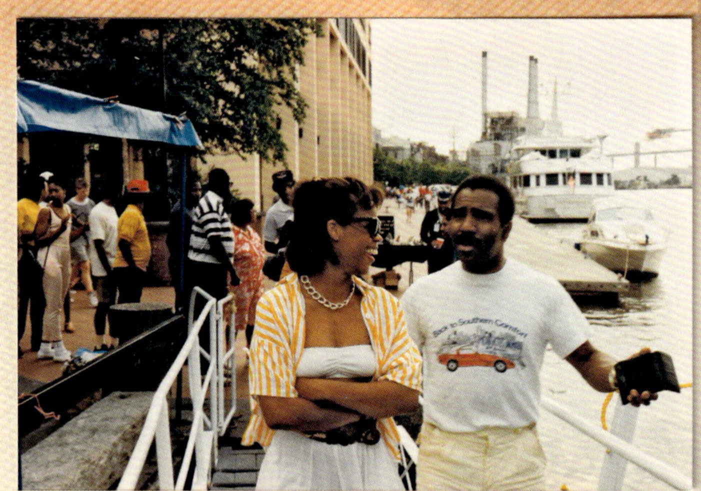

Savannah
Georgia

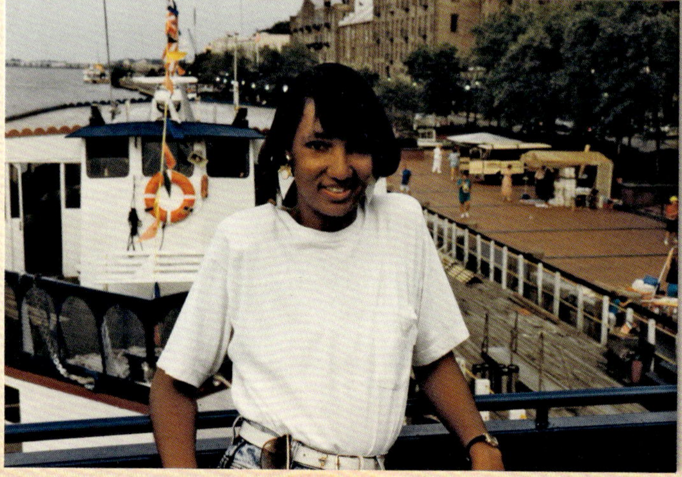

JUNE 1990

Page from the author's family album, curated by her dad
SAVANNAH, GA
1990

The family member who is called upon to gather and curate these images is doing their family – and our collective histories – a great service by pulling together the truth of our existence as people.

One of my most treasured activities growing up was flipping through the pages of our family photo album. Ours was meticulously curated by my dad, Edwin, who thoroughly enjoyed being our designated photographer. I never saw my dad drop a roll of film off for developing and rarely saw the envelope with developed photographs and negatives. I never caught him rearranging the photographs into the album, weaving them through cut-out magazine or newspaper clippings in lieu of writing the date or location alongside the image or on the page beside it. It existed – like magic. Fifteen years after his death, I am amazed at the power of being able to relive these moments and consider his intentionality today. Because of his passion, I am able to revisit and trace our story, to try to see it like he did. Each time I look back, I pick up on something new that I hadn't noticed, or perhaps didn't previously have the language for.

Through the evolution of technology, we are now able to bring these snapshots into the digital realm, where we can share them with our relatives over group texts and social media. This practice allows us to create, cultivate, and share space within online communities and form kinships that reflect a collective familial experience – from things we recognize within our own families and our commonalities, to our differences and the ways our households and traditions are unique. It gives us space to discuss family archival methods, teach one another new ways of storytelling using family keepsakes, and exchange techniques to help us create and sustain our own personal archives. These digital communities help us connect with long-lost relatives while identifying a new generation of archivists, storytellers, ethnographers, and historians. It's a way for us to create new systems to avoid archival loss and erasure.

I recognize that not everyone has access to family photographs, or stories. In many families, particularly Black families, tangible keepsakes have been lost, destroyed, or taken over the years, leaving future generations with the task of piecing together misplaced histories. This can be difficult to reconcile, particularly during a time when there are so many people sharing moments from the past in digital spaces. Those who find themselves without family photos and keepsakes can often find joy and comfort in those of other families. Even in the images of people we don't personally know, we can find so many familiar figures and moments: kids playing in the yard, parents dressed up for an occasion, family gatherings, and celebrations. These images prompt our own memories, allowing us access to both our individual and our collective pasts.

Black Archives: A Photographic Celebration of Black Life explores familial archiving practices, and how we experience kinship and recognize one another through a visual language of the Black experience. This book also fills the chasm of silence between the photos of where truth lives, and the black hole of the unknown. The images in this book were sourced from the Black Archives community and archives held in various institutional repositories. In the spirit of trying to create a collective family album about Black life, I issued a call for photo submissions and received hundreds of incredible family photos from Black folks all over the world. People shared what they knew about the photos, but a lot of the information about the people, locations, and time periods captured was not known or had been lost to time – such is the nature of family photo archives. As such, the scope of information provided about the images in this book varies: some photo captions contain names, locations, and dates; others might only contain locations, names, or may only have estimated dates. This inconsistency is to be expected given the nature of this work, and to some degree, may heighten the experience of this book as a collective family album.

It is my desire that the photographs collected here honor the many stories that were lost in transition, and that by sharing these archiving practices, I can help amplify the stories we do have through collective kinship.

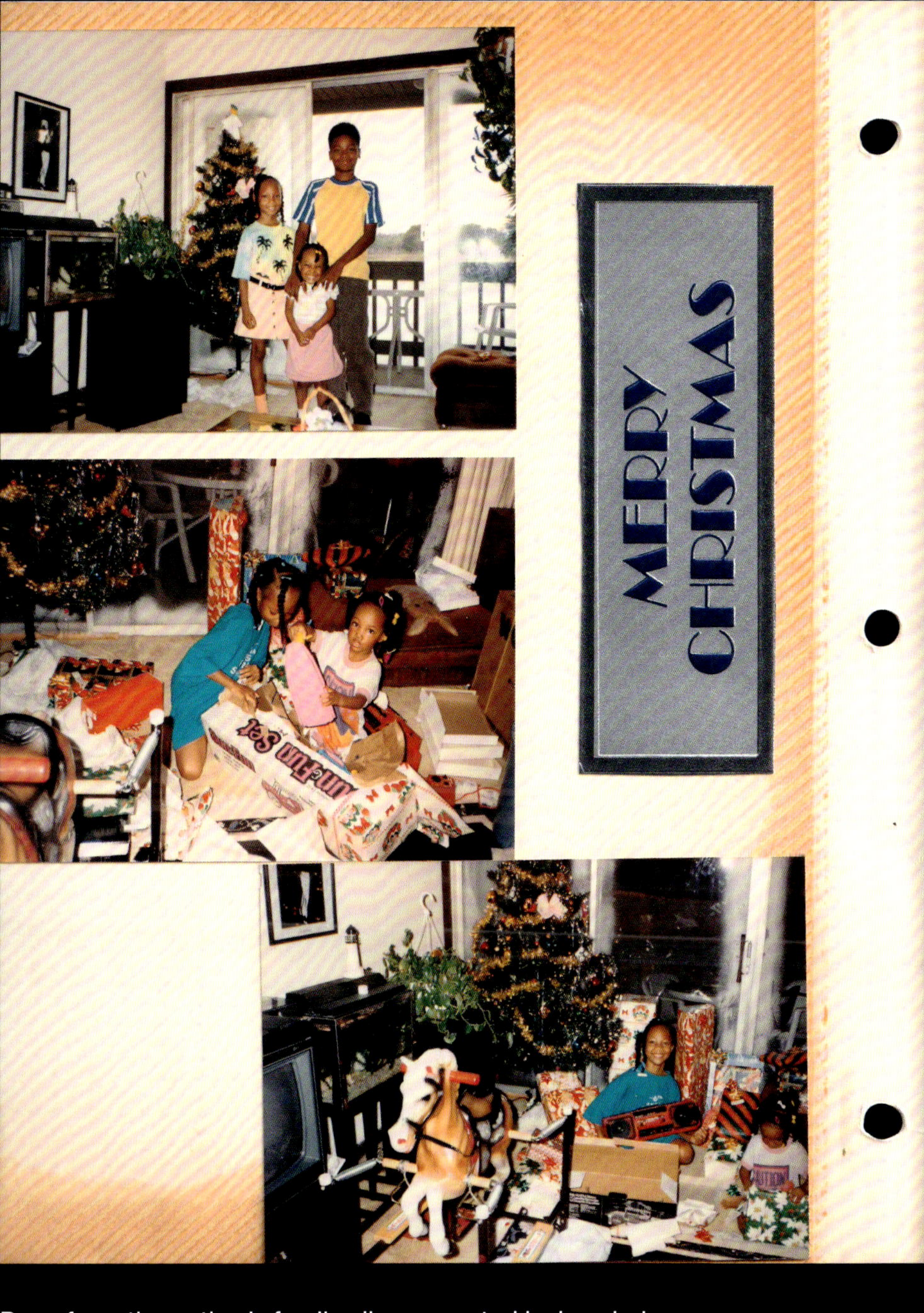

Page from the author's family album, curated by her dad

JACKSONVILLE, FL

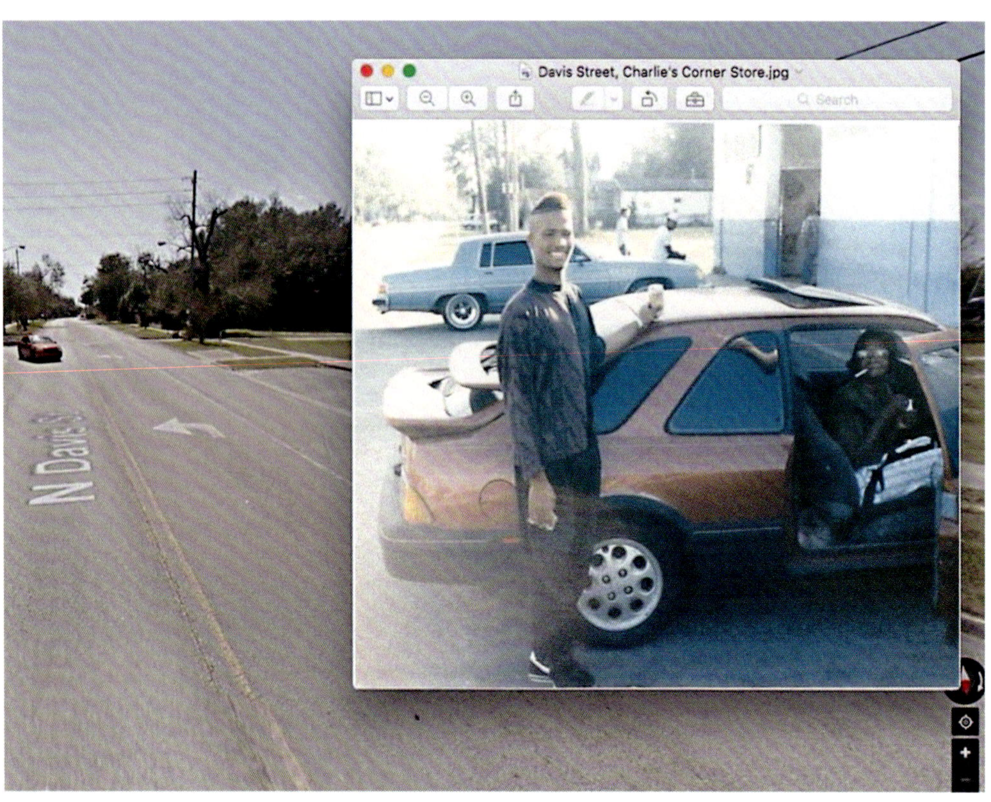

Photo from the author's family collection, with Google Maps background

JACKSONVILLE, FL

1990S

The author's cousin and aunt at the beach
JACKSONVILLE, FL
1980S

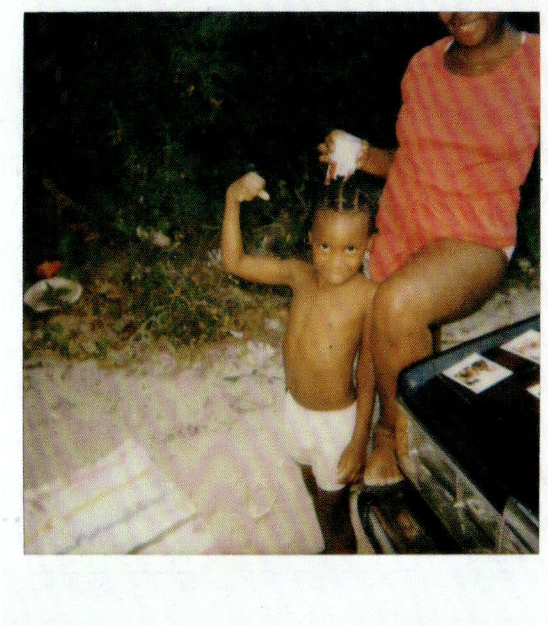

The author's cousins standing on a car
JACKSONVILLE, FL
1980S

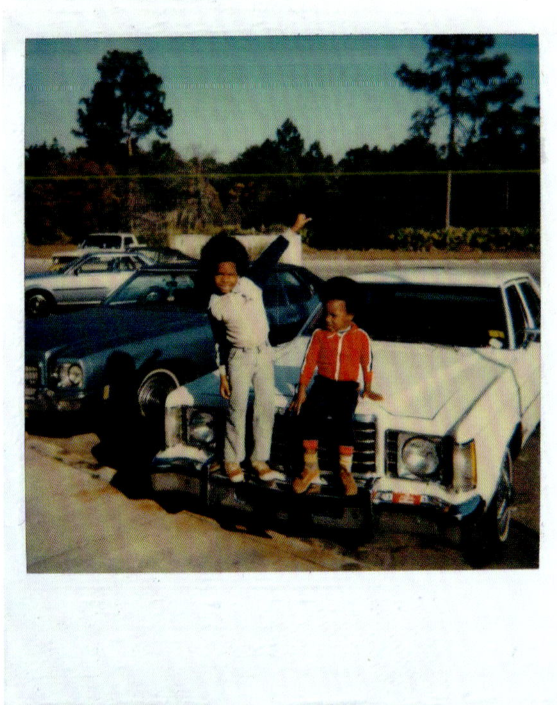

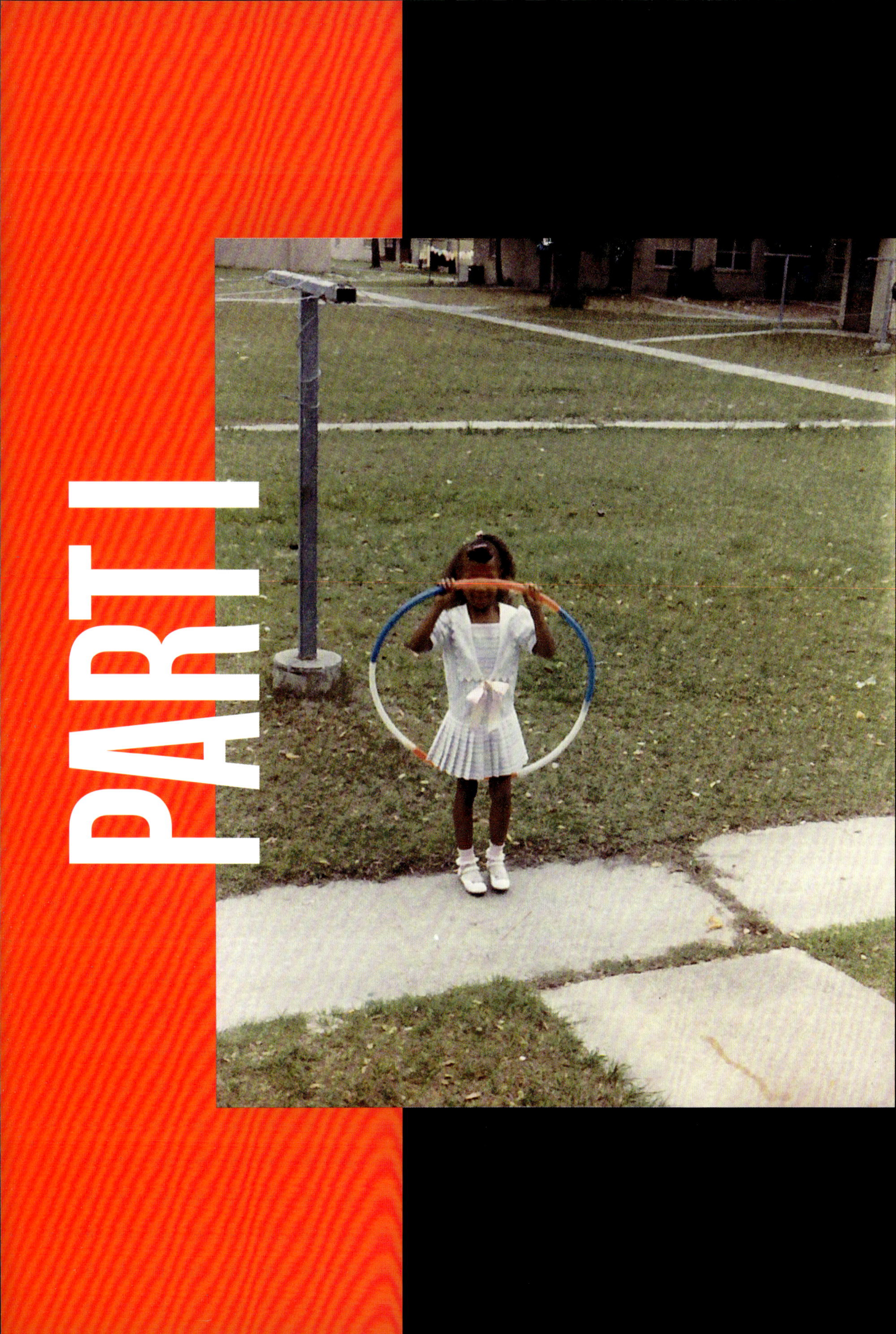

PART I

THE FOUNDATION

KEEPER OF STORIES

← Previous: The author at her grandmother's home
JACKSONVILLE, FL
1988

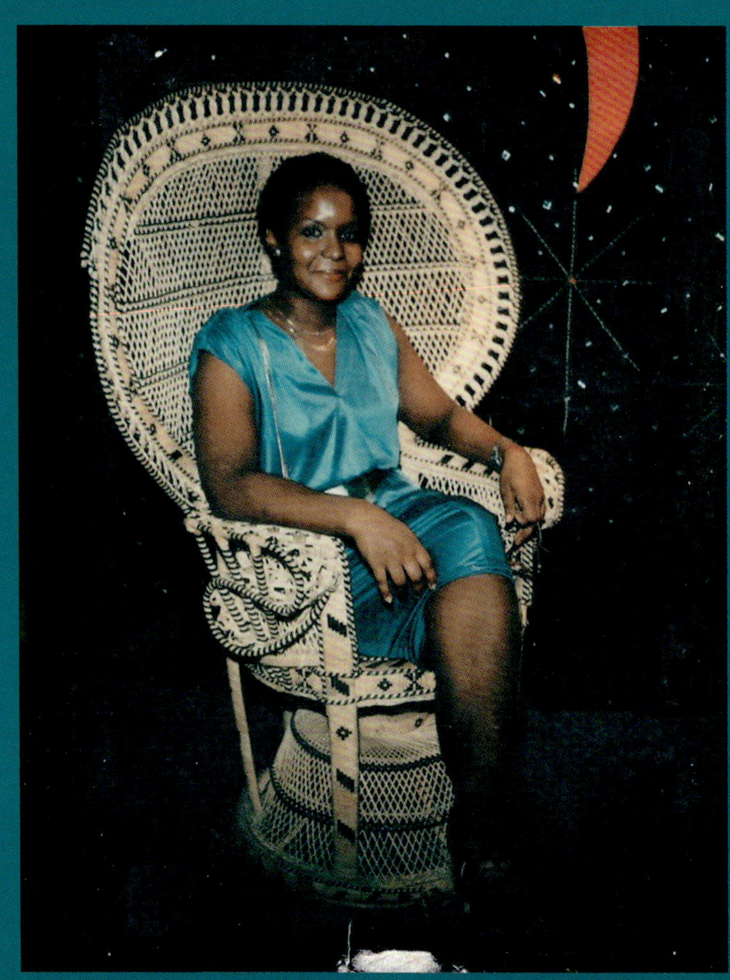

The author's aunt Brenda
JACKSONVILLE, FL
1979

In 2011, I began creating mini stories on the social platform Tumblr by posting and sharing photos documenting the Black experience. Captivated by unearthed digitized images and historical references that I'd never seen in mainstream media or textbooks, I wanted to share the imagery with my online community. So, I began digging – in library, higher learning, and institutional archives – as a form of uncovering and self-exploration, all while learning about the broader visual story of the Black experience.

After a few years, I felt an urge to do more work in this space but didn't know how to approach it without a degree in library science or institutional support. So, I relied on the knowledge held within my maternal bloodline and considered this journey to be one of ancestral work and guidance.

In June 2015, when my mother's sister was rushed to the hospital in Jacksonville, Florida, I flew there from Chicago carrying my late grandmother's worn Bible, which had been in our family for generations.

This Bible wasn't something that my grandmother used for daily worship – it always sat on her dresser. It caught my attention on an ordinary day when I was a child. As I thumbed through the first few pages, I came across a list of relatives – some names I recognized, others I didn't. I saw my own name, along with my date and place of birth. I was mesmerized by the list of names and in that moment, I somehow knew that keeping my family's stories would be an important part of my life, that it was a role I was called to.

Upon my grandmother's death, my mom inherited the Bible and eventually she gifted it to me. That day in Jacksonville, I placed my aunt's left hand on the Bible. After the immediate family said their goodbyes, I rejoined my aunt in the hospital room. I held her hand and shared with her everything that I didn't get a chance to tell her during her time in this realm, including my deepest desires in my artistic work. I told her what I imagined Black Archives could be. I knew that she would get the spiritual family to rally around me. I consider Black Archives to be ancestral work, and it is the reason why I feel such a deep and spiritual connection to my ancestors – known and unknown.

In my role as a keeper of stories for both my family and our collective family, I am also a guardian. Never do I claim to be the owner of the images or stories. But I do feel urgently compelled to take care of the stories – to preserve them, to hold on to them, and to give them back to the community. One of the things that I enjoy most about unearthing and sharing photographs from deep within institutional archives is that, even when there is little to no context available about an image, I am often able to crowdsource information, pulling from shared memories within the Black experience to round out the story.

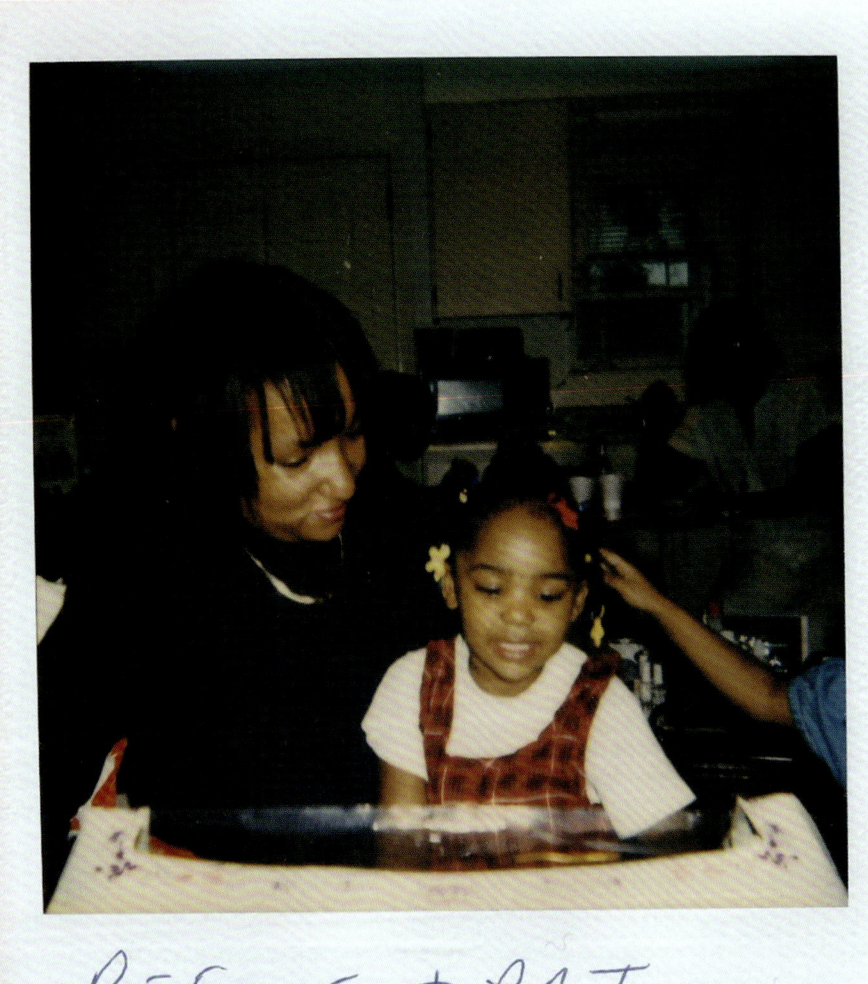

The author's mom and cousin, Pat and Regene, with her grandmother and brother in the background
JACKSONVILLE, FL
1997

HANDWRITTEN STORIES

While documents such as census records, birth certificates, yearbooks, and newspapers can offer vital information to help reconstruct or assist with piecing together a family's story or timeline, photos offer an intimate experience and connection. One of the greatest treasures often found in family photo albums are the handwritten accounts – dates, names, notes – that are folded within the pages, or written on top or on the back of photos. These stories help shorten the bridge between the living and the transitioned, the present and the past. Handwritten notes are gifts to and from ourselves, and to future generations.

We often rely on our memory and imagination to help us piece together (or create alternatives to) the many stories found within our familial lineage. I've learned that photographs carry the answers to questions that we have, even if extracting the metadata we want – like names, dates, and locations – is still a challenge. There are photos within my own family album that I can only wonder about – but it is in that wondering, that meditating on what is shown, that I come away with a deeper connection to my family. My mother is the matriarch; now in her sixties, she is the oldest living family member who can help us name faces and attach stories. It is my family's goal to name as many names as we possibly can. The living archive within my mother's body is all we have to reconstruct and share our legacy.

Unlike the Nikon camera that my dad used to capture family snapshots, my maternal grandmother's camera of choice was the Polaroid. Instant cameras such as Polaroids offered the built-in ease of developing the film in the moment, which saved time and money. Since she was living on a fixed income, developing pictures on the spot was the most accessible option for her. She noted the names, dates, and if space permitted, the occasion on most of her Polaroids. Her curatorial practice was straightforward, grouping her photographs in chronological order soon after the images were captured. Instead of focusing on the free-flowing moments within everyday life, my grandmother focused on capturing the more celebratory ones, like birthdays and holidays. She was a very organized woman so if I had to guess, she was creating a chronological story by intentionally preserving the images by date within their plastic sleeves, one after another.

My grandmother transitioned to the next life just a couple of months after I graduated high school in 2000. I was left with so many questions about who she was, the life she experienced as a Black woman in the South, things that brought her joy. When I trace her handwriting on a Polaroid, sometimes I get a feeling – an indication of what she must have felt at that very moment. I often wonder if she realized that the record she was creating would serve as a pathway to the past from the present. As I flip through her albums, the story abruptly ends – almost mid-sentence or mid-celebration, and unexpectedly, without any warning or indication that the last set of images in the album is the final set that would ever bear her handwriting.

After she passed, instead of using Polaroids and film cameras, my family migrated to digital devices, opting to receive our images back on compact discs, made viewable on our computers. We didn't always preserve these images properly – stories have been misplaced, photos went unlabeled. The digital age shifted the way we stored our images, moving away from albums and tangibility to digital and uncertainty. Technology has advanced so much, and most of us now have a camera at our side at all times through our phones. And yet, when my grandmother's voice escapes me, I feel pulled to her handwriting on her Polaroids. Like unexpectedly discovering a note left inside a picture frame, stashed in a drawer, or tucked between the pages of sacred text, this is an offering of its own. Through time and space, this is an intentional act of love – and a calling for the beneficiary of such gifts to not only consider the story of a photograph or document, but to also join their loved ones in continuing to preserve the narrative. This is how we keep stories. This is how we pass them down – from the transitioned to the living – throughout our lineage.

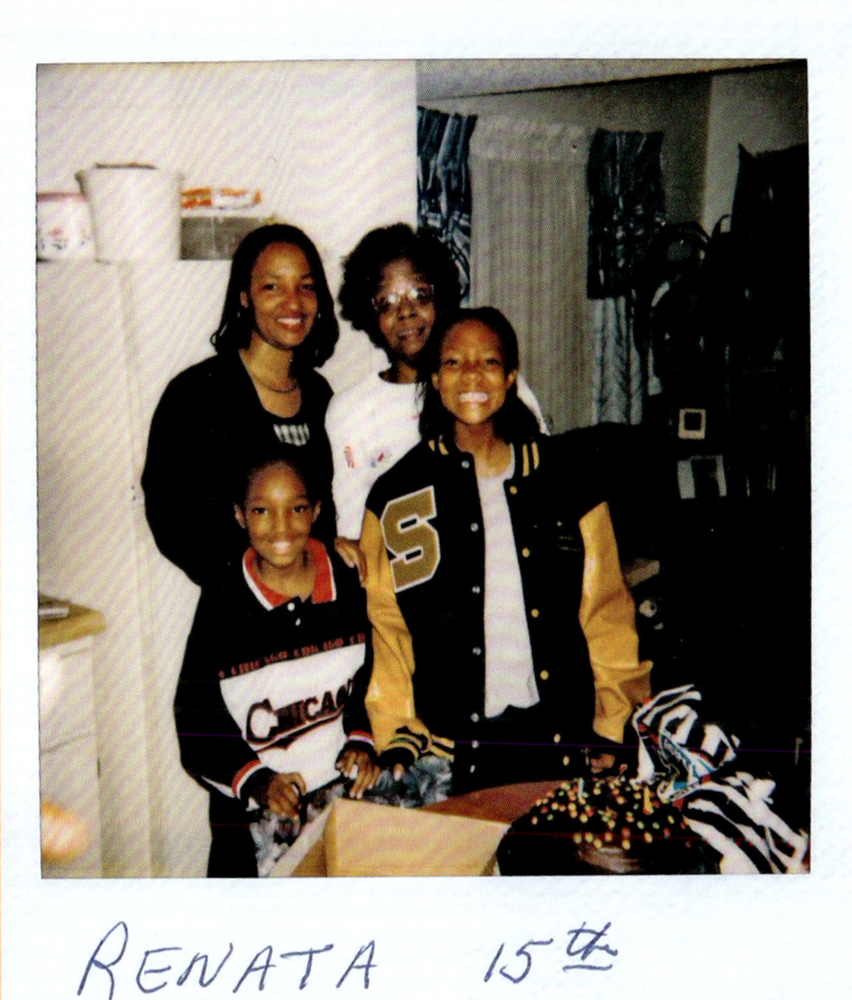

The author and her family on her fifteenth birthday

JACKSONVILLE, FL

1997

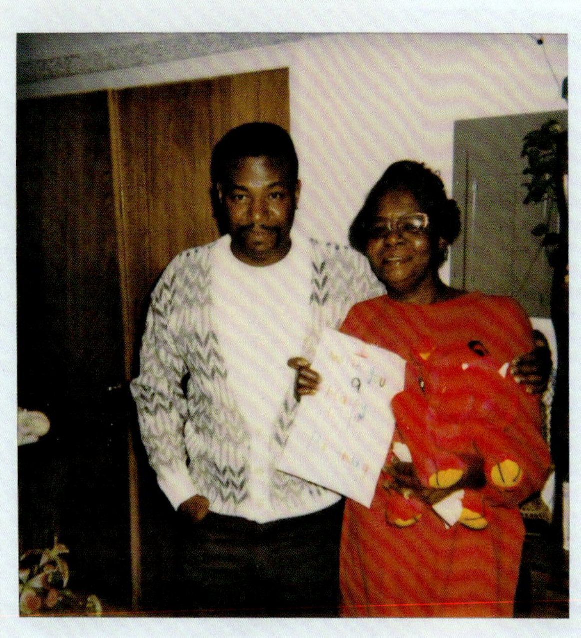

The author's dad and grandmother on
her grandmother's fifty-seventh birthday
1995

The author and her grandmother on
her grandmother's fifty-ninth birthday
JACKSONVILLE, FL
1997

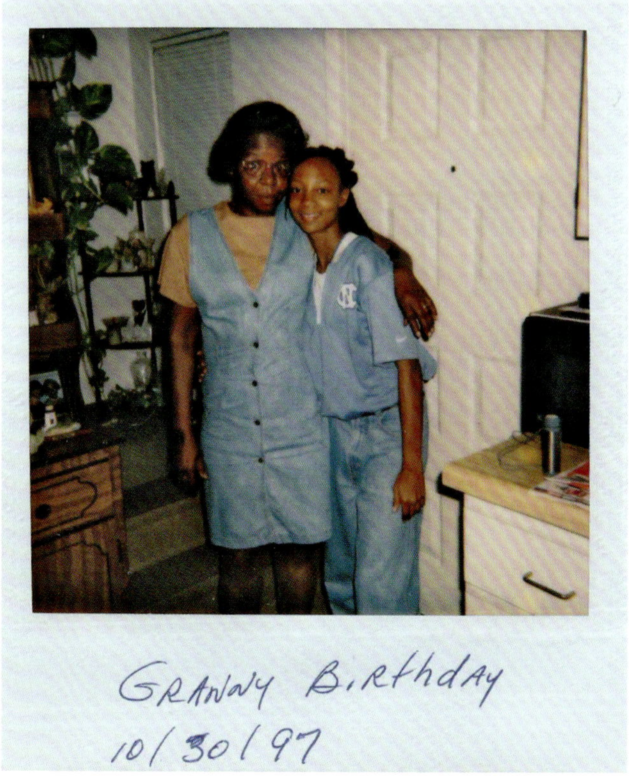

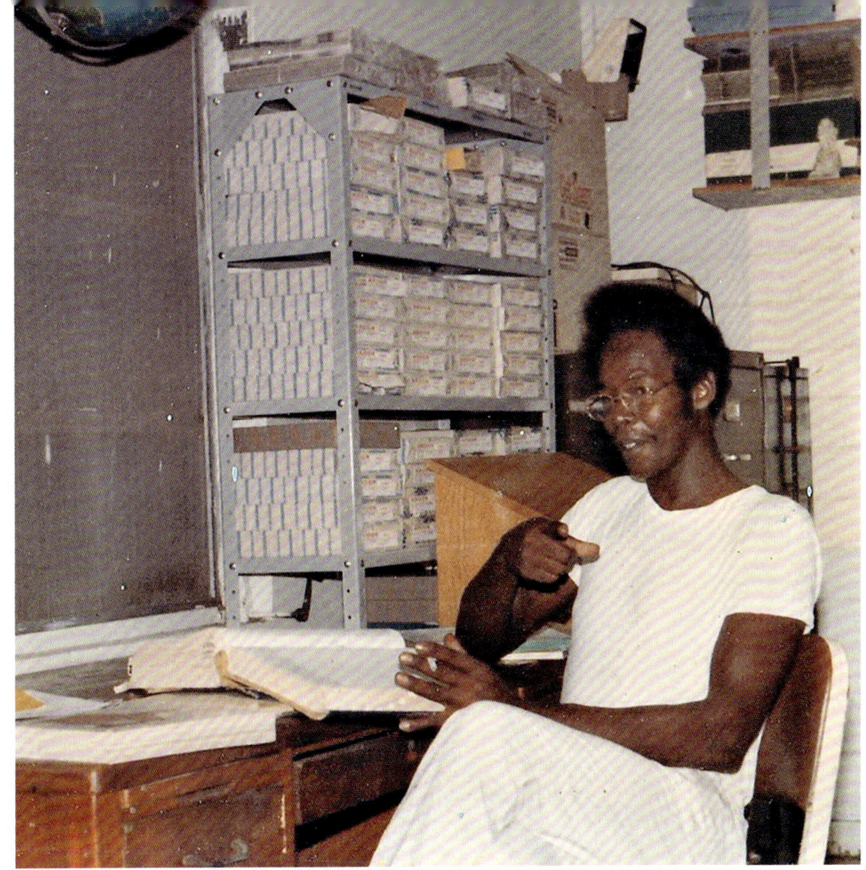

Photo of the author's great-uncle Eddie Jr. while incarcerated in the Florida Department of Corrections
1970S

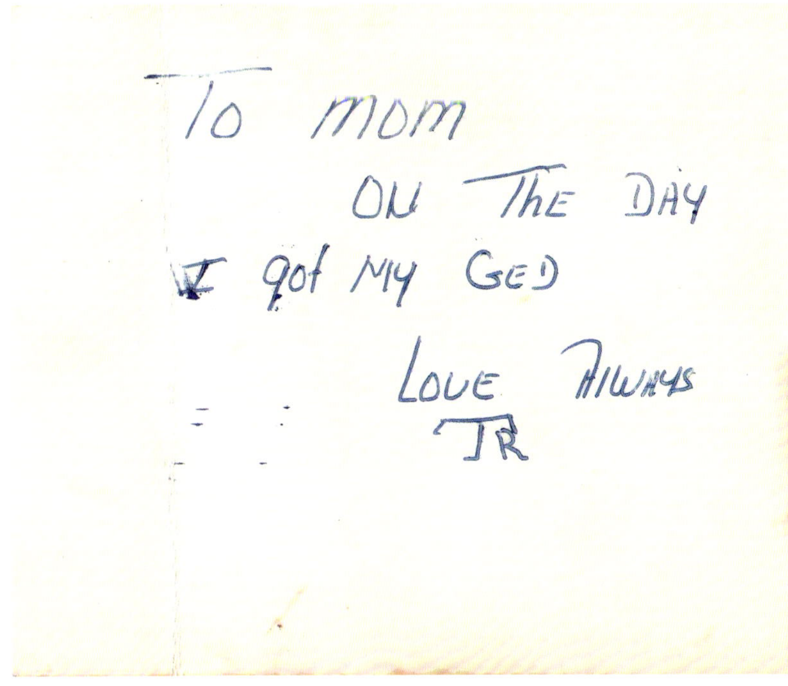

To mom
ON THE DAY
I got MY GED
LOVE Always
JR

Handwritten note, on the back of the above photo, to the author's great-grandmother
1970S

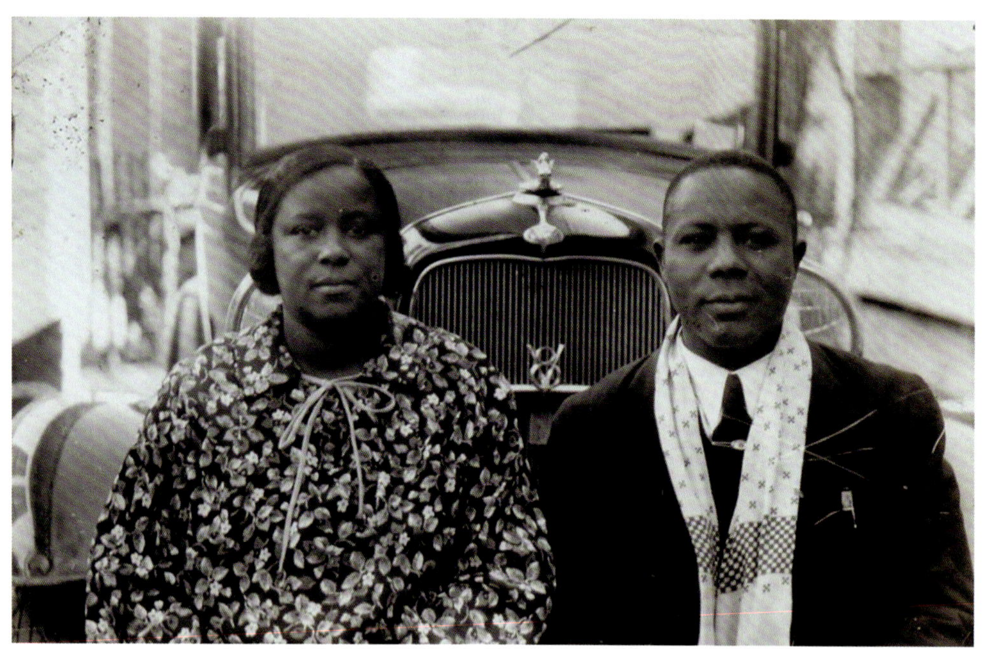

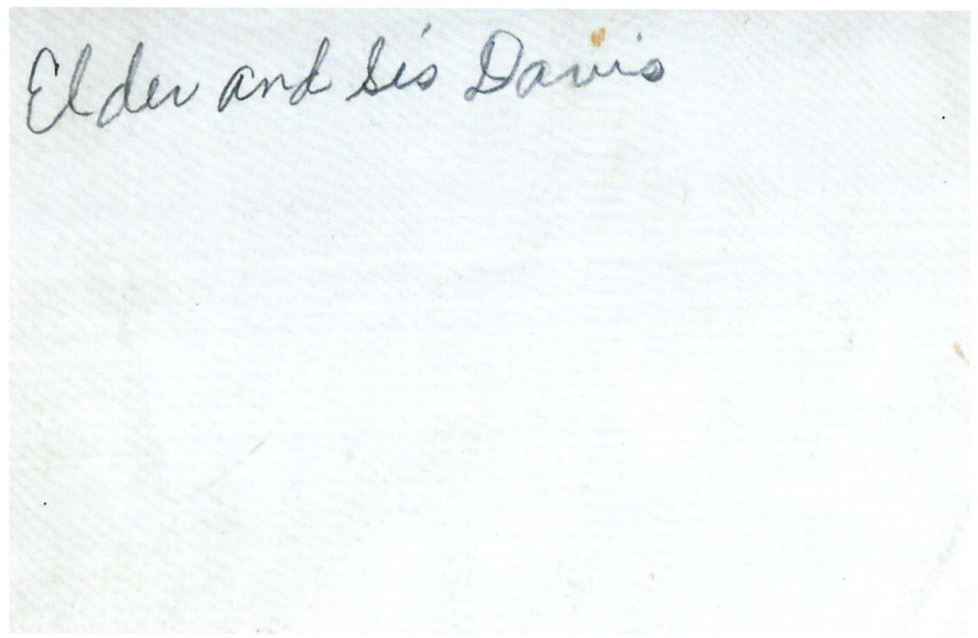

The front and back of a photo of Elder and Sister Davis

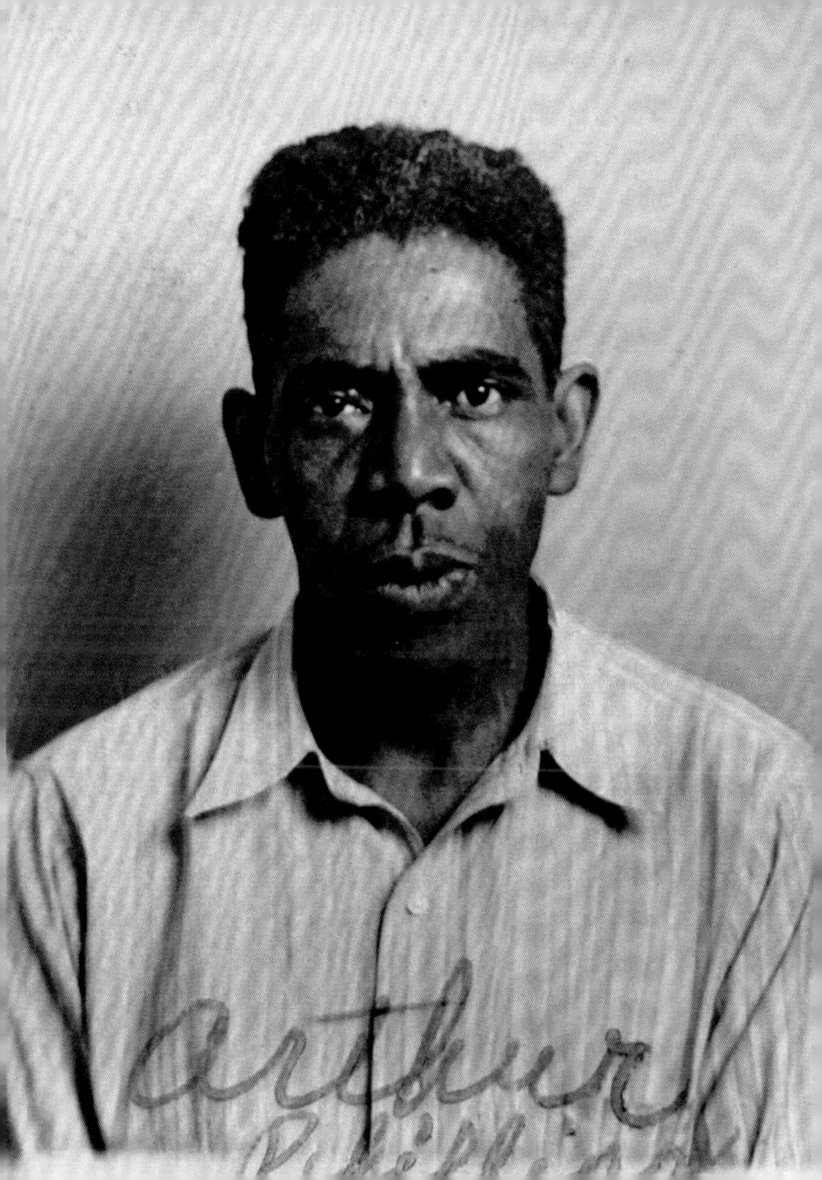
Arthur

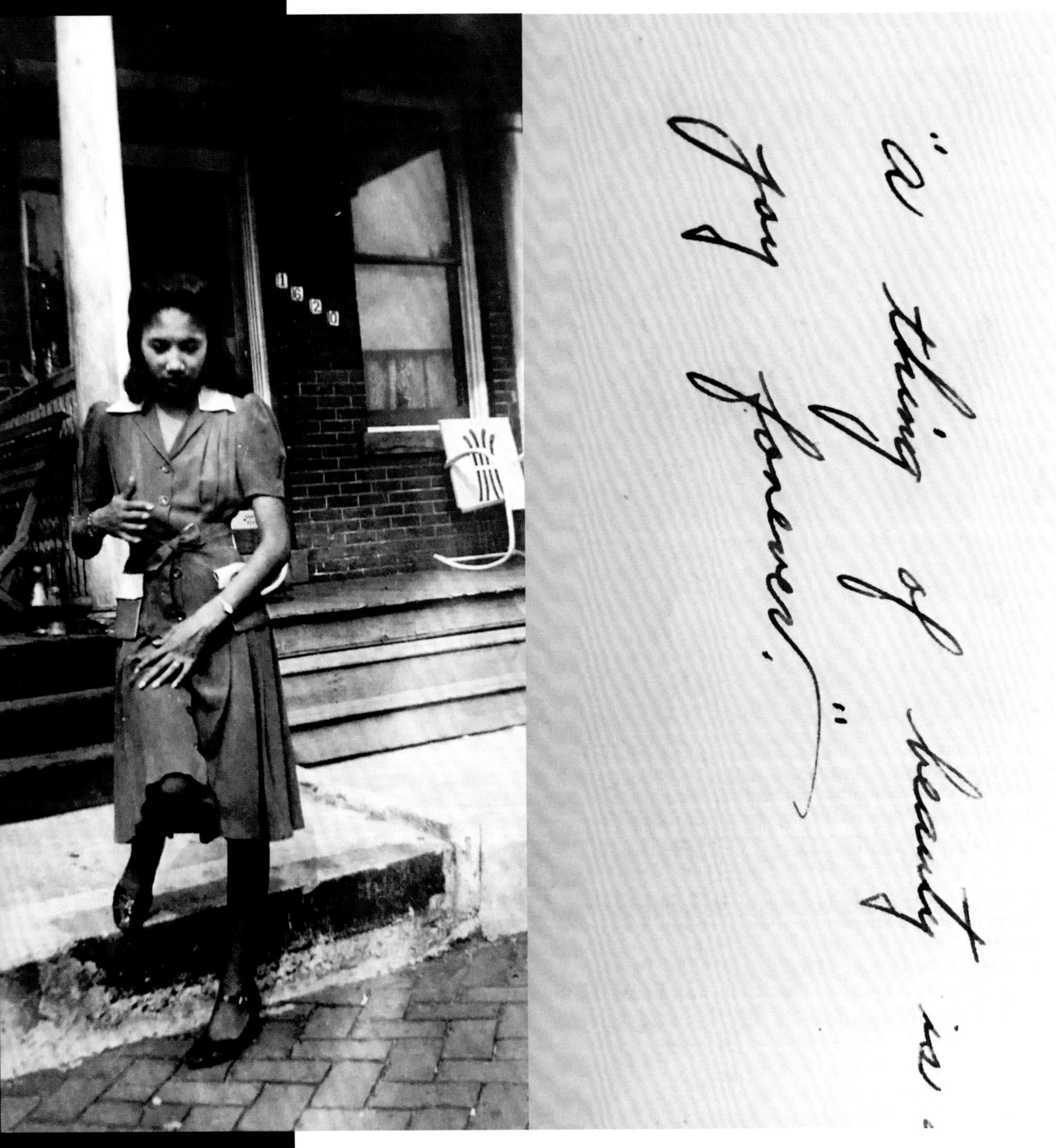

The husband of the woman in this photo wrote a note on the back that reads "a thing of beauty is a joy forever"
1945

Mother Connie Cambridge and son Gerald

MIAMI, FL

1973

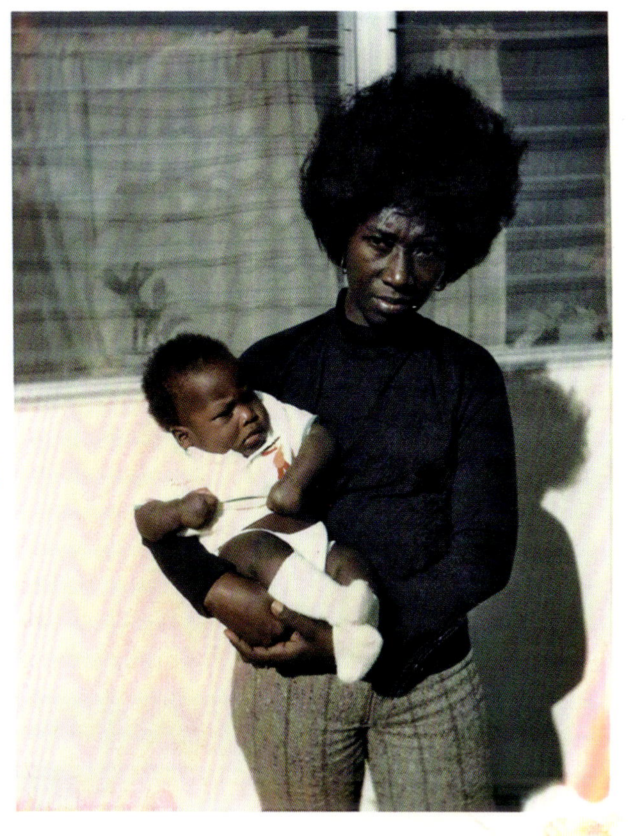

AN ORIGINAL POLAROID® LAND PHOTOGRAPH

SUBJECT Mother+Son DATE 1-73

NAME Connie-Gerald

ADDRESS 3701 N.W. 197 St

REGULAR SIZE COPIES

WALLET SIZE COPIES

5 x 7 ENLARGEMENTS

8 x 10 ENLARGEMENTS

35mm SLIDES

For your convenience when ordering copies, indicate the number of copies desired in the appropriate box for the size(s) you select.

P558A-1 5/70

Printed in U.S.A.

AND I SAW RONALD REAGAN UP CLOSE. HE IS MUCH BETTER LOOKING IN PERSON. STUPID; BUT GOOD LOOKING. THEY HAD A BEAUTIFUL PARADE, BUT BEING THERE IT IS A LOT DIFFERENT FROM T.V. THESE BEAUTIFUL HORSES COME PRANCING DOWN THE STREET AND WHEN THEY GO BY, THE STREET IS COVERED WITH SHIT THEN A MARCHING BAND COMES MARCHING RIGHT THROUGH THE SHIT, AND THAT GOES ON IN SEQUENCE FOR TWO HOURS. IT WAS STILL A BEAUTIFUL SIGHT (EXCEPT FOR THE SHIT) TO SEE.

The man in the opposite photo wrote this note to his family.

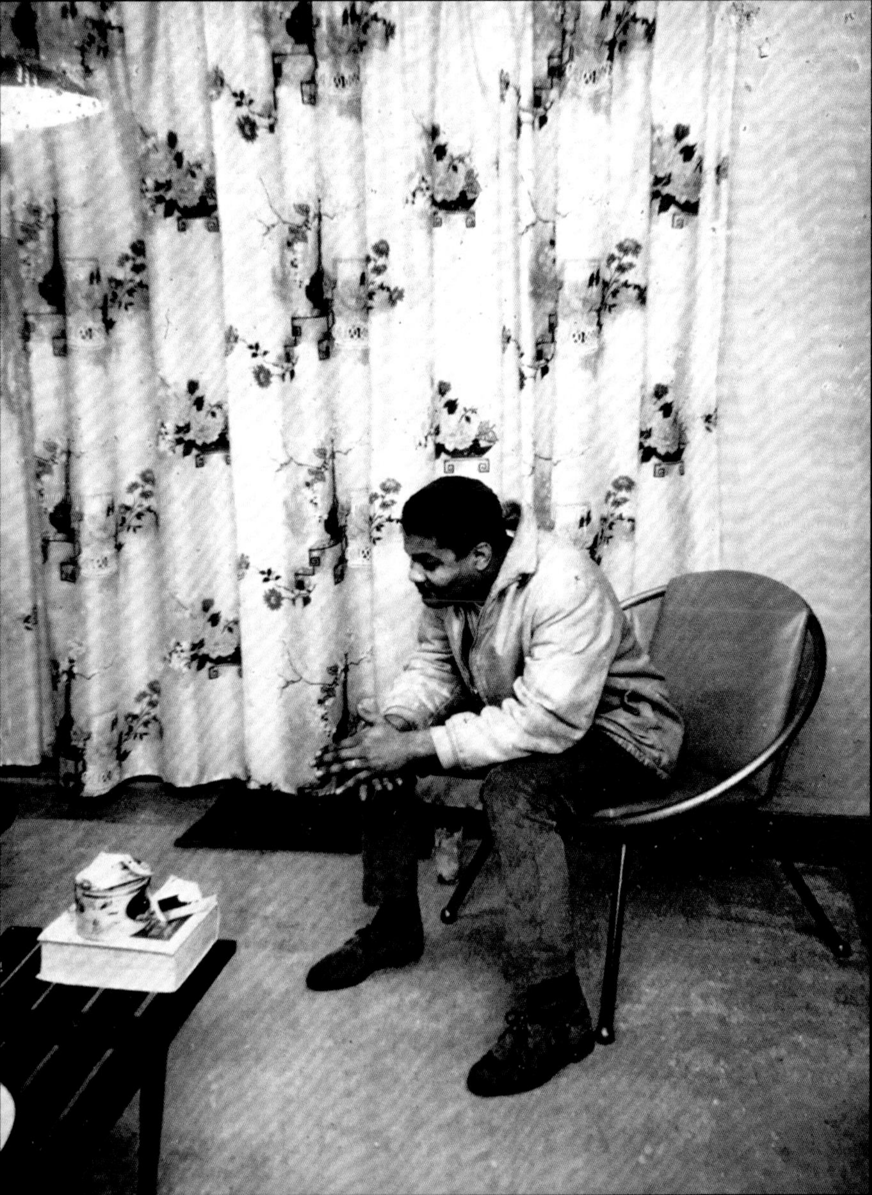

WASHINGTON, D.C

1947

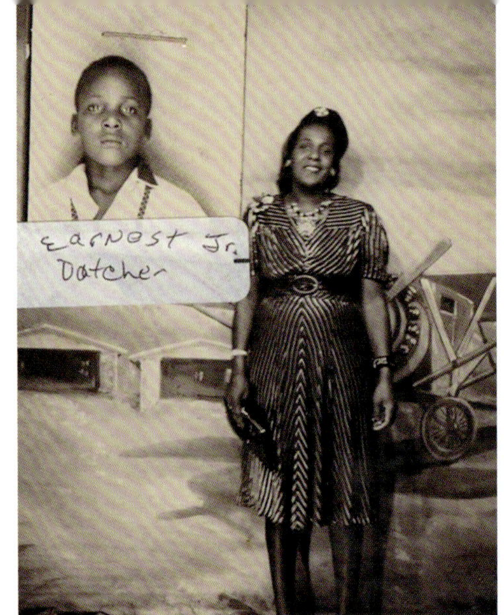

Earnest Datcher Jr. and Cora Datcher

ALABAMA

1940S

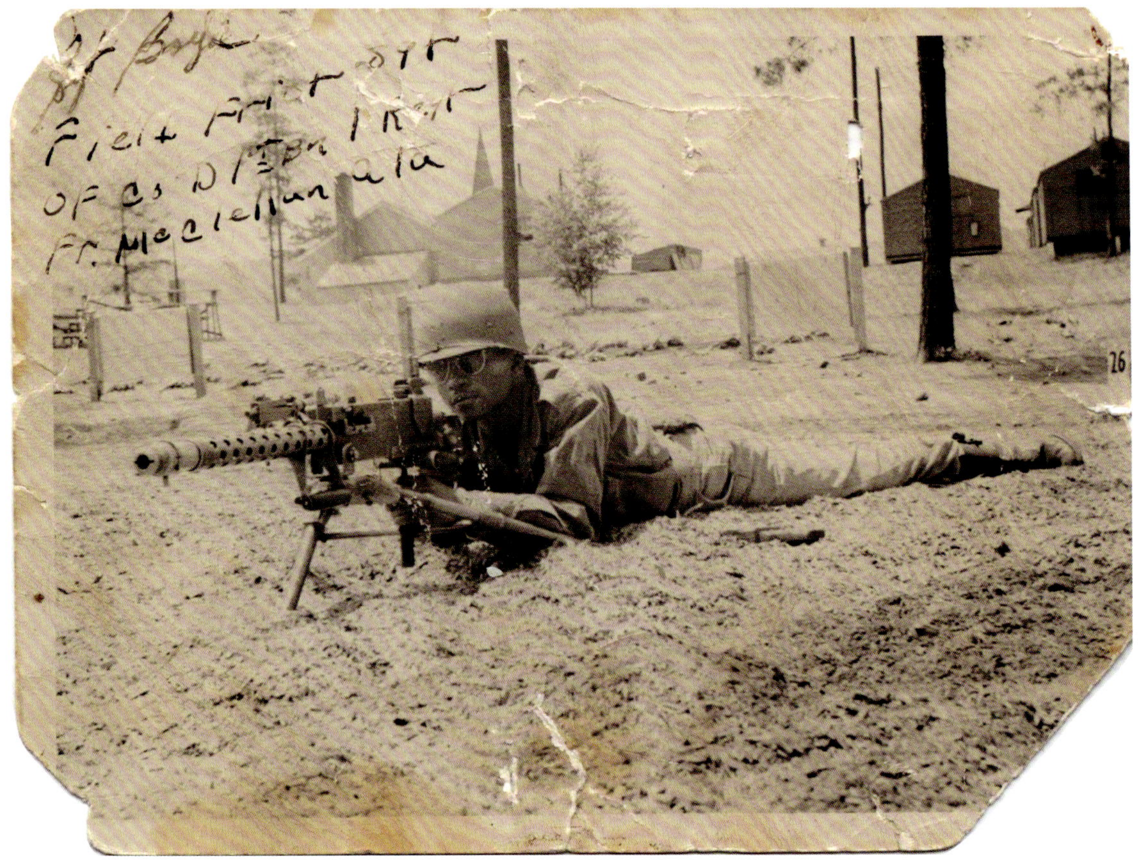

Boyd

1940S

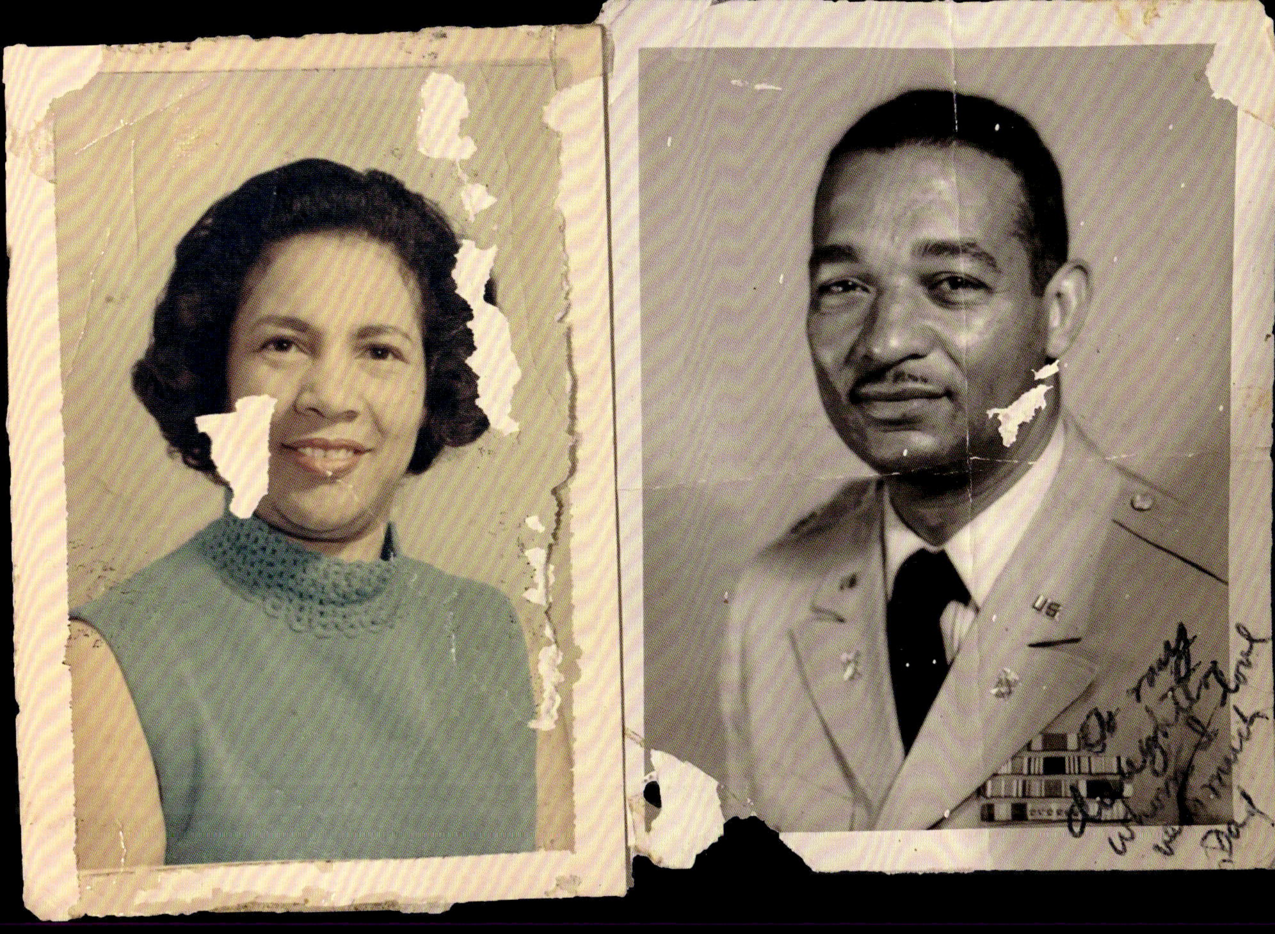

Portraits of Captain Wallace W. Price and his wife, Hortense Price. When he was overseas in the army, he wrote her love poems such as the following:

LOVERS RETURN

Fingers stroking
Through her hair,
Sweet Embraces—-
Close, this pair.
Filled with love—-
Entwined, their hearts
There two lovers—-
Long apart.

1955

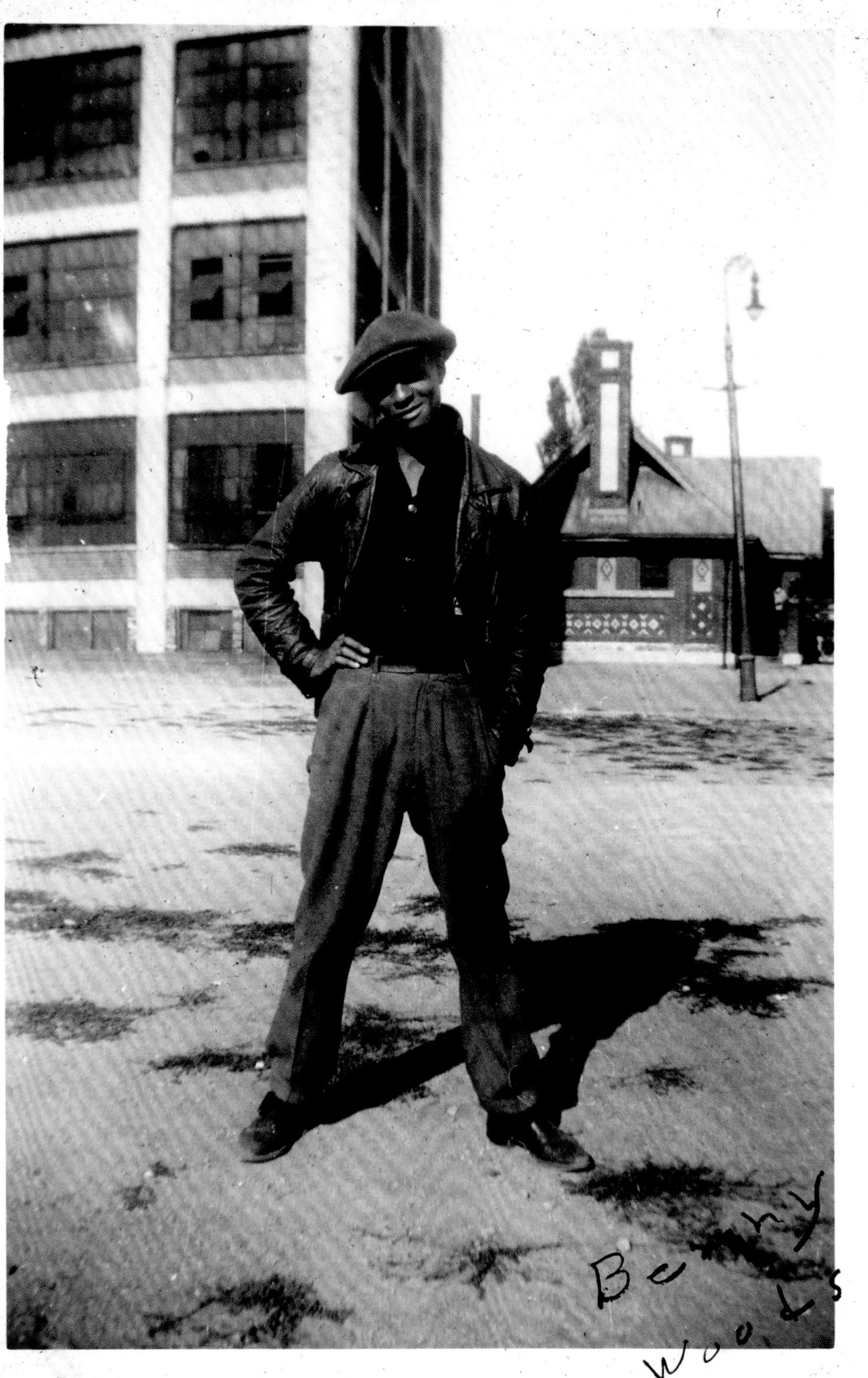

Benny Woo
CIRCA 1940

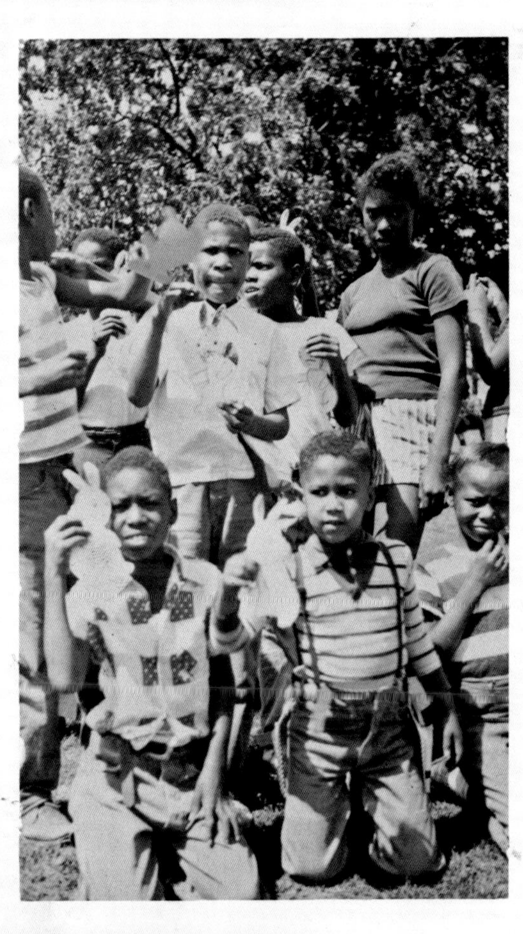

Easter at Griggs Park
DALLAS, TX

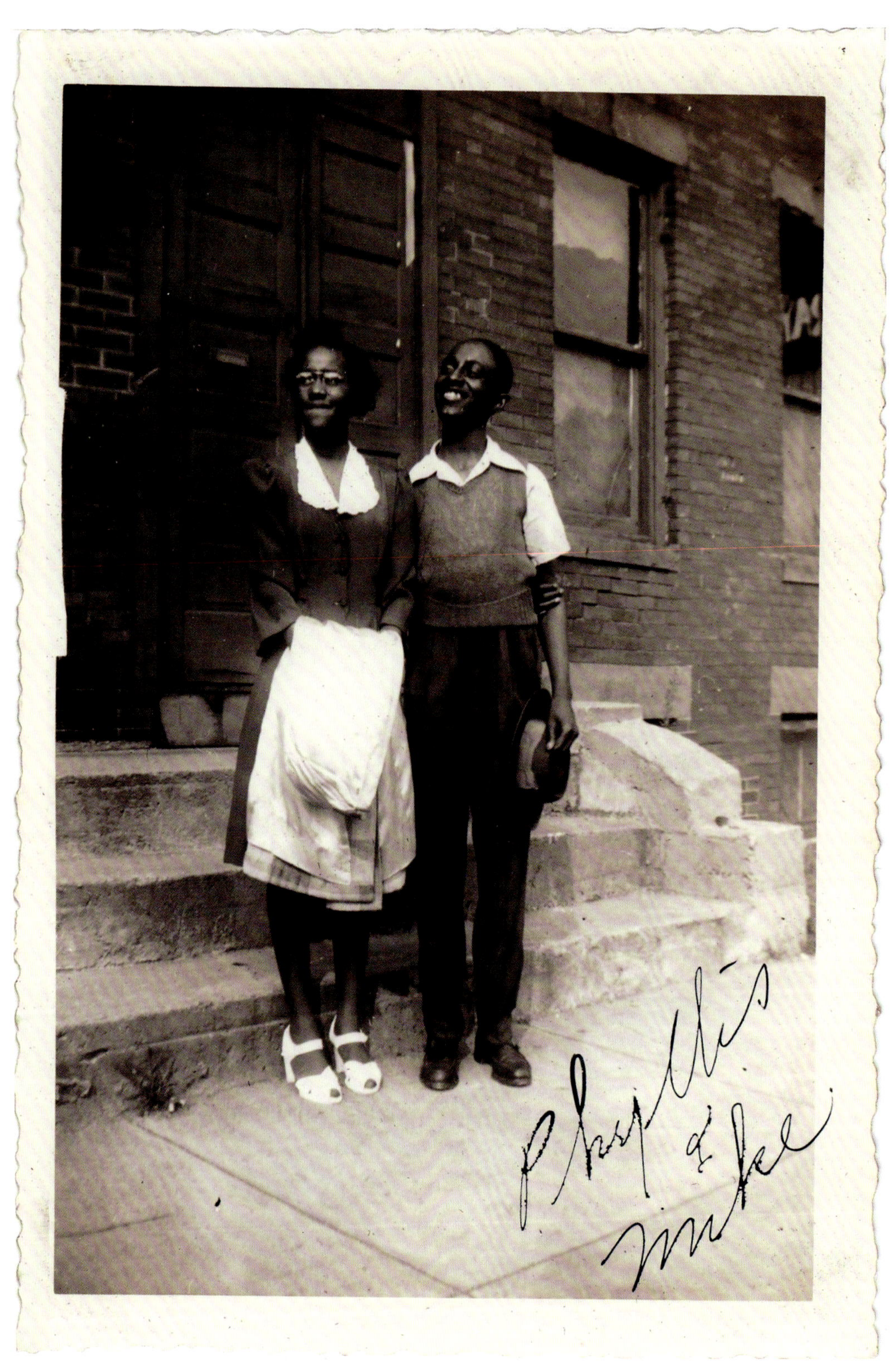

Phyllis and Mike
on Ruggles Street
BOSTON, MA
CIRCA 1940

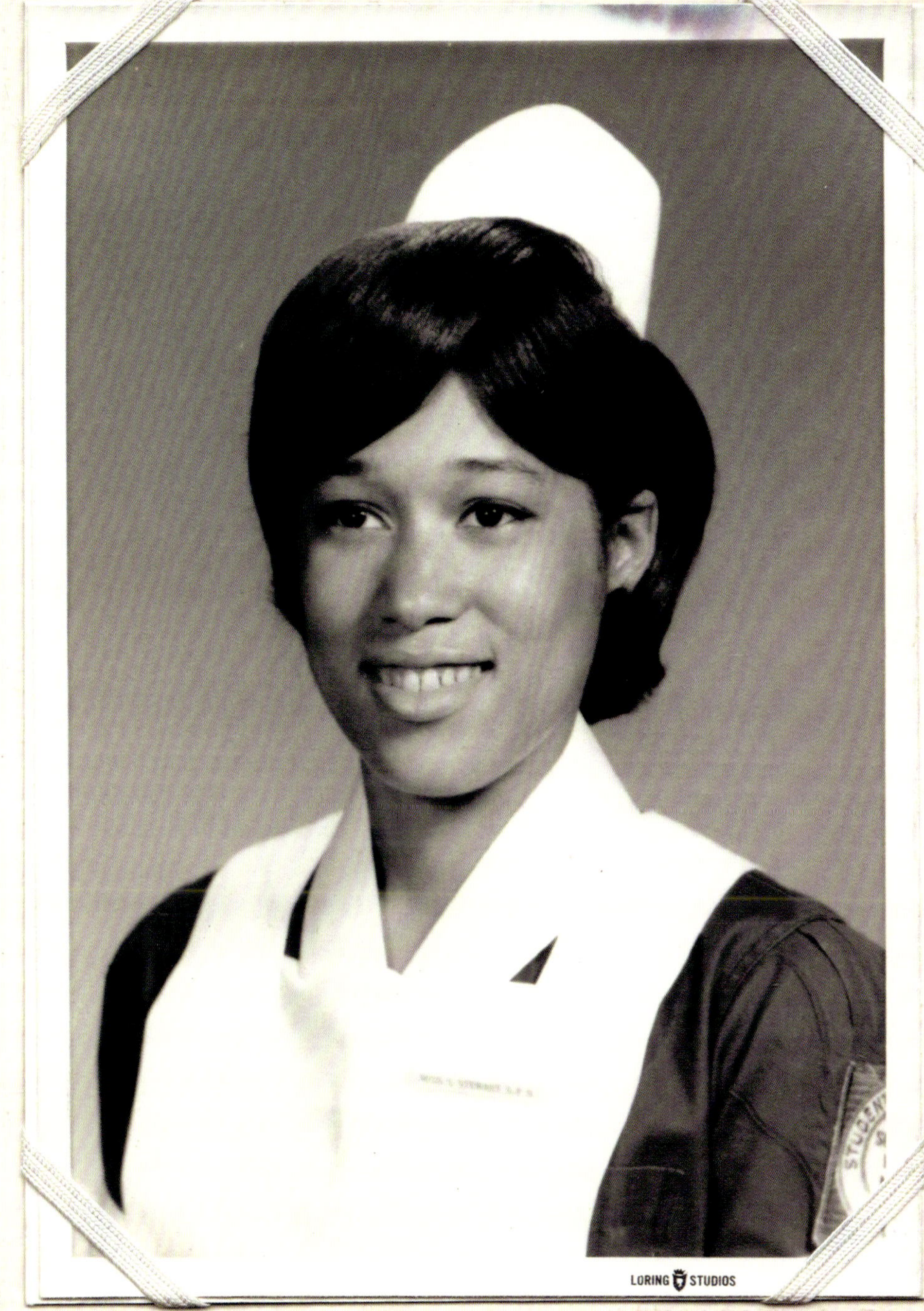

from your
"Cosey"
Sandra
'66

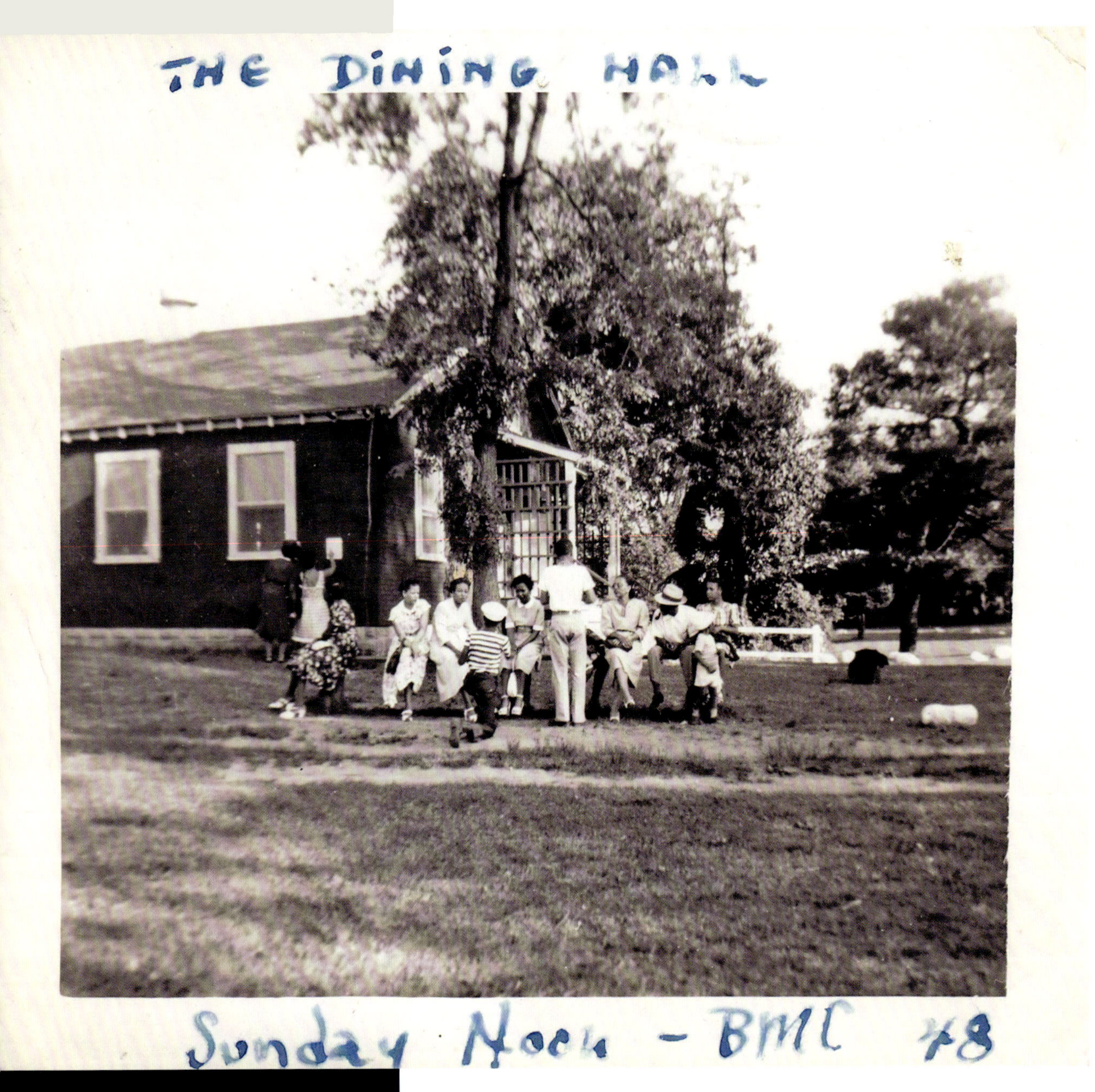

Dining hall at Breezy Meadows Camp
HOLLISTON, MA
1948

Inez and Willie May on the beach

CIRCA 1945

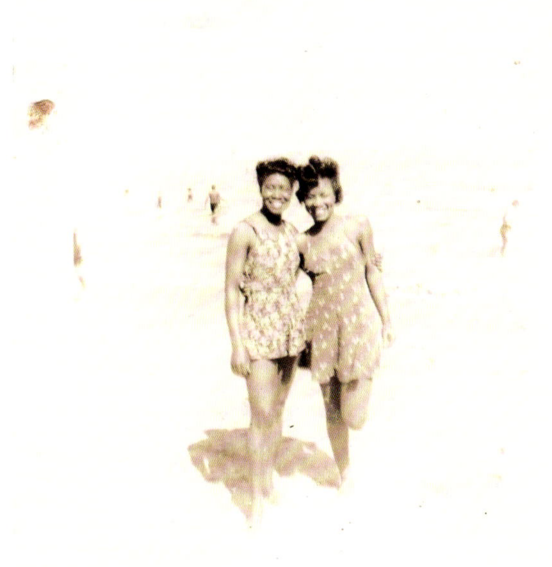

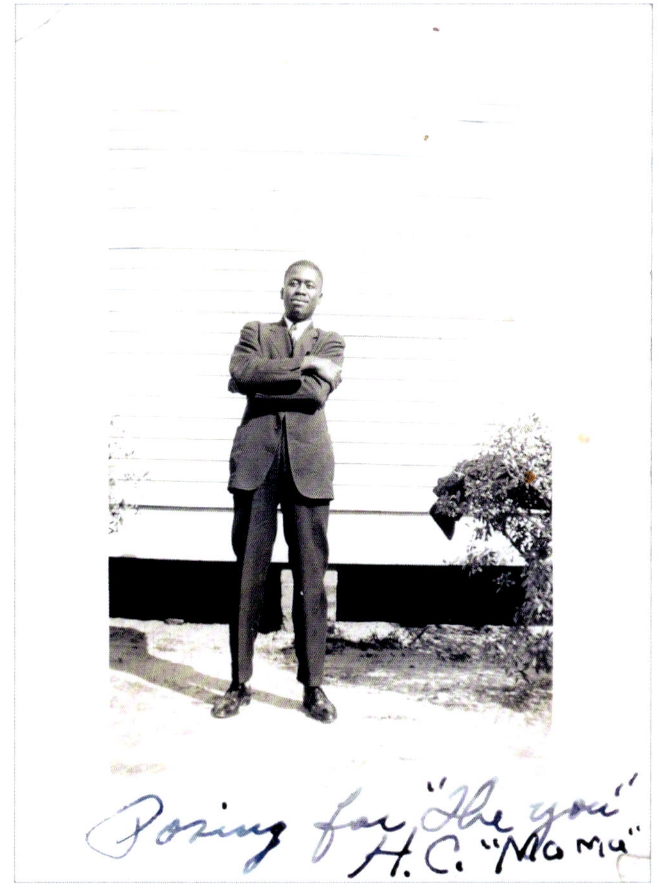

Student at Mather Academy

CAMDEN, SC

1941

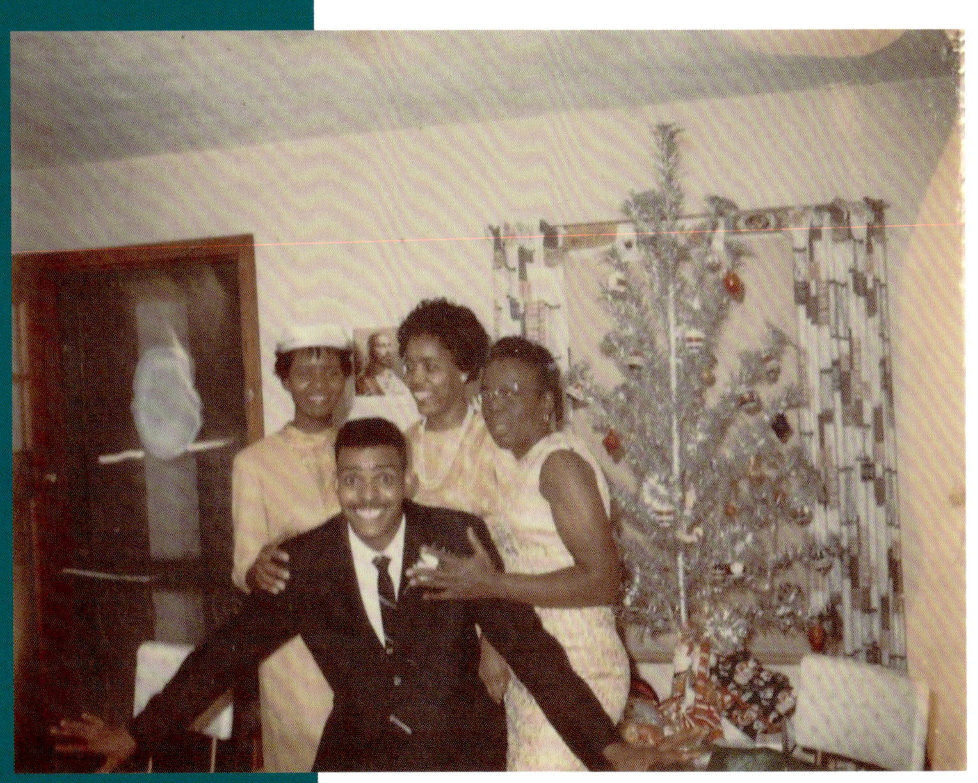

The author's grandparents
on their wedding day
DAYTONA BEACH, FL
1966

PICTURES WITHIN PICTURES

One of the things I enjoy most about family snapshots is identifying the things hidden in plain sight. They often reveal clues of our histories and identities. Scattered across the backgrounds are objects, food, pets, and picture frames that together offer insights into where we come from and the ways in which we have departed. As someone who is constantly drawn to the backgrounds and interiors, being able to admire someone by way of a photo within a photo – or to experience them for the first time because the original photo no longer exists – is a compass for me, offering directional clues to a way home.

I'm thinking of one photograph in particular, taken of my grandmother Cora on her wedding day in the mid-1960s. There are not many photos of her as a young woman, so the first time that I came across it, I was immediately struck by her youthfulness. As far back as I can remember, she always appeared to me as an older woman, largely due to her mannerisms, so when I came across this image of her as a young person, I sat with it for a while, studying everything about it. My grandmother stands on the far left with her hand placed on the shoulder of my grandfather Raymond. Her sister-in law, my great-aunt Louise, stands to her right, smiling and looking away from the camera. Next to Aunt Louise is my great-grandmother Estellar with her left hand placed on my grandfather's chest. Just past the faces of my grandmother and Aunt Louise is an image on the wall of a white Jesus. I remember thinking it seemed out of place. Everyone within my maternal lineage maintained deep spiritual connections that sat outside of a religious sphere, so I found it a bit odd that they'd hang an image such as this on their wall. And while there were always Bibles around and we'd go to church occasionally, I'd been wracking my brain, trying to get to the root of the meaning of this image and its relationship to the people standing in front of the camera. Why was he white? Was there not an image of a Black Jesus around? There's a Christmas tree nearby – is it a seasonal decoration? Is this even their house?

At my parents' home, we had the freedom to form our individual relationships with God. But in the homes of older relatives in the South and friends of the family, every so often, I would come across the same image of a white Jesus. And at one point, it became difficult for me to reconcile this image with what I was being taught about a spiritual relationship with God: that God was a higher power in one's life that did not necessarily take the form of being the father to a white man. It was one of the challenges for me as I came into my own spirituality – trying to separate that image of God's son from my own ideas of this spiritual being. I'd later learn from my mom that this photograph was taken in Daytona Beach, Florida, at the home of my aunt's godparents, the Baileys. Because everyone in the photograph has since passed on, I still find myself with unanswered questions.

Pictures within pictures tell stories within stories. The intentional curation of photos of family members and friends along walls, positioned across mantles, on nightstands and dressers, or stuck to the refrigerator door raises so many questions: Why is this photograph by the bed, instead of that one? Why were certain pictures selected for framing while others live only in the sleeves of albums?

Now, as I curate imagery along the walls of my own home, I am reminded of the intentionality of my selections, their placements, and what these images mean or represent to me – the power within them and what they may say about me after I'm no longer around to explain them.

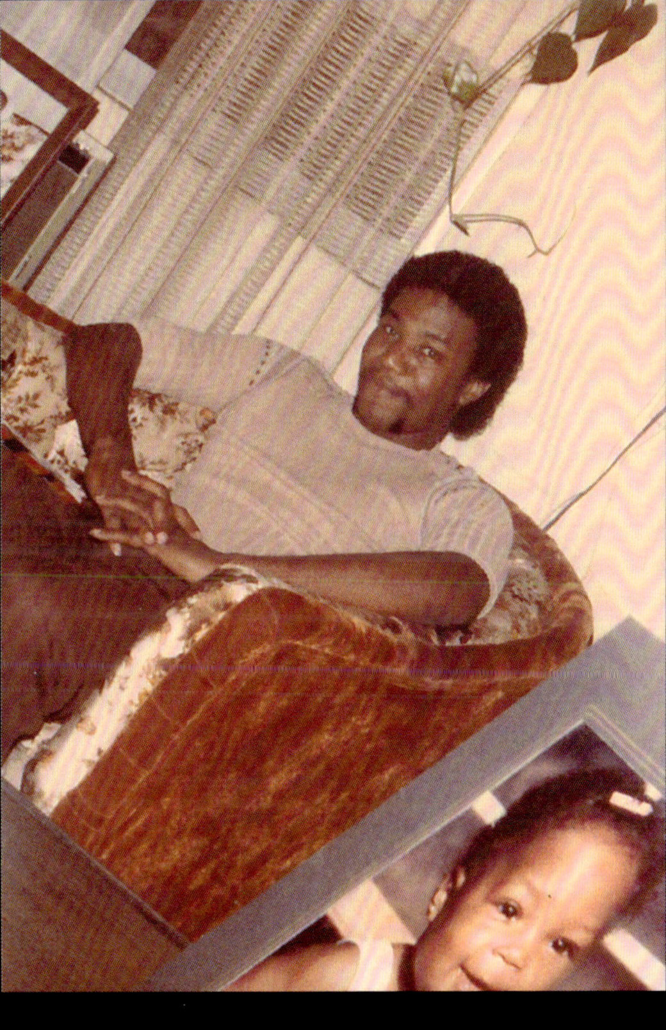

The author's dad sitting with a
baby photo of the author in view
JACKSONVILLE, FL
1980S

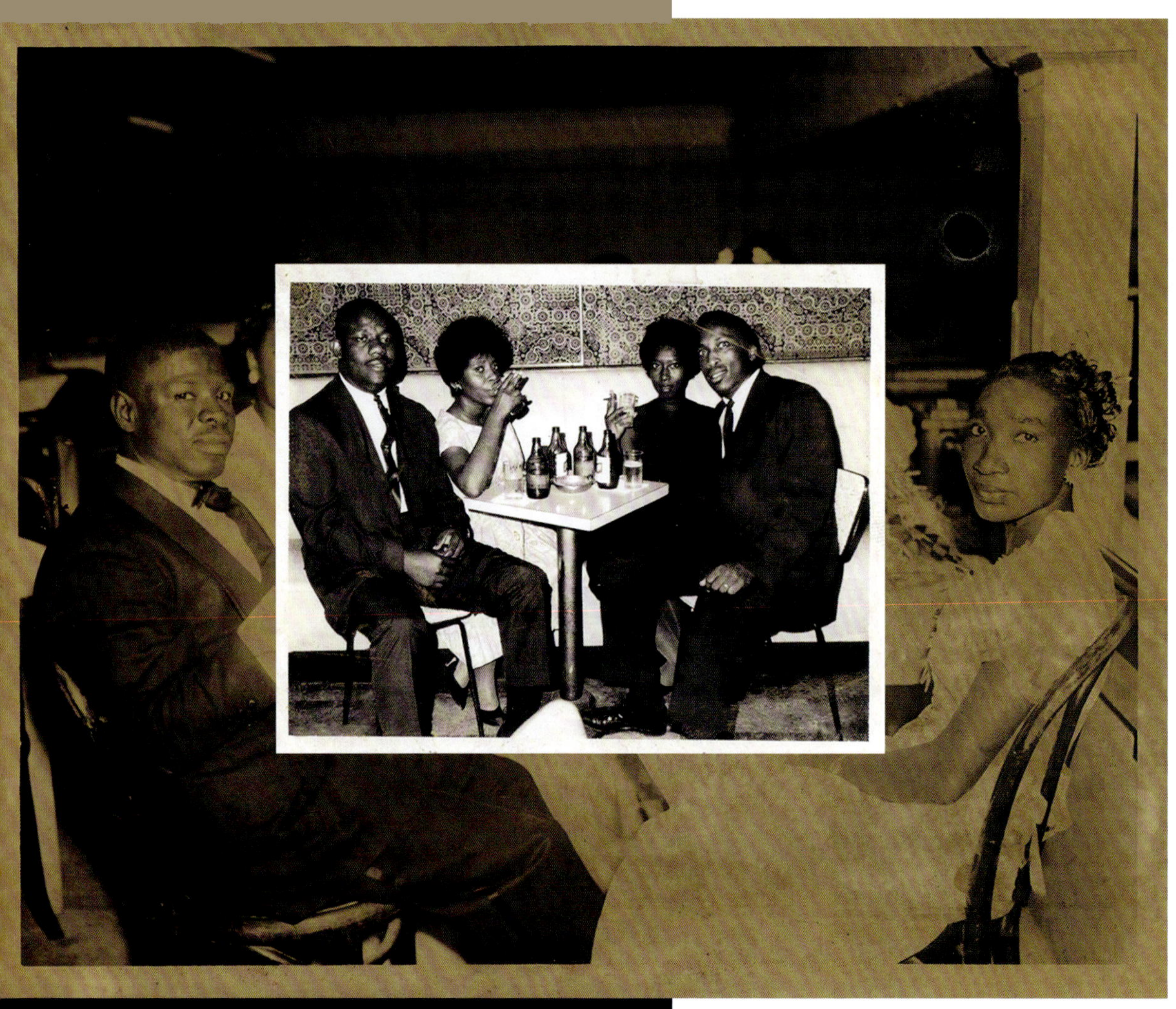

Outside image: David and Velderia Sawyer on a date
Inside image: Joseph and Connie Cambridge on a date
MIAMI, FL

Mother and daughters
BALTIMORE, MD
1958

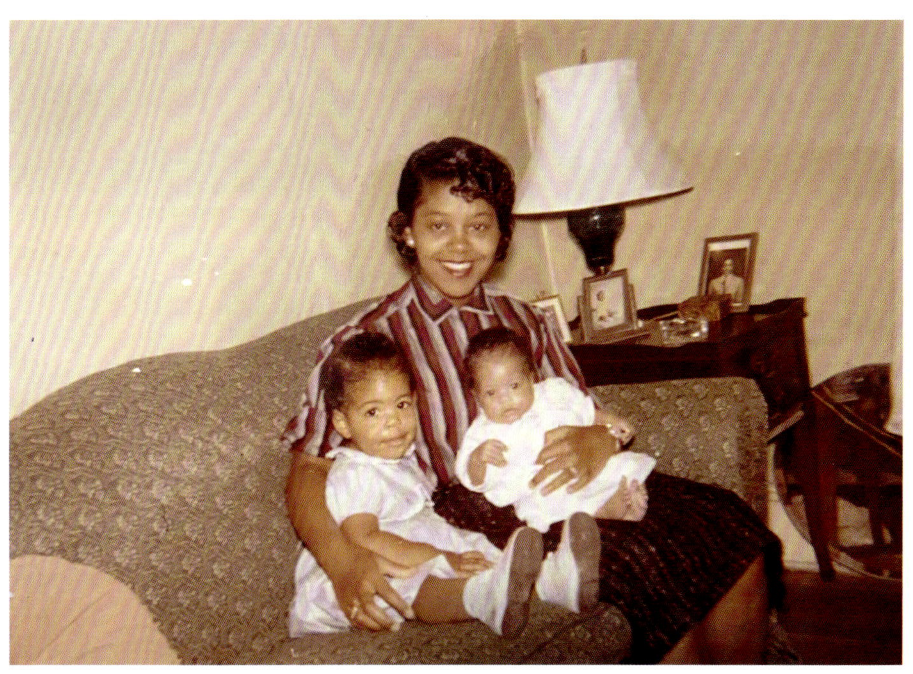

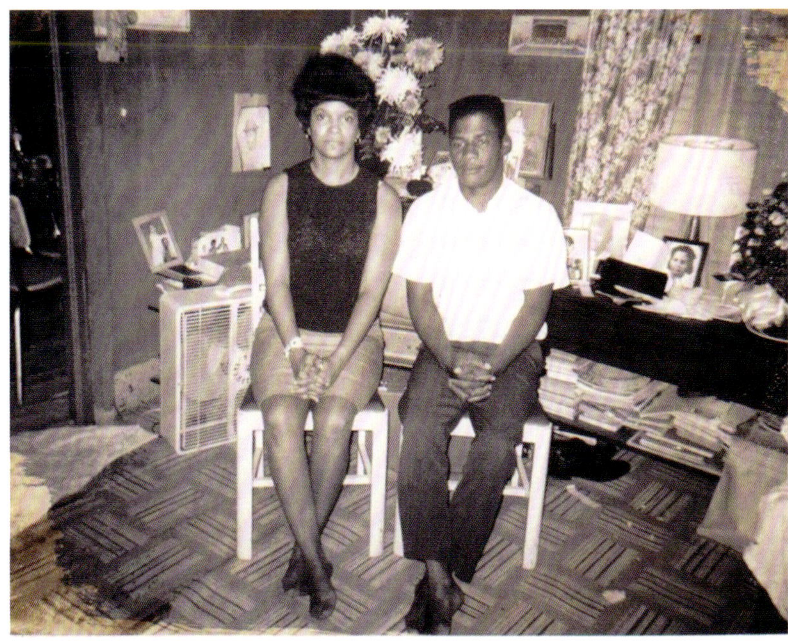

ARDMORE, OK
1950S

Samuel Johnson Sr.

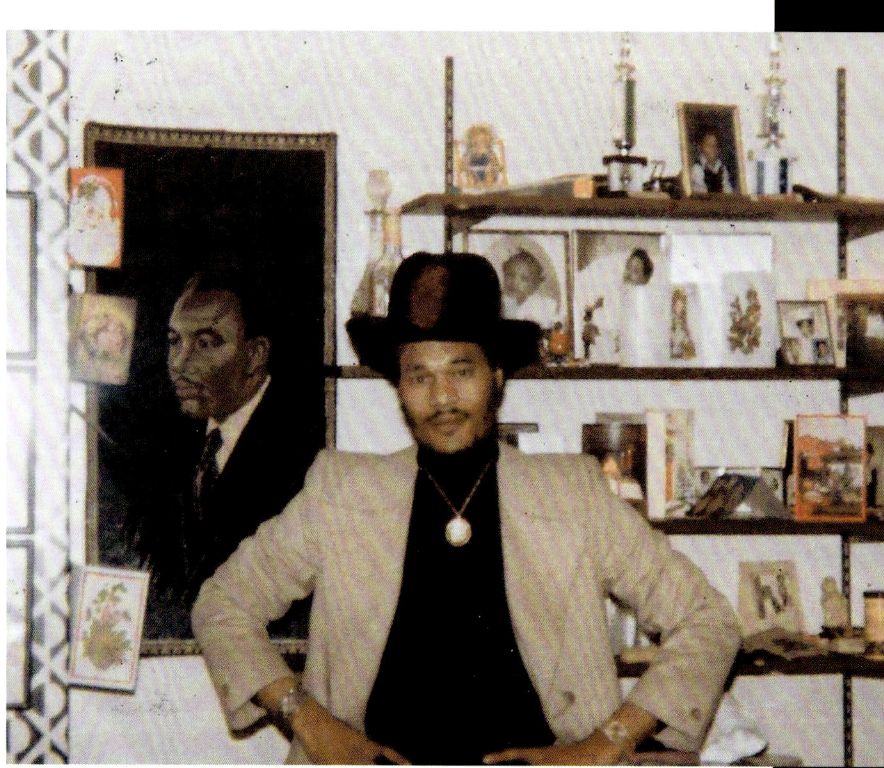

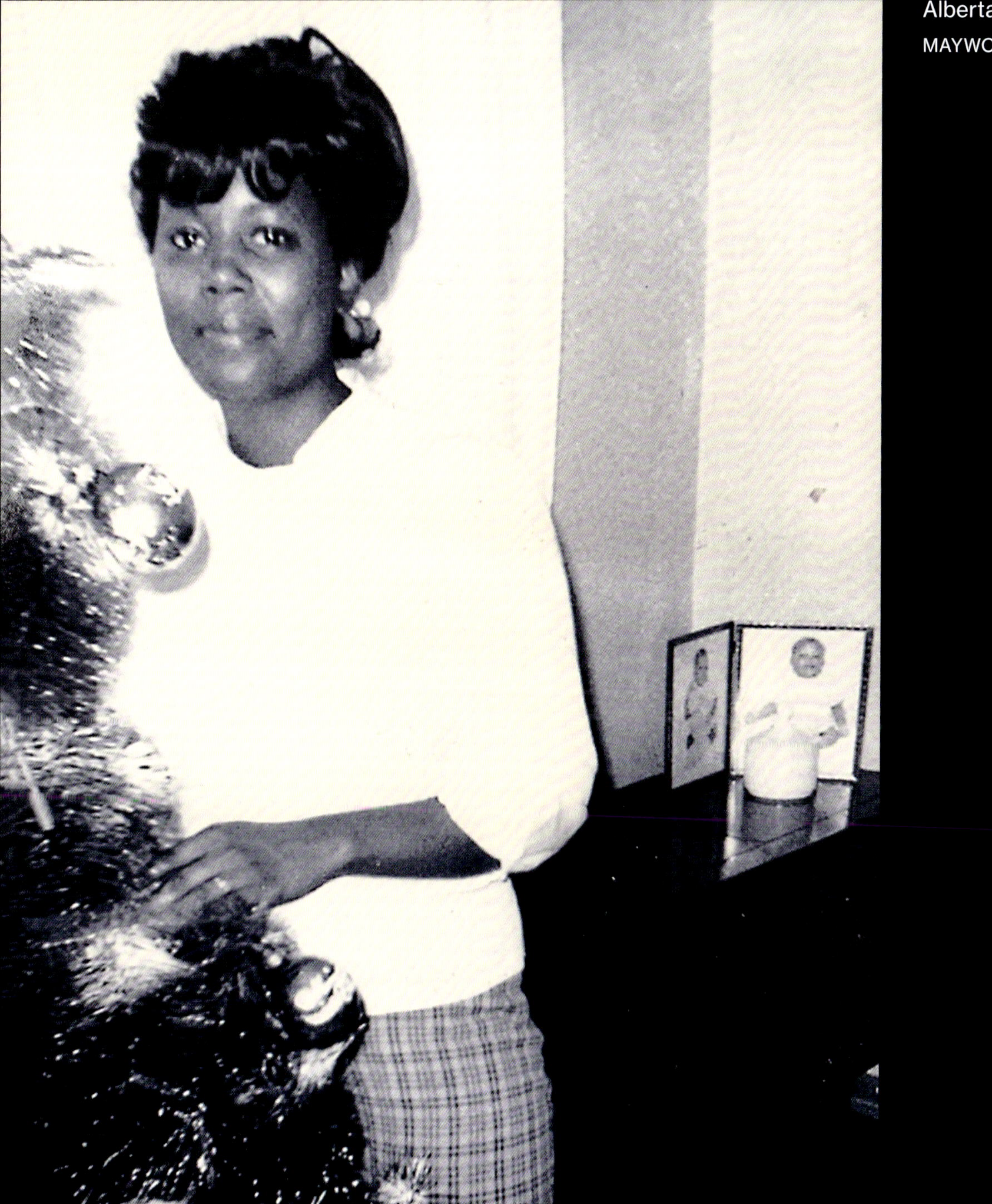

Alberta at home
MAYWOOD, IL

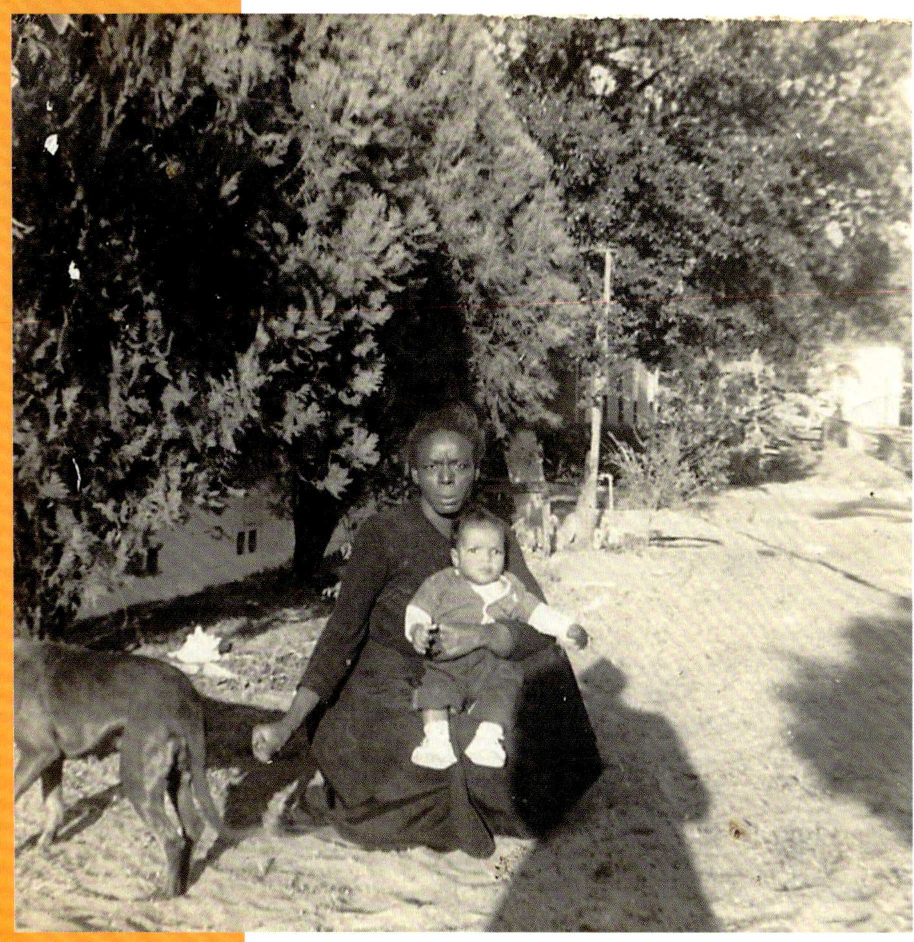

The author's great-grandmother Estellar Beatrice with an unidentified baby
DAYTONA BEACH, FL
CIRCA 1960

LIFE BETWEEN LIFE, IN BLACK AND WHITE

Color photography dates back to as early as the 1800s, and research and development continued throughout the twenty-first century to create the best formula for analog picture-making. However, before there was color, there was black and white. In black-and-white photos you may not be able to tell when a photo was taken, the ages of the sitters, or what time of year it was. There's no red alarm clock to distract, no gold sequined dress, no hazel eyes that draw you in. Black-and-white photos allow for the subject's emotions to be the central focus, bringing our attention to certain elements using shadows and light. Perhaps that is why it is the most timeless form of photography.

Almost all of the photographs in my family albums from the 1970s through the mid-1980s were in color and appear to have been taken through a combination of disposable and compact film cameras. Many of these photographs have date stamps from when they were developed at the local photo laboratory, and these dates are a valuable resource – particularly when reconstructing timelines without context. By the mid-1990s, most of our family photographs were captured on color film by my dad's camera and on Polaroids by my grandmother. By the late 1990s we shifted to digital photography. During this time, my siblings and I were coming of age and alternating between using digital and disposable cameras for color photography.

For me, color photography creates a sense of urgency and can be used to fulfill an immediate need or desire. The rich colors and details make the images pop and appear more relatable. Even if a color photograph precedes my birth, there's still something within the image that feels present, alive, and vibrant. It wasn't until I began studying photography that I came to learn more deeply about black-and-white photography and its use within news reportage and various artistic mediums. The essence of beauty captured within black-and-white images serves as a bridge between space and time. These photos display a timelessness that creates reactions in the body – causing one to change their posture, alter their breathing patterns, and even gasp as they guide their eyes back and forth, in and out of shadows, compositions, and framing.

Whether an image was captured by an amateur photographer or one who had studied their craft for many years, a black-and-white photograph offers a different way of seeing – especially to someone who is not on either side of the lens, but rather a witness to the resulting image.

Covering a wide range of photography styles, this section takes us through everyday moments captured in black-and-white with tones of sepia – a process applied to black-and-white photography to help prolong its life span. Black-and-white photography is always living and breathing the truth.

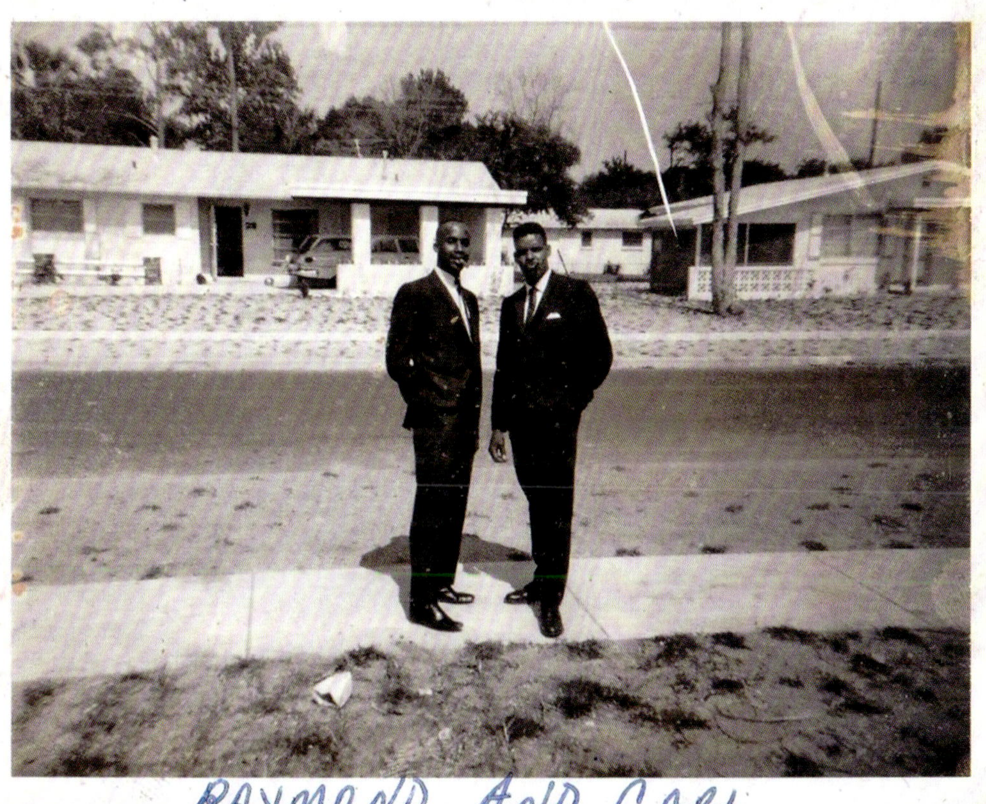

The author's grandfather Raymond (right) and his friend Mr. Carl (left) standing in front of her grandparents' new home

DAYTONA BEACH, FL

1936

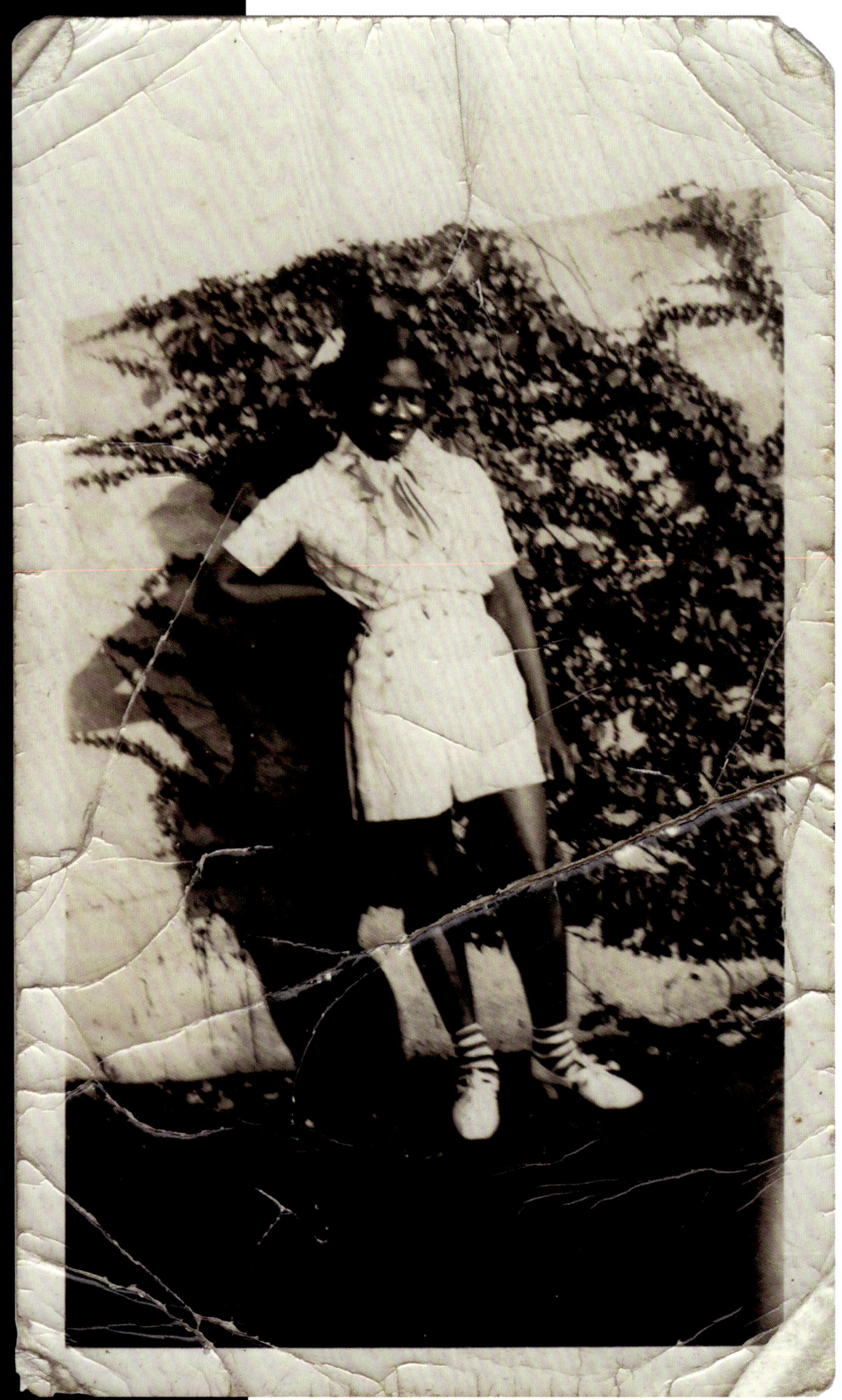

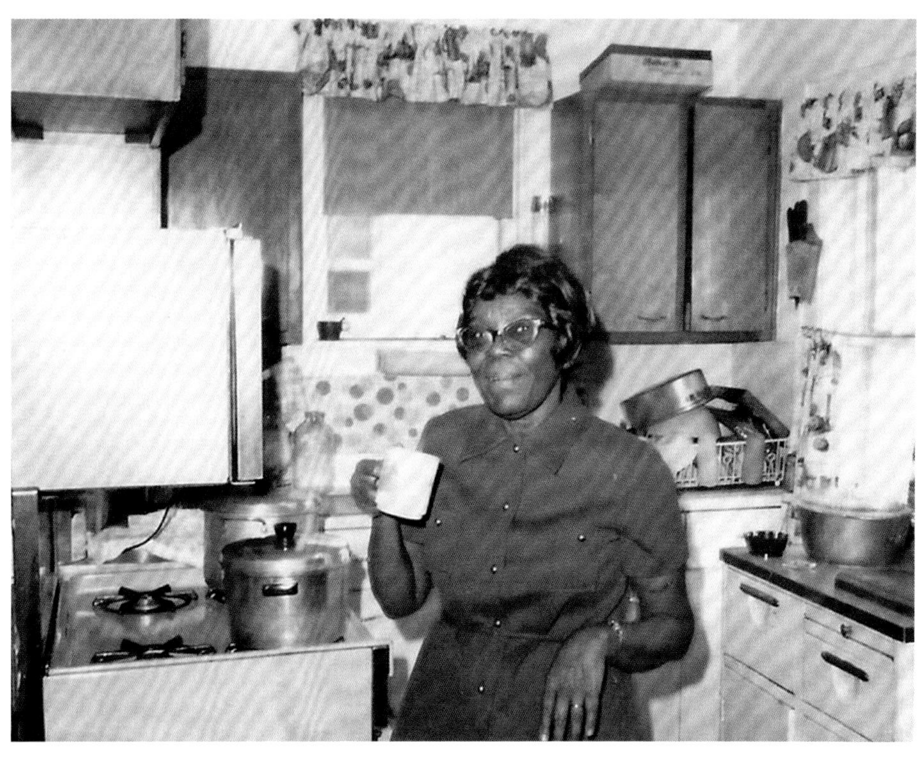

Tressie Knox in her daughter's kitchen

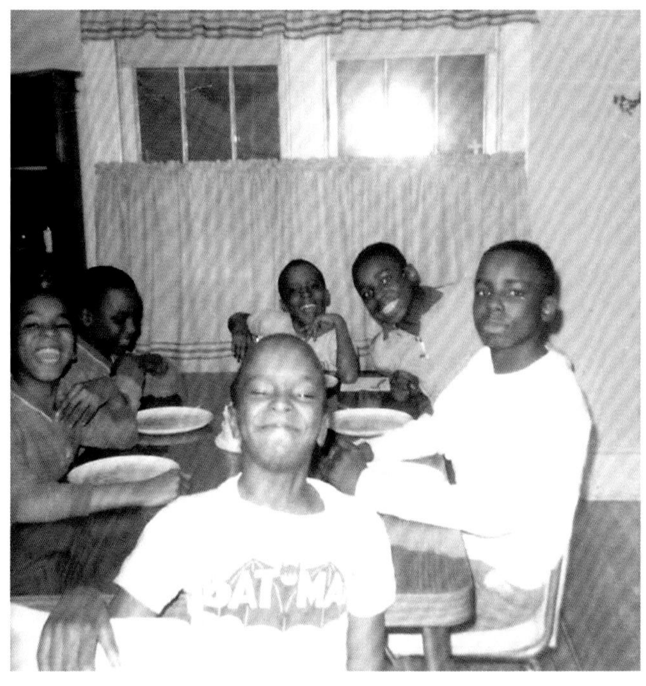

Six brothers at the dinner table

1960S

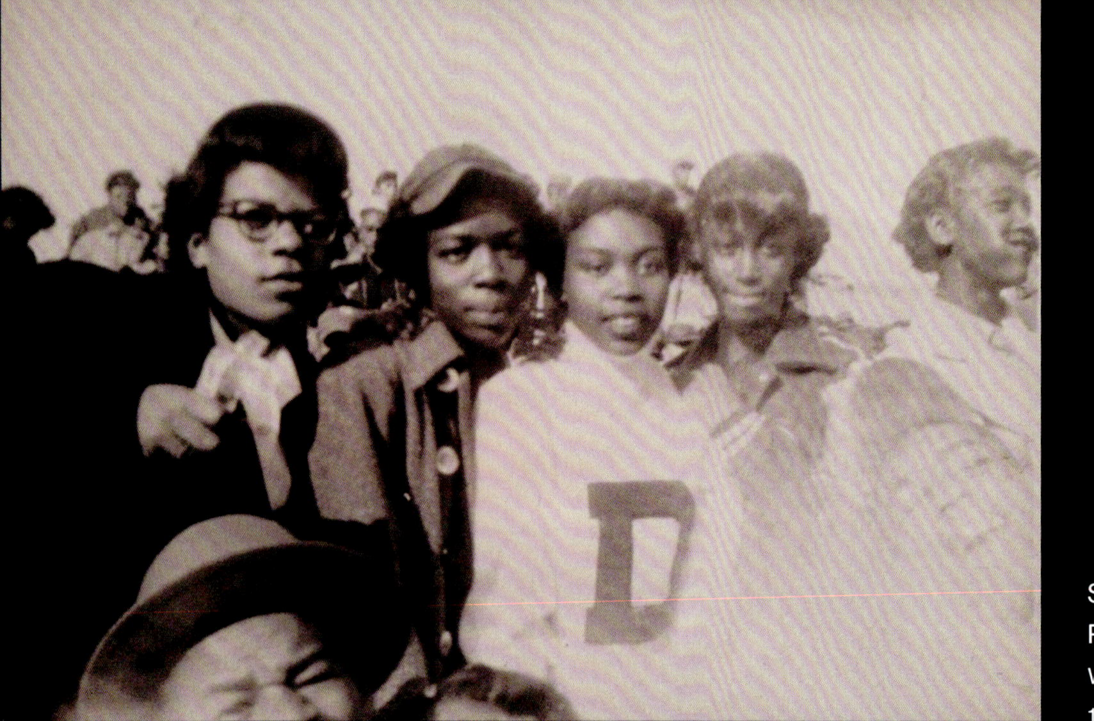

Students at Dunbar
Public High School
WASHINGTON, D.C.
1950S

Party for Delores
FRENCHTOWN, FL
1960

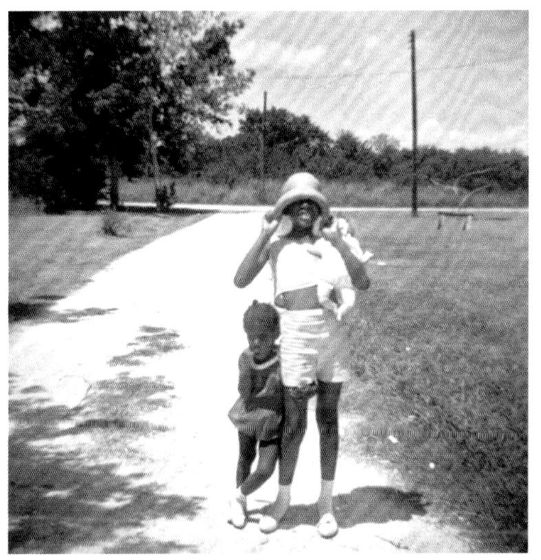

EAST COLUMBIA, TX
1960S

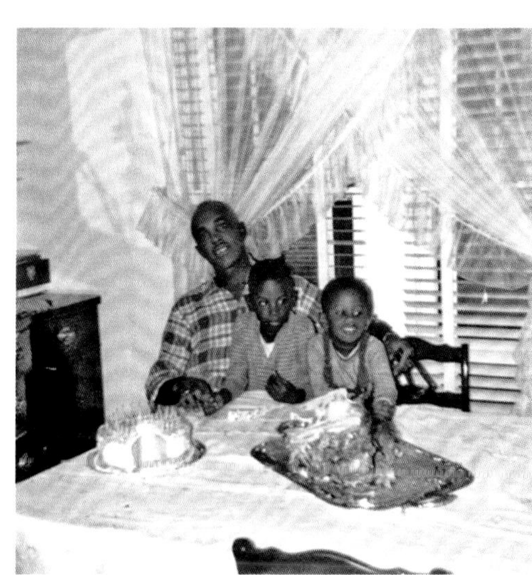

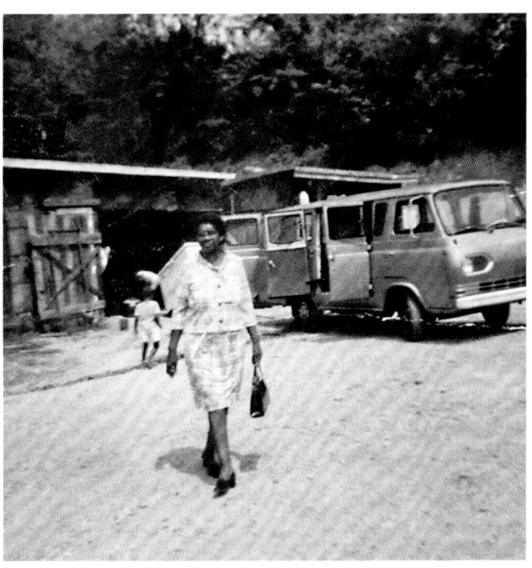

JAMAICA
1950S

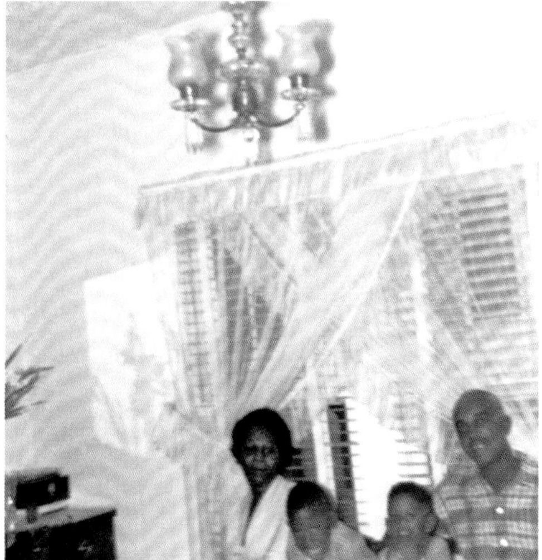

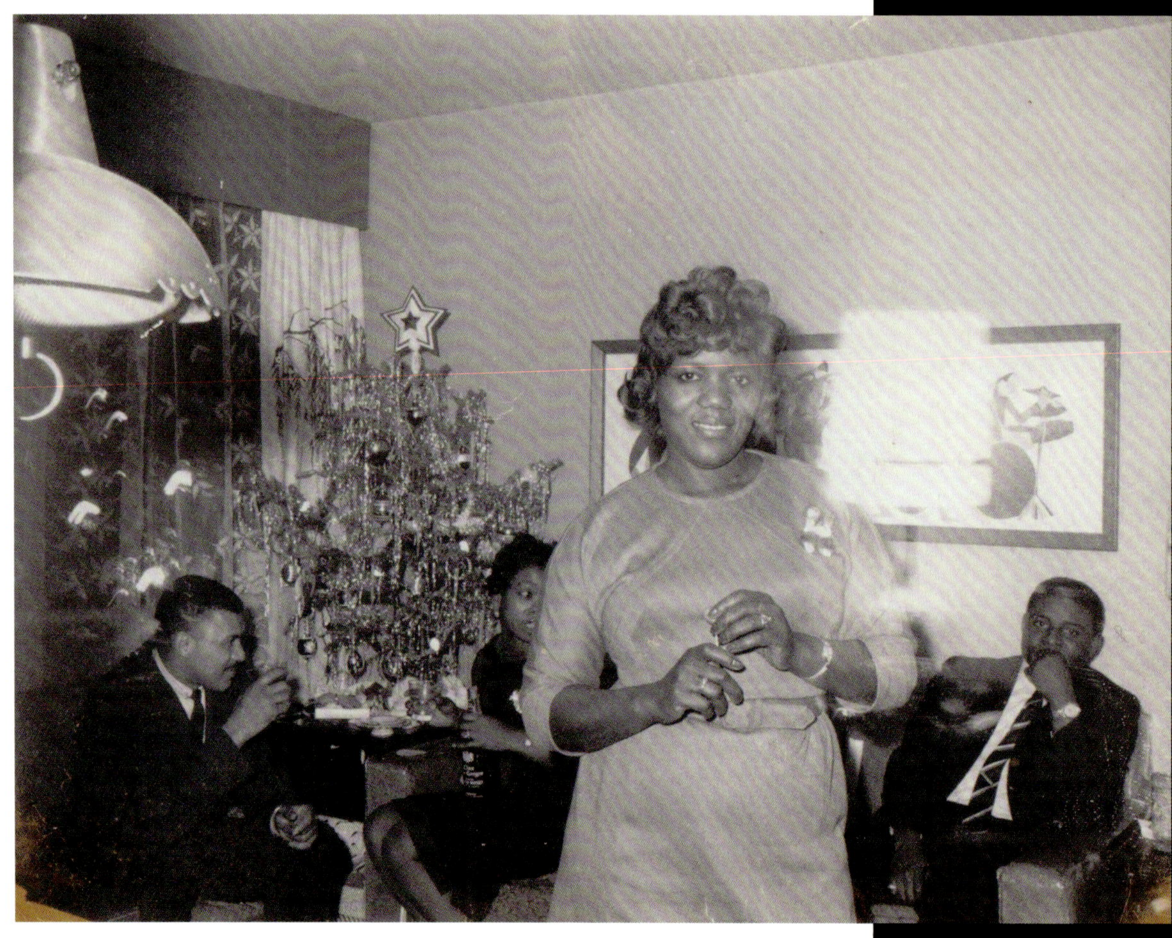

Grandma Q

1960S

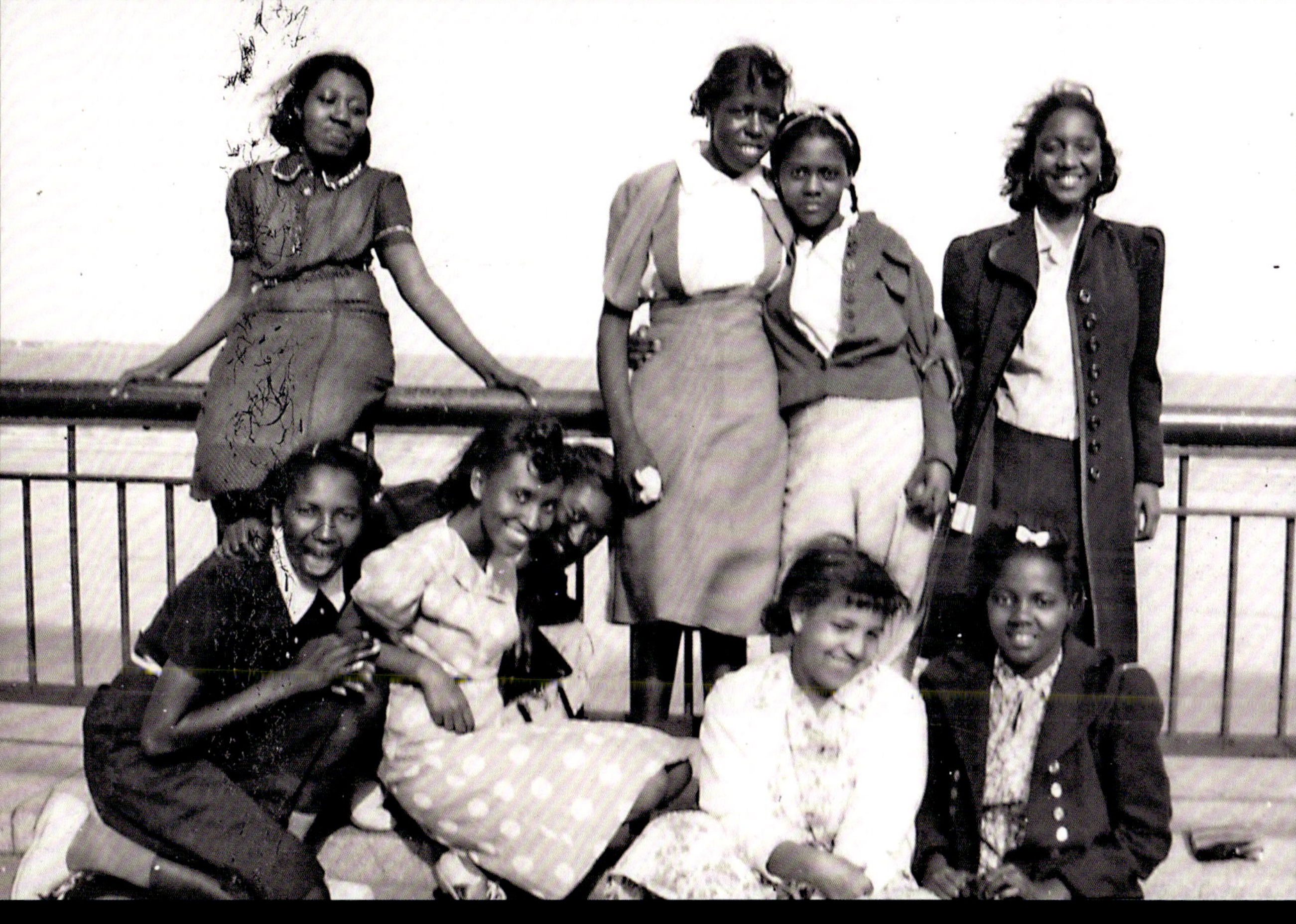

At the beach

1930S

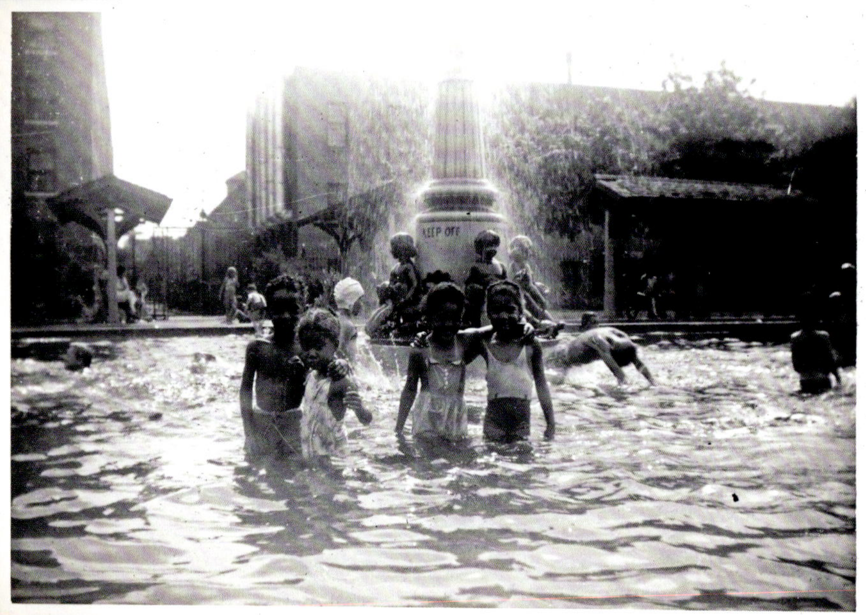

In the fountain
BOSTON, MA
CIRCA 1940

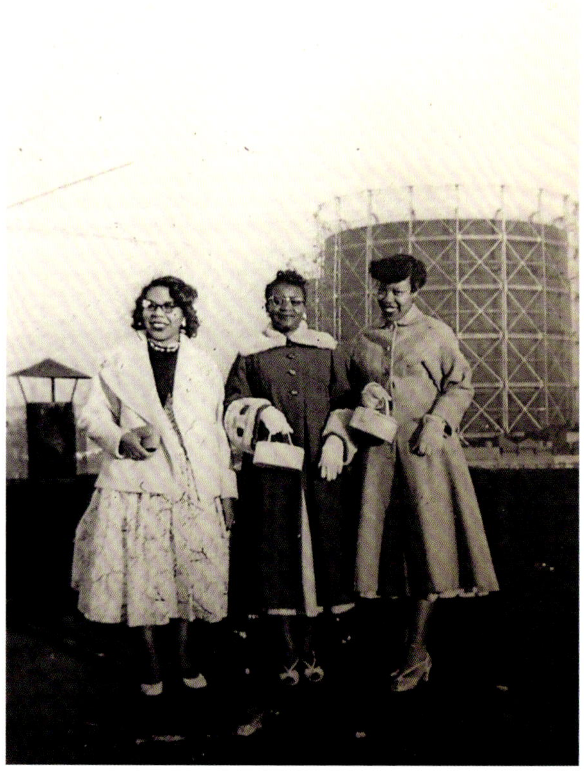

1950S

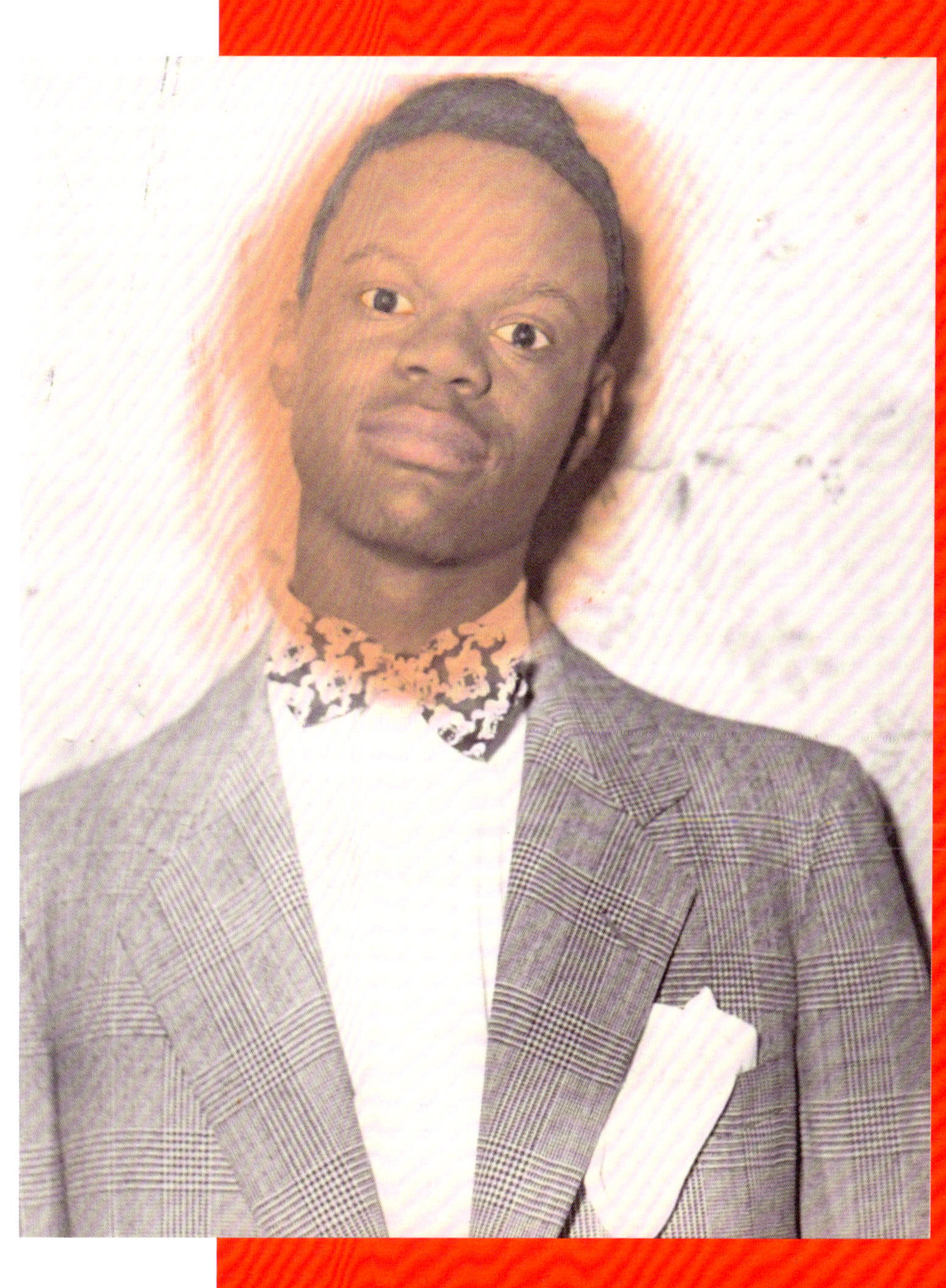

Recolored photo of
Abraham Parham
BALTIMORE, MD
1950S

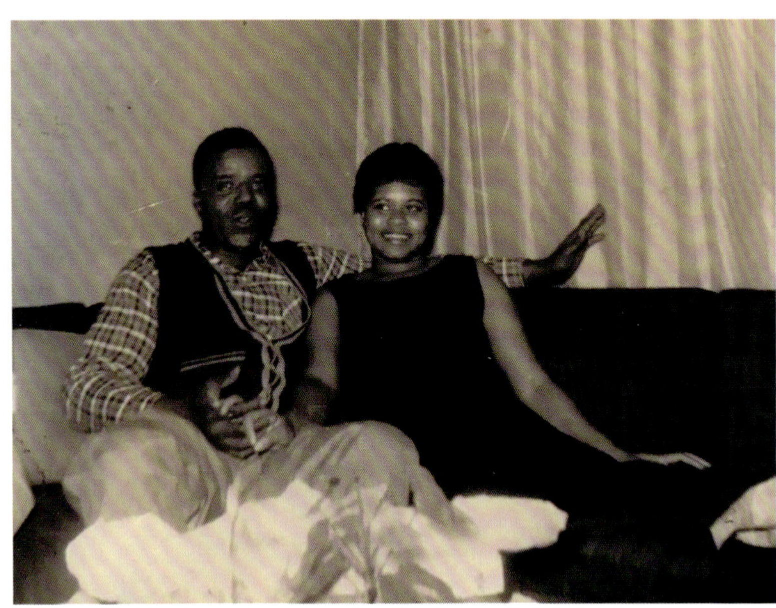

Ernest and Annette Winbush
NEWPORT NEWS, VA
1962

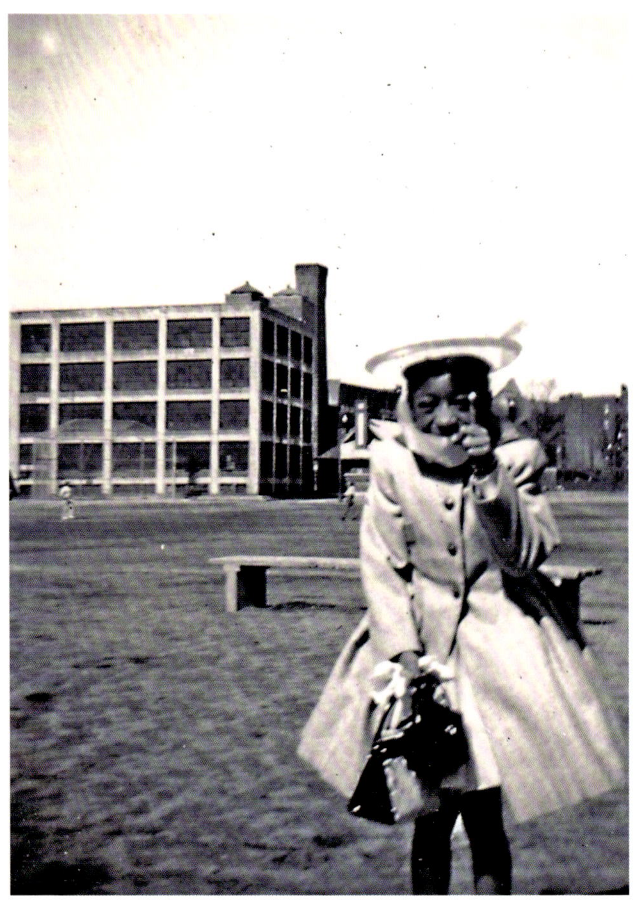

Cheryl Hall in
Columbus Park
CIRCA 1940

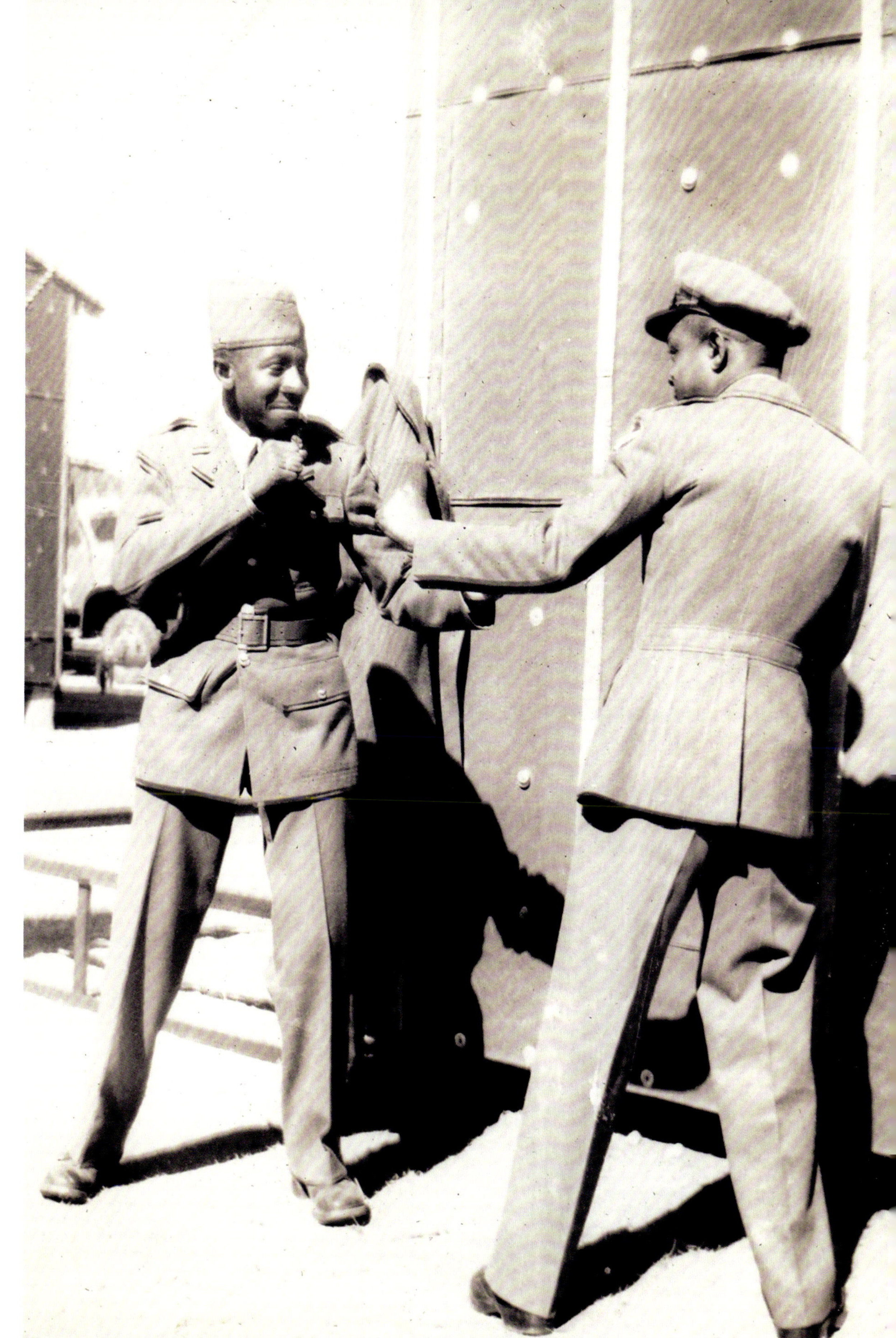

Army base
CIRCA 1940

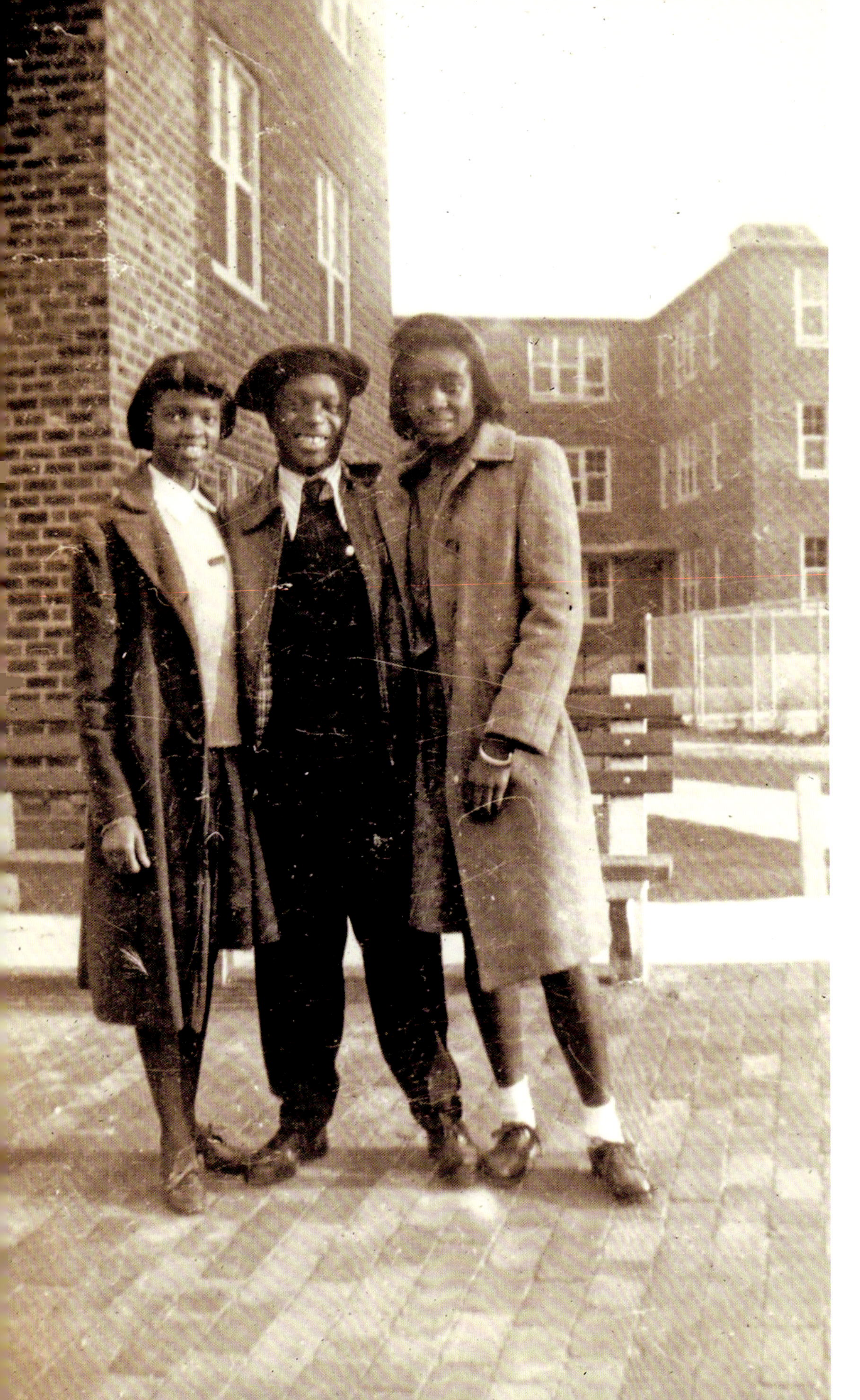

Lenox Street Housing Development
BOSTON, MA
CIRCA 1940

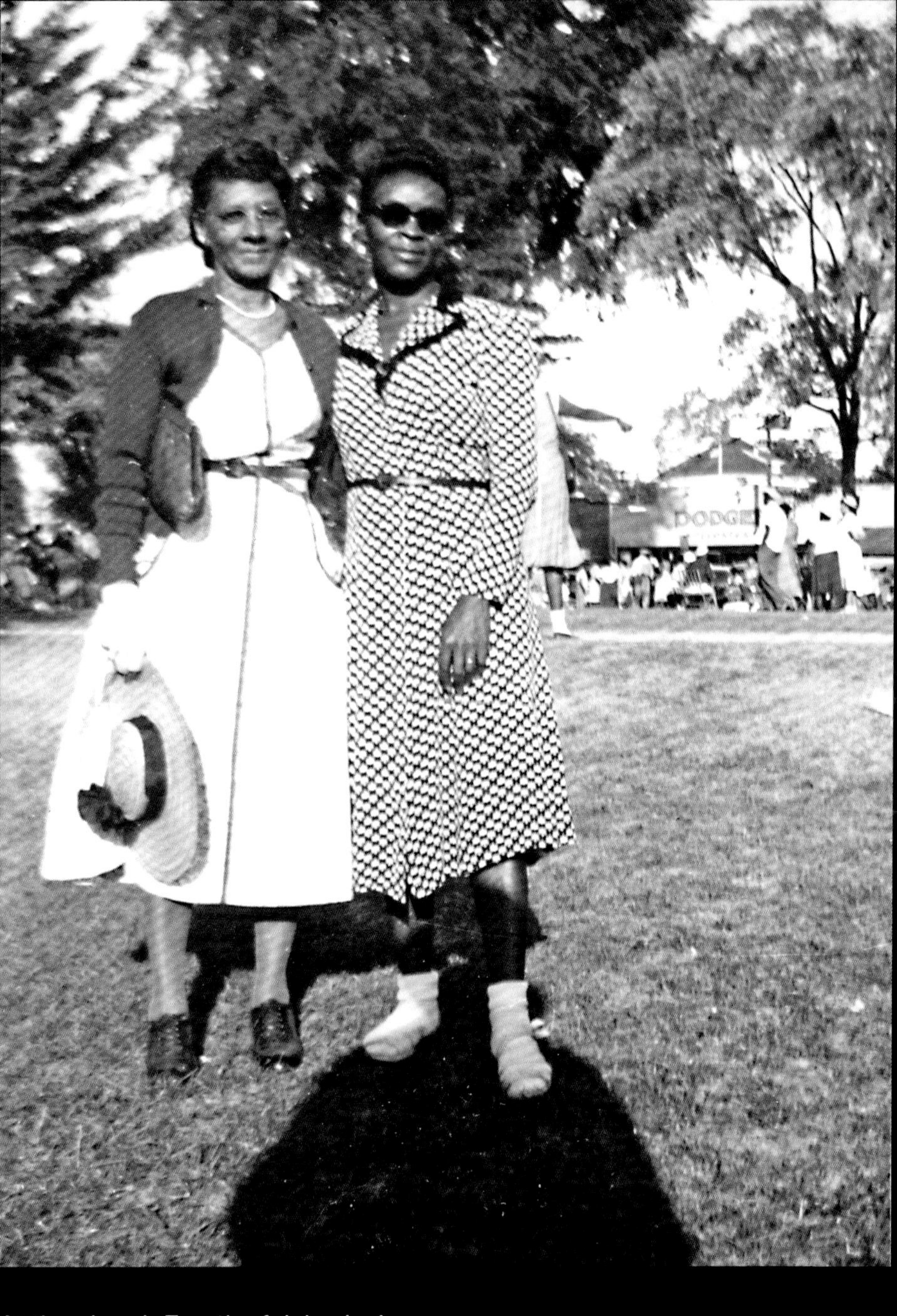

At the church Fourth of July picnic

1953

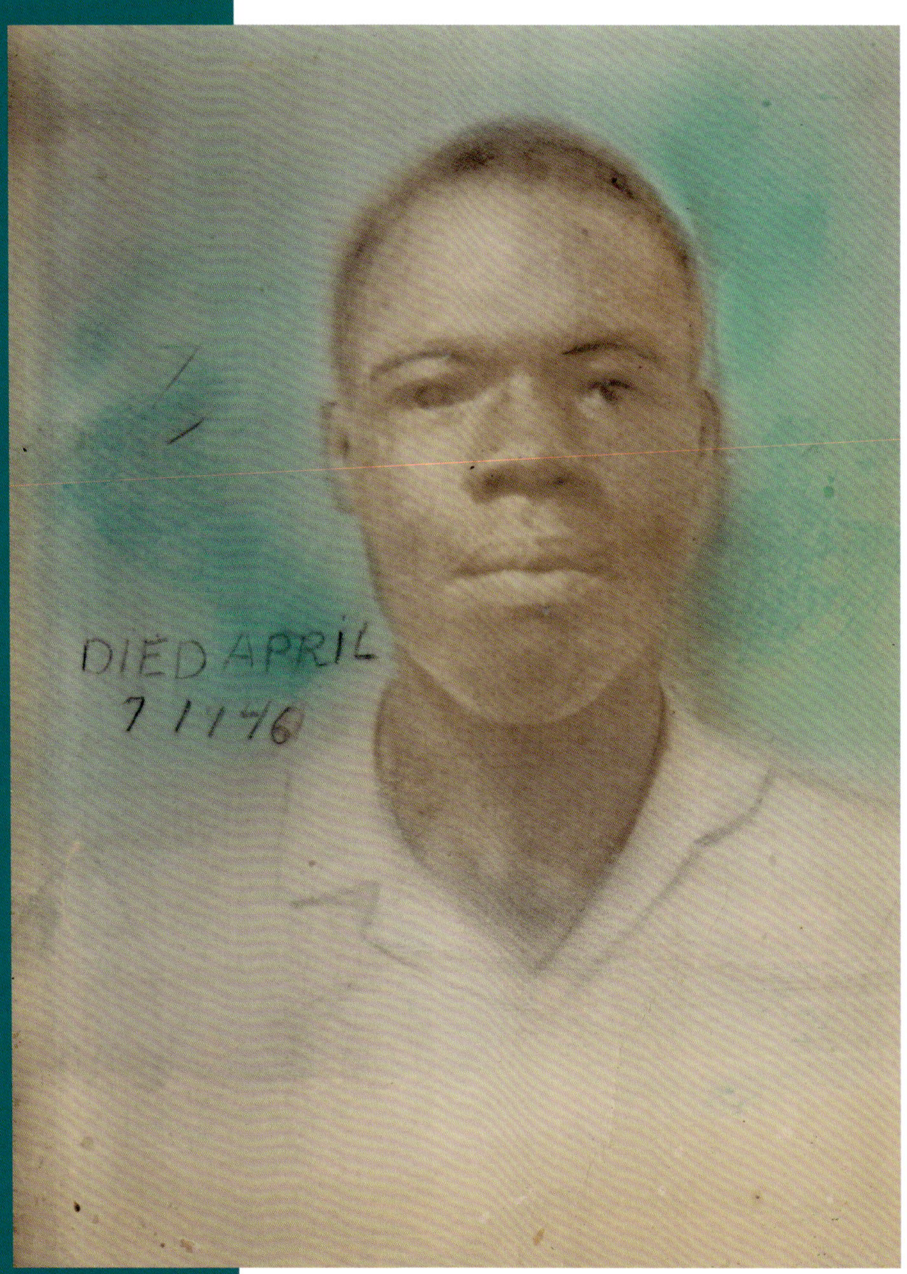

Portrait of the author's great-grandfather Eddie Amerson Sr.

THINGS WE LEAVE BEHIND

How do we memorialize lives fully lived outside of family photographs? Keepsakes are one of the most treasured artifacts within my family, particularly after someone's passing. There's a section in my family album dedicated to funeral programs paired with dried roses, personalized napkins, and ticket stubs in protective sleeves marking the date and location of an occasion. There's also a hand-drawn portrait of my maternal great-grandfather Eddie, who died in 1946 at 30 years of age. It's the only image of him known to exist and the only thing left behind that carries his face.

The ability to experience a person through something that belonged to them, something that they touched or cherished, overwhelms me with gratitude. The preservation of these keepsakes gives us an opportunity to share in the beauty of the things left behind while we celebrate the life of a loved one, whether it's an article of clothing, a part of their music collection, a book, prayer, or highlighted page of scripture.

I inherited my dad's favorite red robe, his old keychain with my baby picture on one side and his boating license on the other, and the fifty-dollar bill that was in his pocket at the time of his passing. Each of these keepsakes has a different meaning, but all of them connect me to my dad.

This section explores the ephemera in family archives, the spirit of our family history, the part that lives beyond the body.

Alexander Facey, 1924–2019

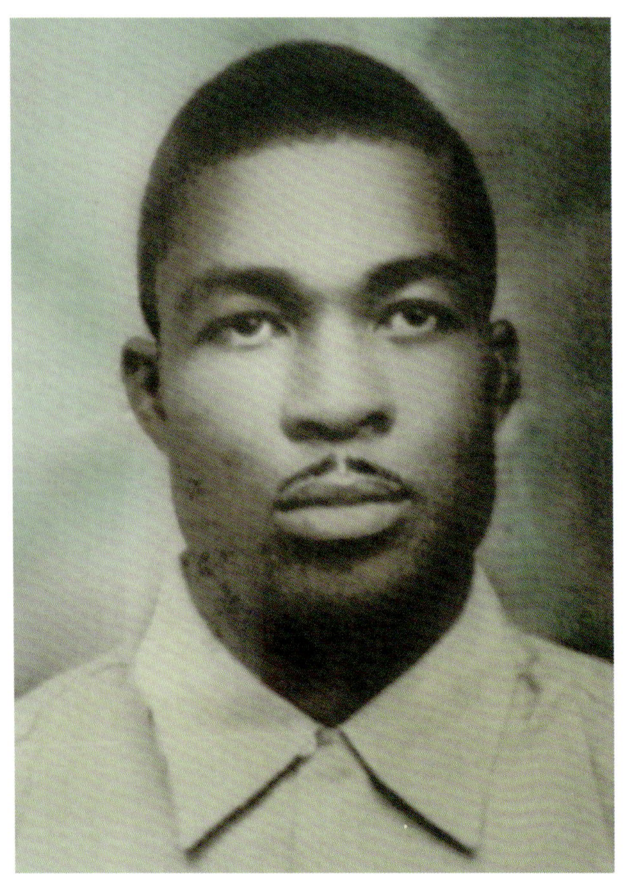

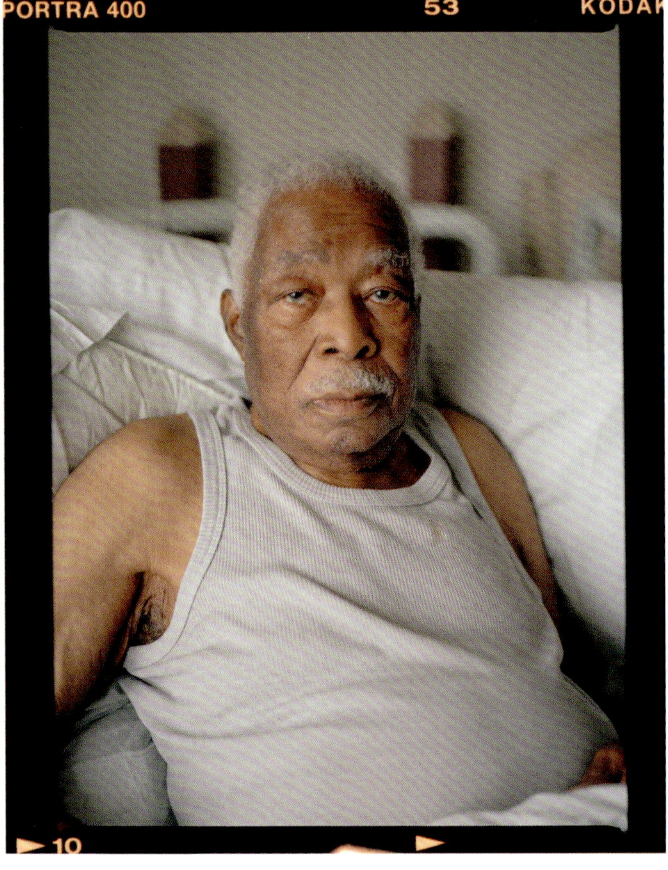

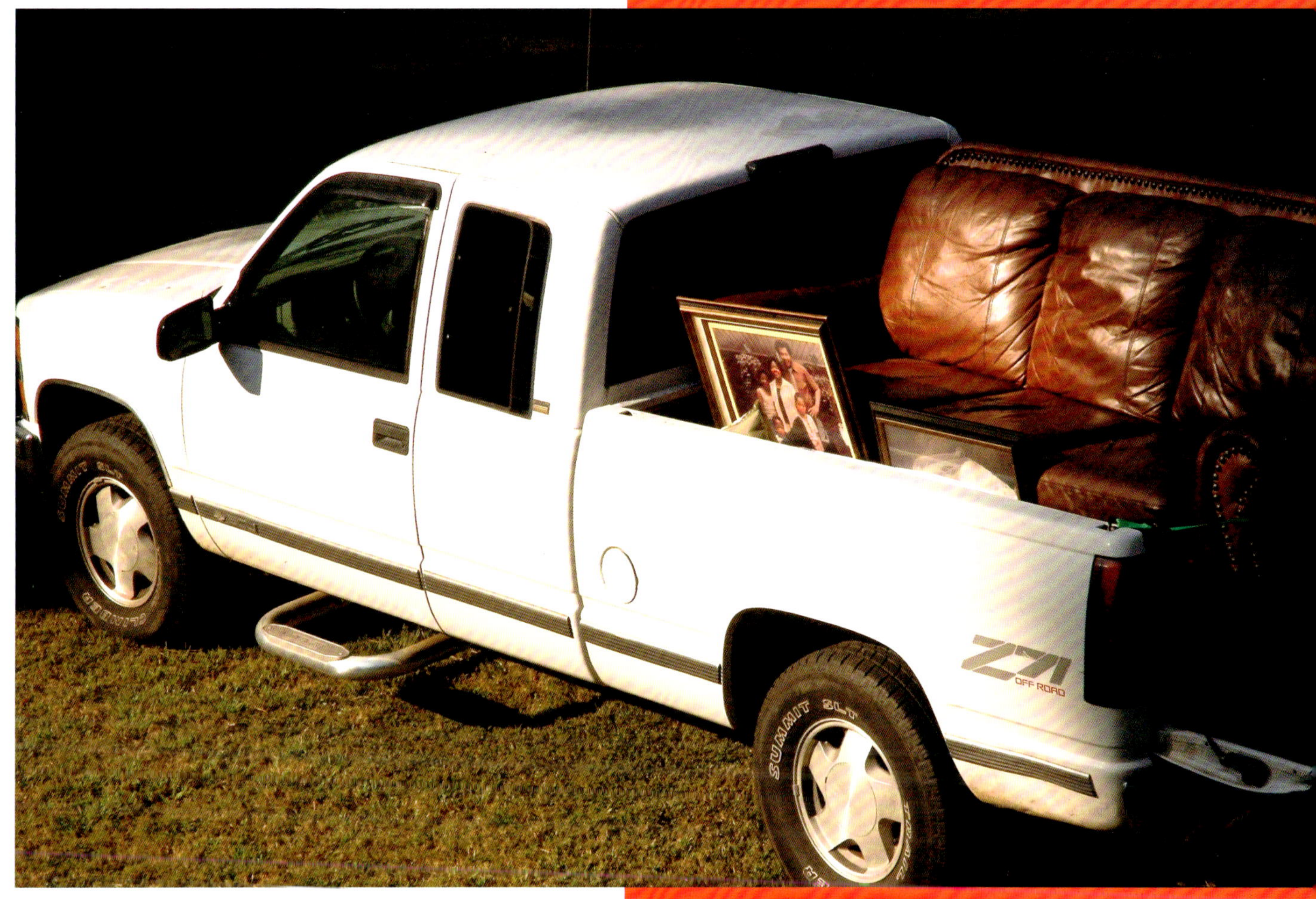

Ernestine Miles Mann's possessions – including her husband's brown leather couch and a family portrait from the 1970s – being transported to a relative's home when she moved to an assisted-living facility.
2019

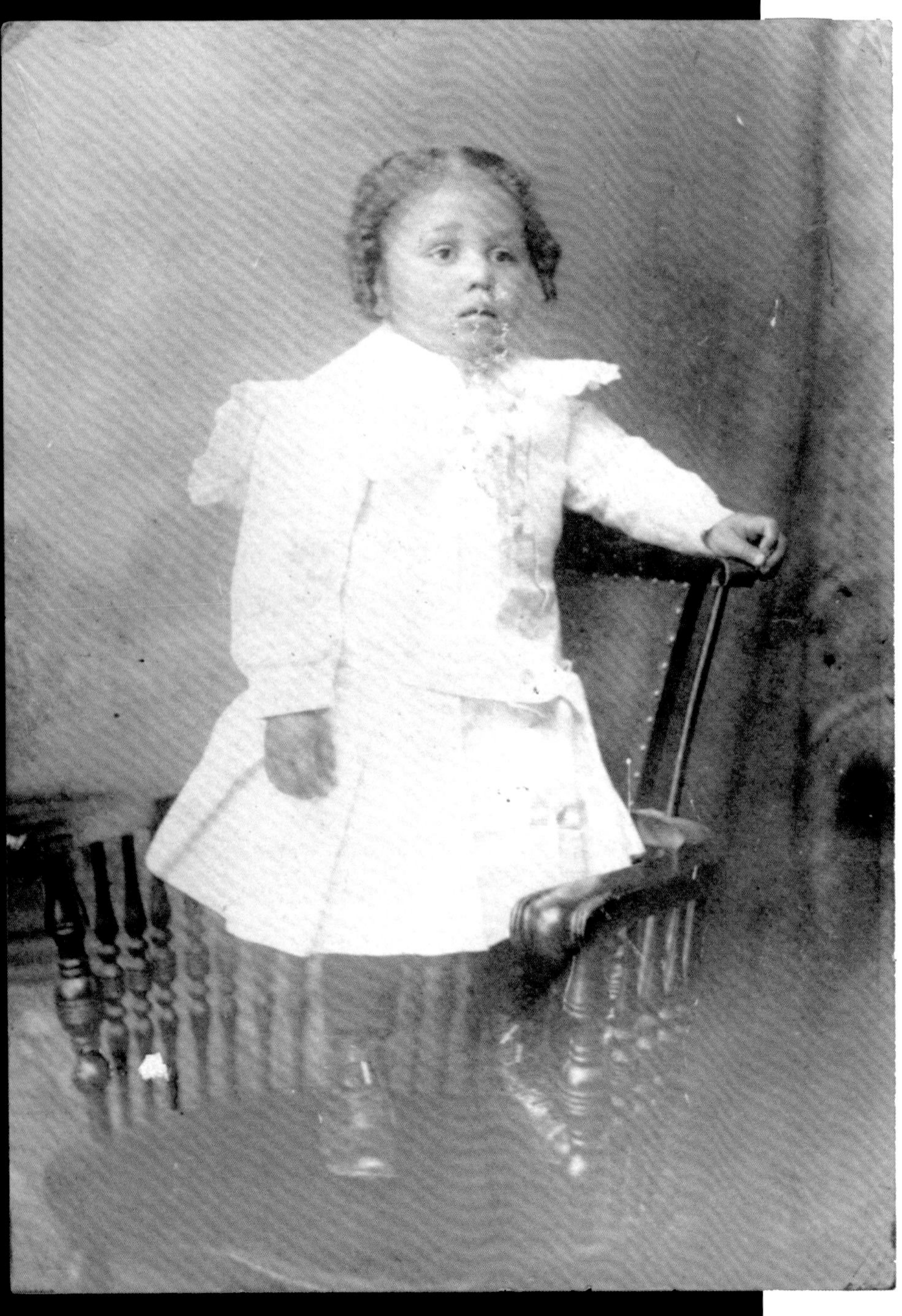

→ Letter from Dr. Edwin D. Moten to his daughter Myrtle Bell Moten explaining why he sent her money although she did not ask, and telling her that she may call anytime at his expense.
1947

Myrtle Bell Moten
1911

March.I6, '47.

My dear daughter Myrtle:-

I received your most recent letter yesterday which I could not give my full attention until today. I have read and reread it and perhaps I have the information you desired me have.

No, you did not ask for aid in your recent letter, but it was in part as this one before me; stressing your sacrifices and hardship under which you have had to live for several years without the proper assistance from the proper source. Knowing I could help you in your apparent distress, it was just a part of me as a father to do what my conscious bade me. I was happy to do so and did not feel encroached upon in the least.

From the memorandum you made in this letter before me; I must say you have really done well and made tremendous sacrifices. I think some one should encourage you and have you know you have done a wonderful job, let it be appreciated or not by those whom you were making this sacrifice,to make your home pleasant, comfortable and co opporative. The Lord has much in store for those who honestly serve Him and try to do the right and fair thing by every body.

The other night when you were talking over the phone, I did not know at the time you were having the charges transfered to me, otherwise I would not have said a thing. I thought you were paying the call amd I did not wish you to have a big bill to pay and going away too. I was surprised when I came out of the bath room when wife and Annetta told me the call was to be paid here and you had said you had to make it short. Now be sure to call us at our expense before you leave and talk as long as you choose, as it will be far less than me making a trip to see you off. try to make your call around IO P.M. any night.

Everything is going on alright with us all and happiness and good will continue to abide. With best wishes, I am

Devotedly

Dad.

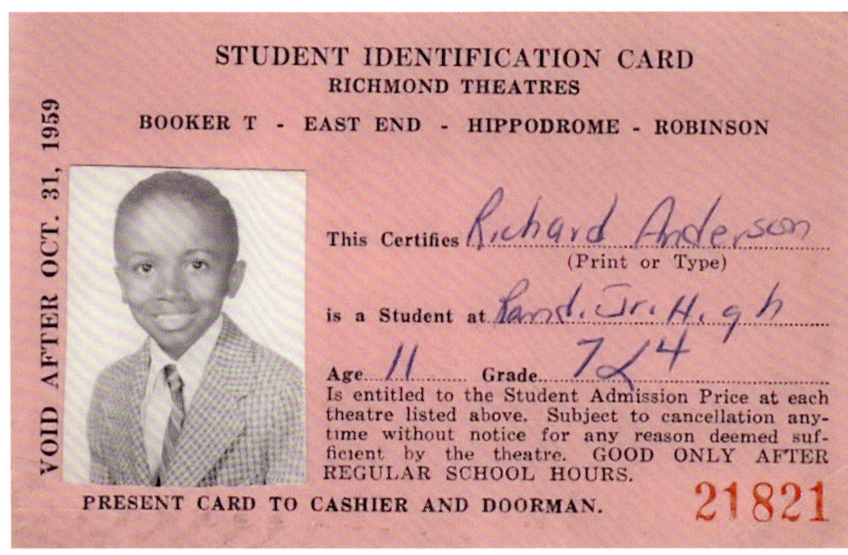

STUDENT IDENTIFICATION CARD
RICHMOND THEATRES
BOOKER T - EAST END - HIPPODROME - ROBINSON

VOID AFTER OCT. 31, 1959

This Certifies Richard Anderson
(Print or Type)
is a Student at Rand. Jr. High
Age 11 Grade 7L4
Is entitled to the Student Admission Price at each theatre listed above. Subject to cancellation anytime without notice for any reason deemed sufficient by the theatre. GOOD ONLY AFTER REGULAR SCHOOL HOURS.

PRESENT CARD TO CASHIER AND DOORMAN. 21821

Richard Anderson's student identification card. In order to get discounted tickets for theaters in Richmond, Virginia, students had to have these identification cards. The theaters listed at the top of the card were the only ones Black people were permitted to enter.

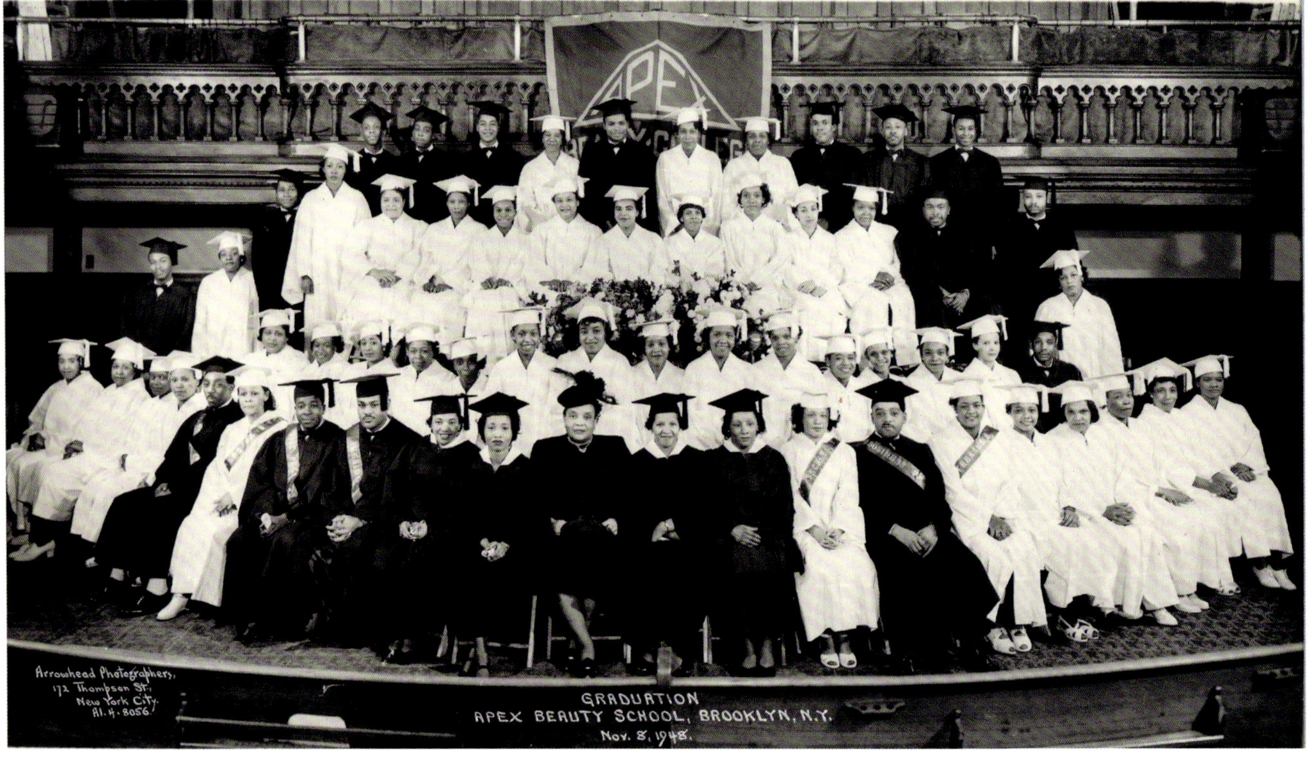

Class photo from Apex Beauty School
BROOKLYN, NY
1948

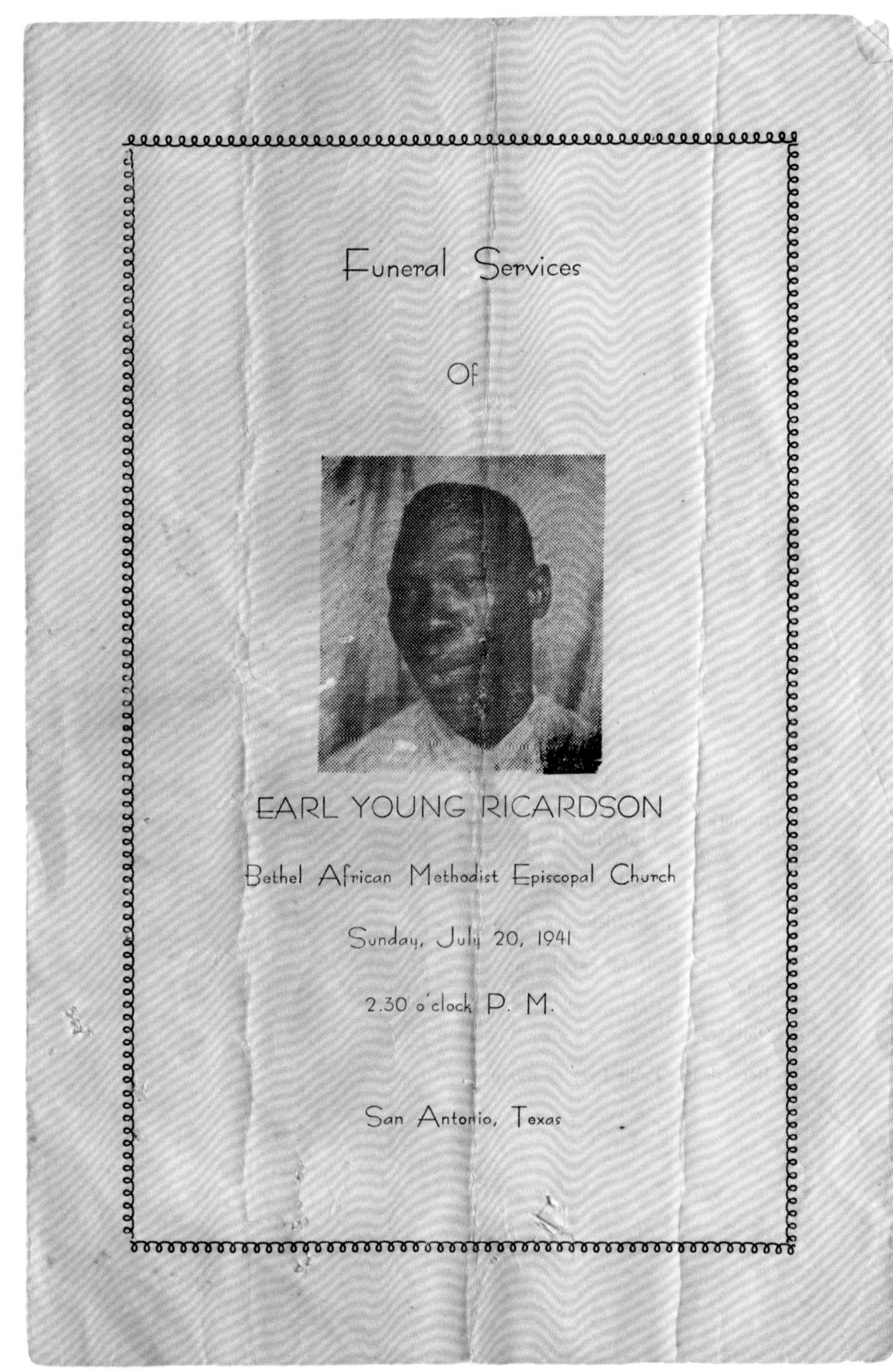
Funeral Services

Of

EARL YOUNG RICARDSON

Bethel African Methodist Episcopal Church

Sunday, July 20, 1941

2.30 o'clock P. M.

San Antonio, Texas

Funeral program
for Earl Young
Ricardson
SAN ANTONIO, TX
1941

PART II

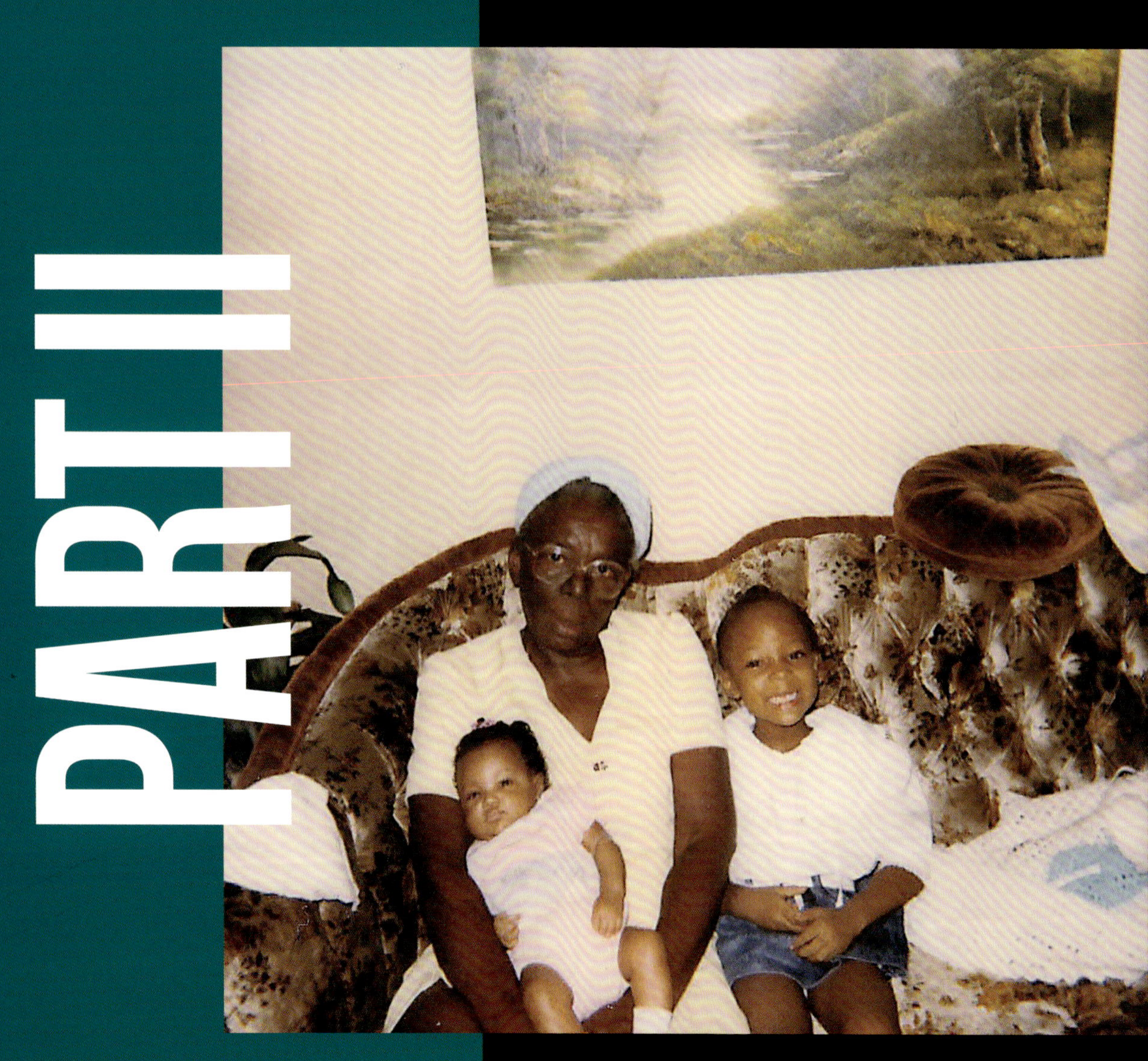

INTERIORS

HOLDING SPACE AND KEEPING TIME

Sharing space with loved ones is a love language all its own, a comfort to the soul. Like many Black family's homes, my grandmother's home was the center of all centers. No one held you as tight as she did; her hugs gave us the permission to either lose ourselves or find whatever it was that we needed. Her laugh filled every crevice of her home. These are the things I miss most about her: the way she felt and the sound of her laughter.

By the mid-1990s, our family began pairing our cameras with a camcorder to record films as a way to bridge and record life lived between photographs. The digitization of these 8mm films that documented movement and sound has brought me so much joy. It has also offered powerful insights to younger family members who were not yet around to spend time with our elders in the flesh giving a sense of their personalities and how they took up space in the world. But I also like to consider the sound we can only access through memory, when there are no home movies or other forms of audio to pull from or return to. Often a photo or still can help activate that memory and bring us back to a certain time and place. Photography helps us track the time of our loved ones in addition to ourselves. We can see their joys and interests, how they gathered during the holidays, how they worshipped, the ways in which they smiled in family portraits. This series gives us a look into Black people and all of the ways that we take up space through time.

← Previous: The author sitting on her grandmother's couch with her younger sister and great-grandmother. Her great-grandmother was visiting from Daytona Beach, Florida.
JACKSONVILLE, FL
1988

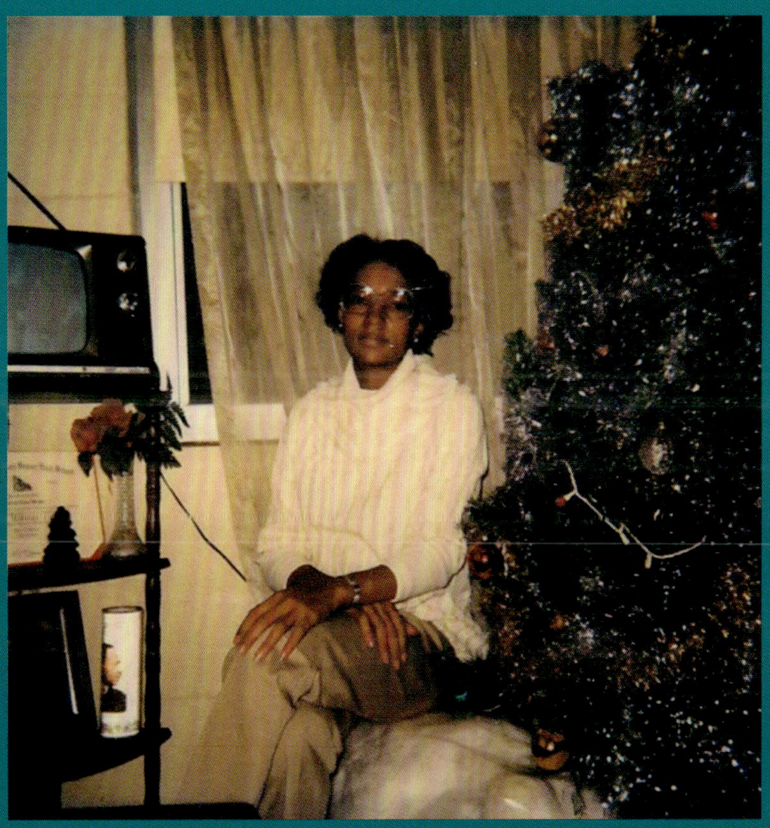

Patricia, the author's mother,
while pregnant with the author
JACKSONVILLE, FL
1981

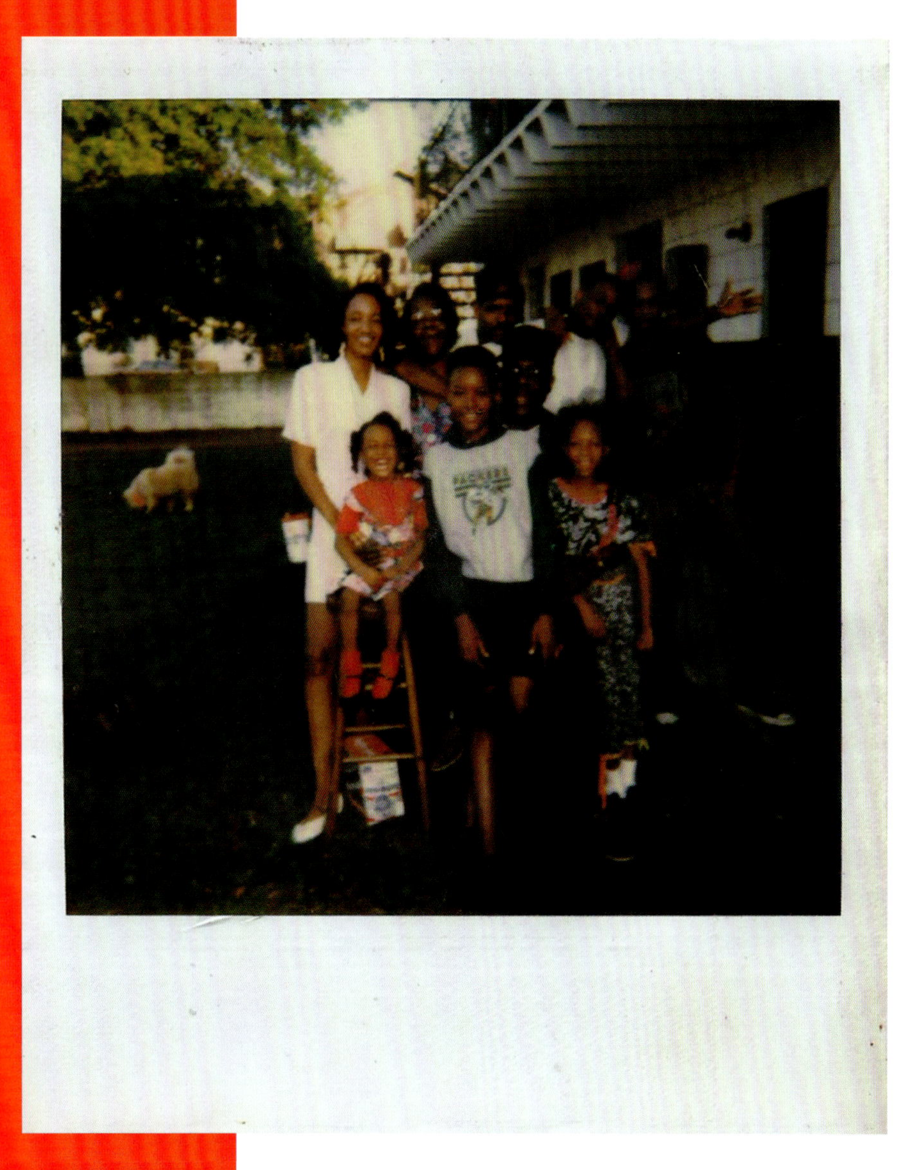

Portrait of the author's family
JACKSONVILLE, FL
1990S

SOUNDS OF BLACKNESS

I am proud to hail from a loud and boisterous family. All of our gatherings, regardless of size, are filled with jokes, debates, laughter, and most importantly, music. But one of things that makes Black families so special is that our very existence is also music – a unique sound so melodic that even if absent from speakers, the rhythm in our voices can still fill rooms. The sound of Blackness is undeniably one of the greatest things that you'll ever experience, and even when there is no sound, the vibrations of Blackness can still be felt.

The impossible but possible capturing (nearly) of sound through photography is a delightful thing to witness. I am immediately transported when looking at an image that evokes sounds and even smells: I suddenly remember the ripples of my grandmother's laughter or the scent of one of her cakes baking in the oven. Such experiences are true testaments to the power that photography holds to activate these memories and heighten our senses.

These photographs are a visual representation of how Blackness sounds.

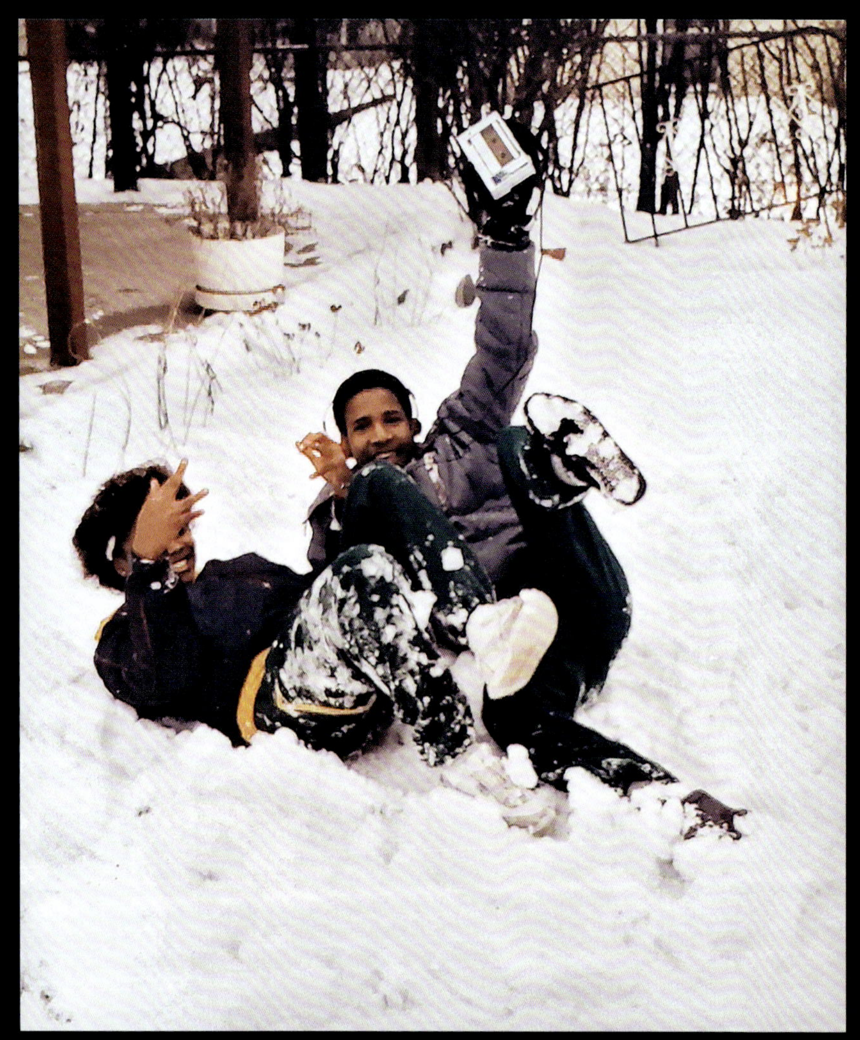

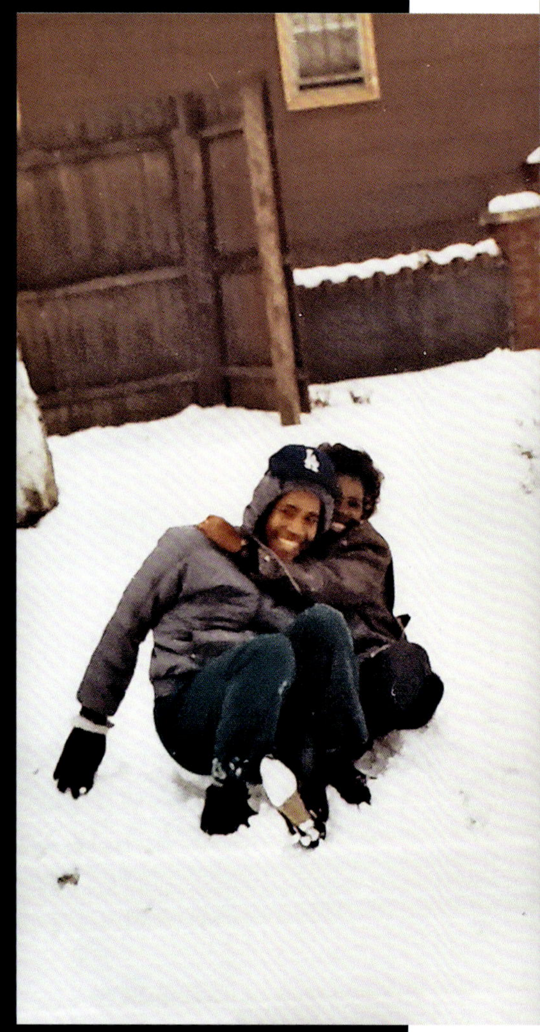

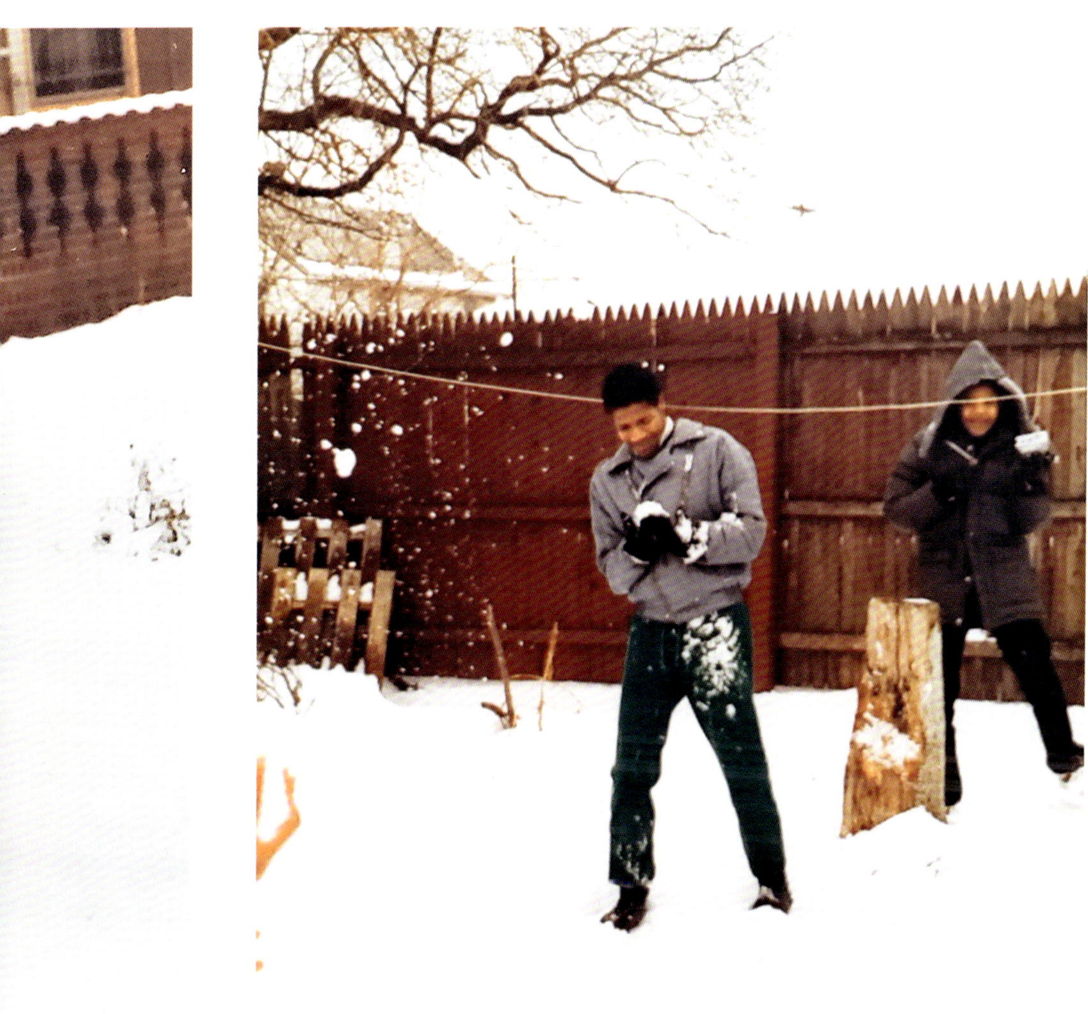

Siblings from Jamaica experiencing snow for the first time
QUEENS, NY
1984

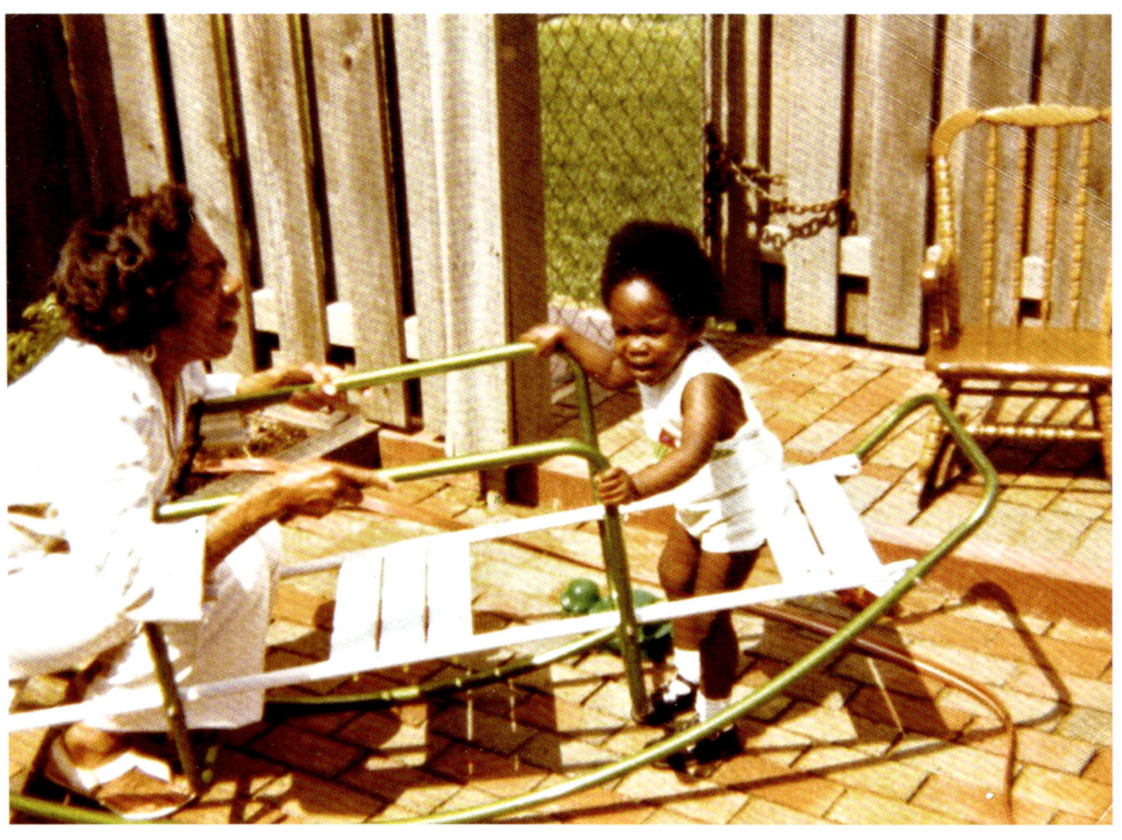

Grandmother and grandchild
1978

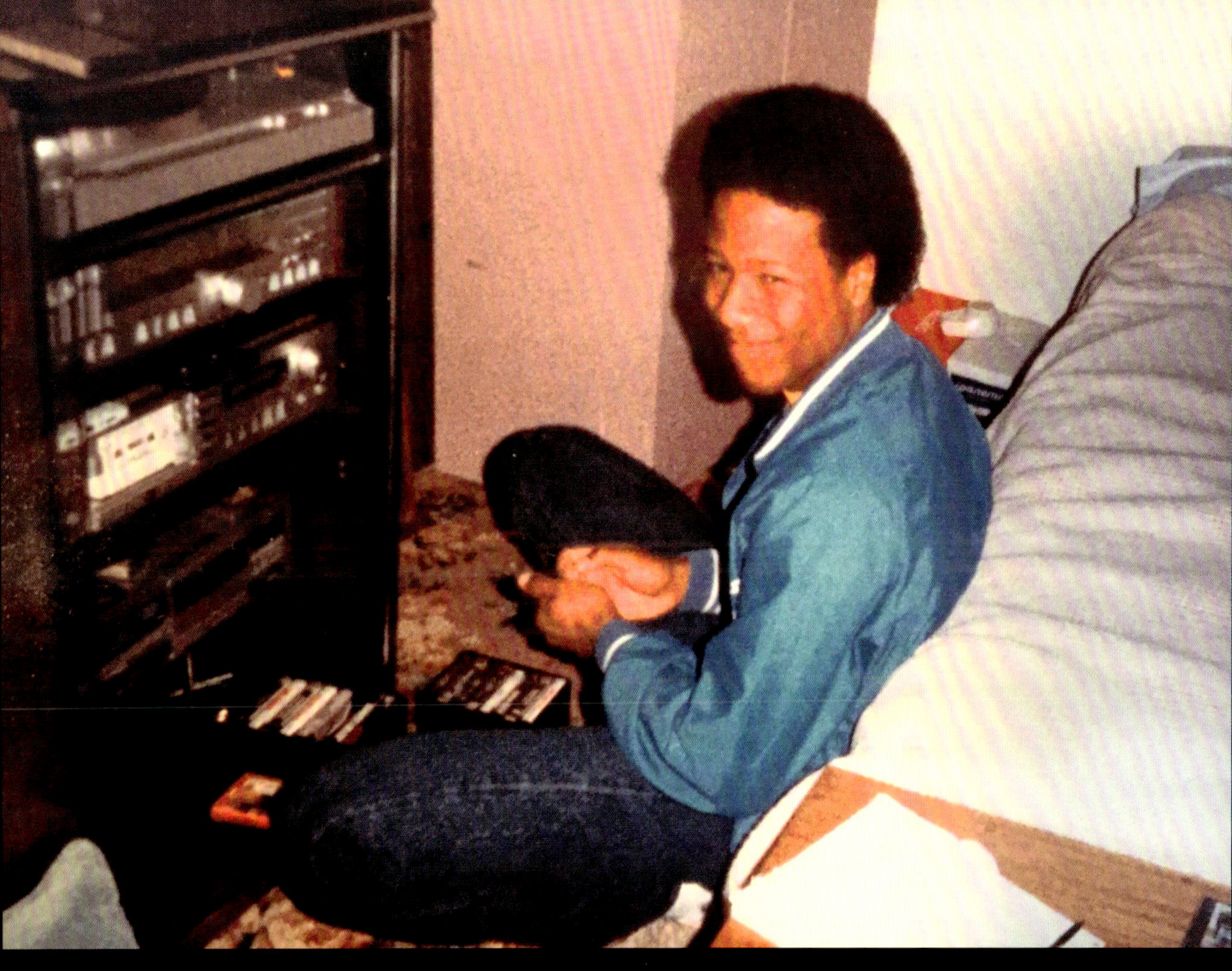

SANTA ROSA, CA

1983

MILWAUKEE, WI
1980S

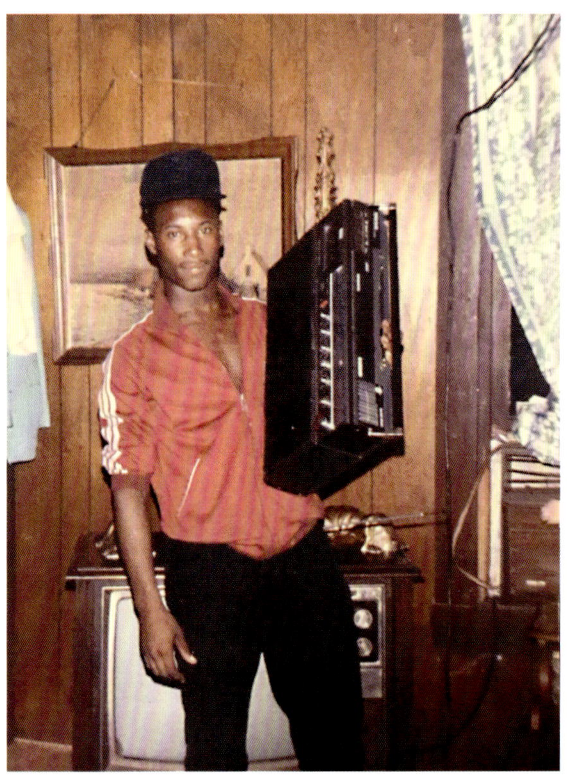

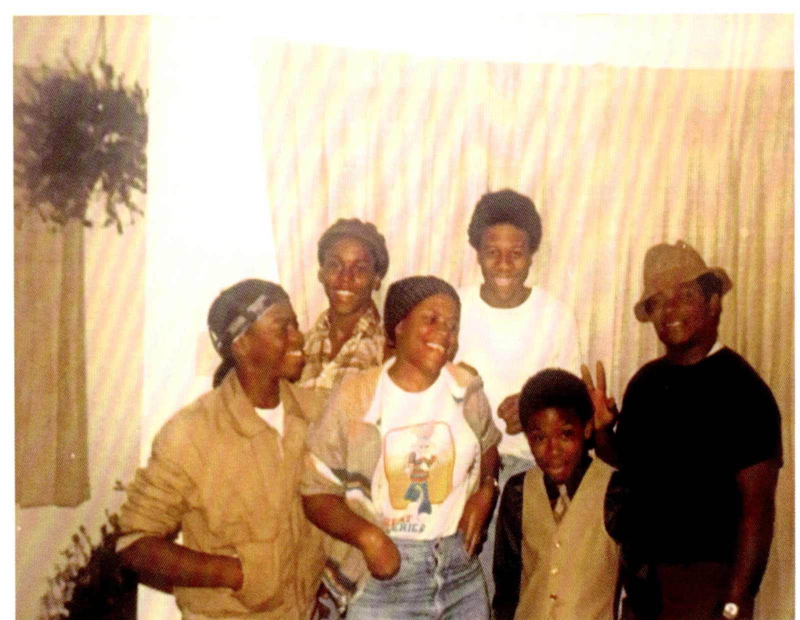

James, Eddie, Sallie Ann, CJ, Harold, and Pops at home
SANTA ROSA, CA
1970S

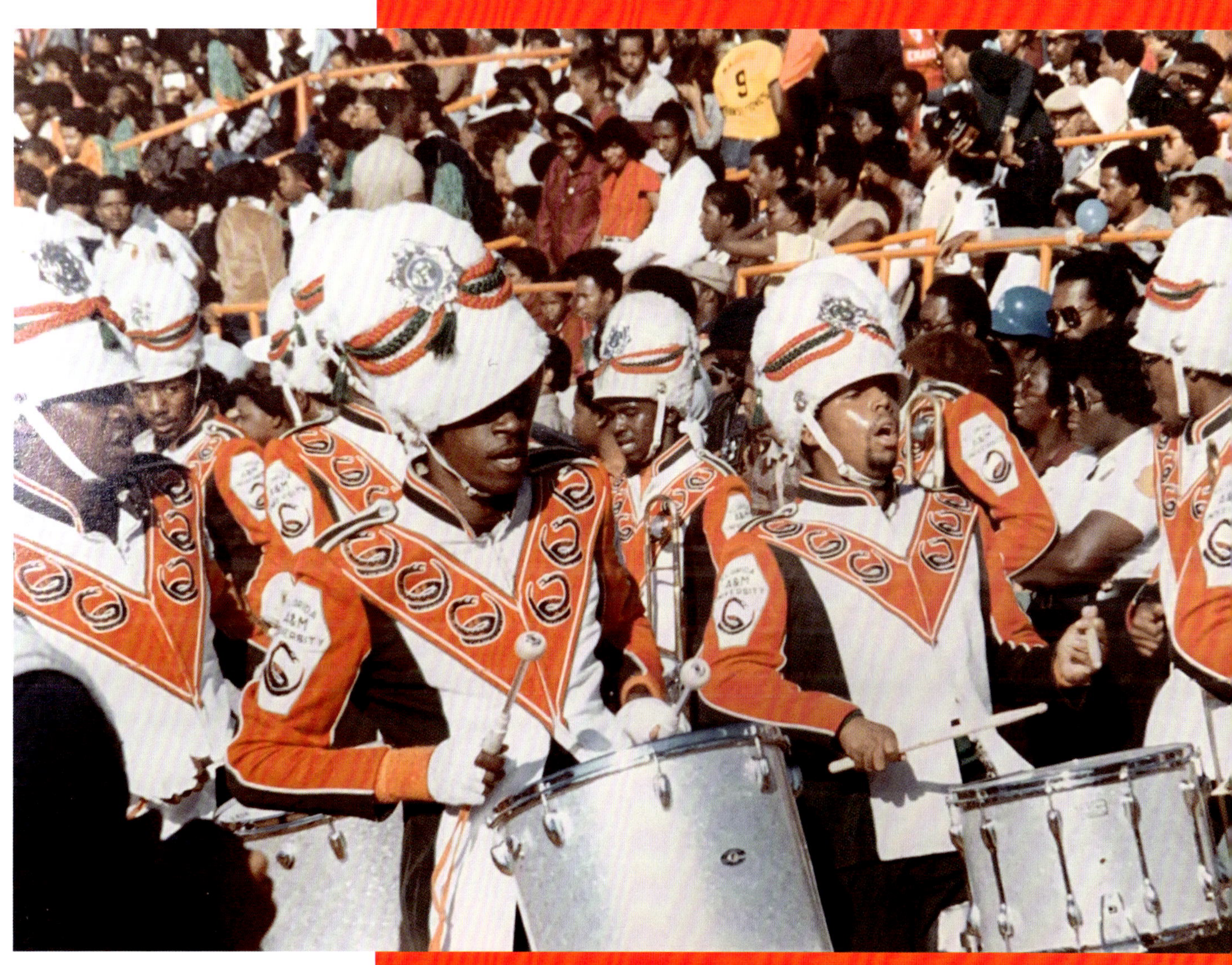

Florida A&M University
marching band
1980S

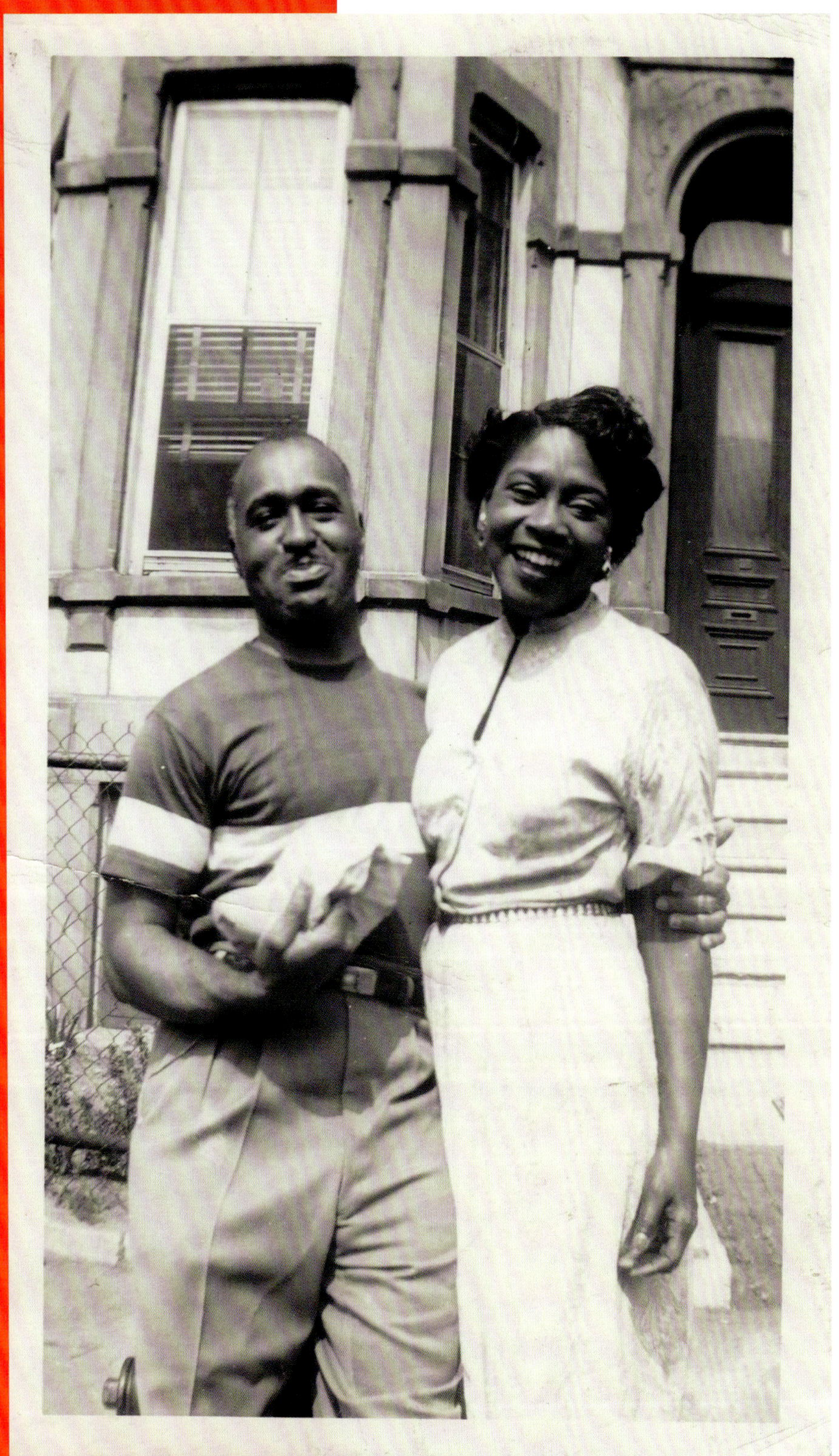

Laymon and Inez

CIRCA 1955

Columbus Park

BOSTON, MA

CIRCA 1945

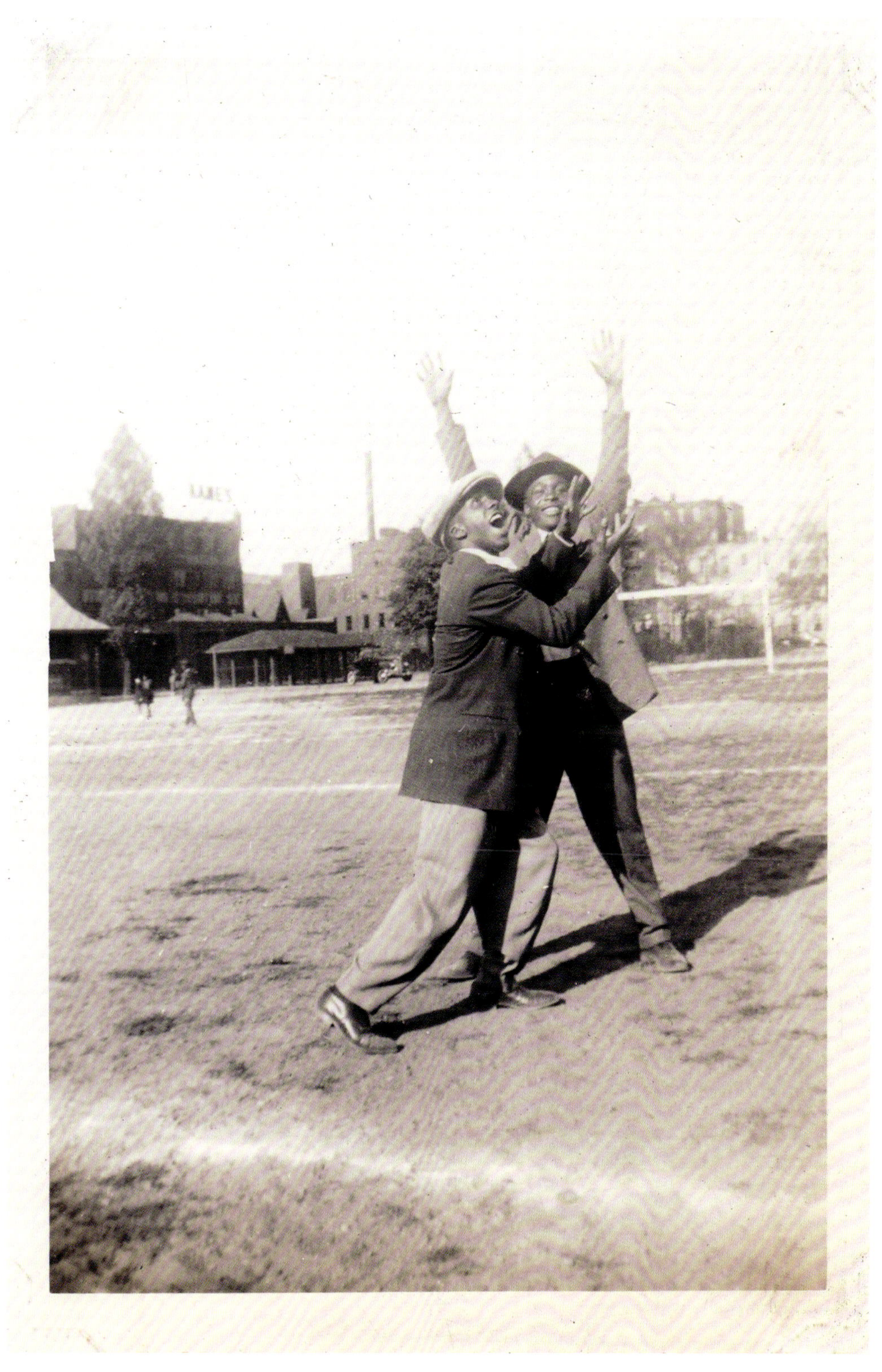

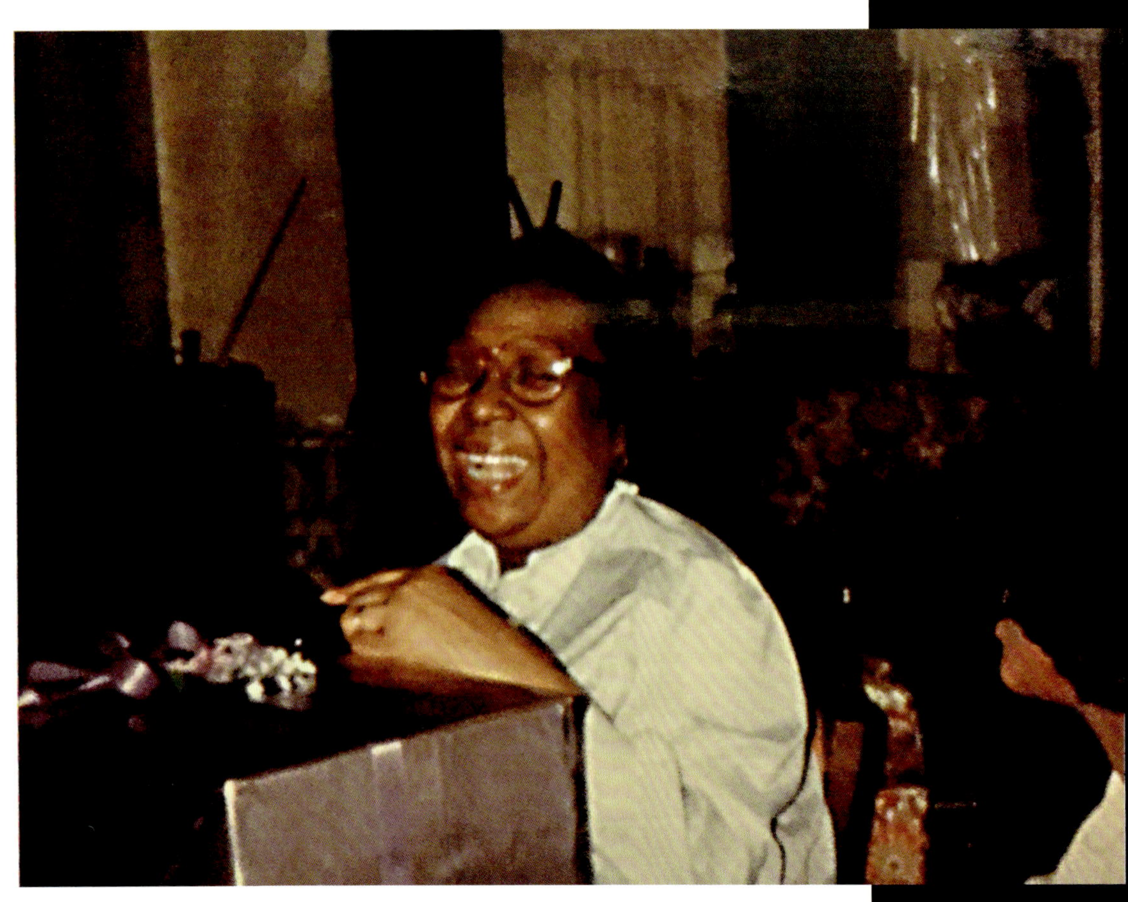

LOS ANGELES, CA
1980S

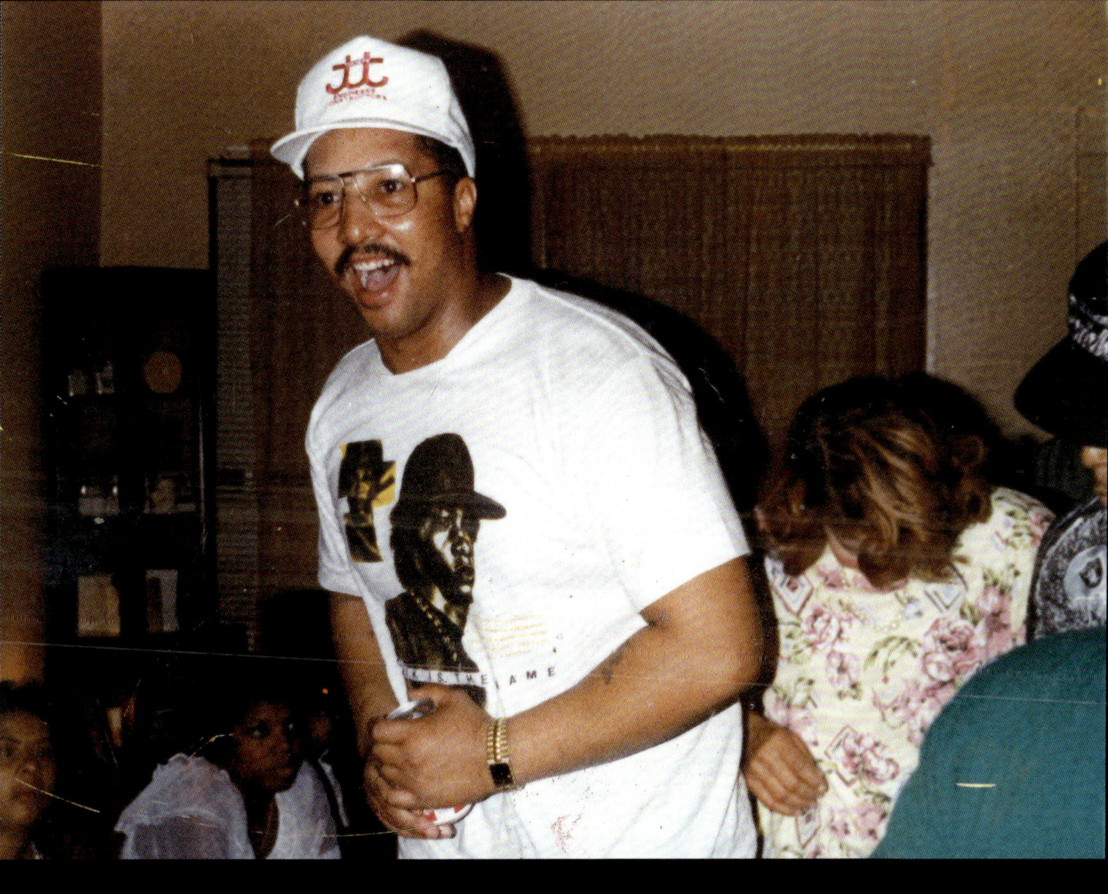

House party in the Goosport neighborhood of Lake Charles

LAKE CHARLES, LA

1992

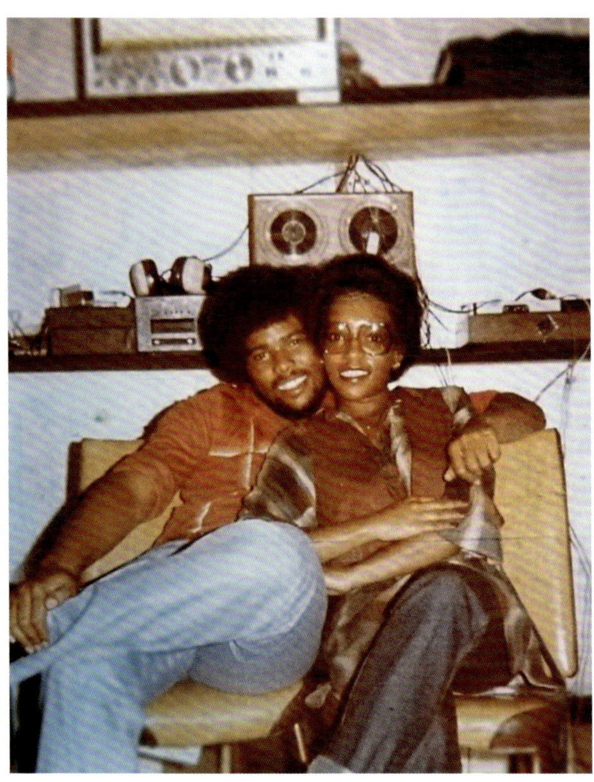

MIDLAND, TX

1977

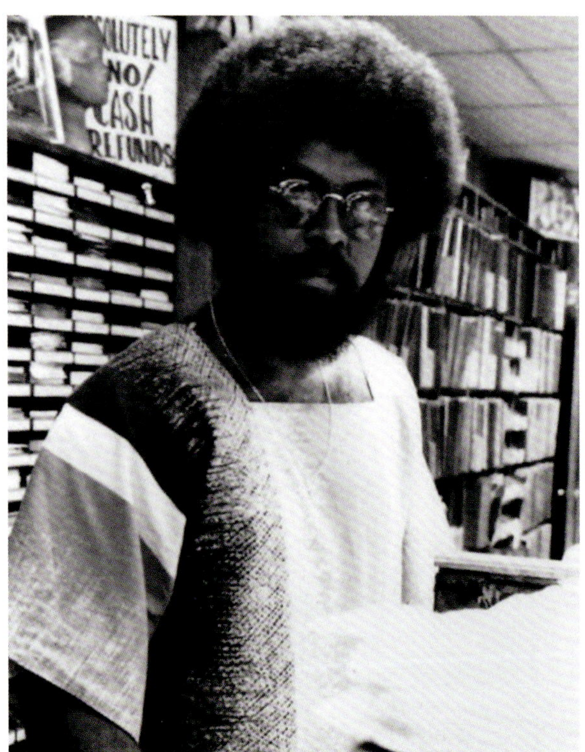

Sherman Lewis in a record store

WILMINGTON, DE

CIRCA 1975

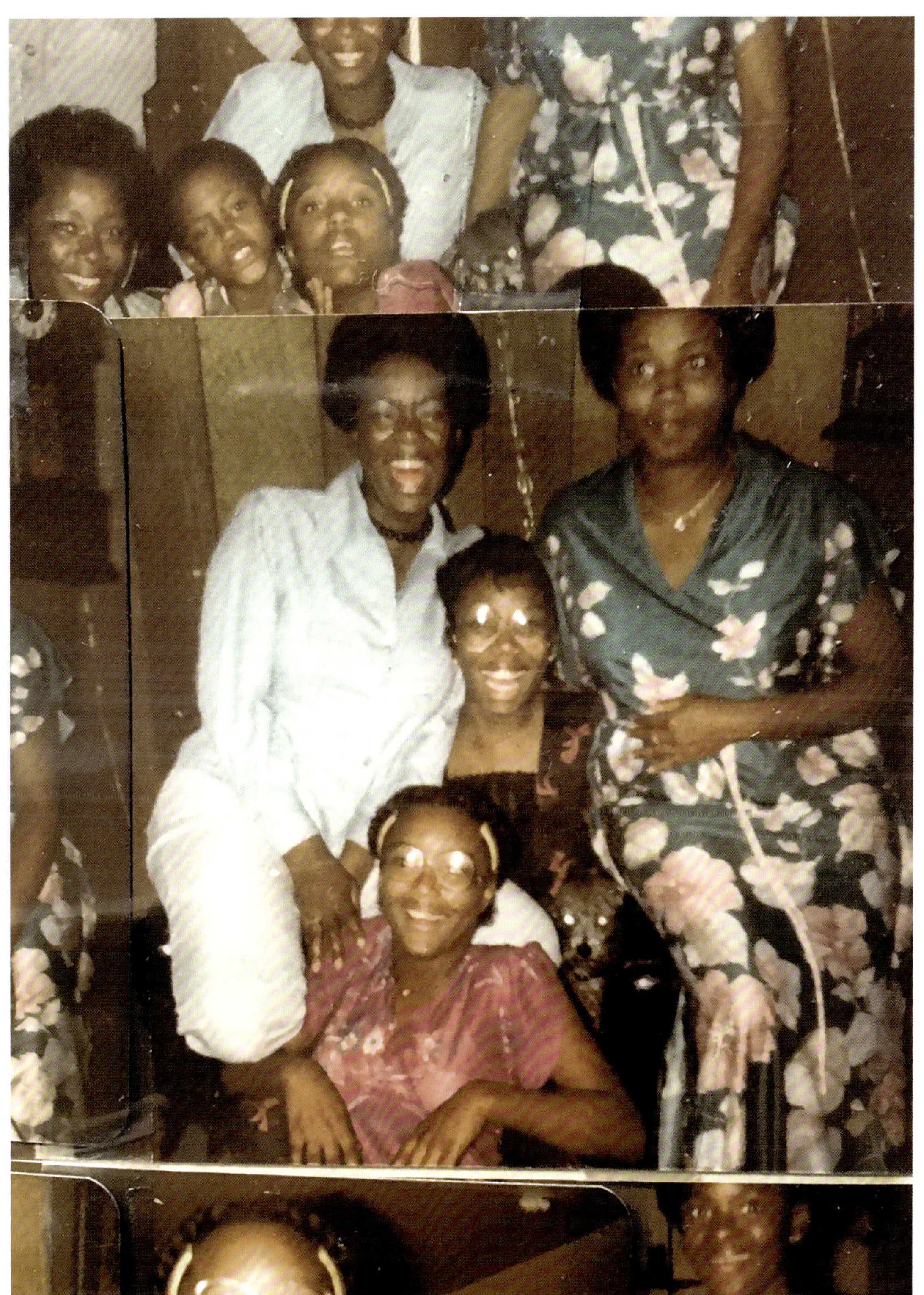

Sisters Margaret, Sylvia, Carol, and Denise
COMPTON, CA
1980S

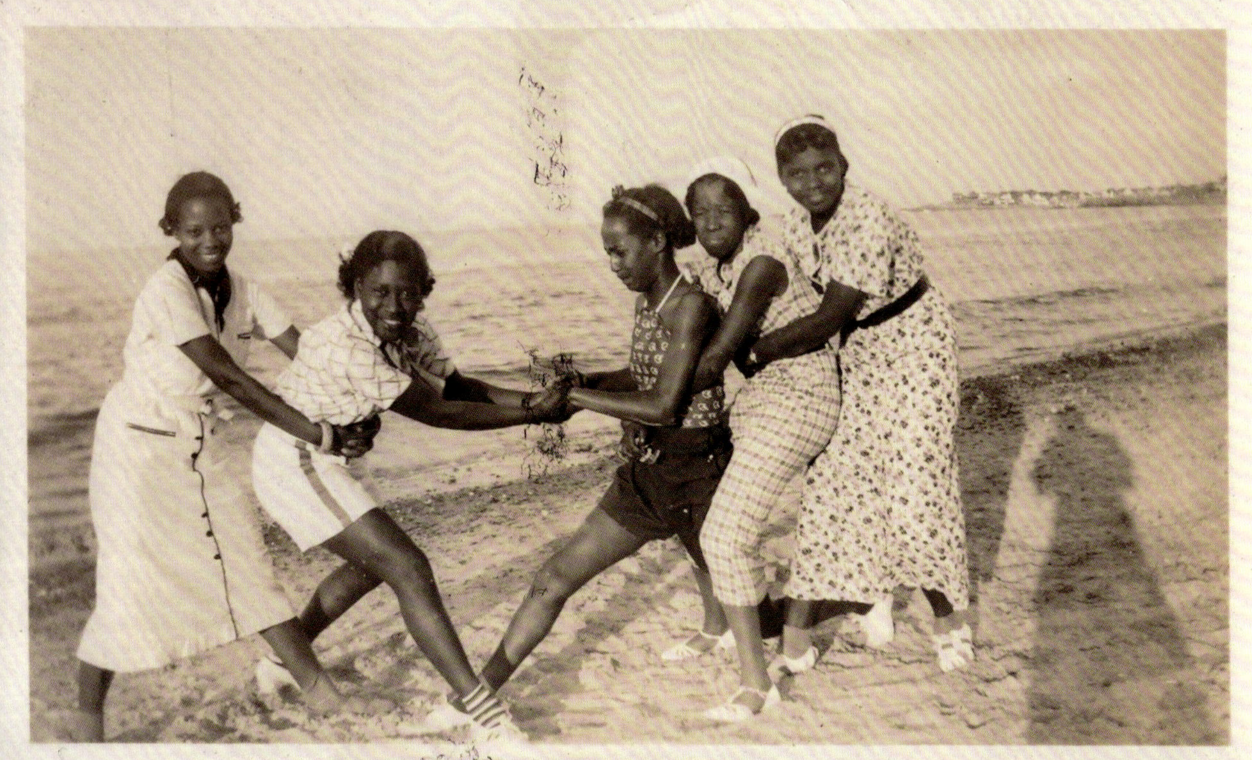

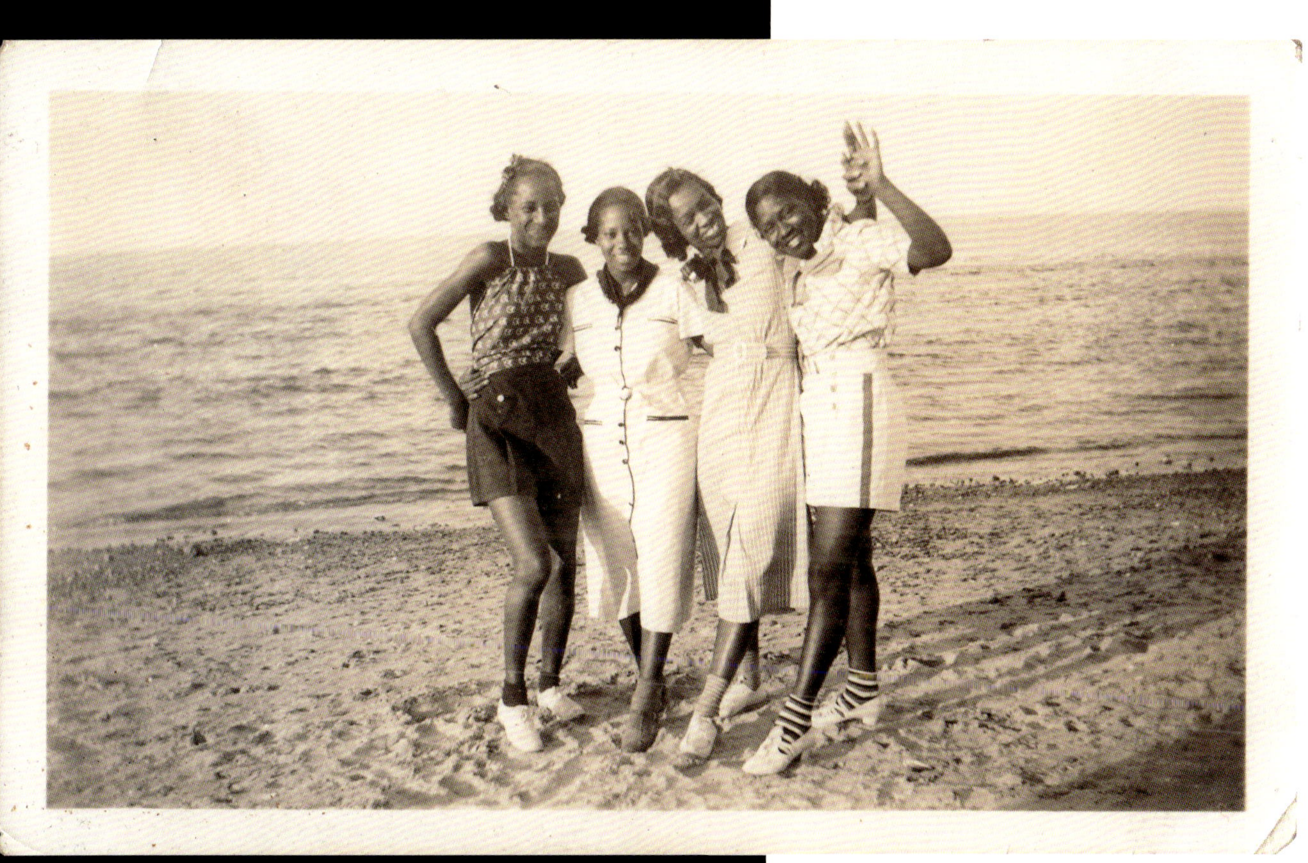

At the beach
1936

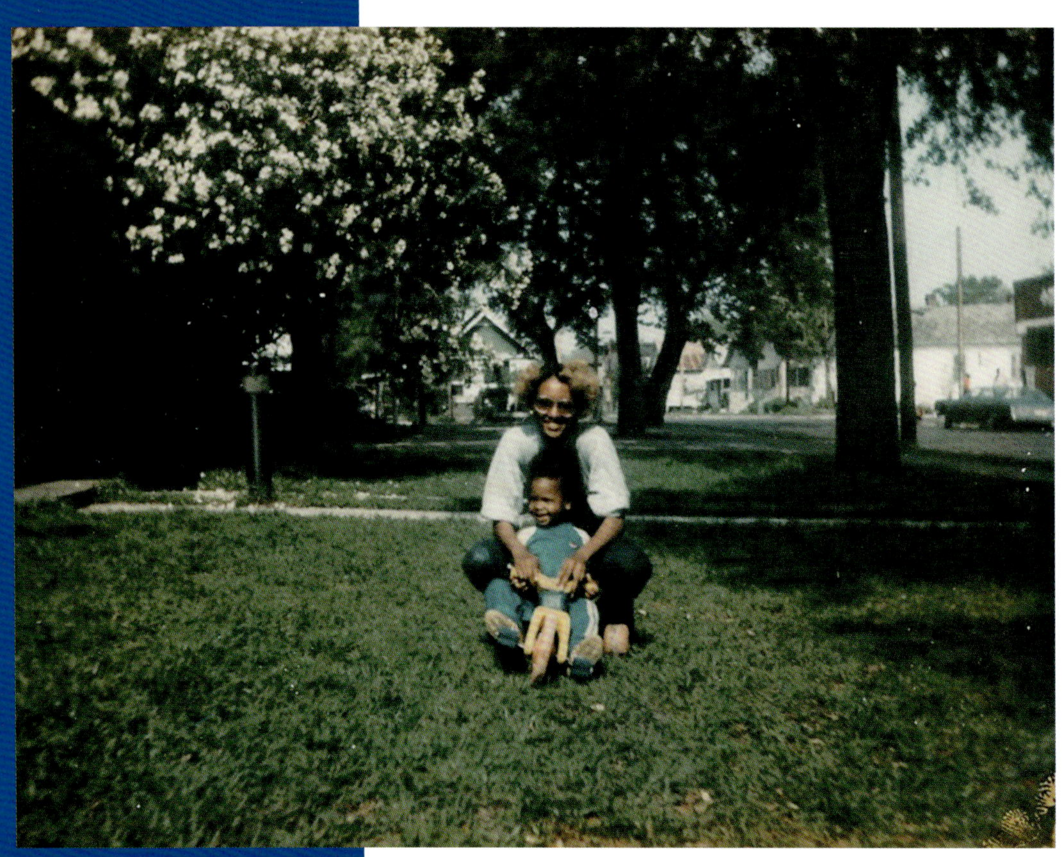

The author's mom and cousin Chauncey
JACKSONVILLE, FL
1979

HOLDING JOY, LOVE, AND TENDERNESS

Joy, love, and tenderness are some of the most radical and important things a Black person can demand, experience, or give. If you imagine the act of holding joy, love, and tenderness what do you see? I imagine a series of photographs where the holder and the ones being held are equally celebrated and lifted in the moment. For Black people, especially when faced with the burdens of the world around us, holding these things is a radical act and a way to resist what doesn't align with our spirits. Holding joy means that we get to experience, and hold onto, an everlasting power – if even for a moment's time. To capture the essence of tenderness in a photograph is a gift to all who bear witness. The best part of love lives in the spaces in between what can and cannot be defined. We remember love more than we remember anything else.

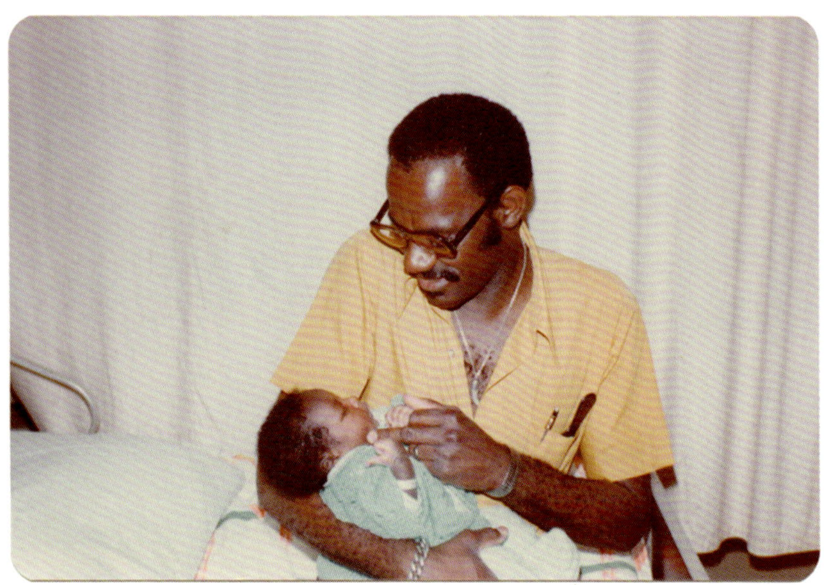

The Anderson family
JAMAICA
1976

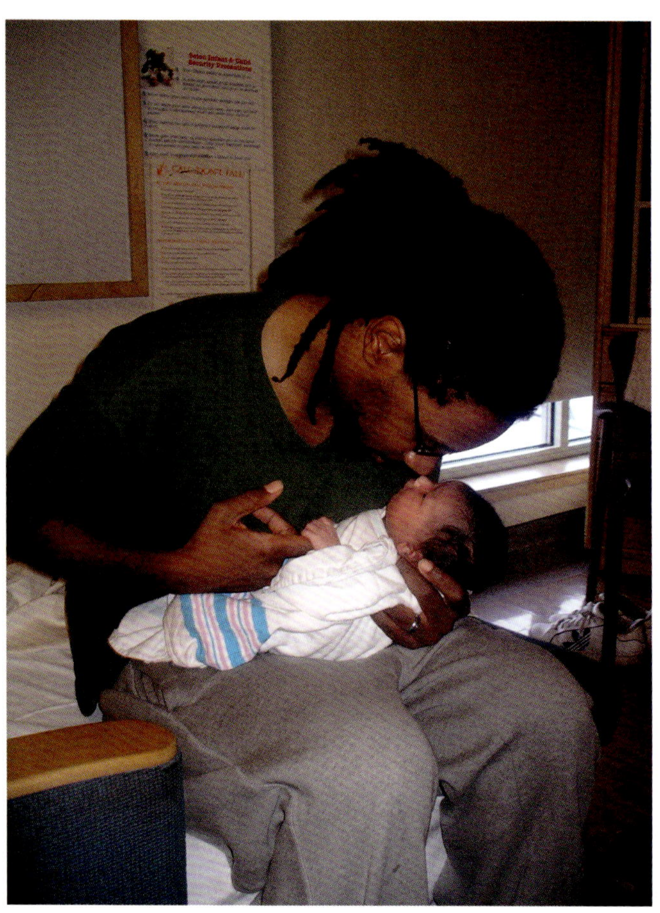

The Anderson family
THE UNITED STATES
2008

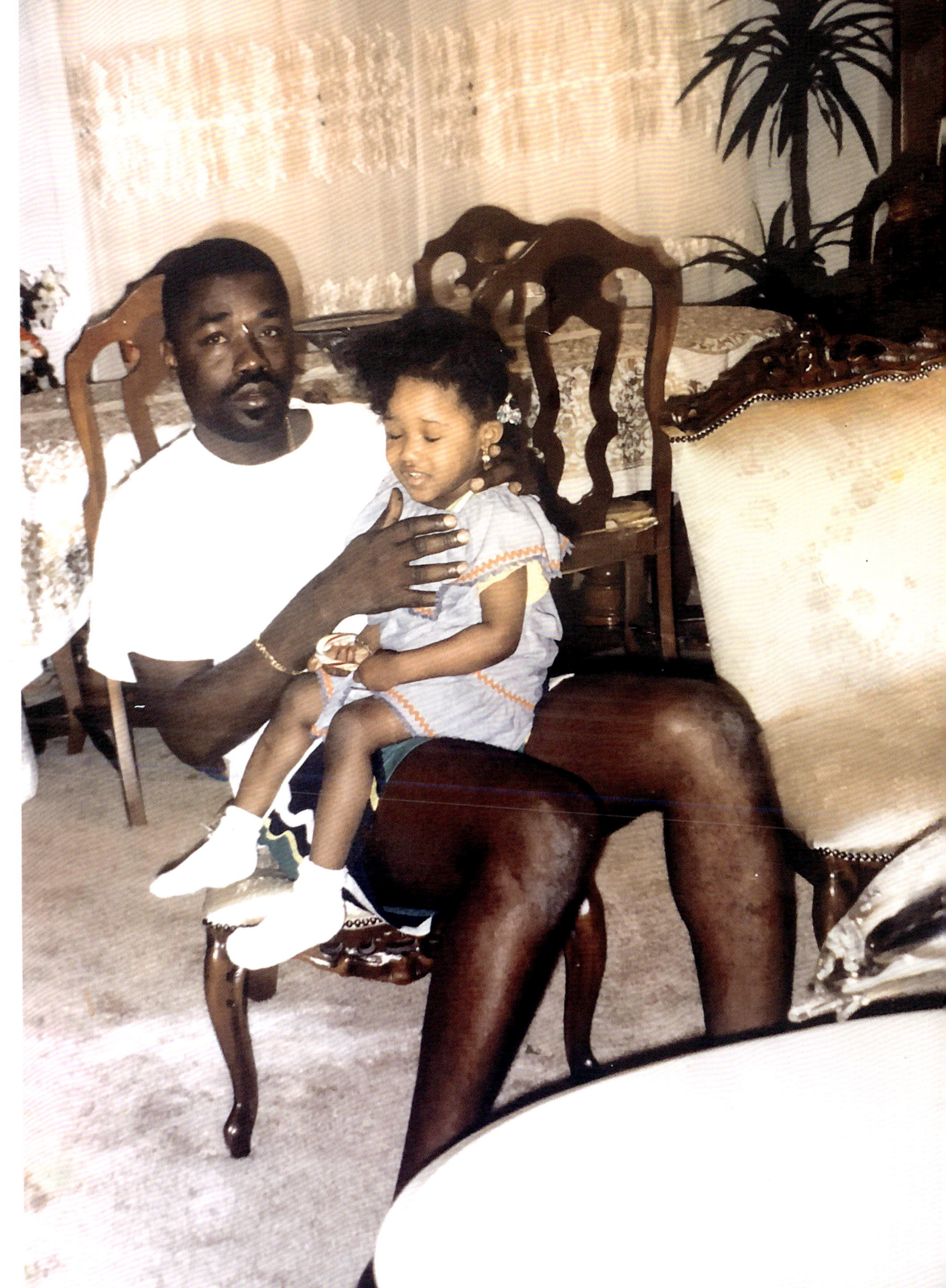

1990S

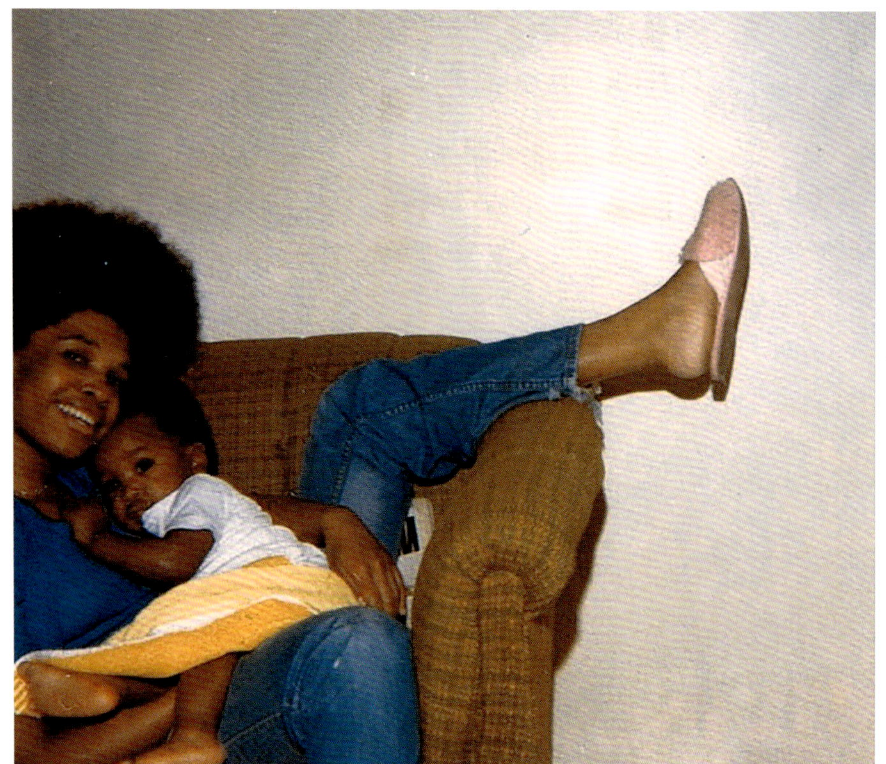

Mother and son
TORONTO, CANADA
1978

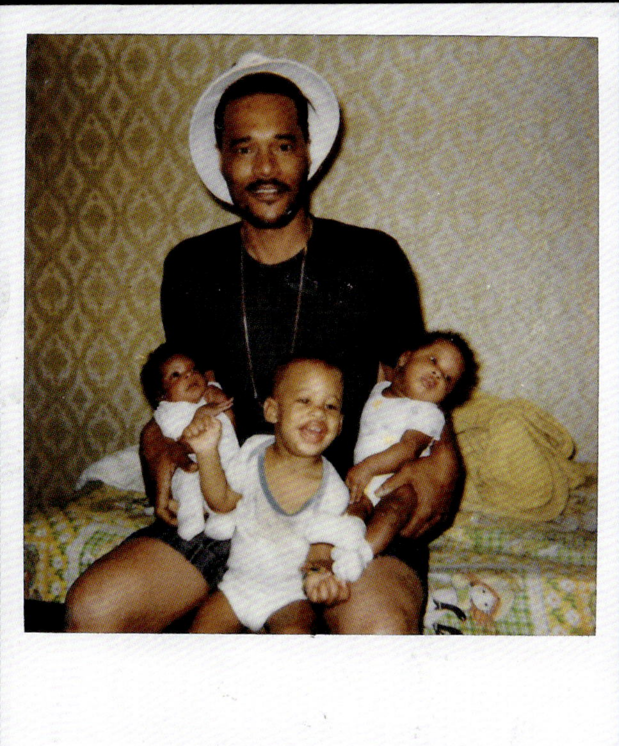

Samuel Johnson holding his grandchildren Shanice, George, and Shernelle

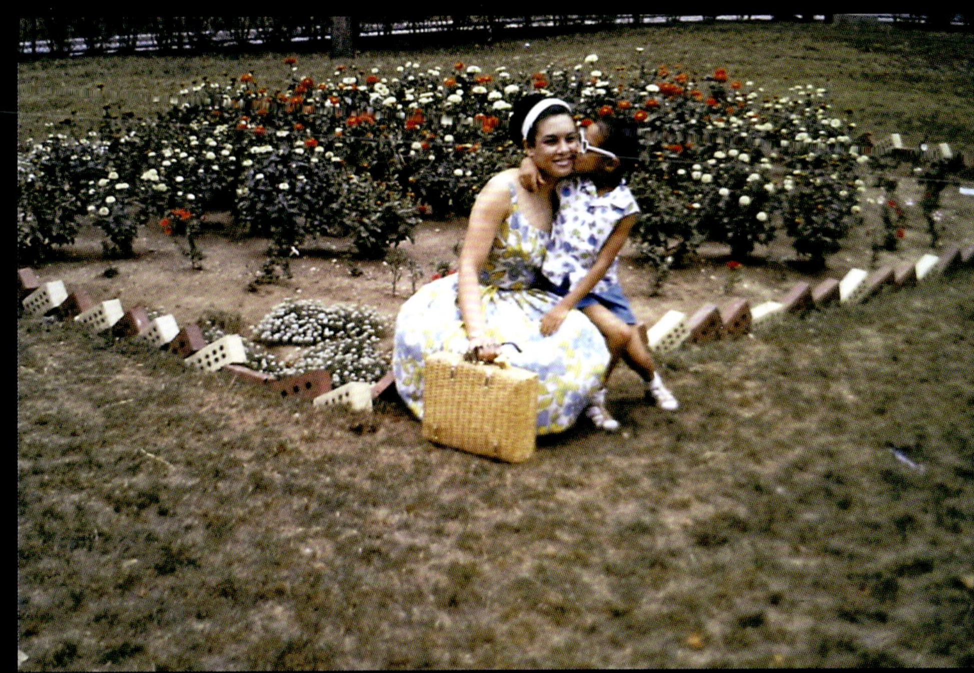

NEW YORK, NY
1960S

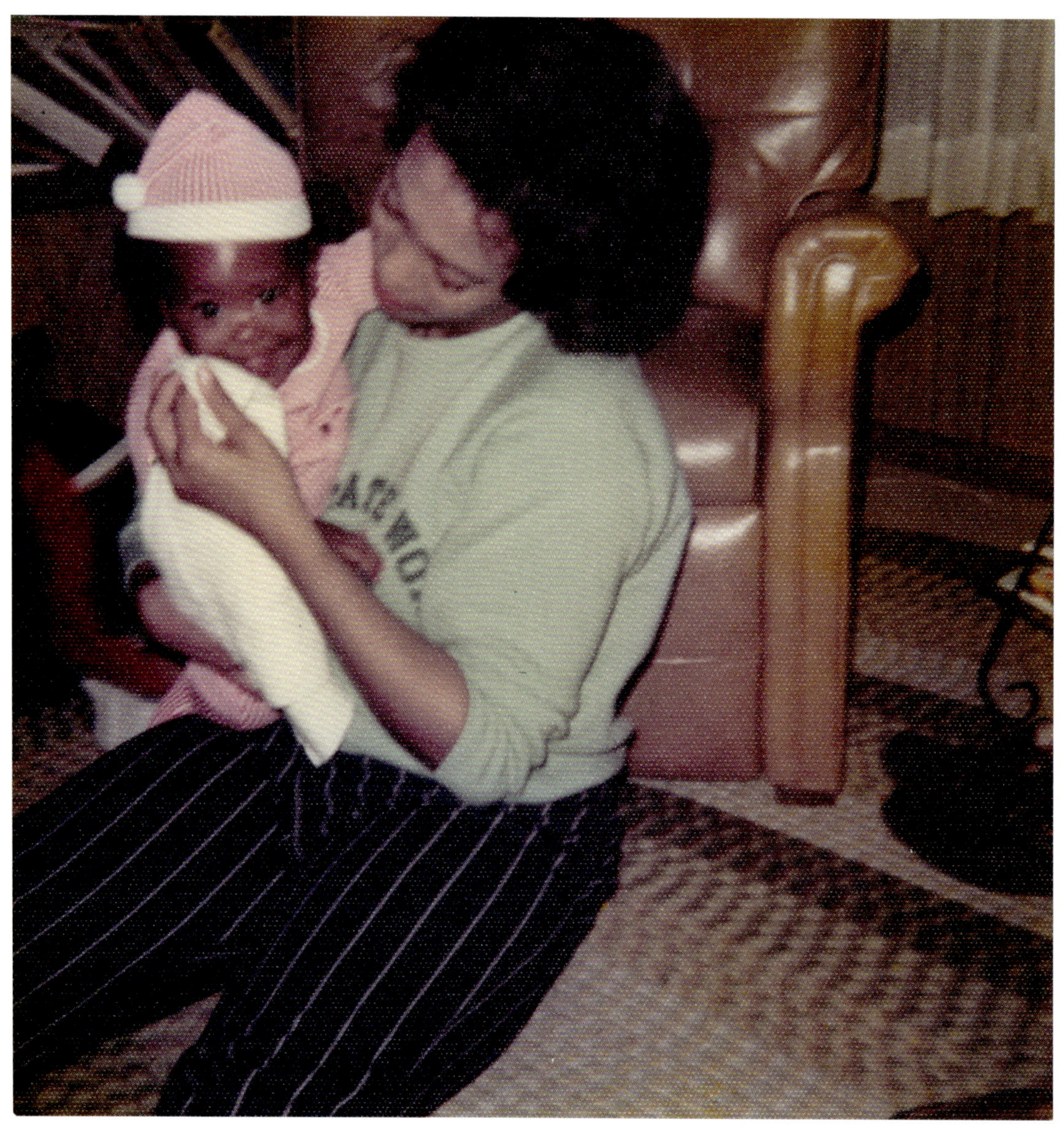

The Odom family
1970S

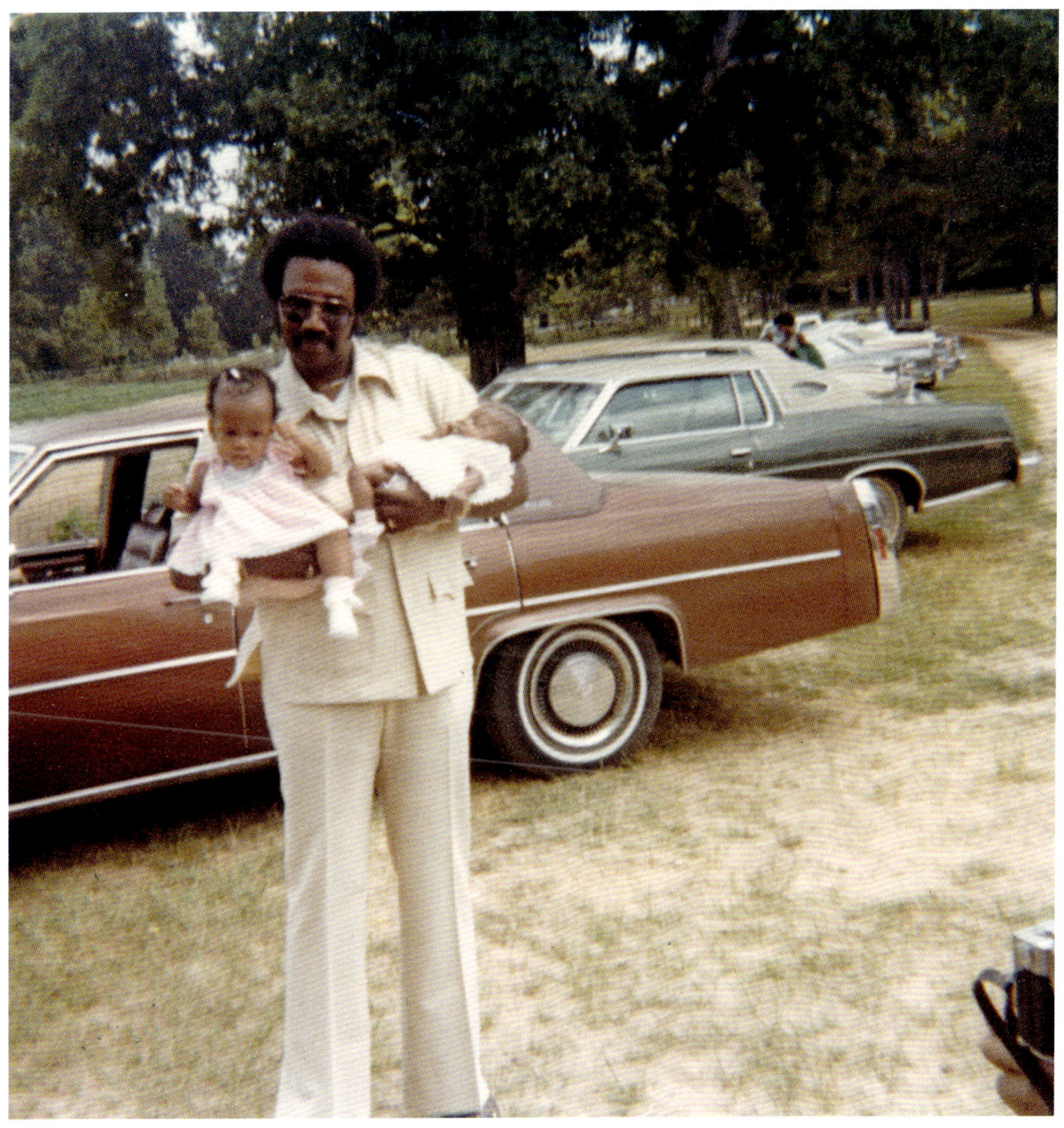

The Odom family

1970S

MIAMI, FL

1980

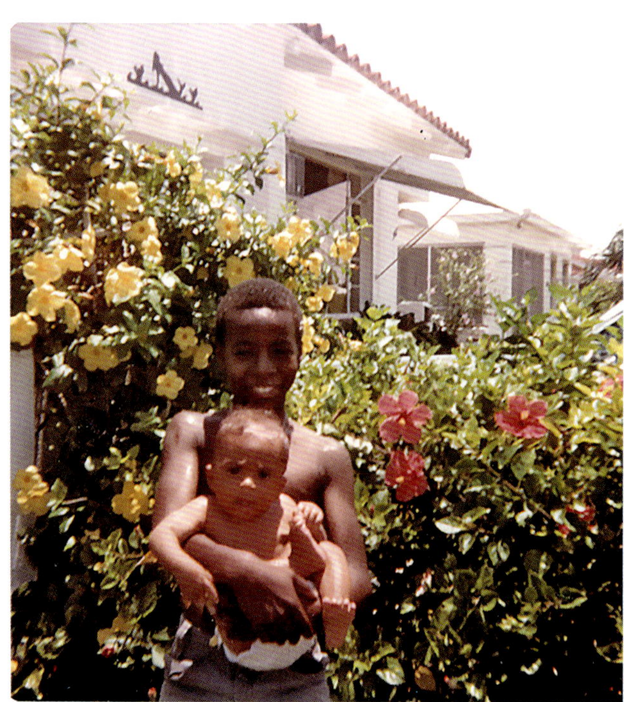

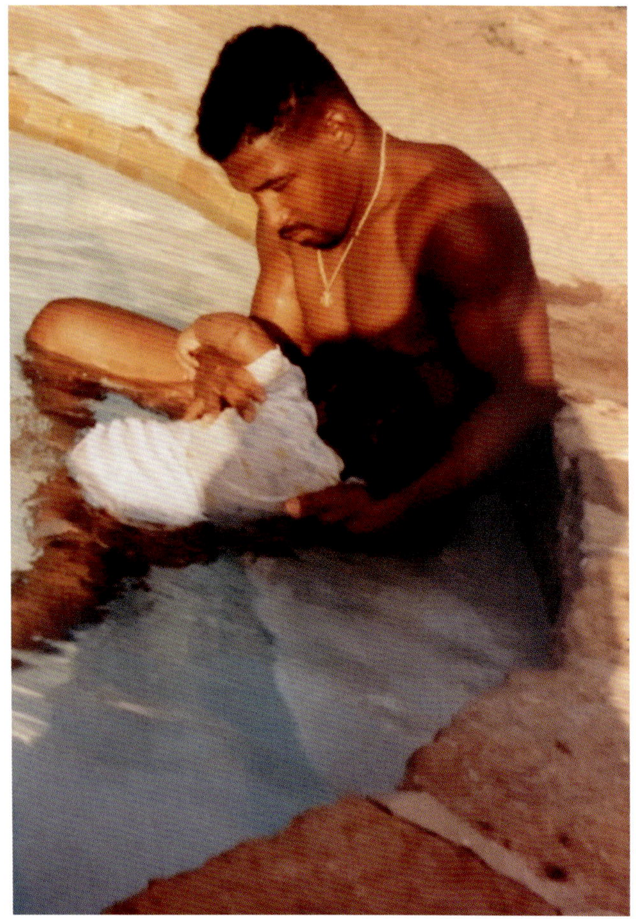

1990S

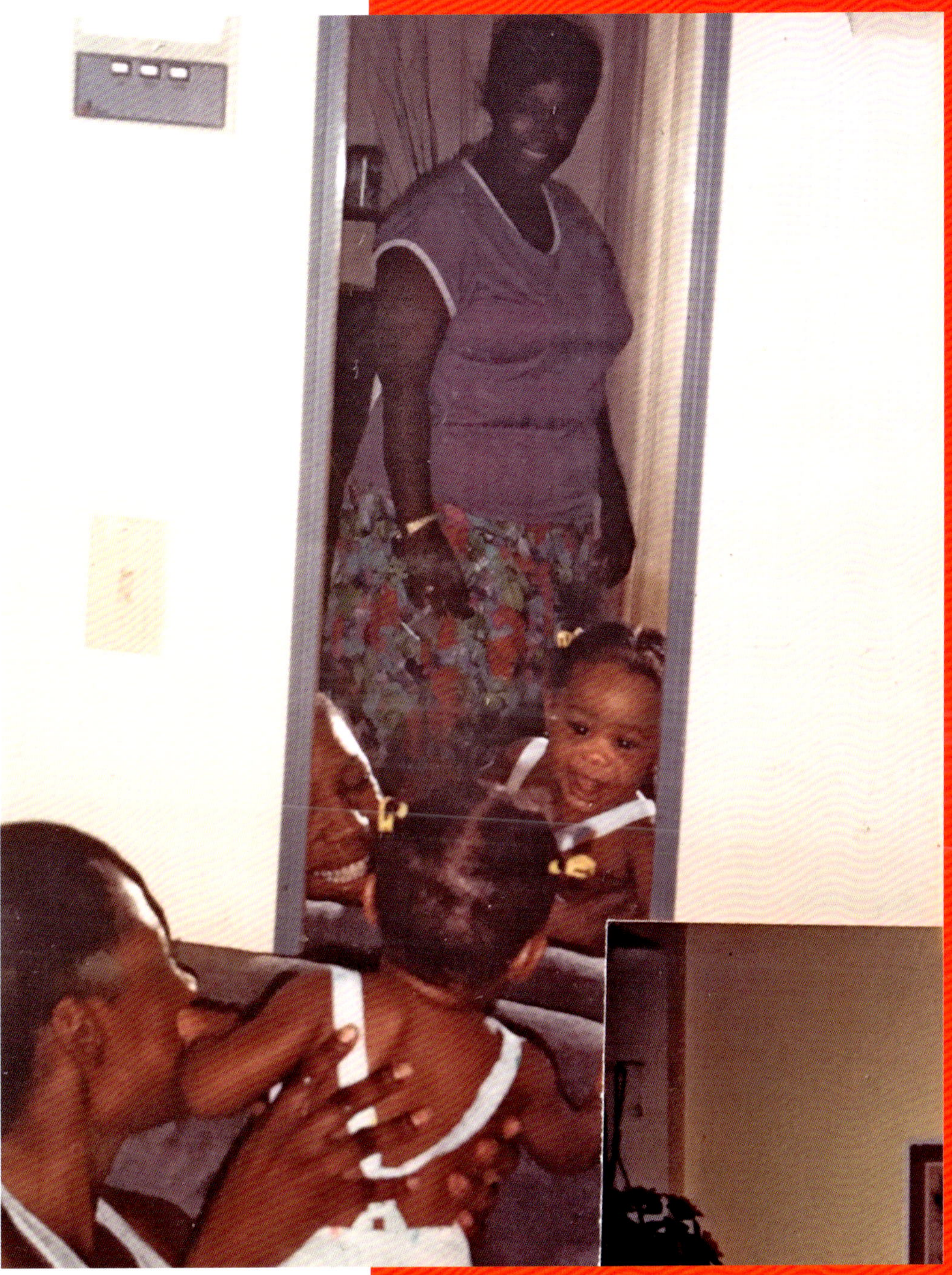

Mother,
daughter, and
grandmother
1990S

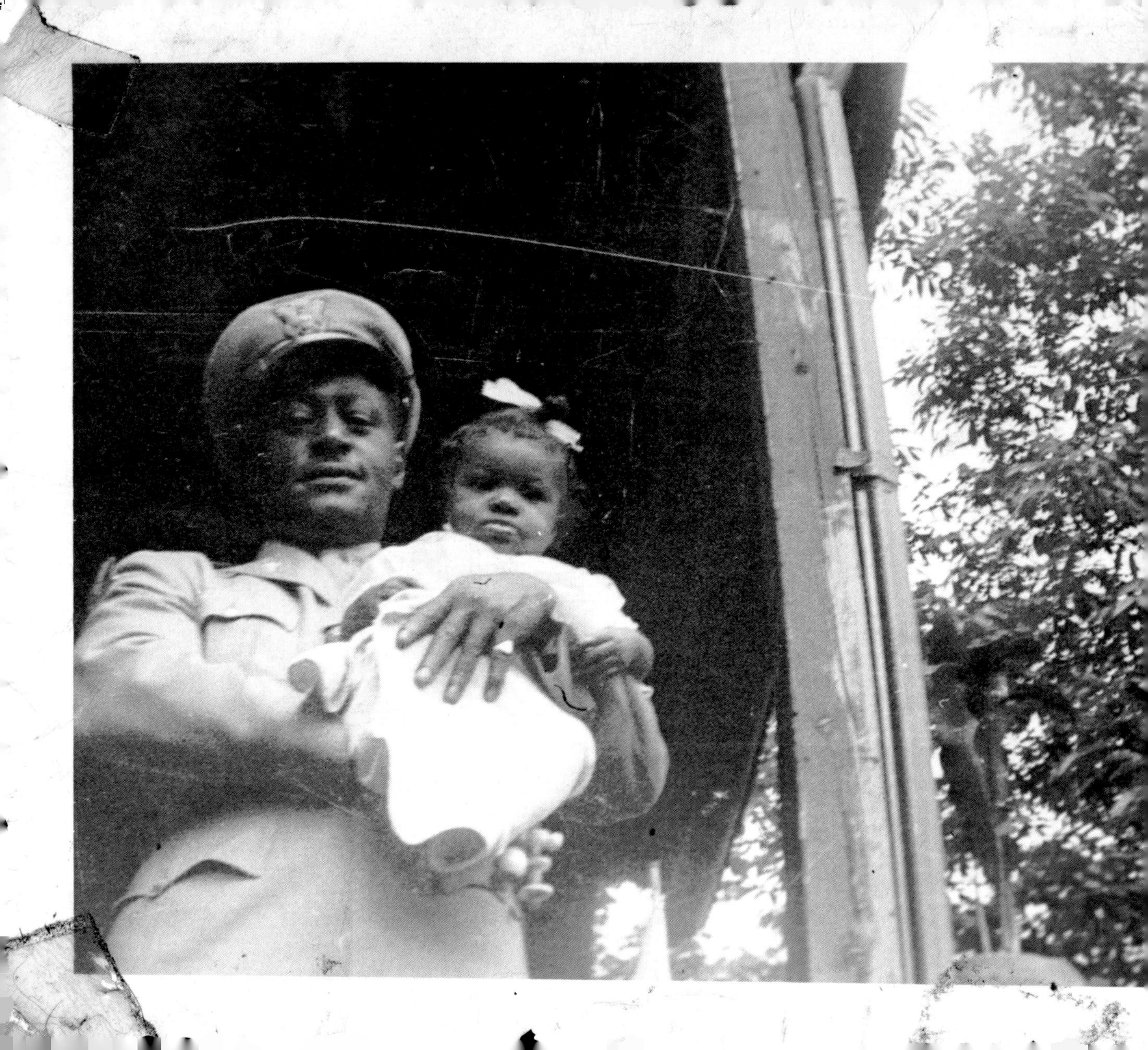

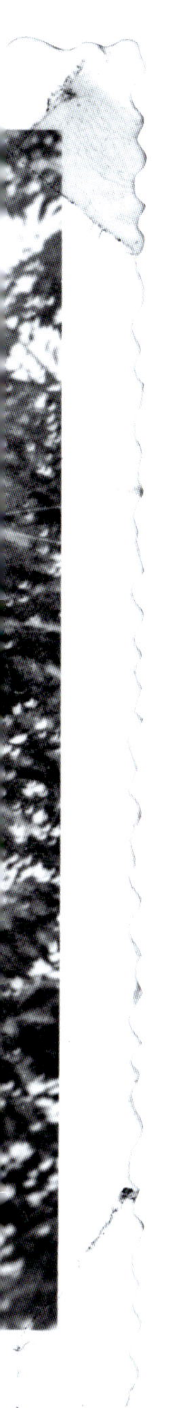

ROXBURY, MA

CIRCA 1940

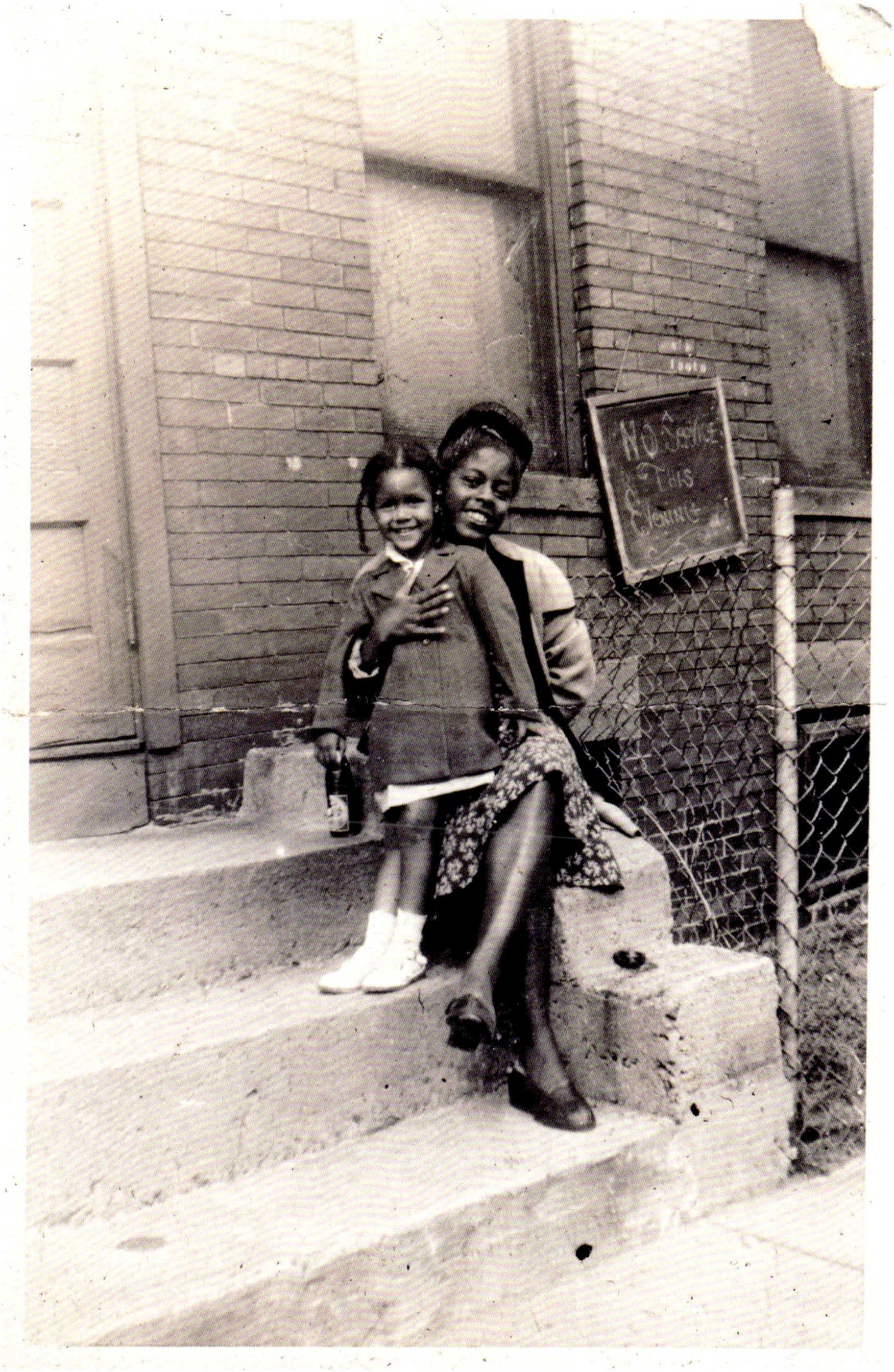

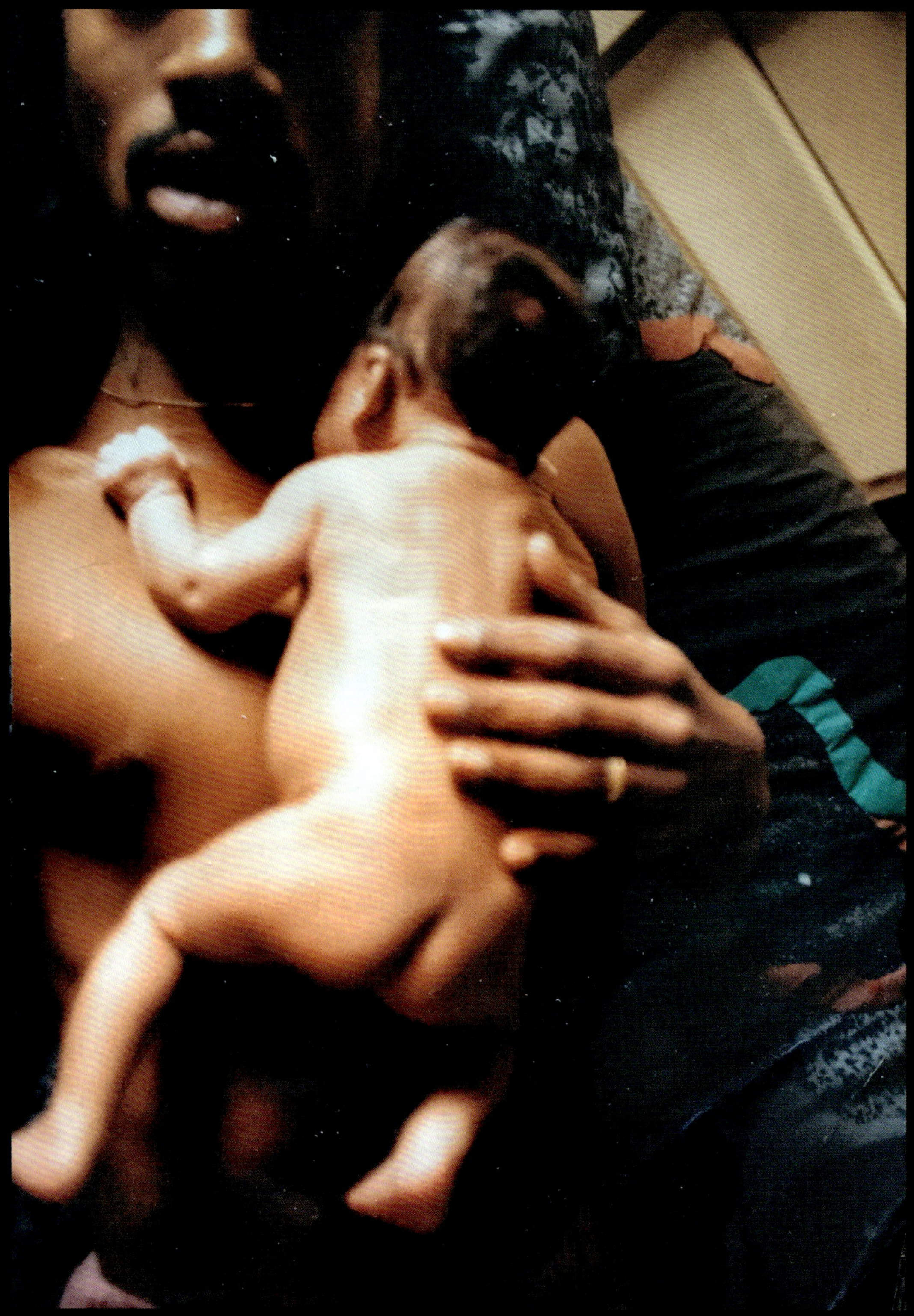

Carl Counts and
his newborn baby,
Nicole Counts
NEW JERSEY
1991

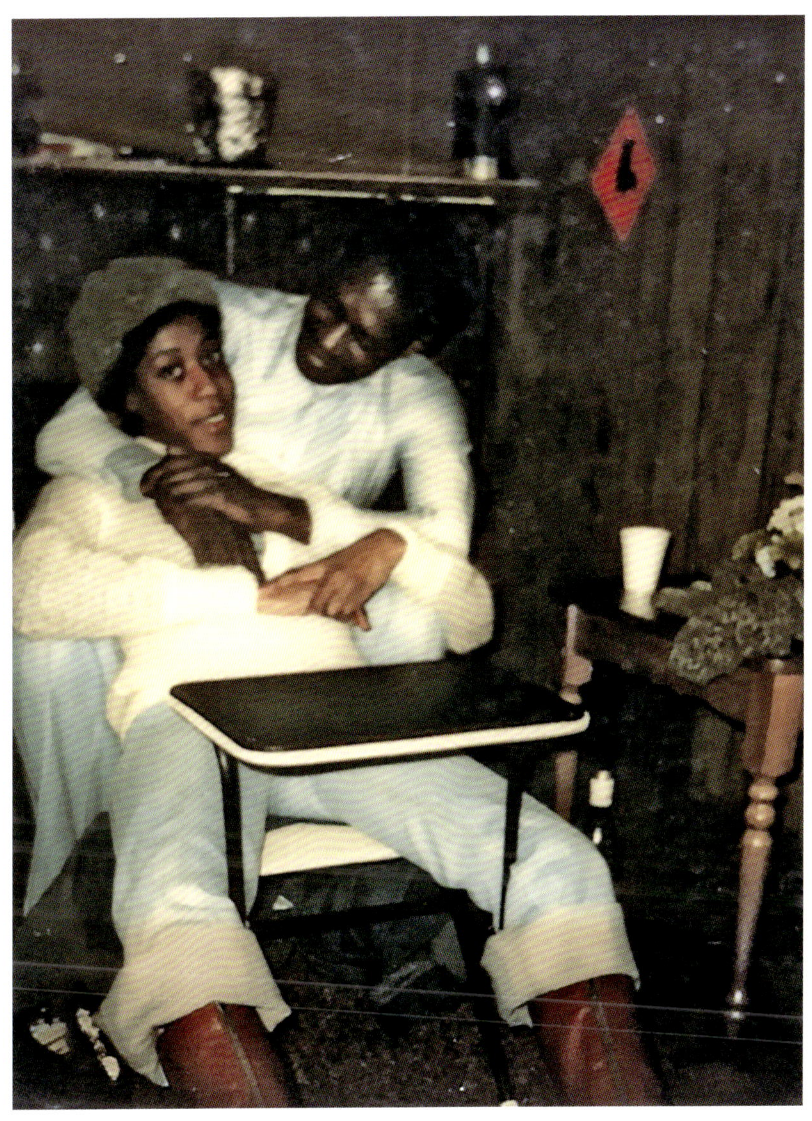

1970S

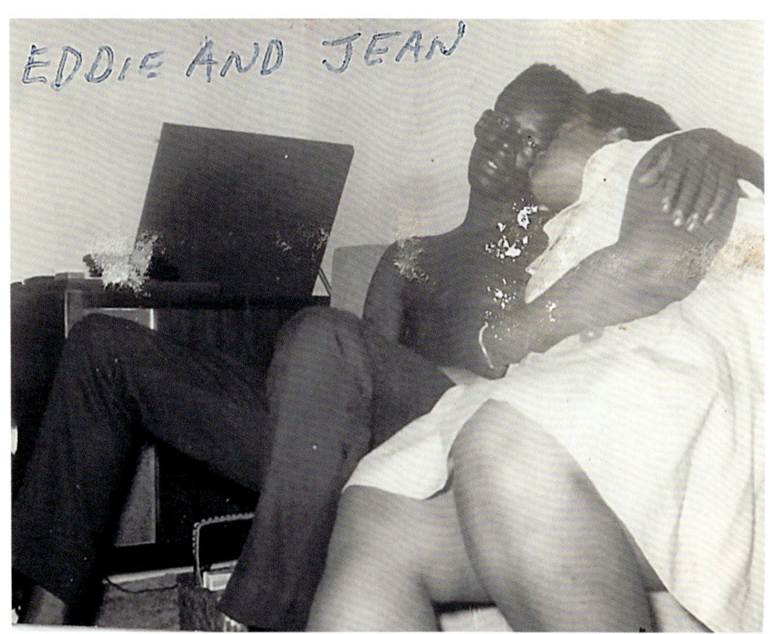

Eddie and Jean

DAYTONA BEACH, FL

1960S

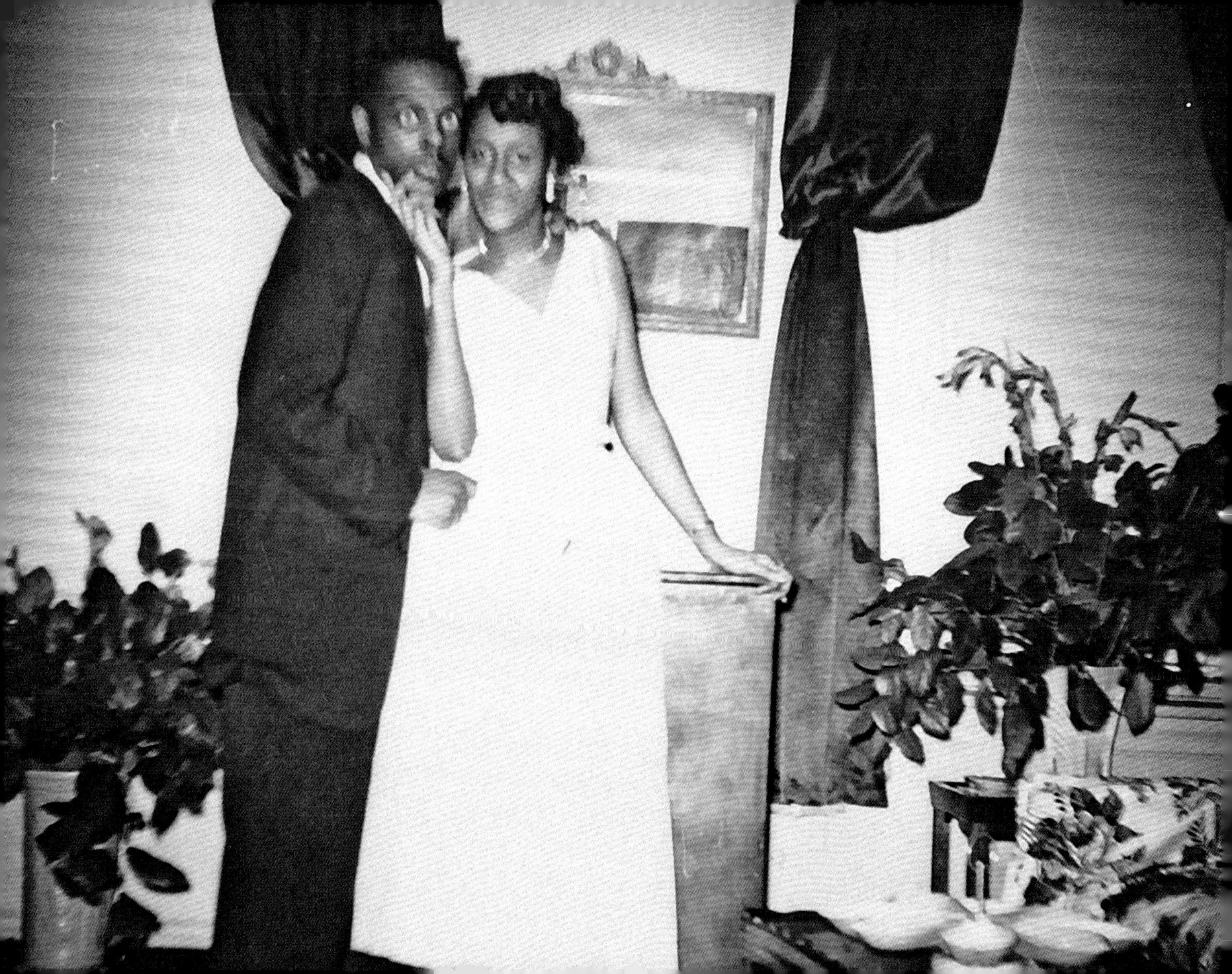

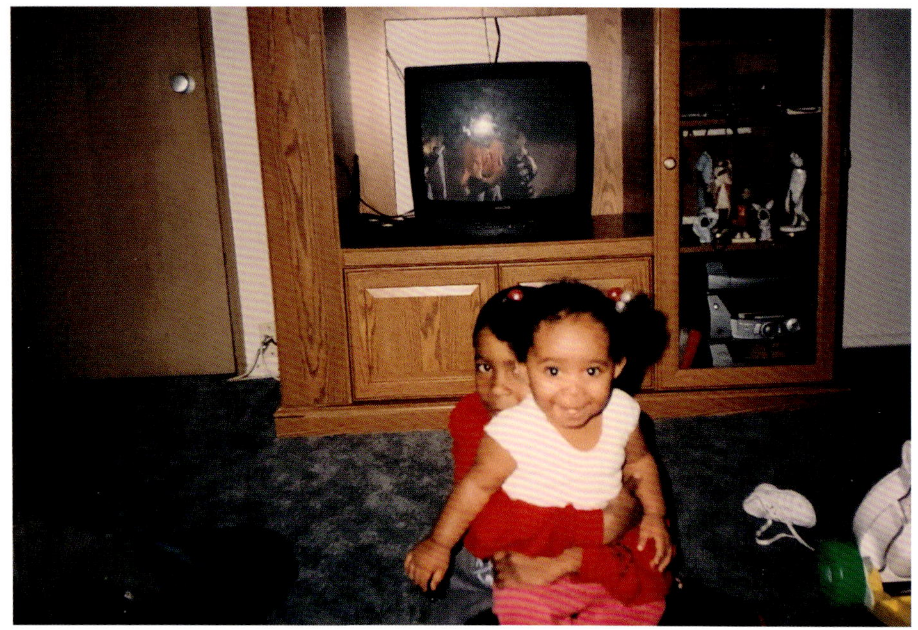

Siblings at home
FERGUSON, MO
2002

VIETNAM
1970S

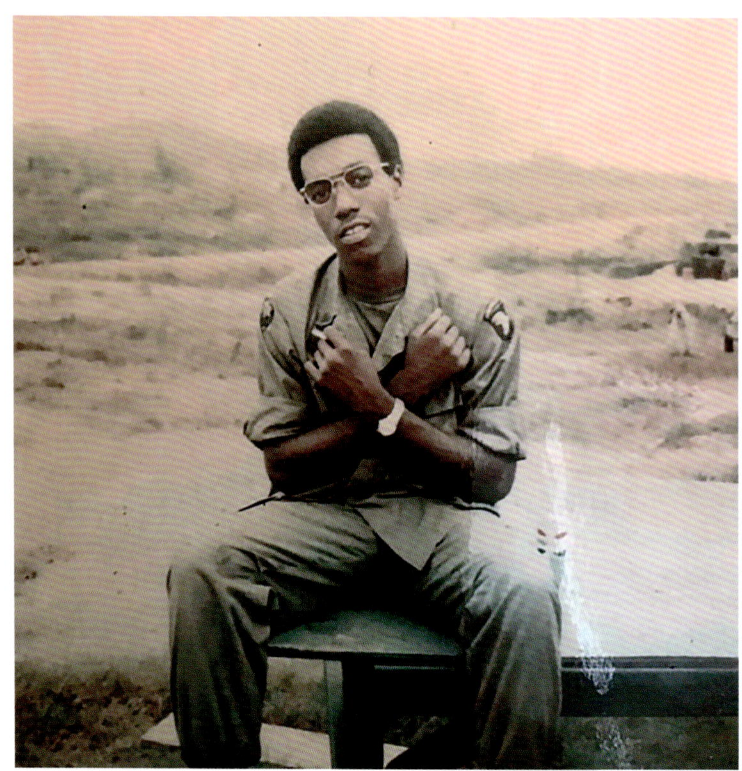

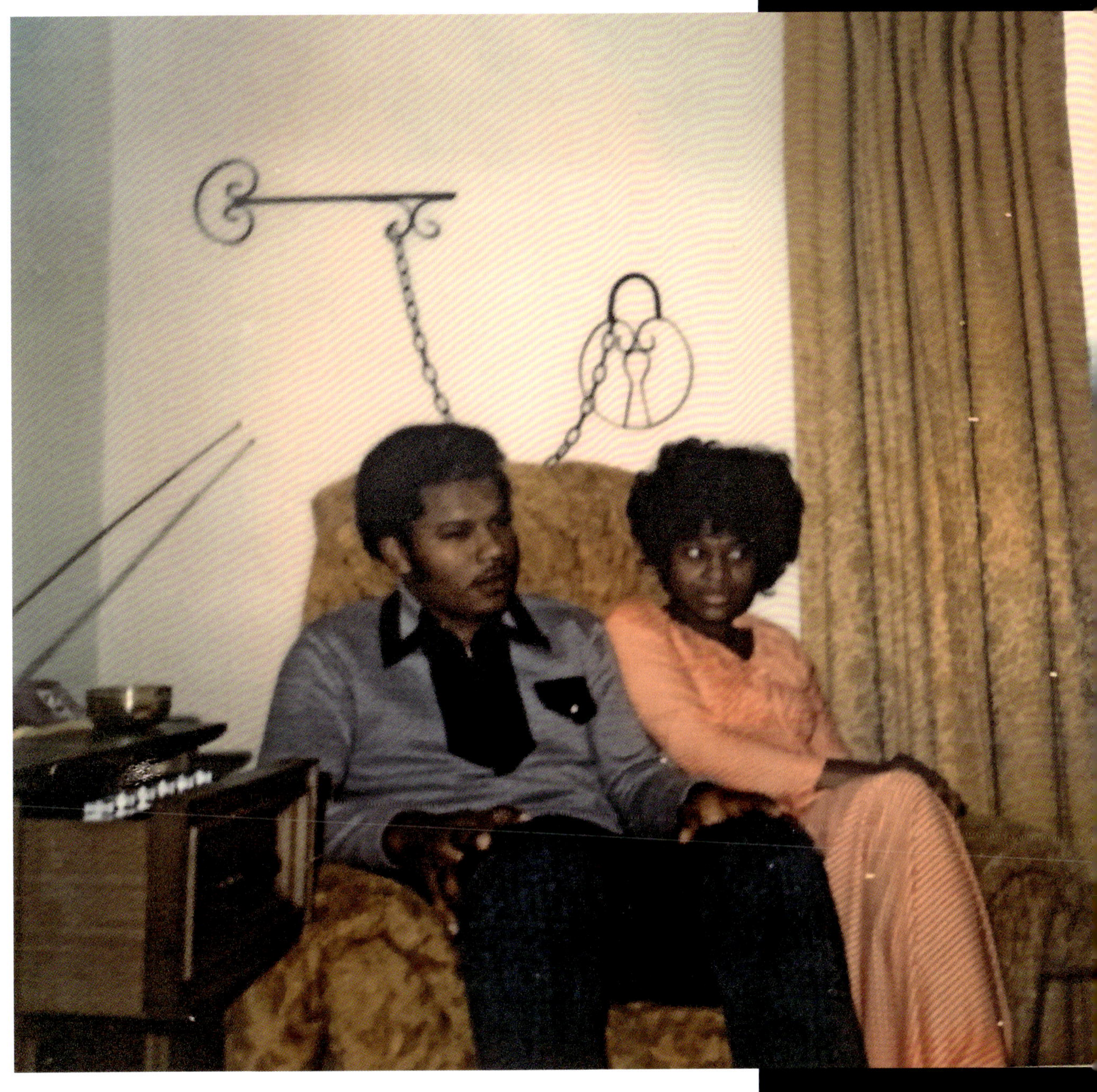

1970S

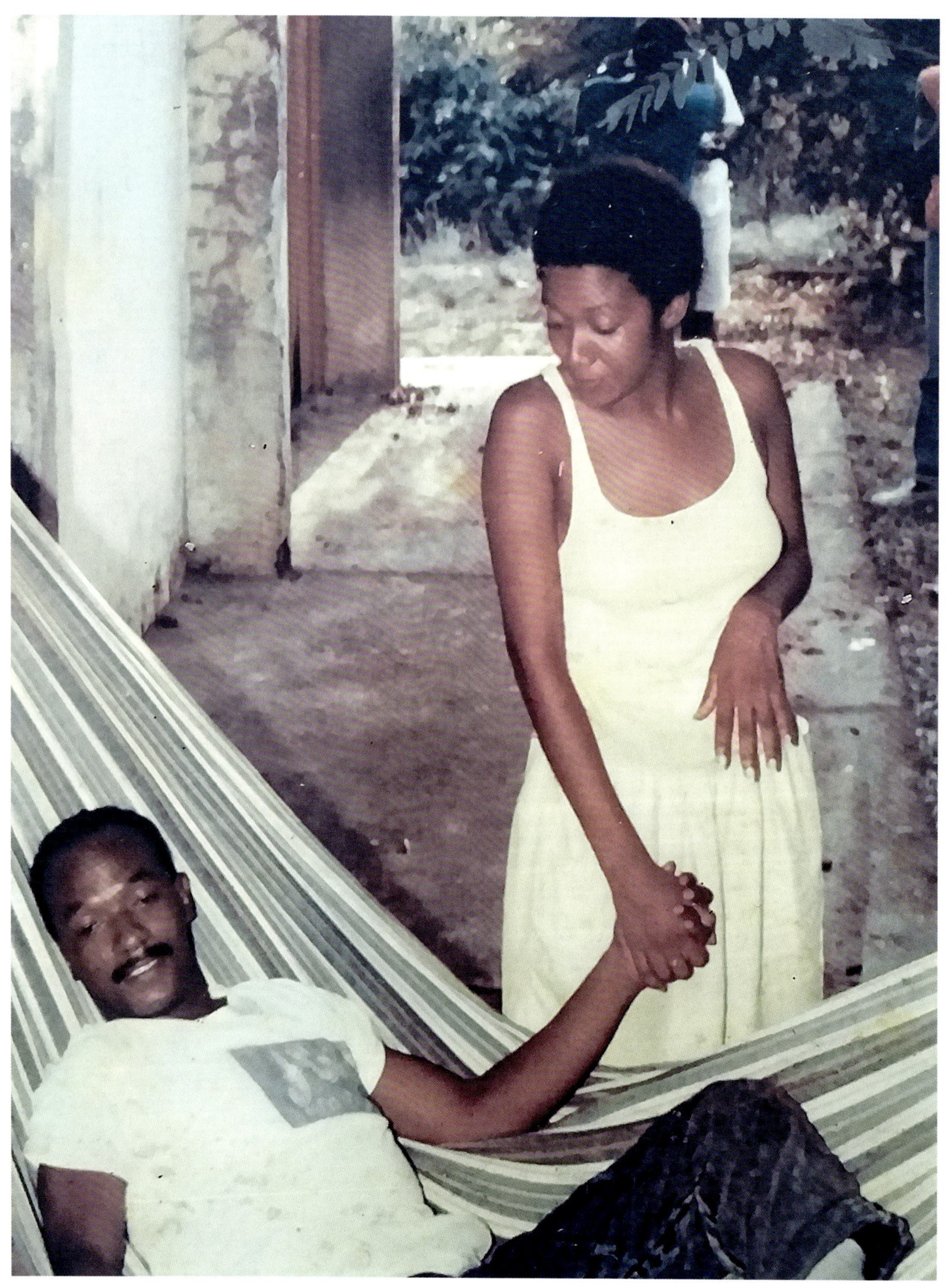

QUIBDÓ, COLOMBIA

Juanita helping her daughter
Nyesha get ready for the prom
1992

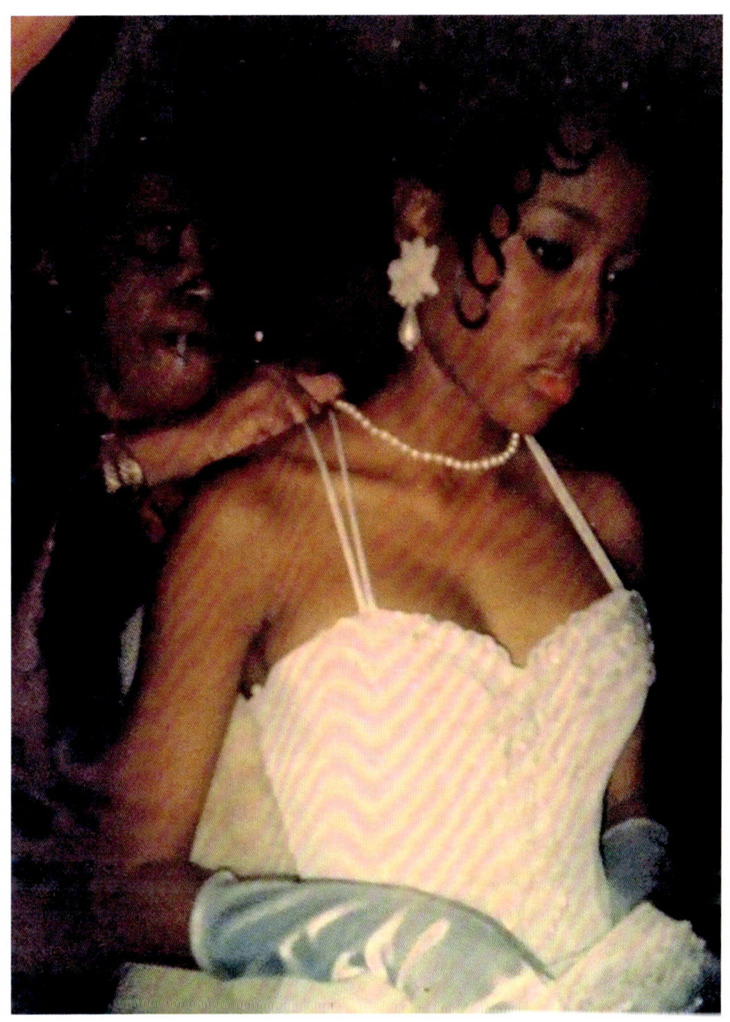

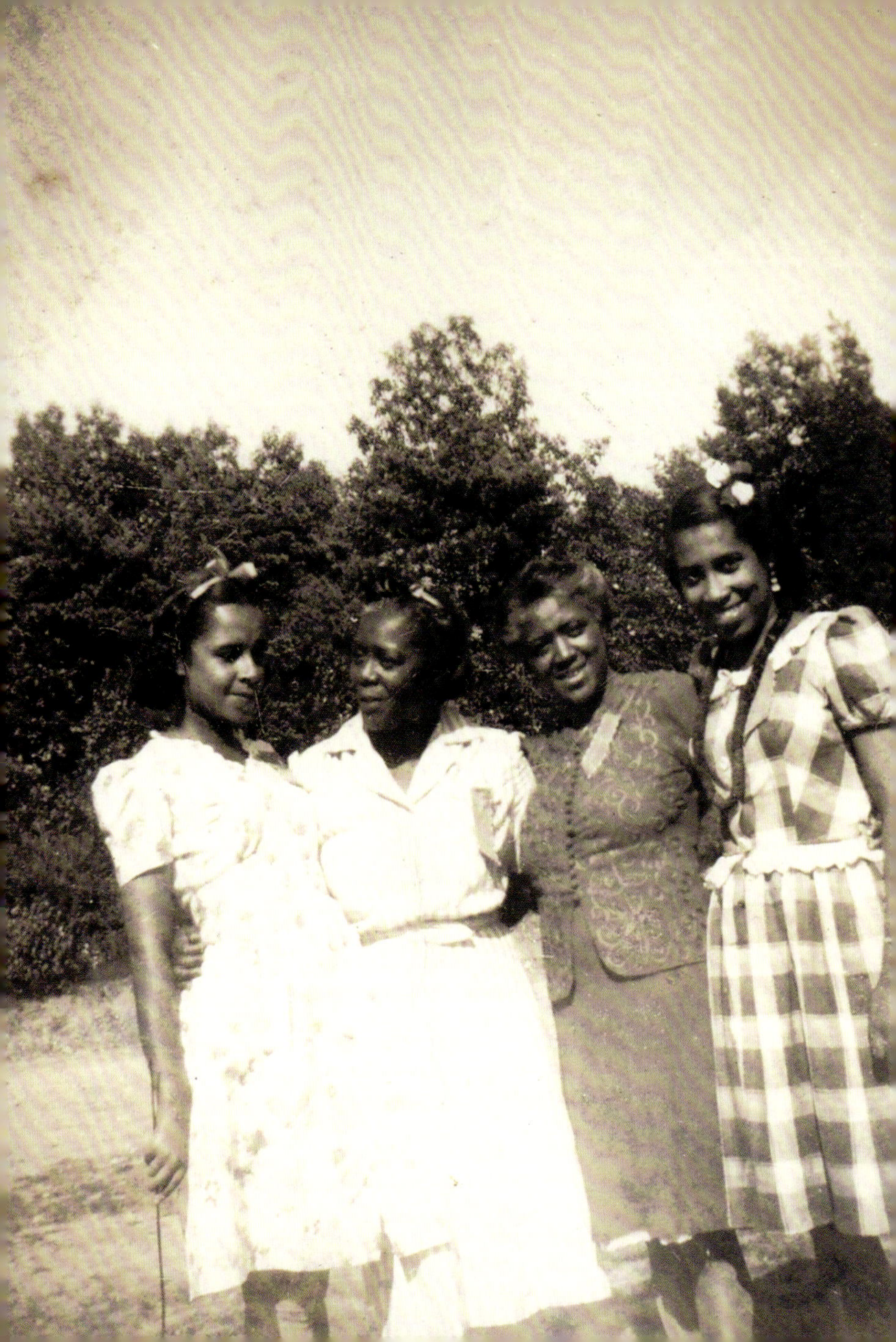

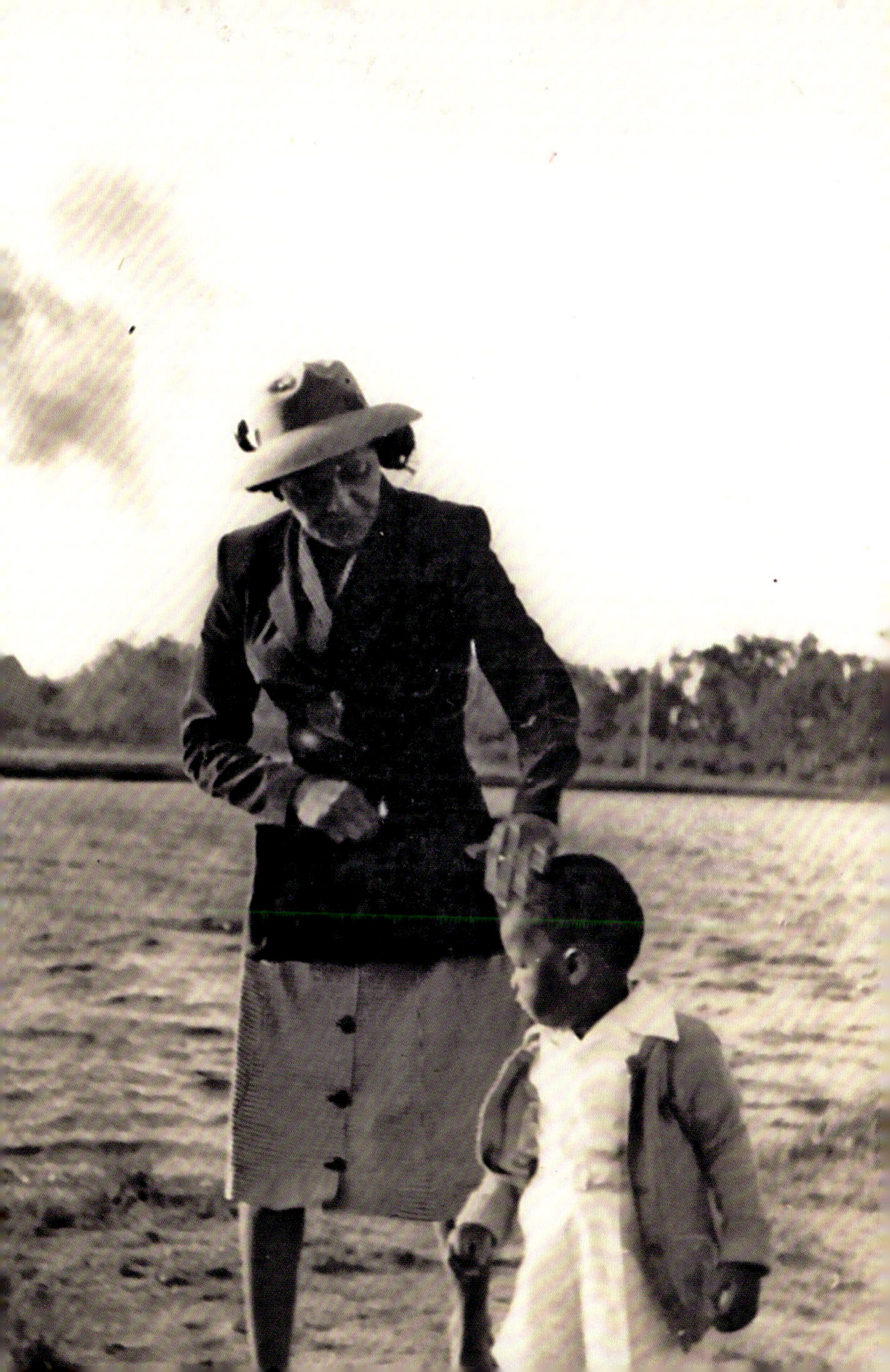

Grammy, grandchild, and stuffed koala bear collection
1981

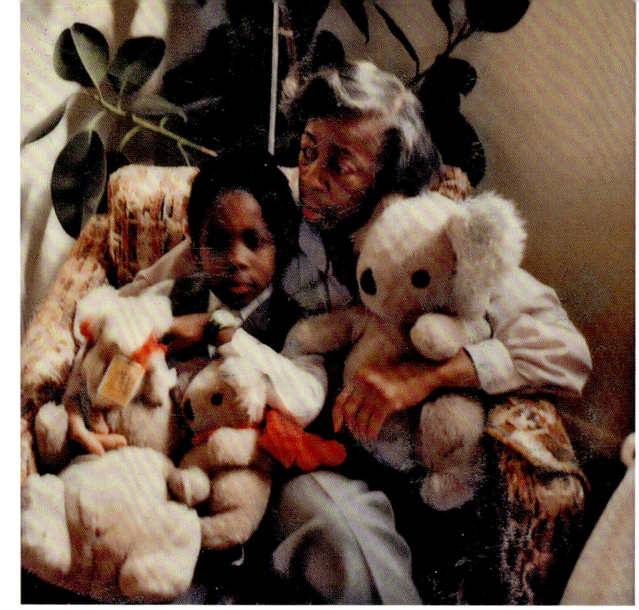

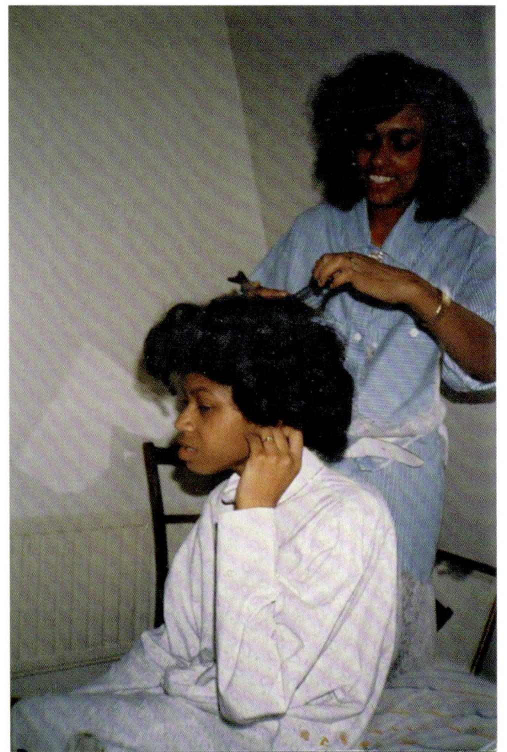

LONDON, ENGLAND
1980S

Jennifer (left) and her best friend, Bobbie

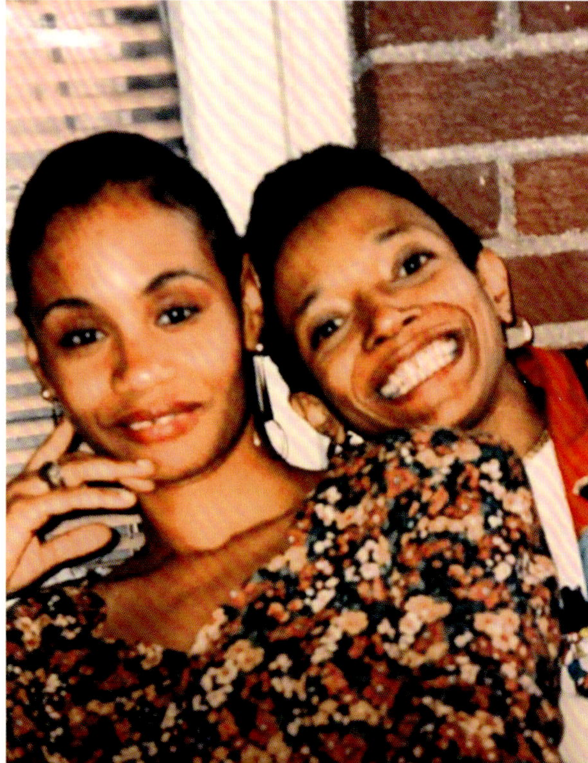

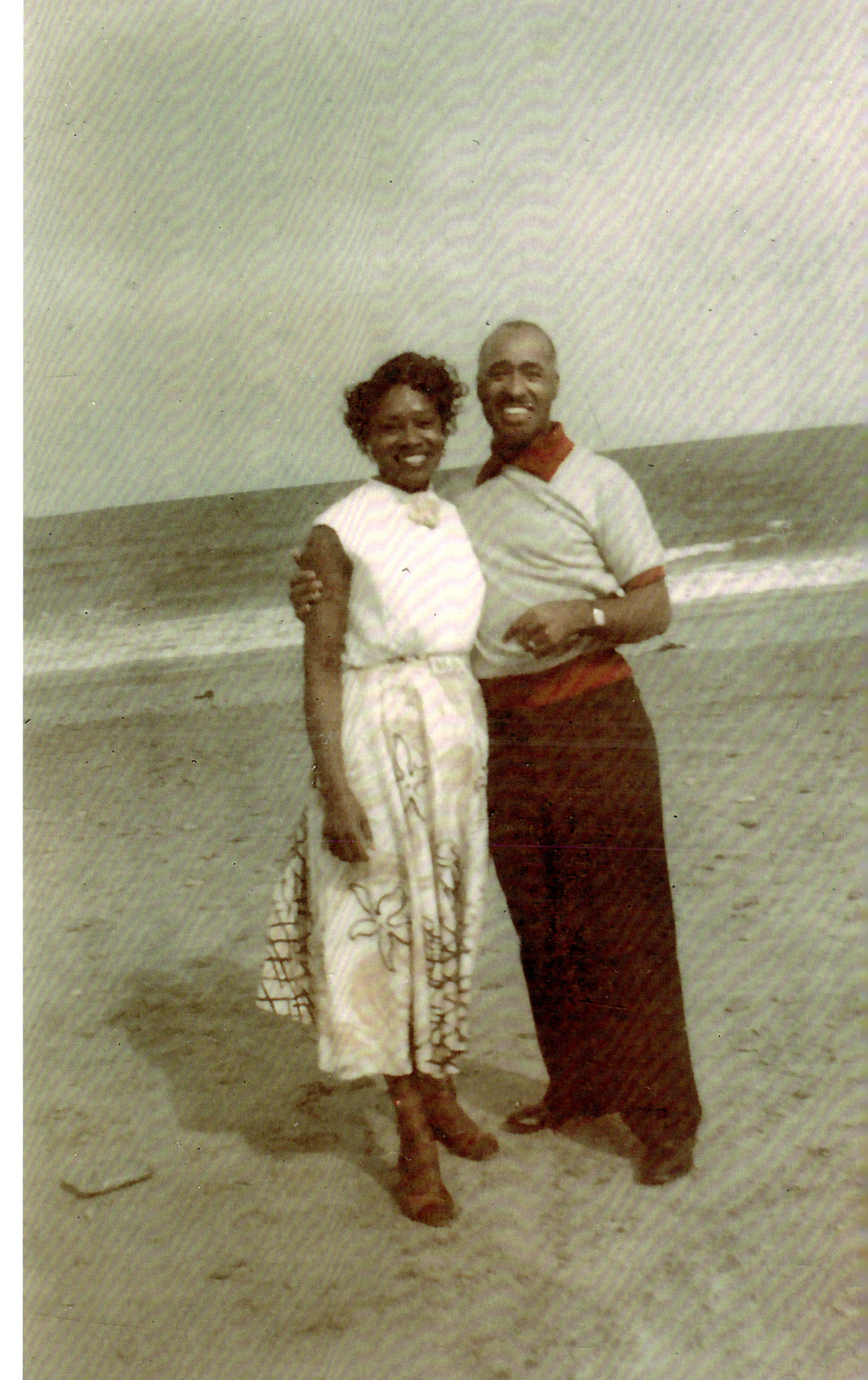

On the beach

CIRCA 1945

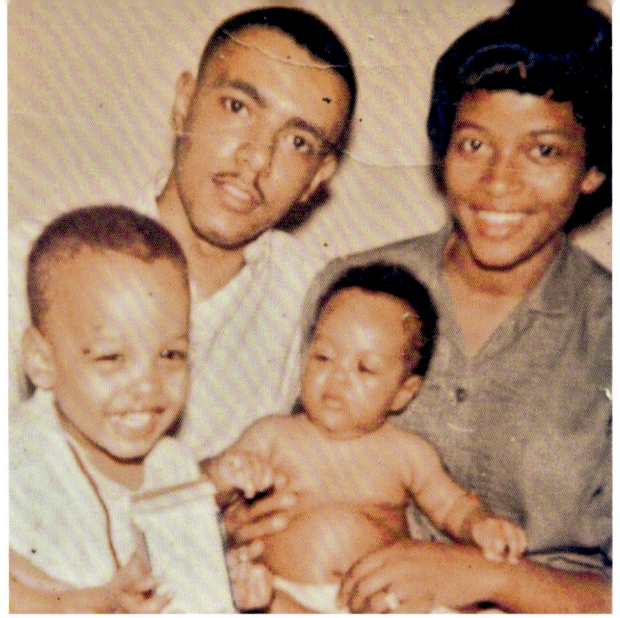

1960S

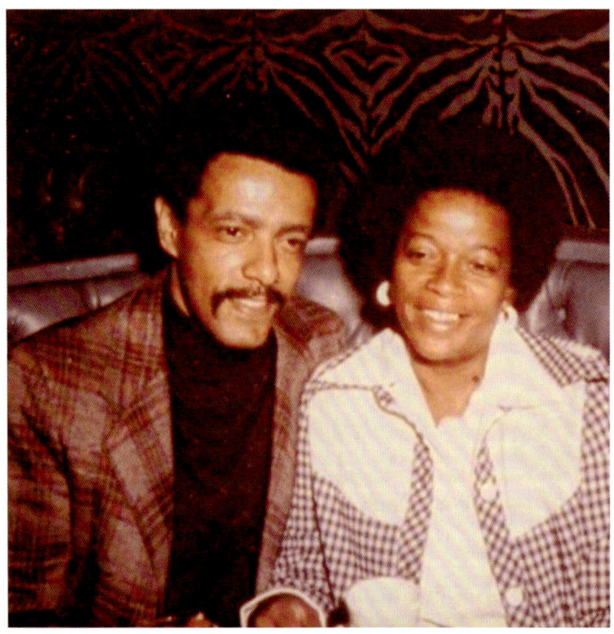

1970S

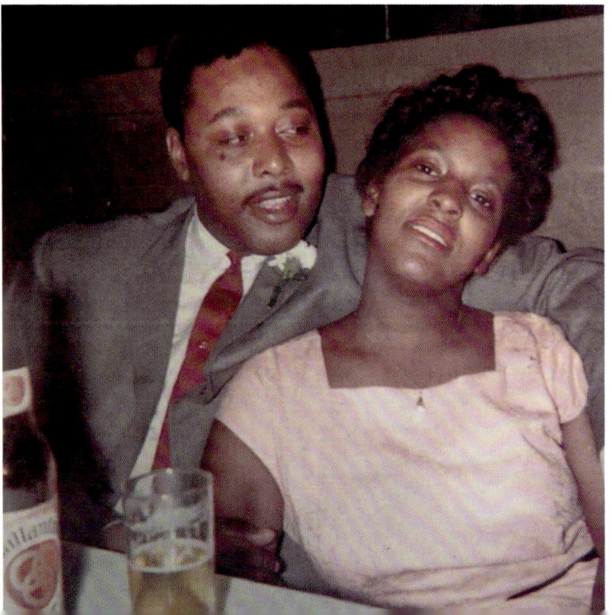

Joseph and Lennette

BROOKLYN, NY

1964

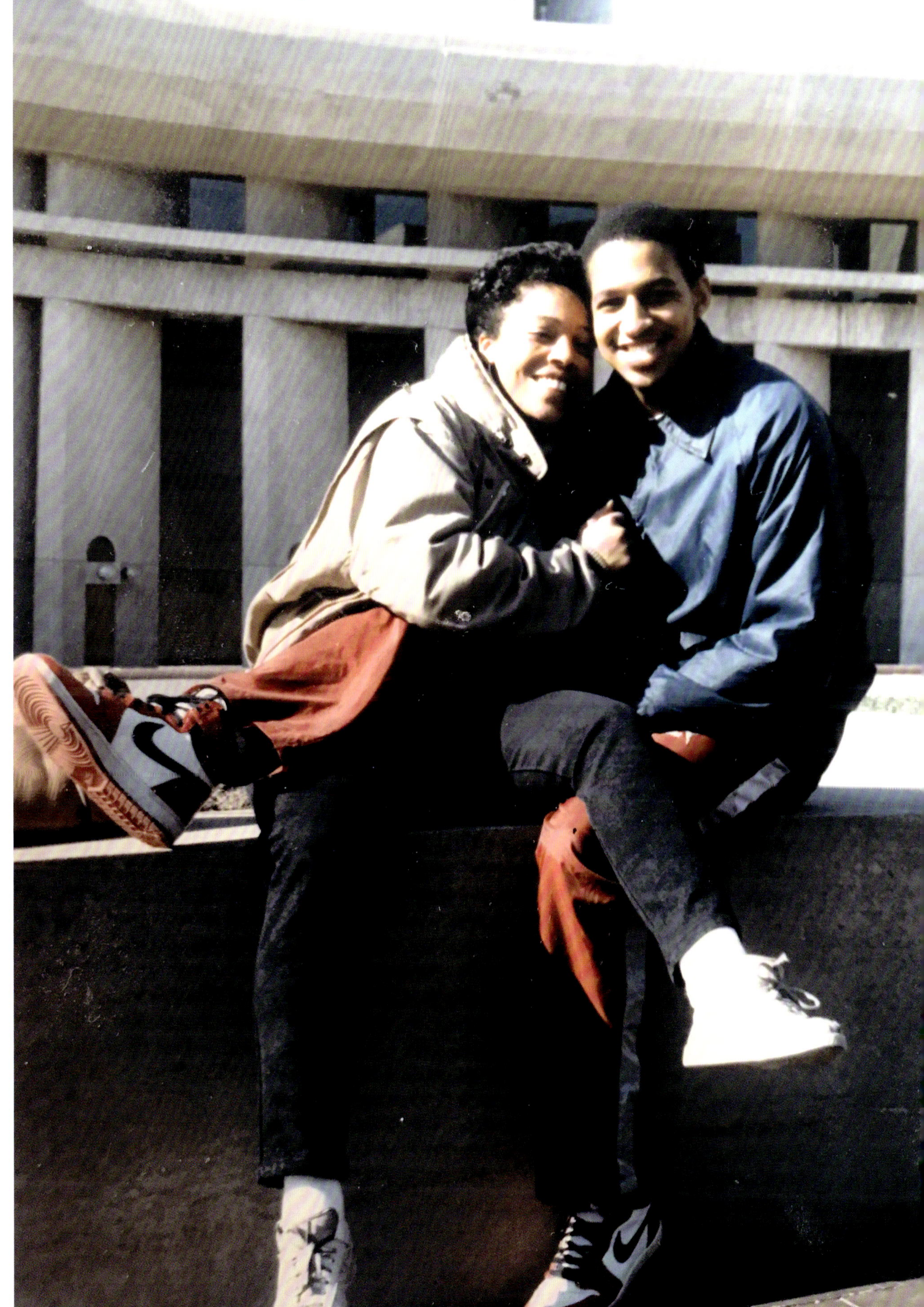

1980S

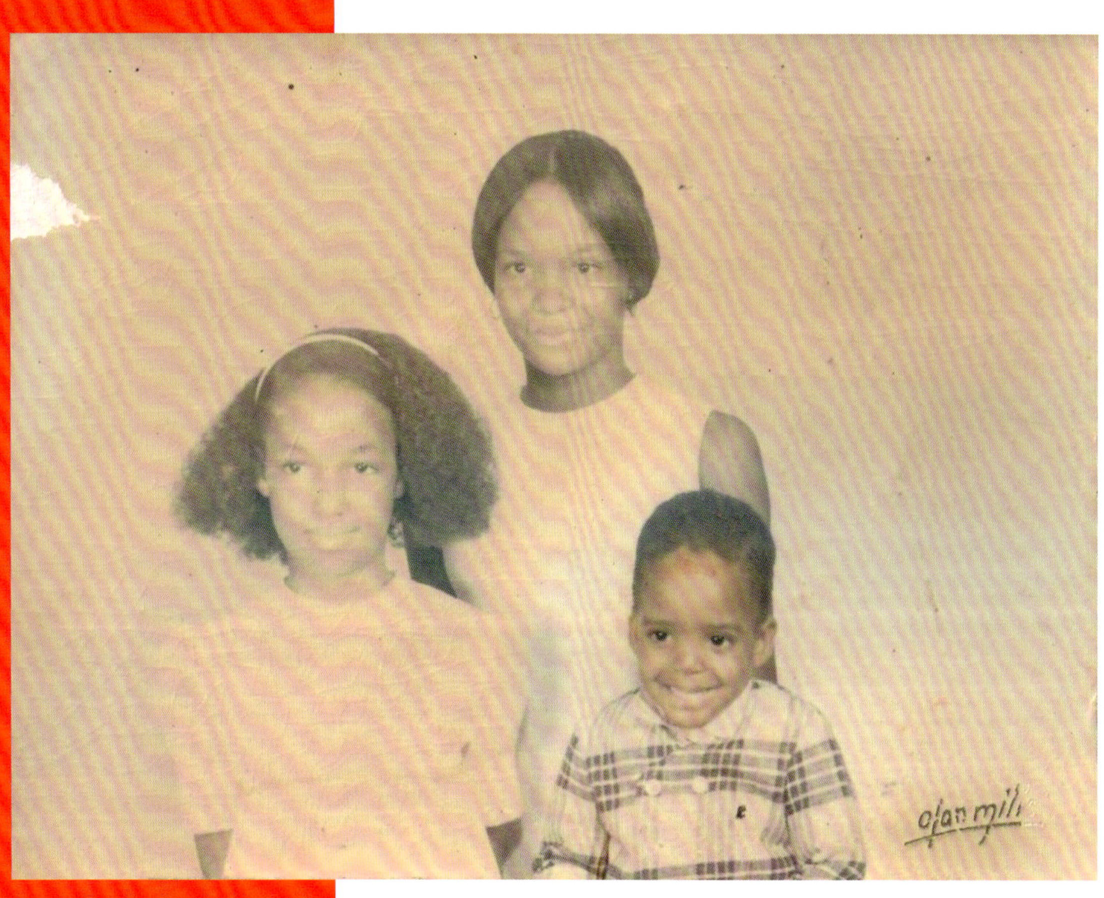

Studio portrait of the author's mom
Patricia, aunt Brenda, and uncle Gilbert
DAYTONA BEACH, FL
1970

FAMILY AND STUDIO PORTRAITS

Family portraits reflect the importance of the family unit and represent the intentionality and sophistication of creating a record of being together. Additionally, family portraits offer an accounting of "who all was/is there" that can be used in family genealogy and record-keeping. Portraits often show who was considered family – who was someone's partner, child, or friend; who raised whom; and so on. In a familial archiving context, a group portrait can be particularly useful when estimating the approximate year an image was taken, especially if clothing or other background clues prove to be unhelpful when attempting to date an image without context.

For example, there is a fading photograph of my mom, aunt, and uncle taken at an Olan Mills Studio in Daytona Beach, Florida, when they were children. The photo is undated, and the only prior knowledge that I had about it was the birth years of the people in the portrait. My uncle, born in December 1968, appears to be at least one, but no older than two years old. His presence in the image strengthens the approximation of the date, where the discoloration and wear and tear of the image create a bit of uncertainty. After conferring with my mom, it was determined that this family portrait was taken for Easter in the spring of 1970. She remembers her yellow Easter dress and the piece of yellow yarn she wore around it as a sash – contextual clues not privy to me beforehand.

Portrait studios offer picture packages: photos taken at the same place and time, in different poses and against an array of backdrops, some in group settings, and others as solo portraits marking the existence and celebration of oneself. Traditionally, the photos from these sessions were printed in various sizes, with the favorites typically reserved for the larger frames, and the others divided between friends and family as wallet-sized keepsakes that found homes in smaller frames and photo albums across town and state lines. Framed and curated along walls and down hallways, family and studio portraits are staples in Black homes. But as digital photography technology has evolved, taking and exchanging these types of portraits has become a rarity. Now, we tag our relatives on social media apps, like Facebook, to show off a graduation photo or a prom picture. We view and download these photos at our convenience, but rarely do we print them.

If only for a moment, this series makes space to reflect on a lost or fleeting tradition of getting dressed up to take professional photographs and passing them out as keepsakes.

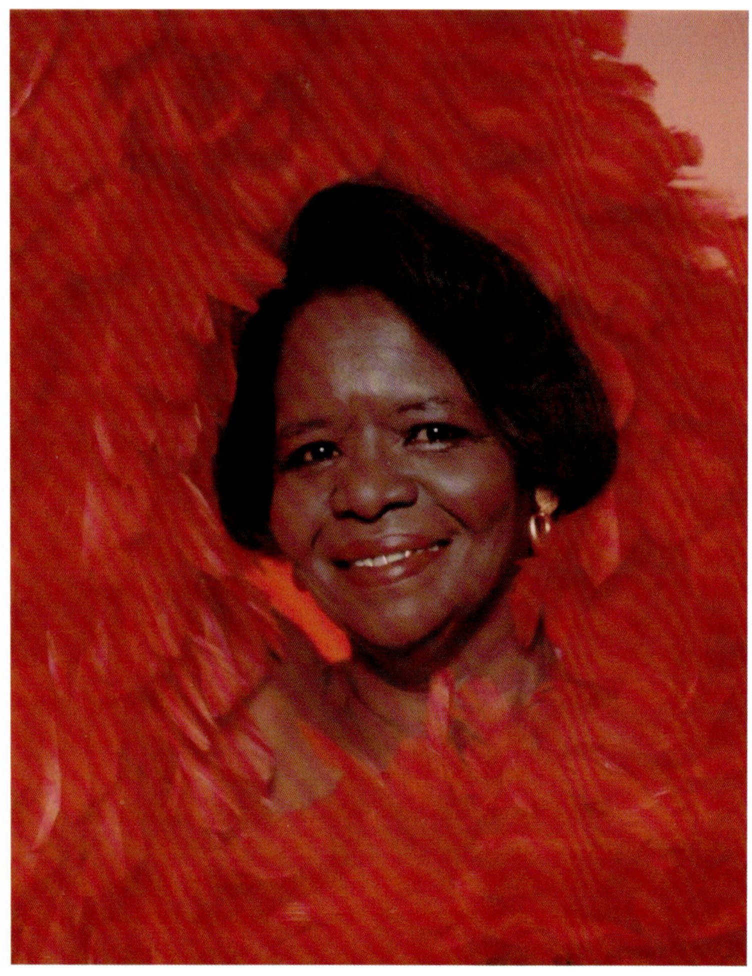

Portrait of the author's grandmother Cora at a Glamour Shots studio
JACKSONVILLE, FL
1990S

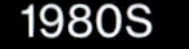
1980S

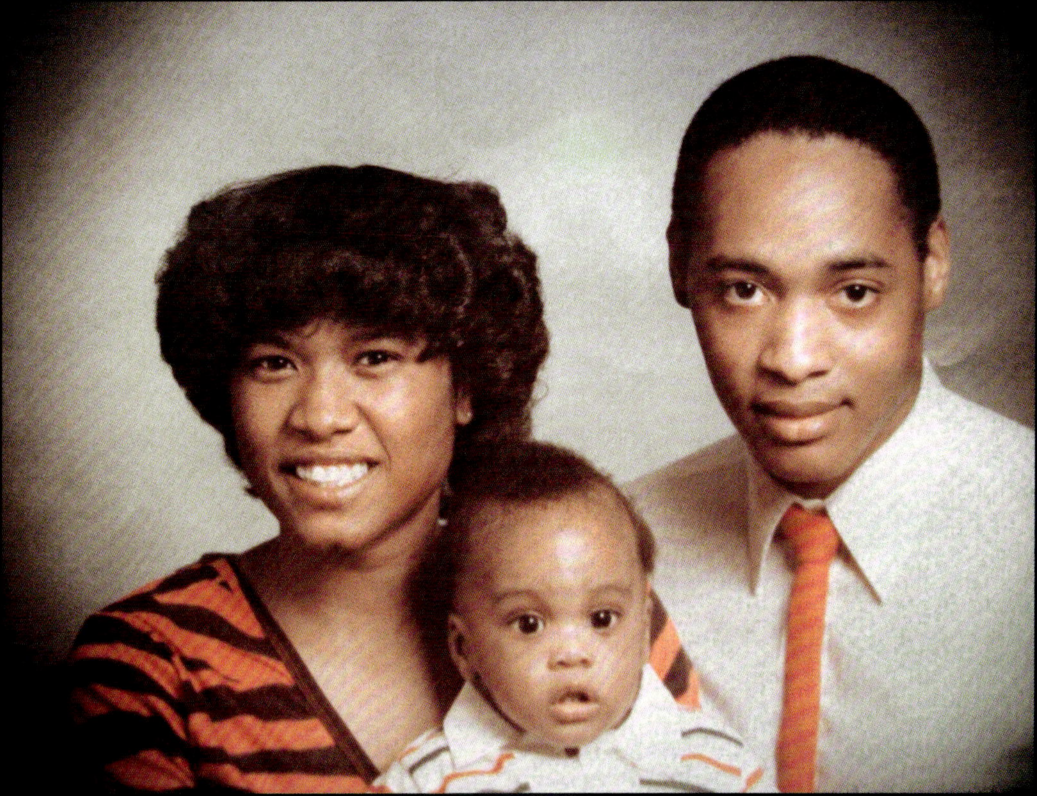

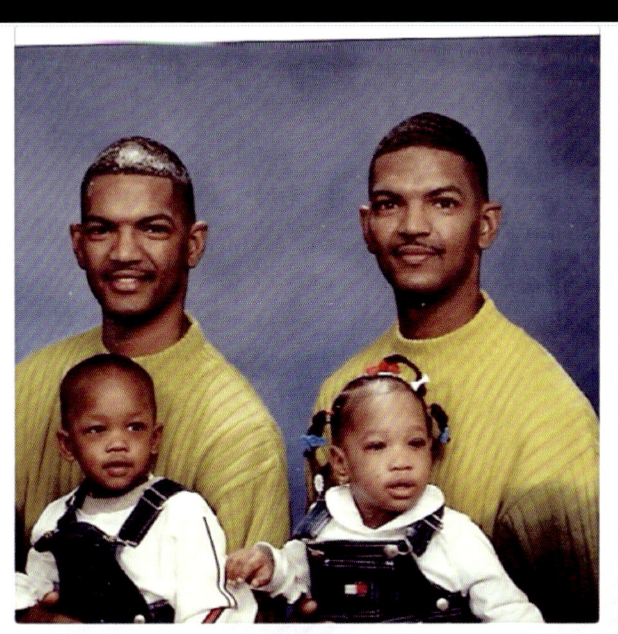

1990S

→ The grandchildren of Samuel and Stephani (top to bottom, left to right): George Johnson, Shanice Johnson, Shernelle Hall, Samuel Johnson, and Shawdell Taylor
1991

The Weatherall family
LAFAYETTE, LA
1996

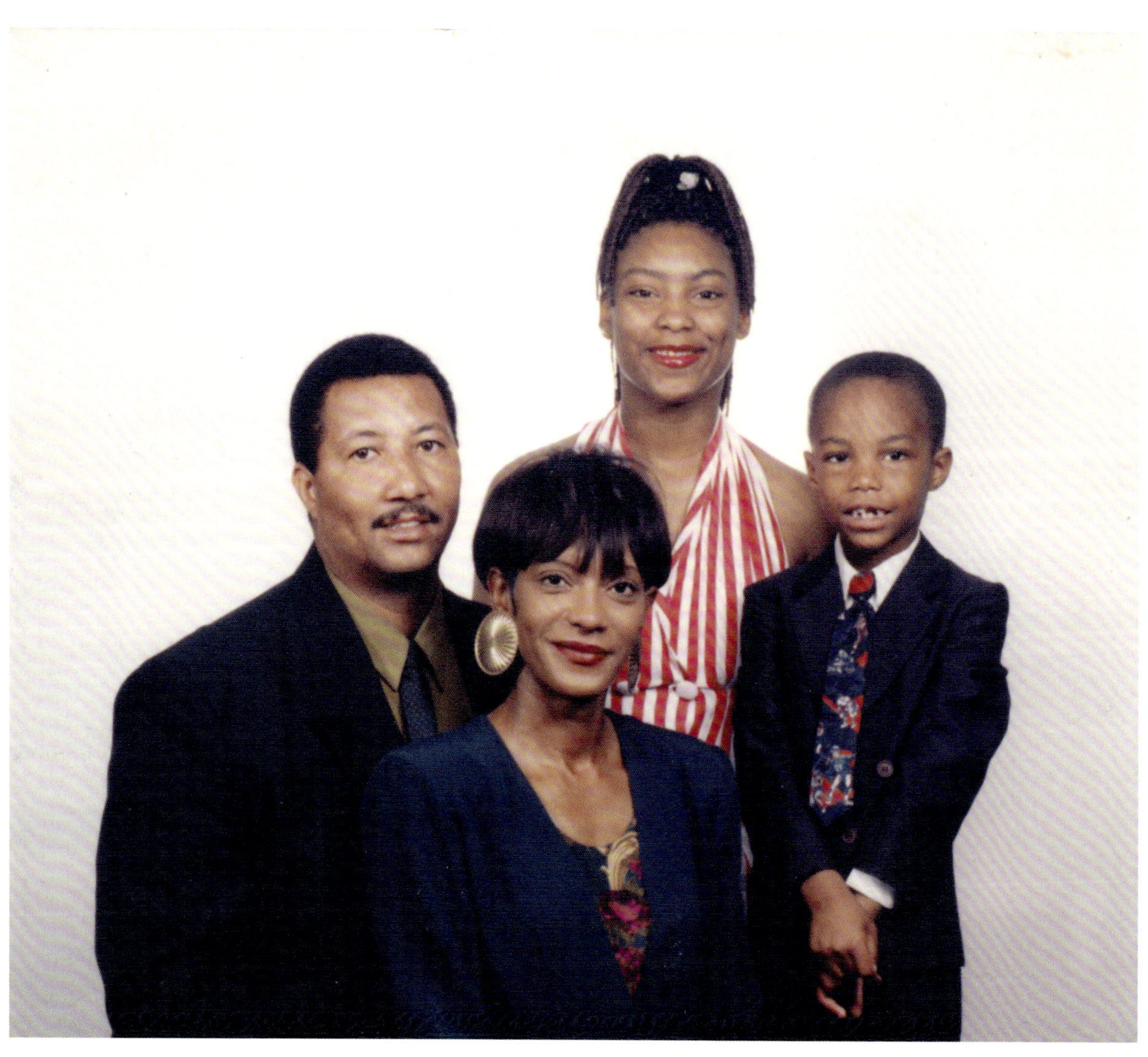

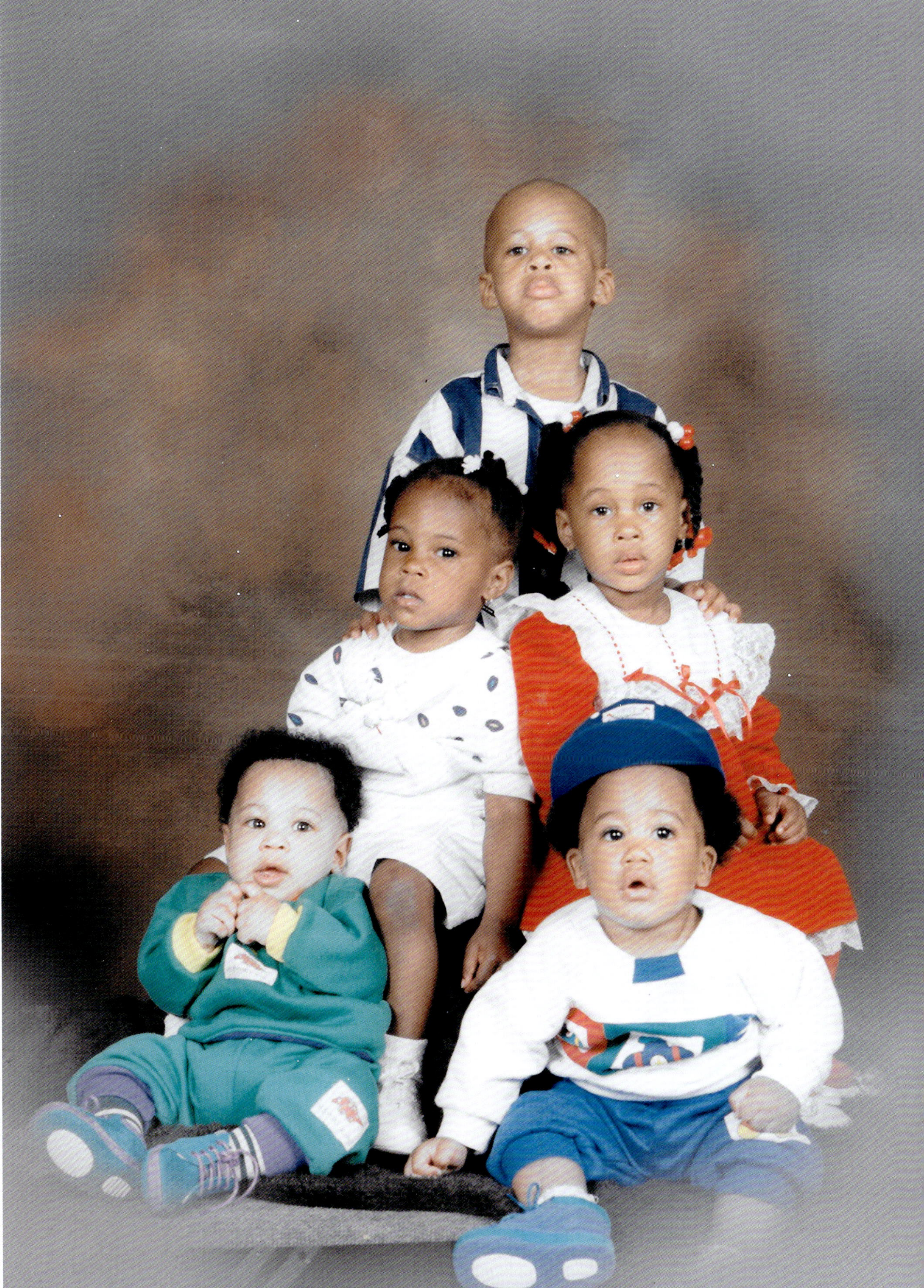

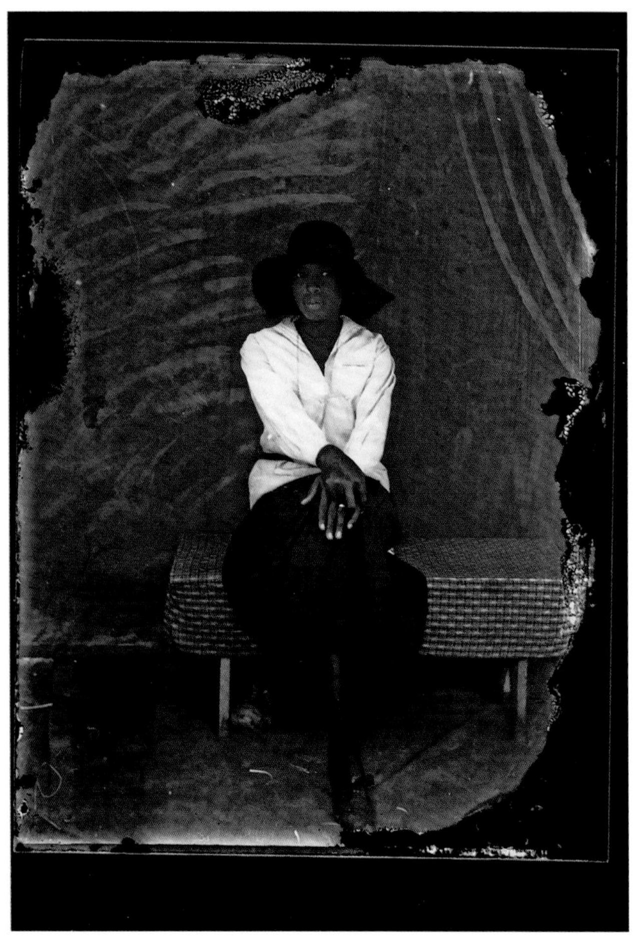

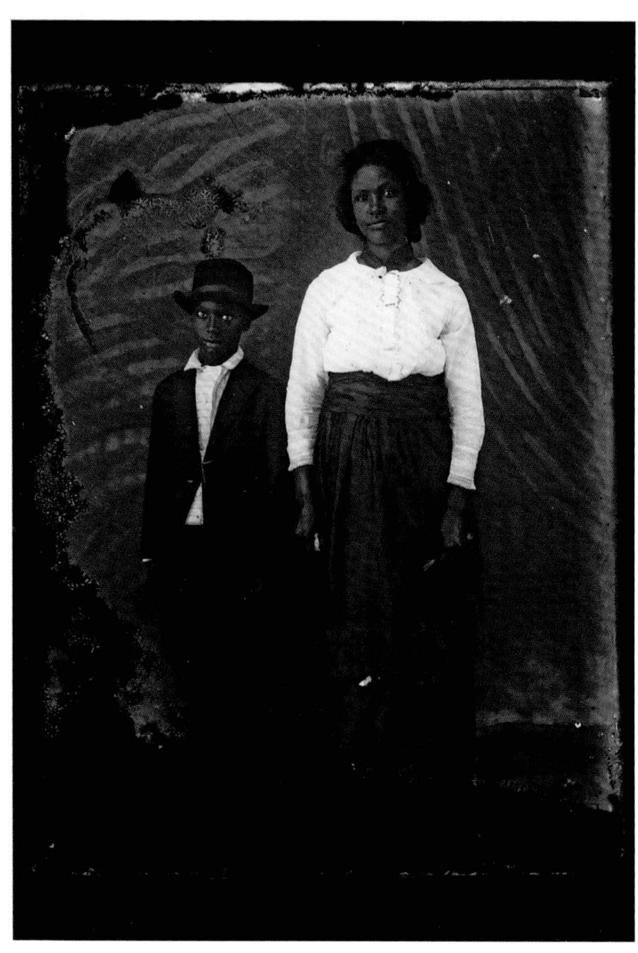

SOUTH CAROLINA

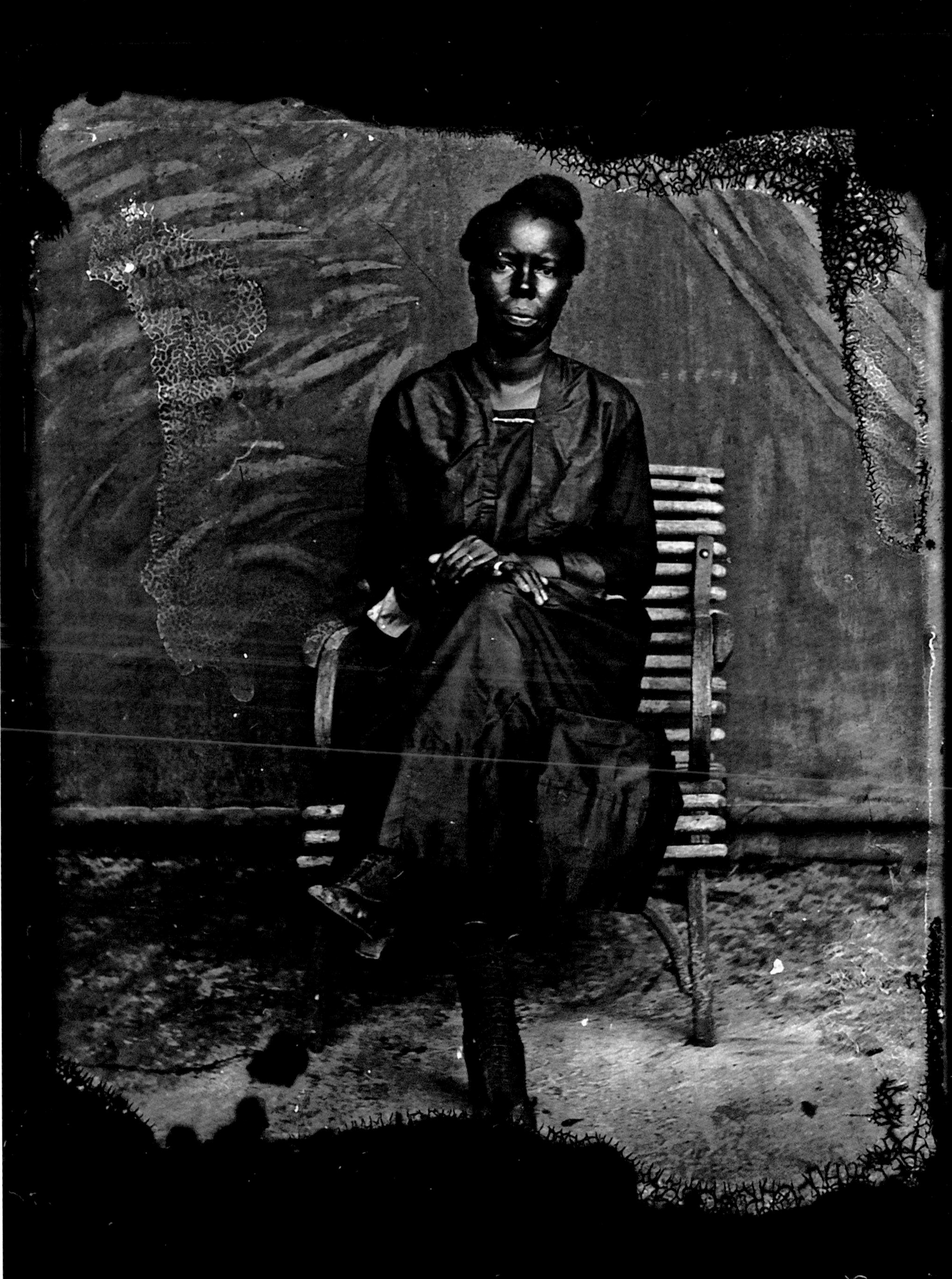

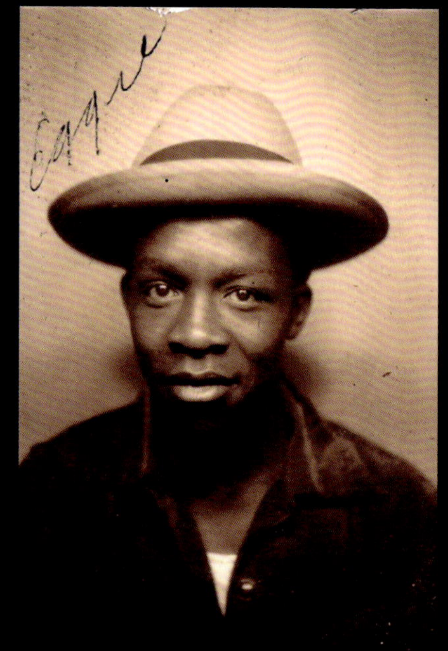

Eggie

CIRCA 1940

Yvonne

CIRCA 1940

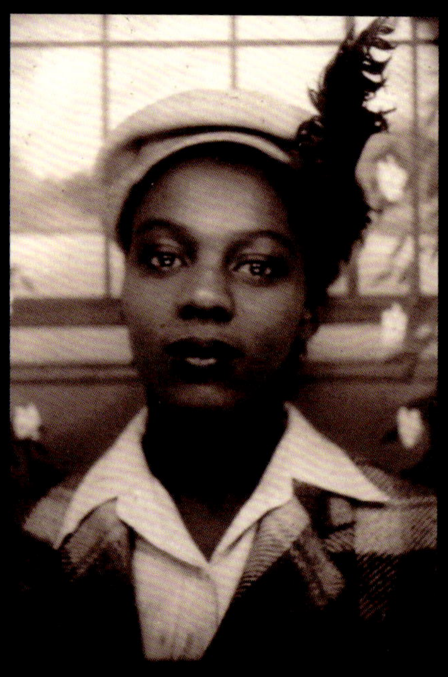

CIRCA 1940

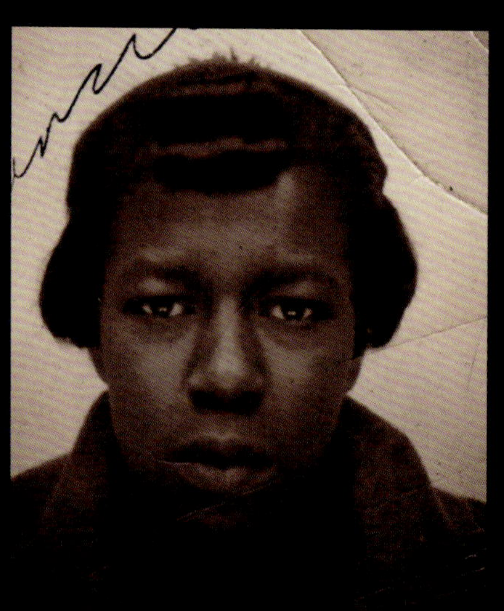

Francis

CIRCA 1940

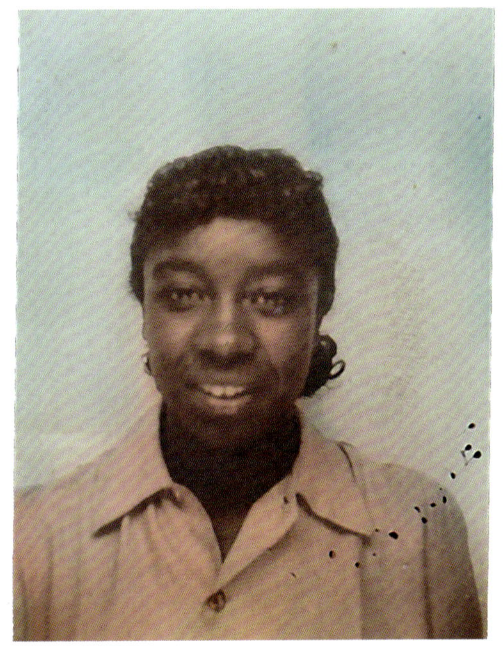

Winnie Irish

CIRCA 1945

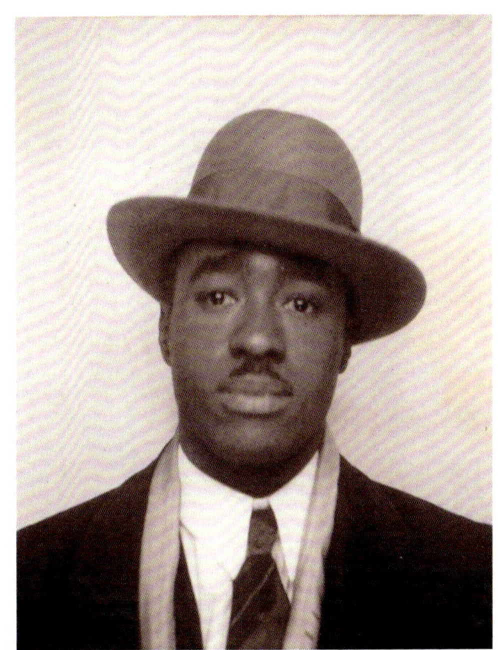

CIRCA 1940

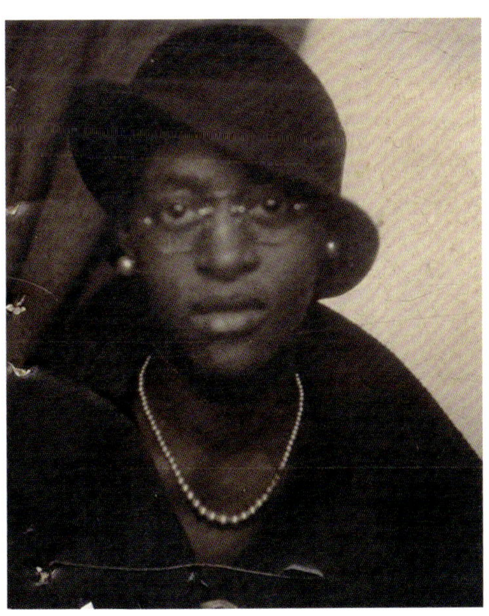

Claudie May

1930S

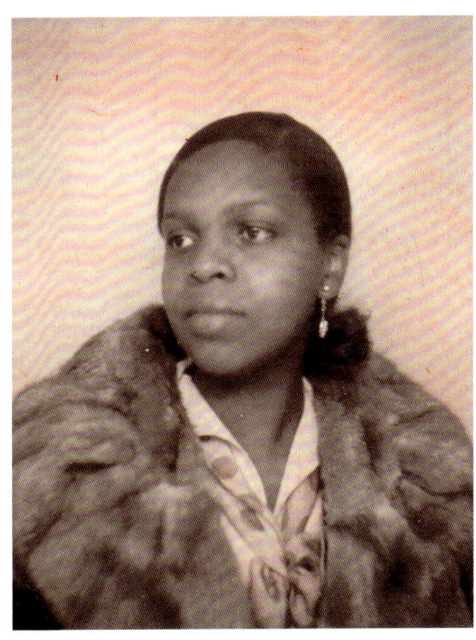

Ethel May Stewart

1933

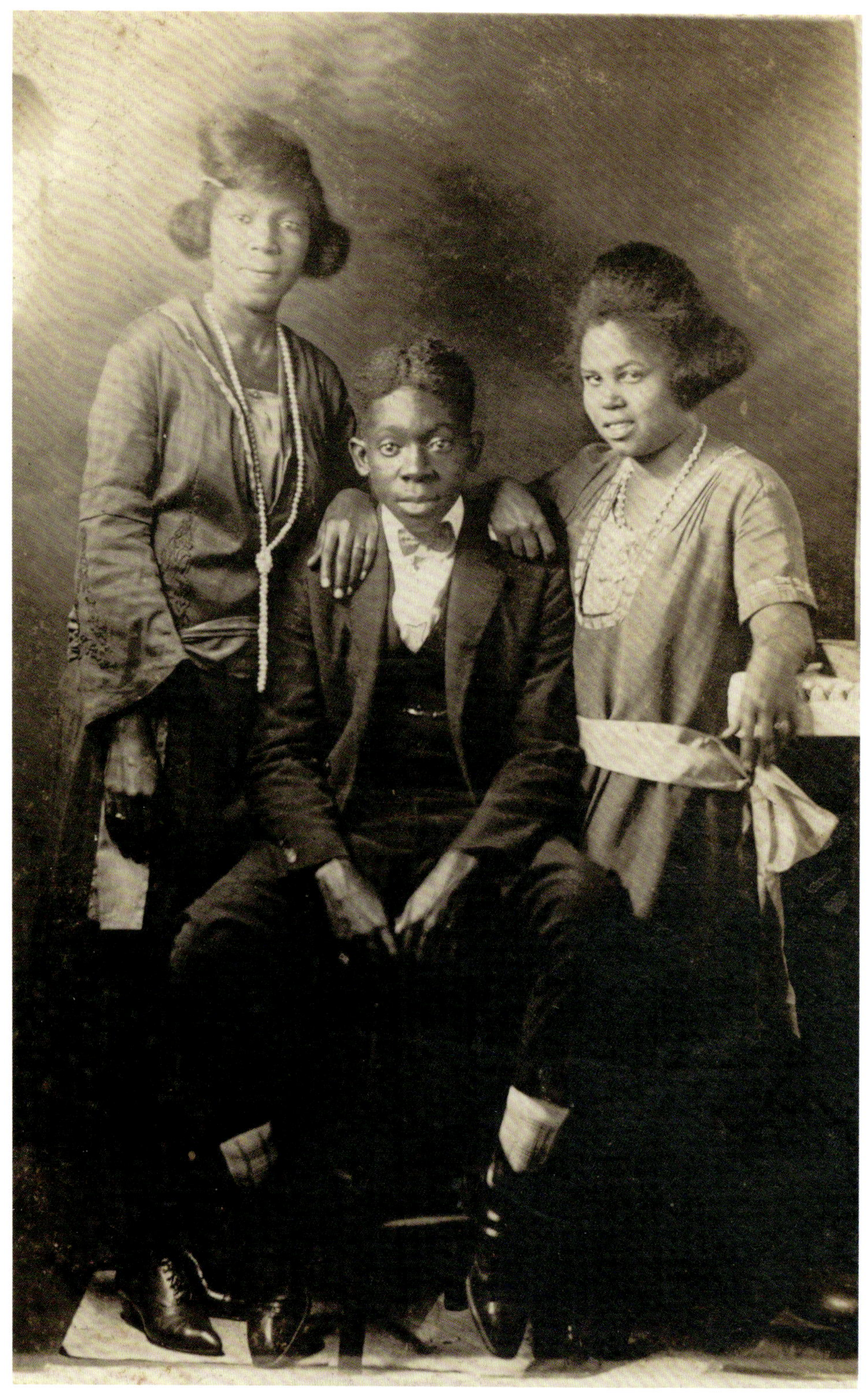

CHARLESTON, SC

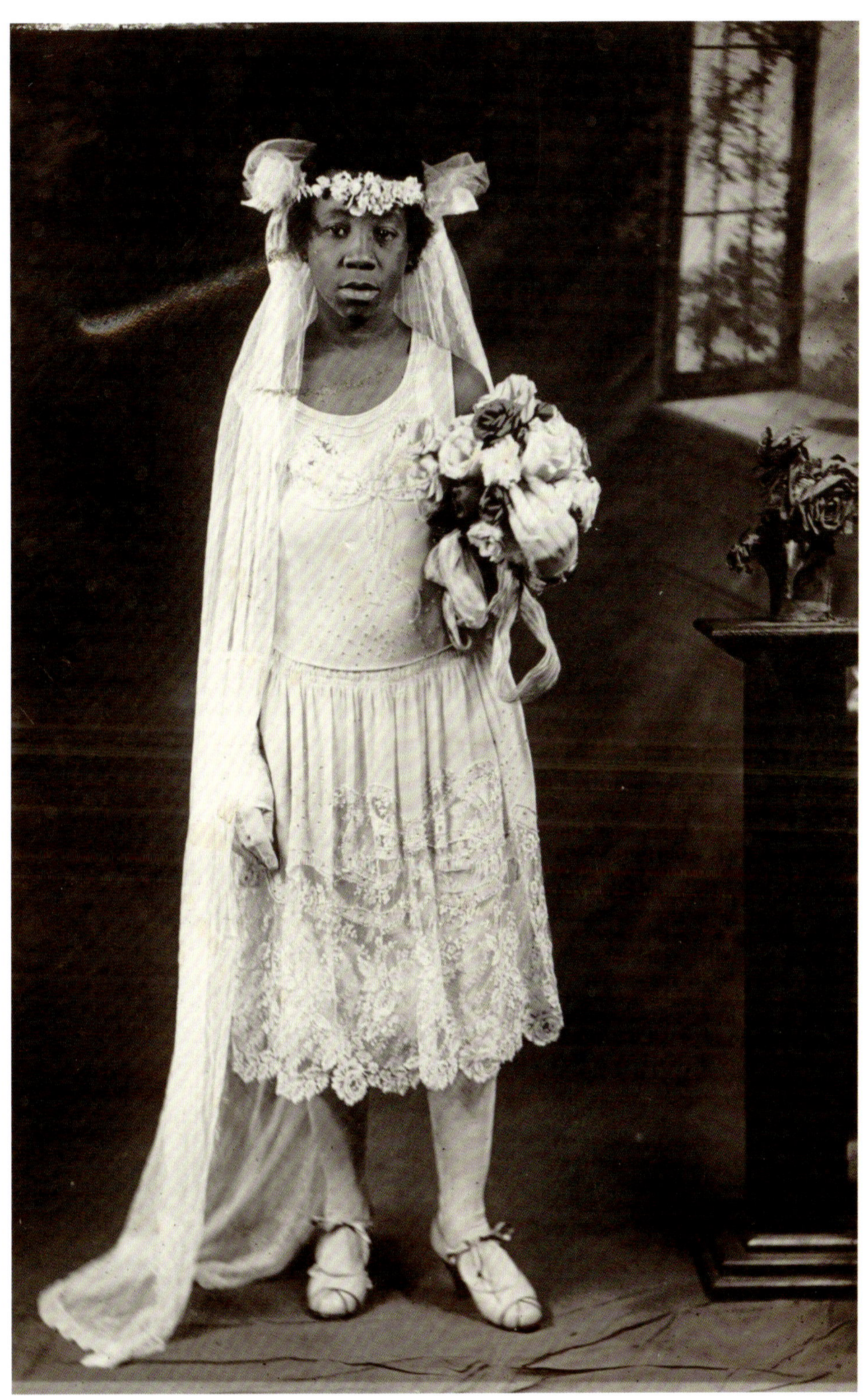

SOUTH
CAROLINA

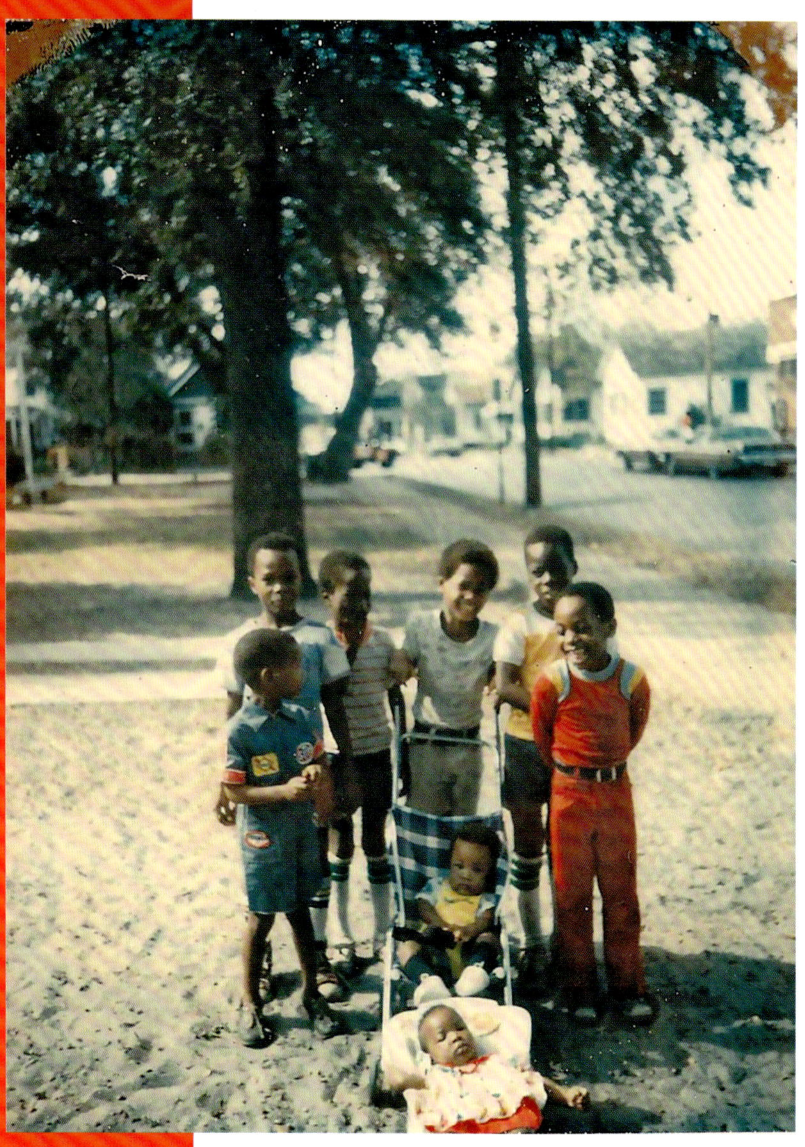

The author's cousins Damion and
Markale with neighborhood children
JACKSONVILLE, FL
1978

YOUTH

Mainstream media frequently strips Black young people of their innocence and quickly forces them into adulthood, where their entire existence is measured against stereotypes of what Black people represent. And this is connected to – and in addition to – being criminalized based on the color of their skin. These images of Black youth are then accepted as the truth by people of varying backgrounds, particularly those who have never experienced a Black childhood. Growing up in a society where you're constantly seen as a threat, regardless of age, is never accounted or adjusted for in these mainstream portrayals.

As a mother, it's important to me that my personal and professional work reflects intentionality in my celebration and love of Black youth, while reminding Black folks of the sweet moments tucked away within the memories of their own Black childhoods. My desire is to protect the sacredness of Black youth, and it is my hope that one day, the kinds of images we see in this series become the norm for how Black children and young people are witnessed: as beautiful, joyful, and free.

WACO, TEXAS
1950S

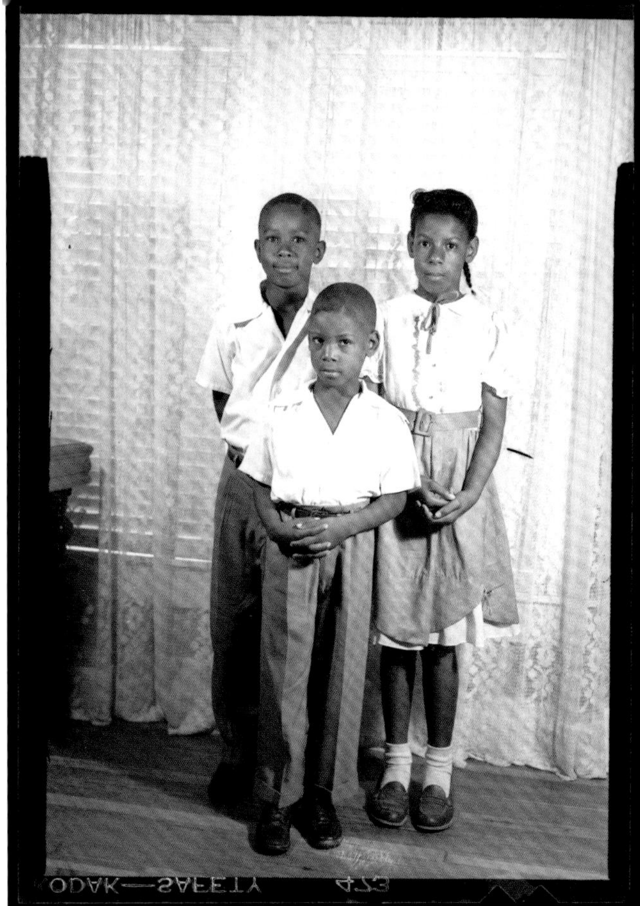

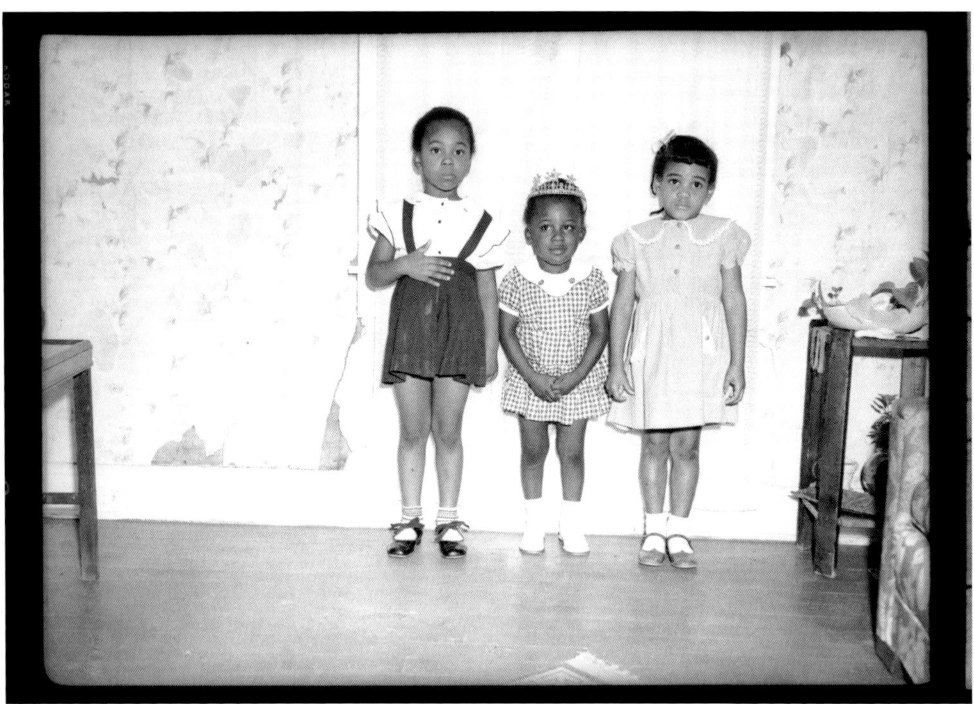

Portrait of three girls
TEXAS

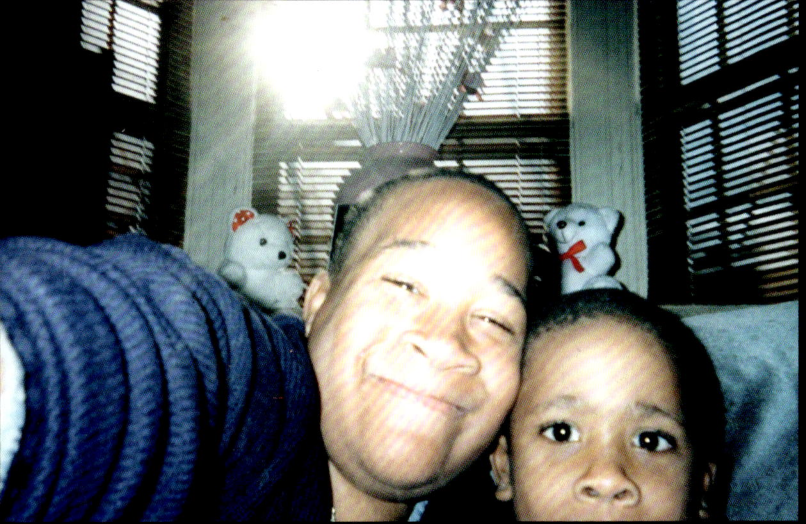

1990S

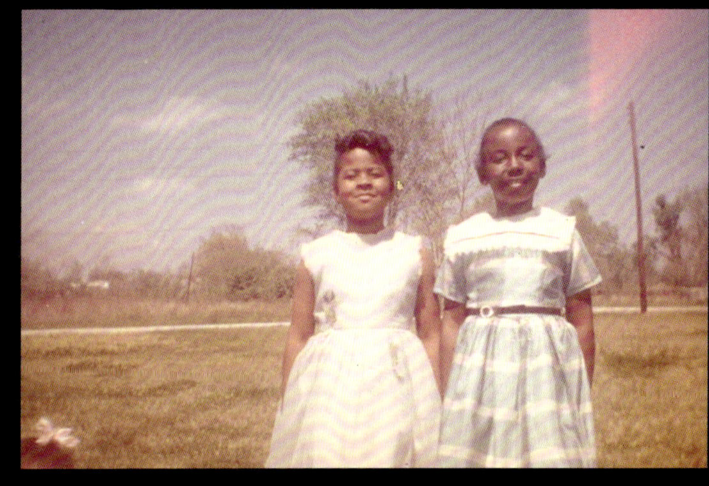

EAST COLUMBIA, TX
1950S

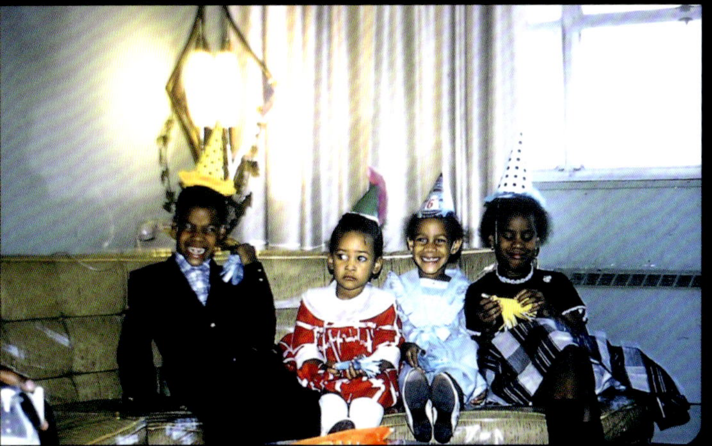

NEW YORK, NY
1960S

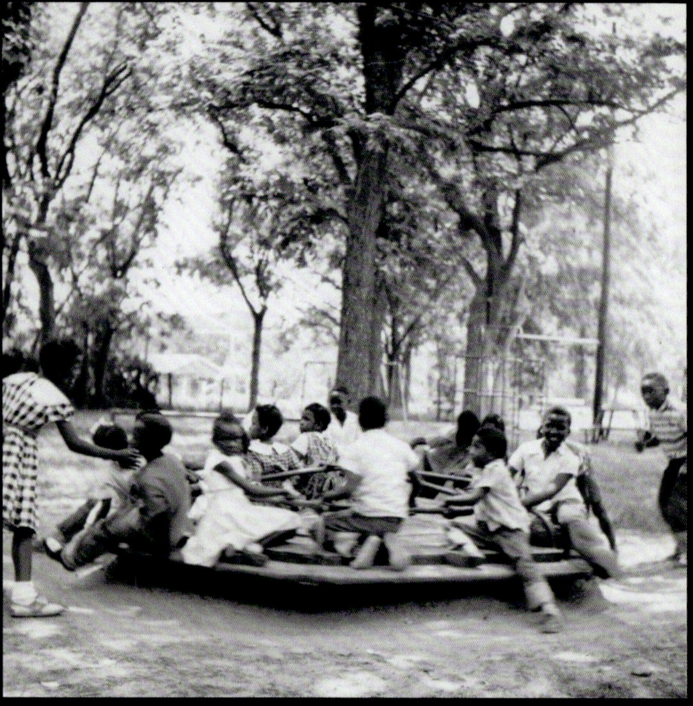

TEXAS

1958

A group of children pose

MASSACHUSETTS

CIRCA 1945

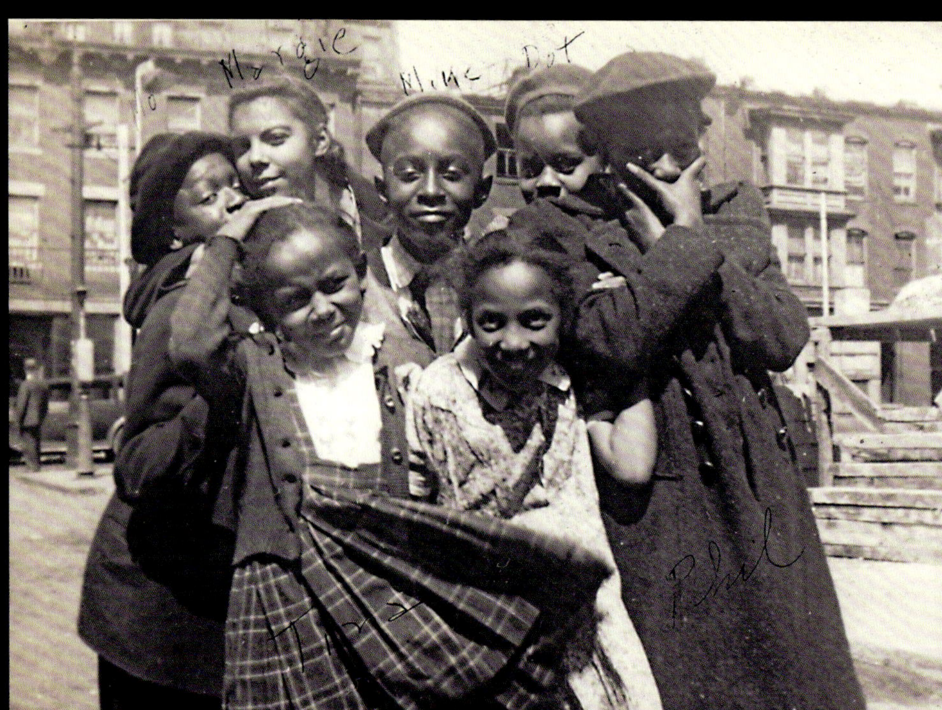

Sunday after church
CLEVELAND, OH

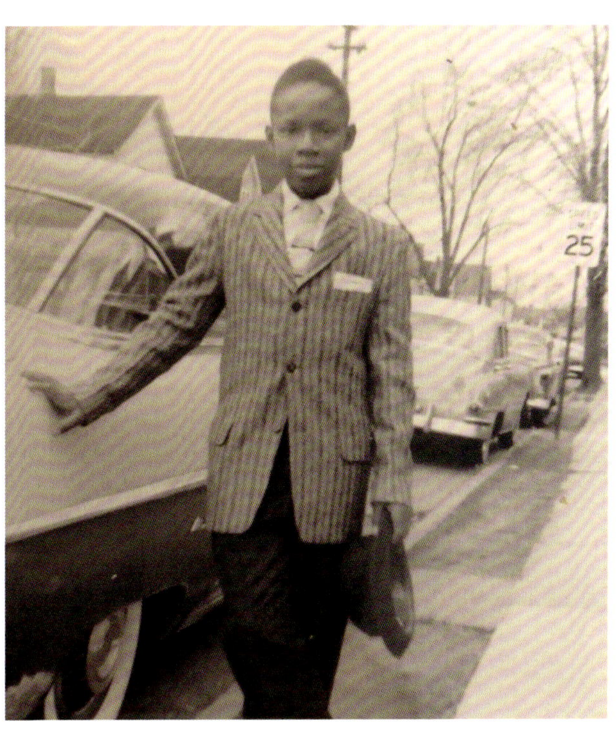

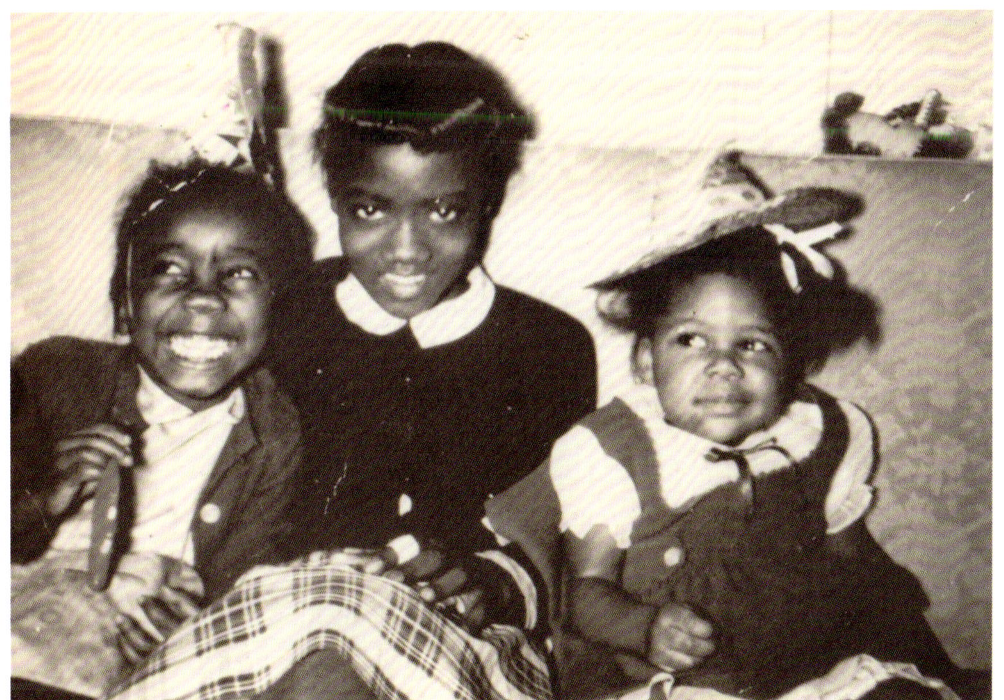

Vikki, Brenda, and Regina

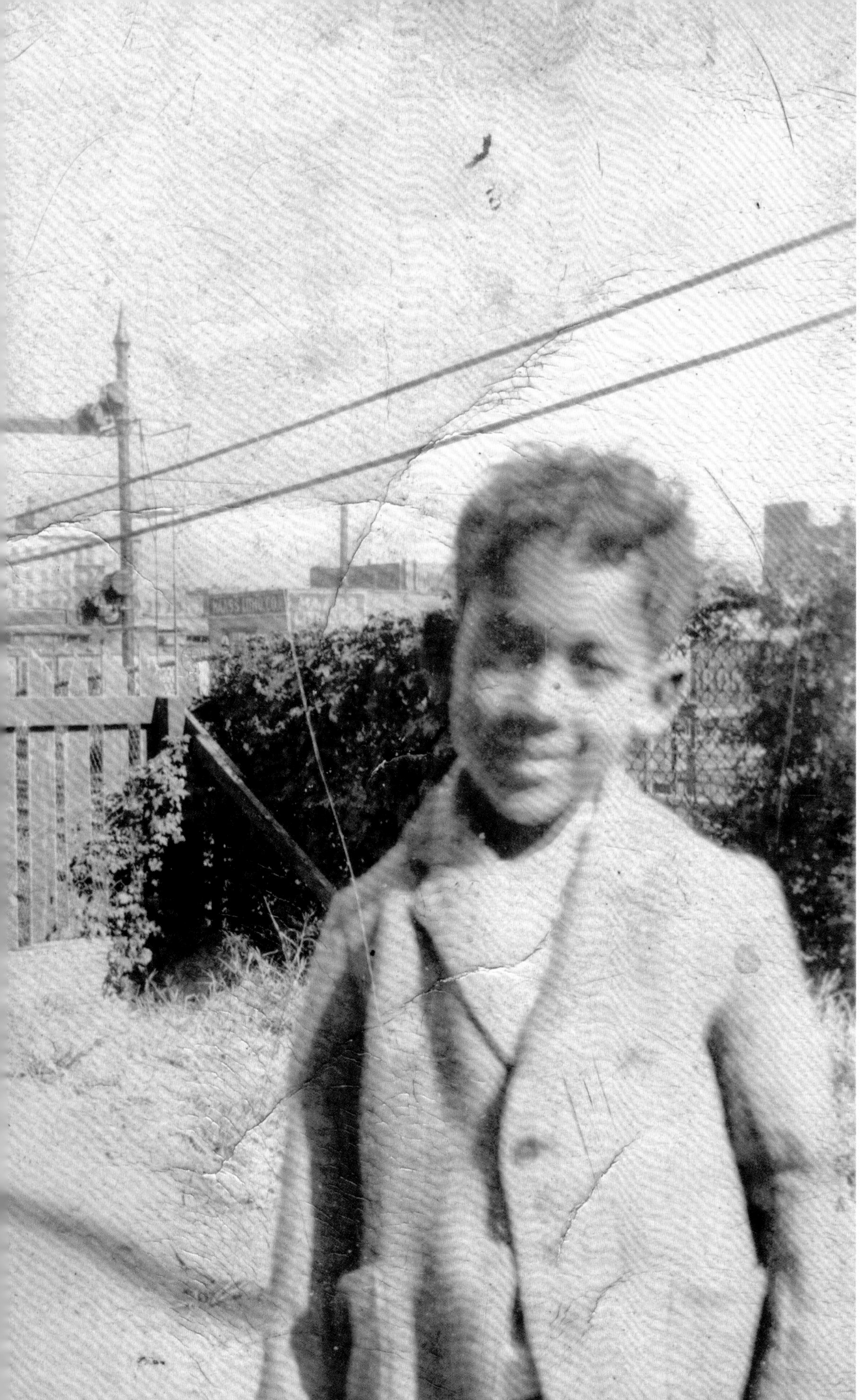

CHARLESTON, SC

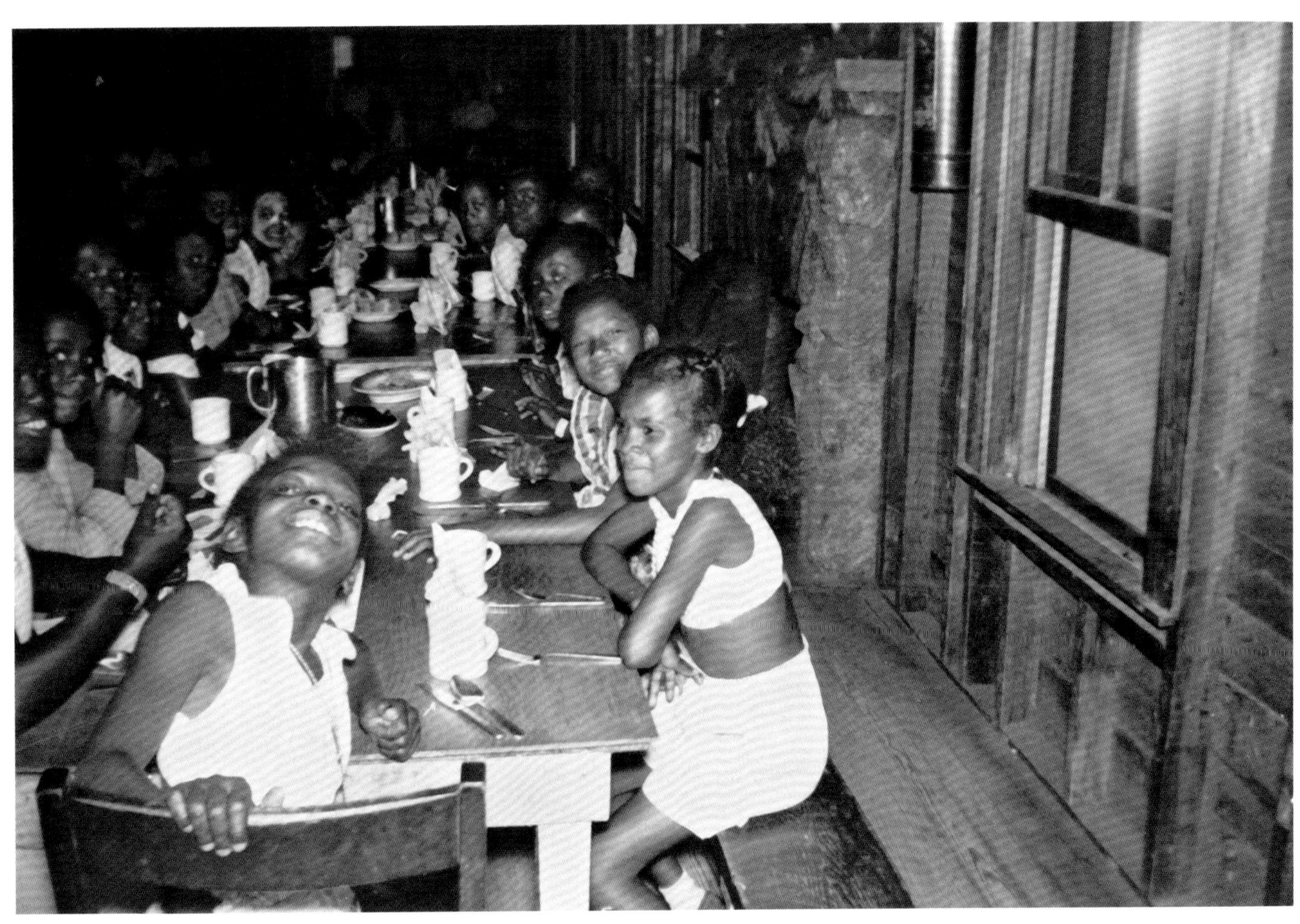

Breezy Meadows Camp

HOLLISTON, MA

1950S

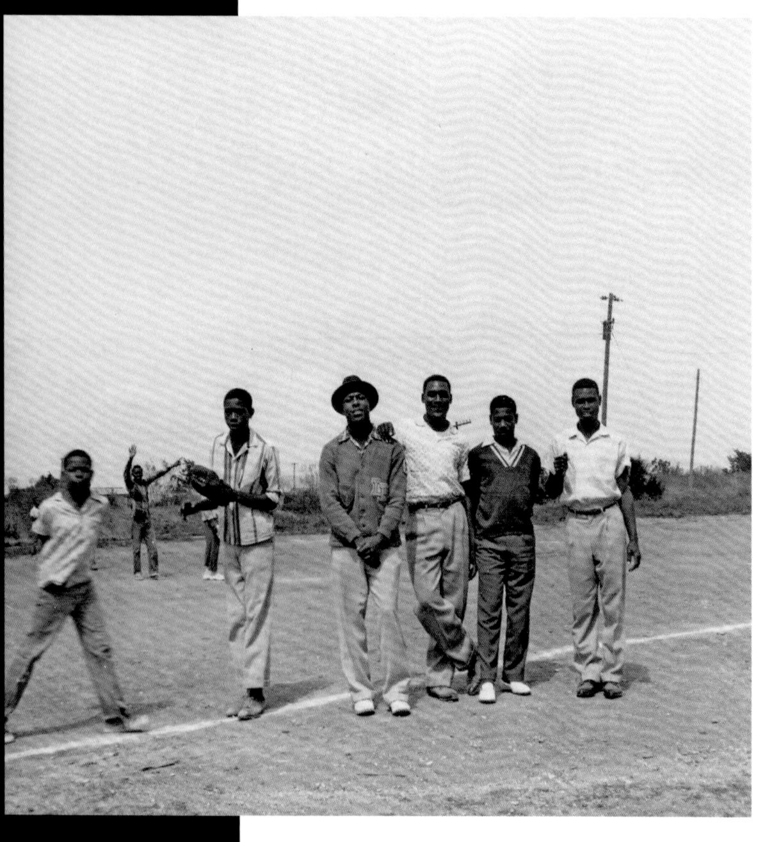

TEXAS
1958

→ Breezy Meadows Camp
HOLLISTON, MA
1948

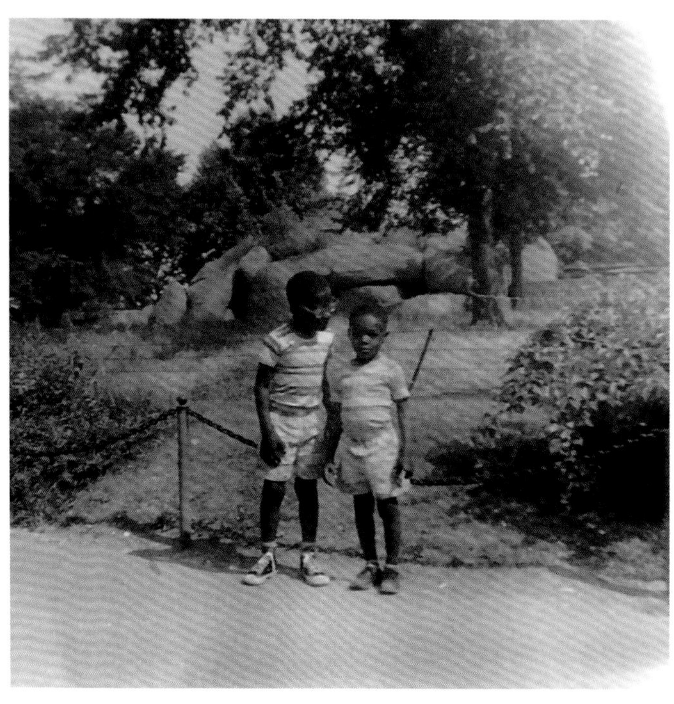

David and Stephen Hunter
BOSTON, MA
CIRCA 1955

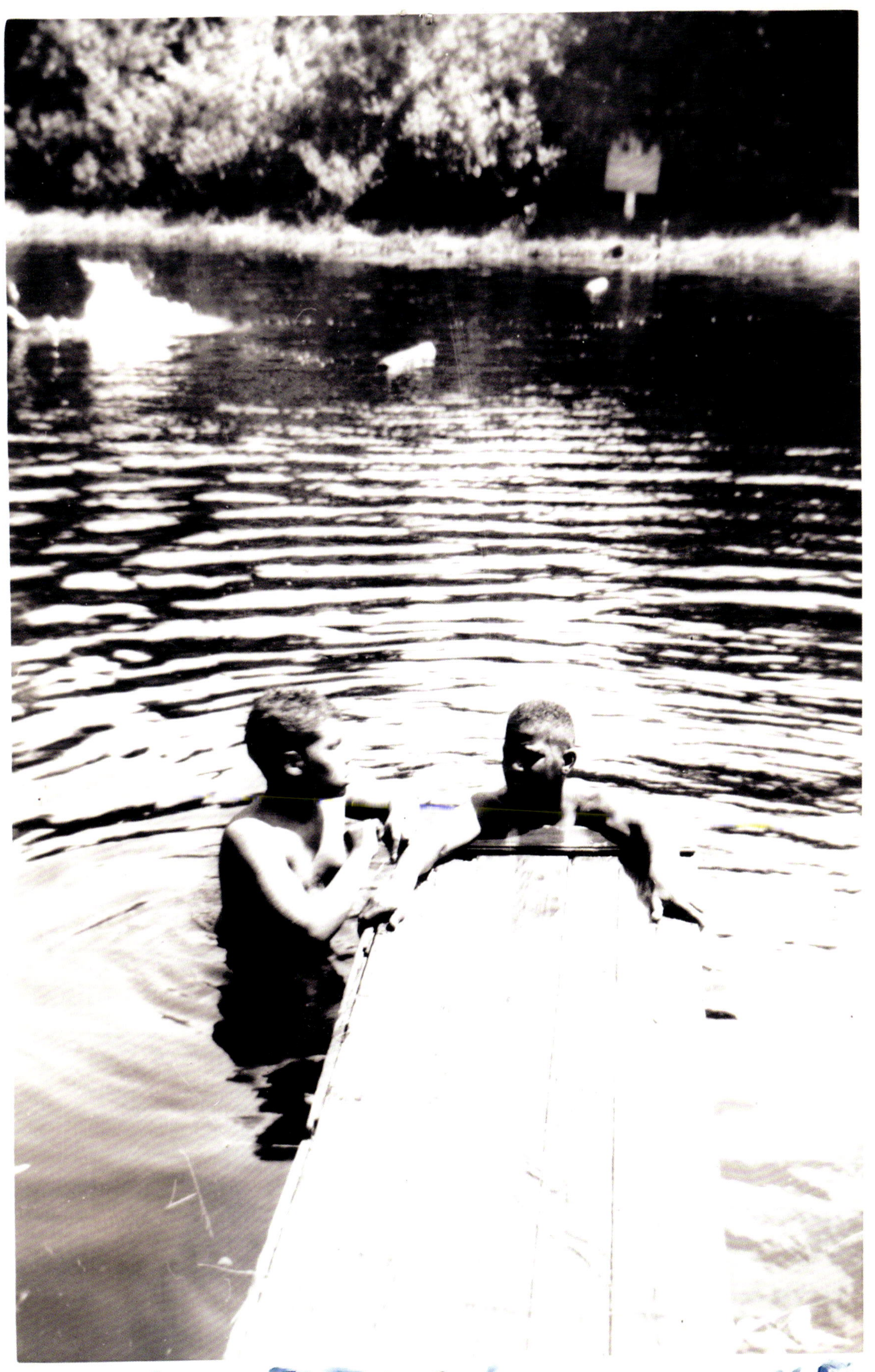

LANN + BROWN BMC 48

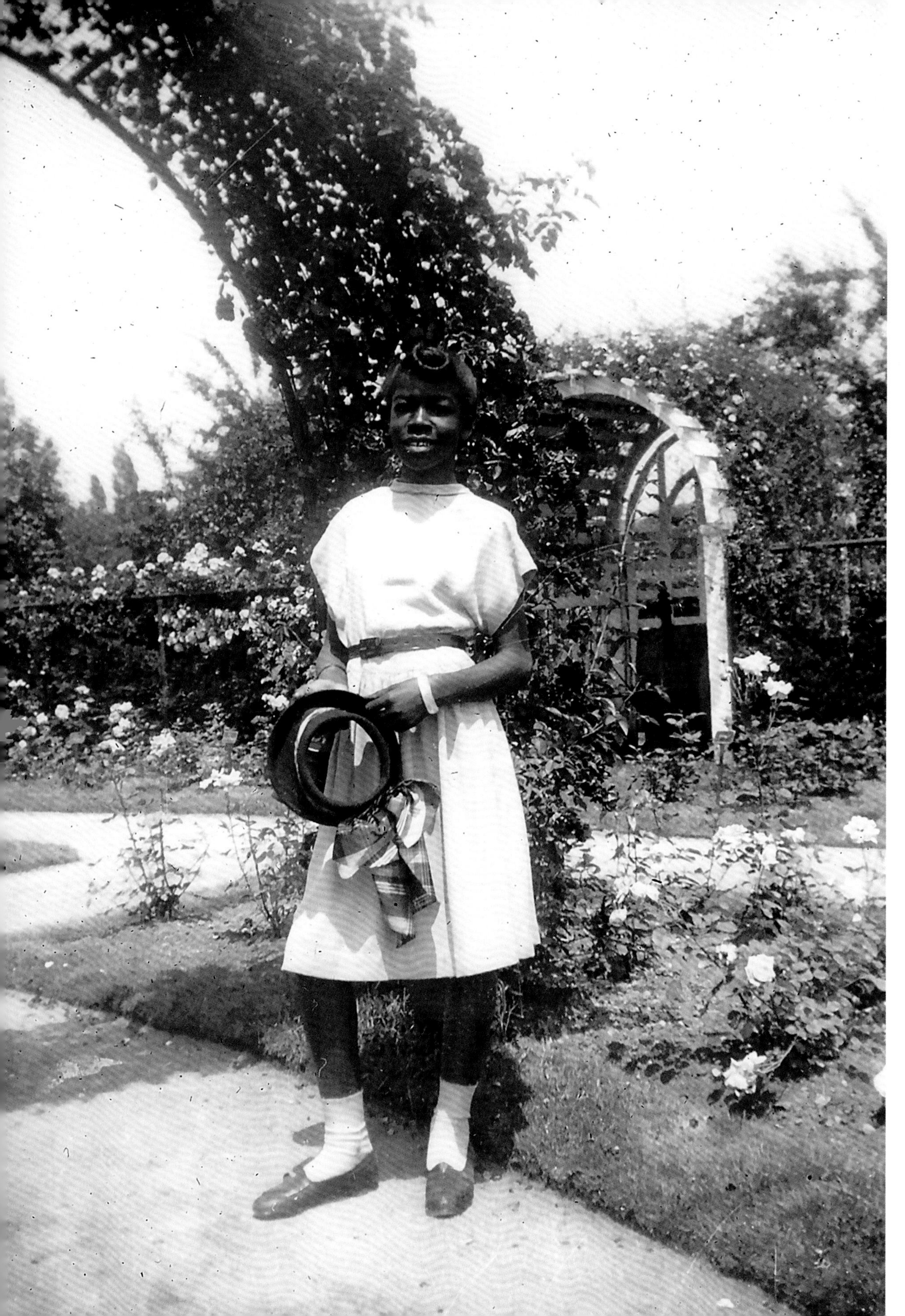

Lower Ninth Ward
NEW ORLEANS, LA
1954

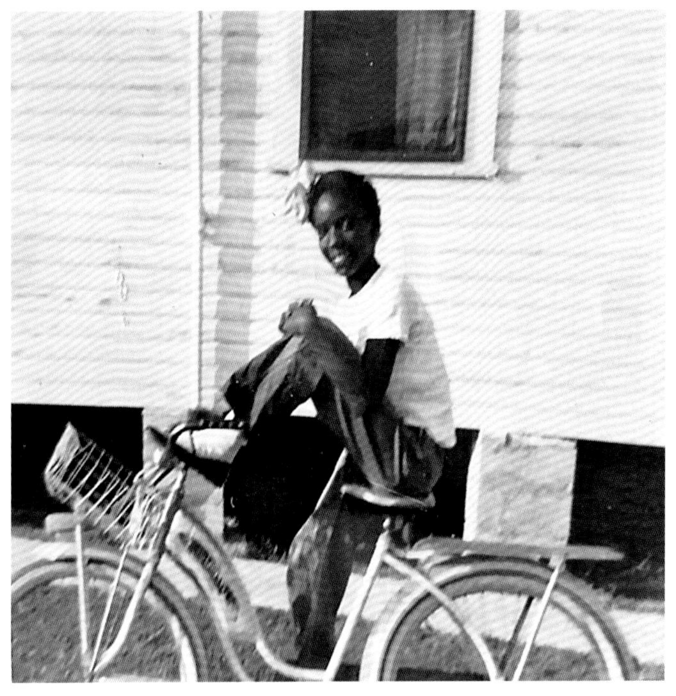

← Winnie in the Fenway Rose Garden
BOSTON, MA
CIRCA 1940

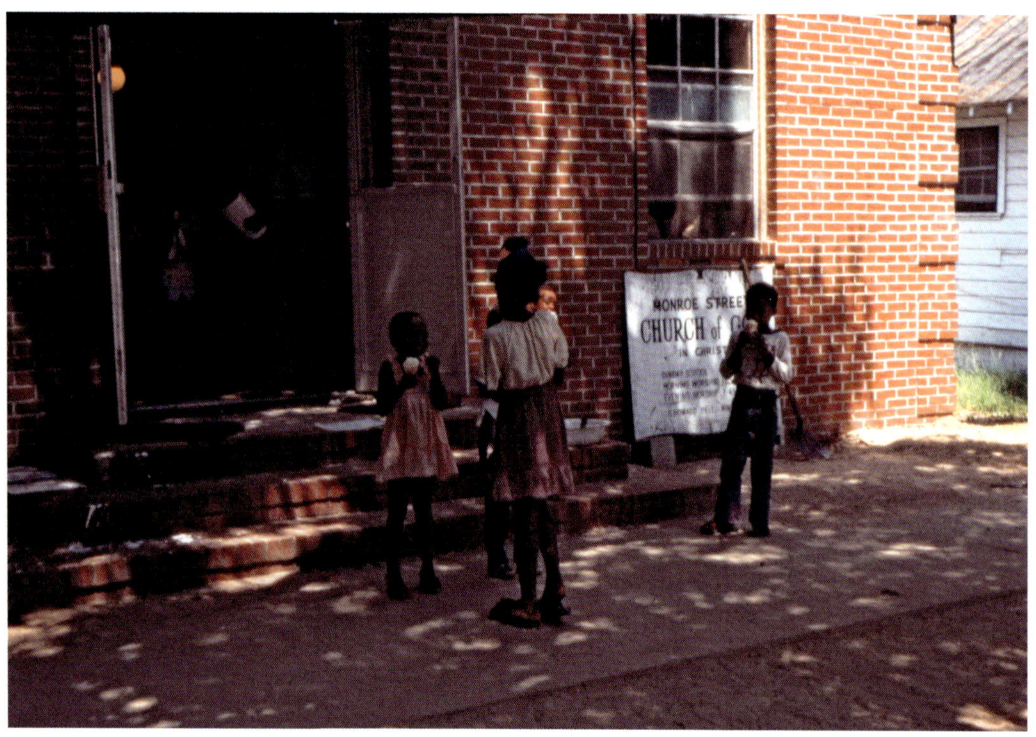

Monroe Street Church of God in Christ

ALBANY, GA

CIRCA 1980

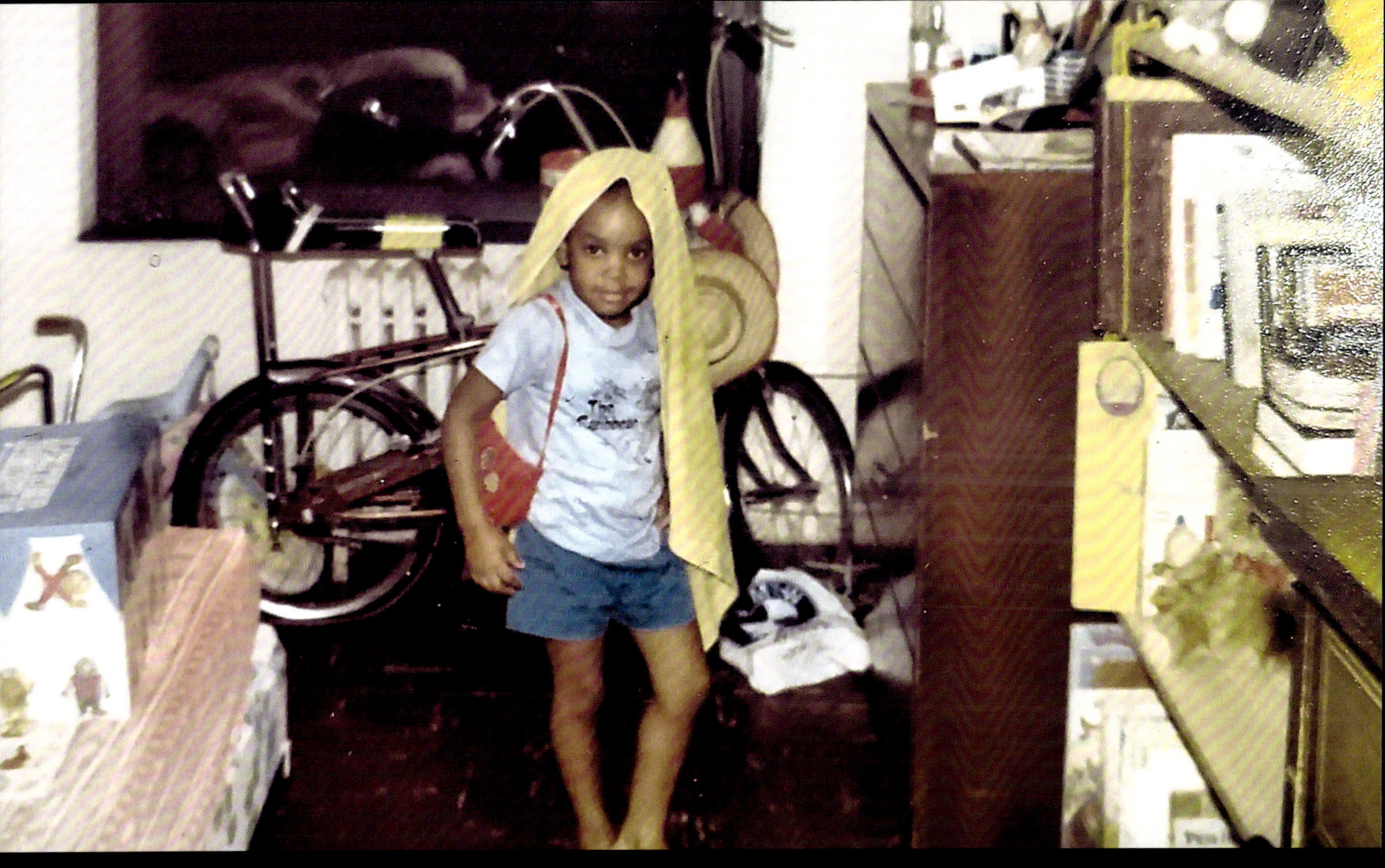

Jennifer pretending with “long hair”

BROOKLYN, NY

1984

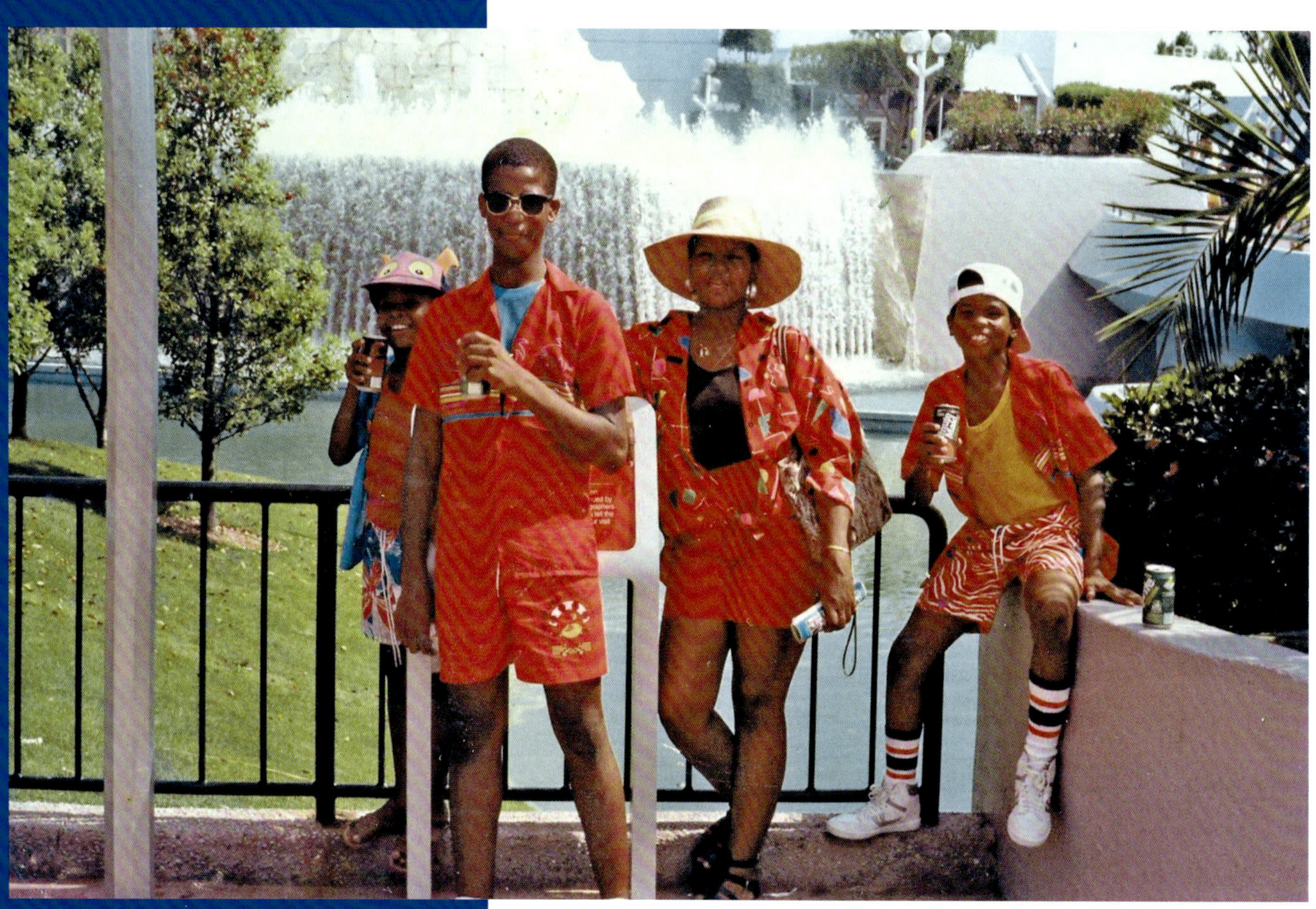

The author's aunt and cousins at Disney World
ORLANDO, FL
1980S

FAMILY GATHERINGS

From reunions and cookouts to backyard parties and celebrations, traditional family gatherings create new memories and rejuvenate old ones. Family gatherings offer a sense of belonging and it's important to document them so that when we feel untethered, we can relive the moments that made us feel most loved, cared for, and held. Family gatherings are a time to listen to the stories of our elders: the matriarchs, patriarchs, and older friends of our families. They offer a time to witness and learn not only by observation, but also by engaging and being in fellowship with one another – by learning how to create, pass, and carry on family traditions.

At my own family gatherings I am without a doubt the person behind the camera, the person who is actively documenting to create the record. But I am also intentional about showing up in the record, to mark my presence, too. This series serves as a reminder of the various ways we can actively show up to do the work in documenting and preserving our family traditions and archives, while finding ourselves in the process.

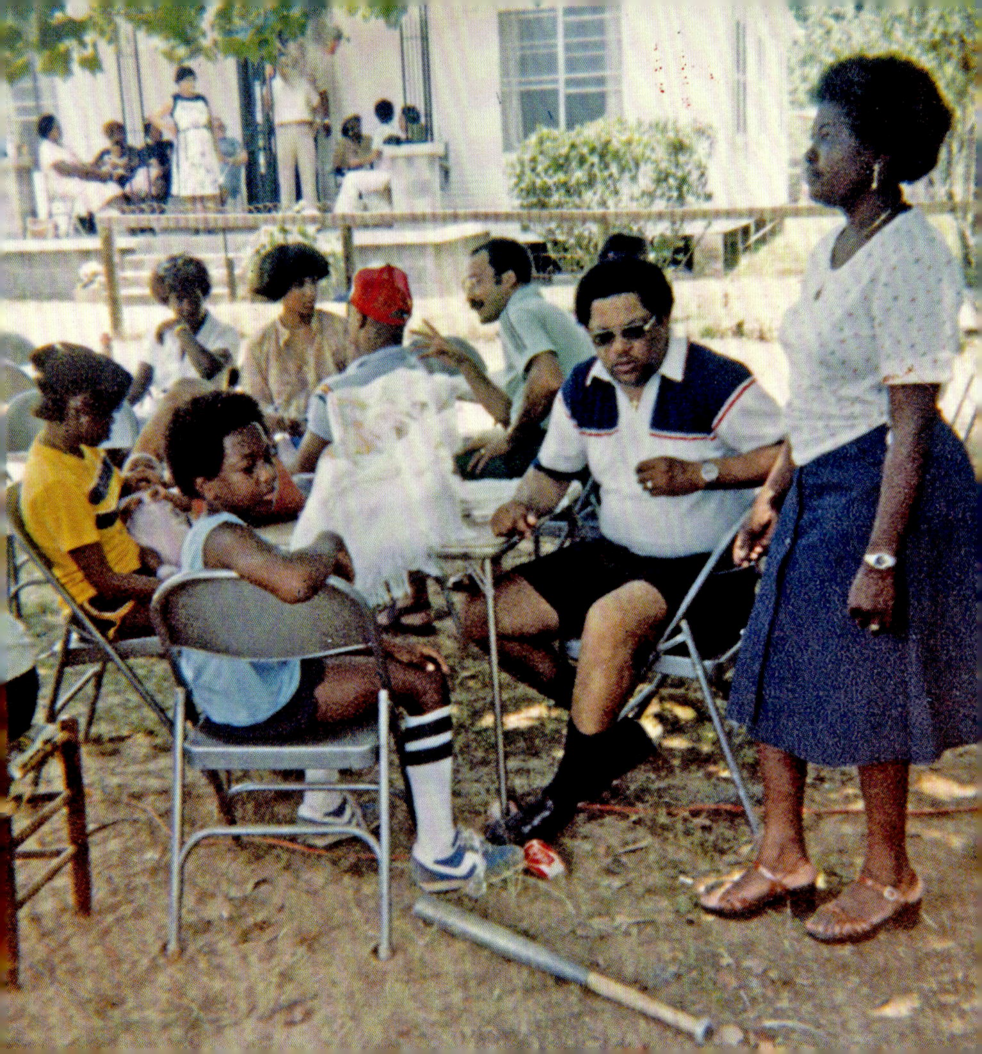

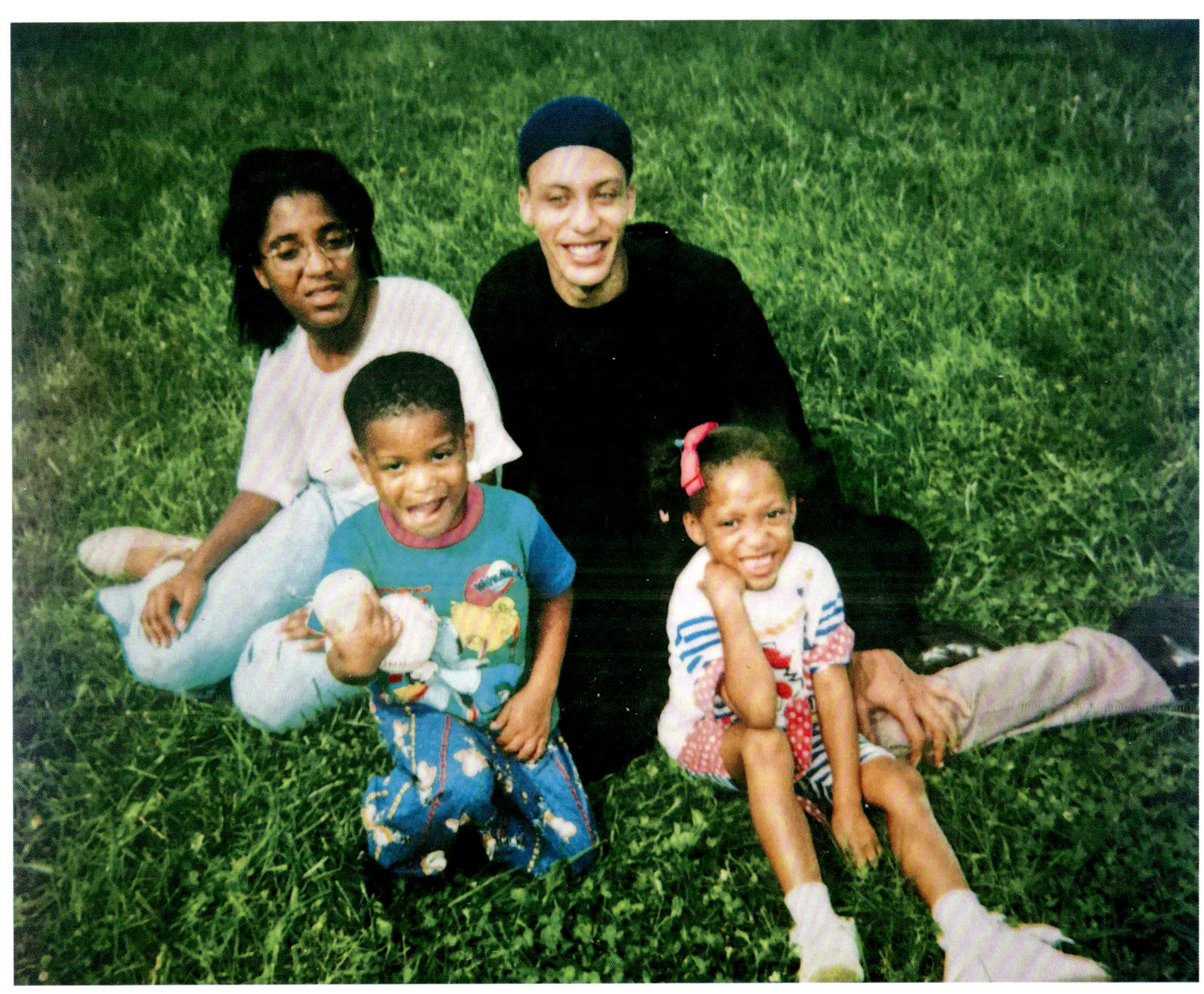

Visiting father in prison

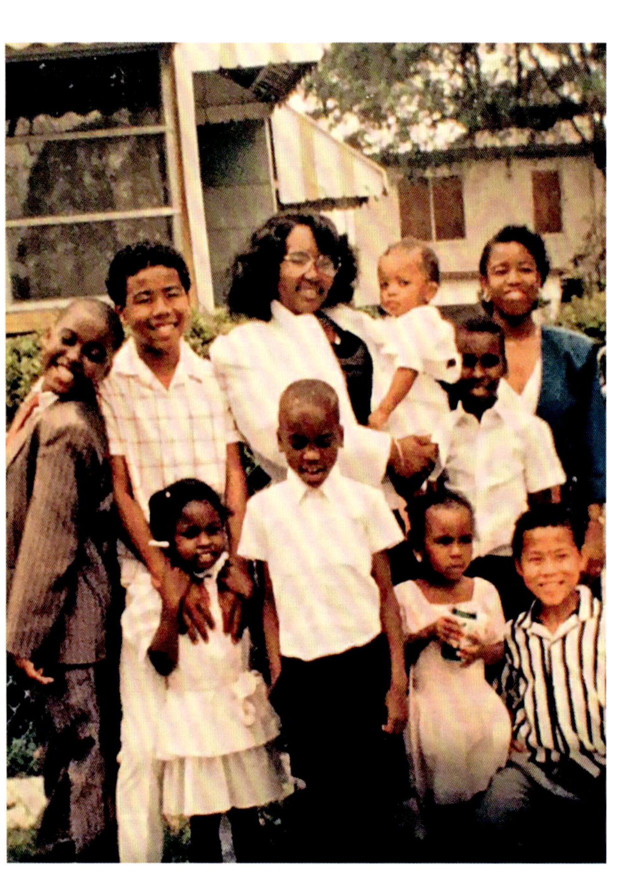

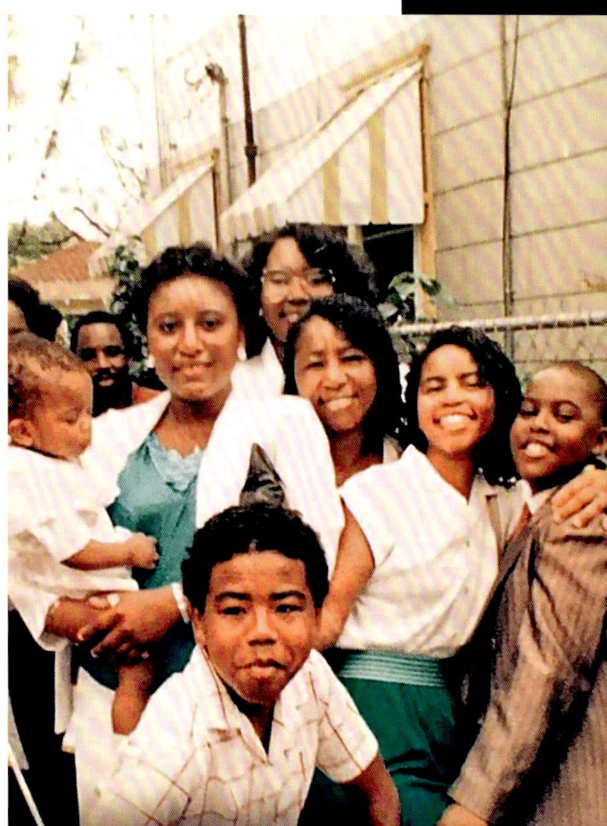

The Chambers family at a family gathering
ORLANDO, FL
1987

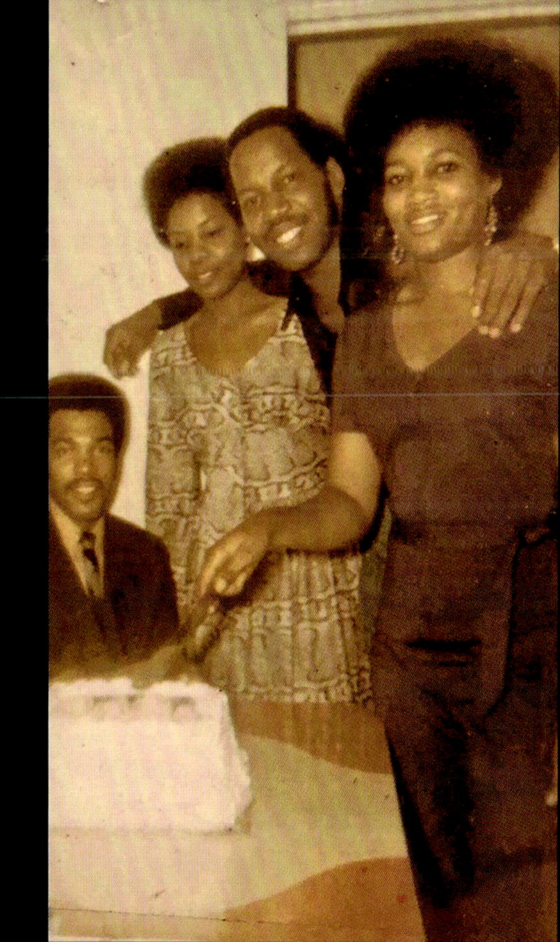

Stella (right) cutting her birthday cake with her husband, Everett (center), her sister Eileen, and Eileen's boyfriend at the time

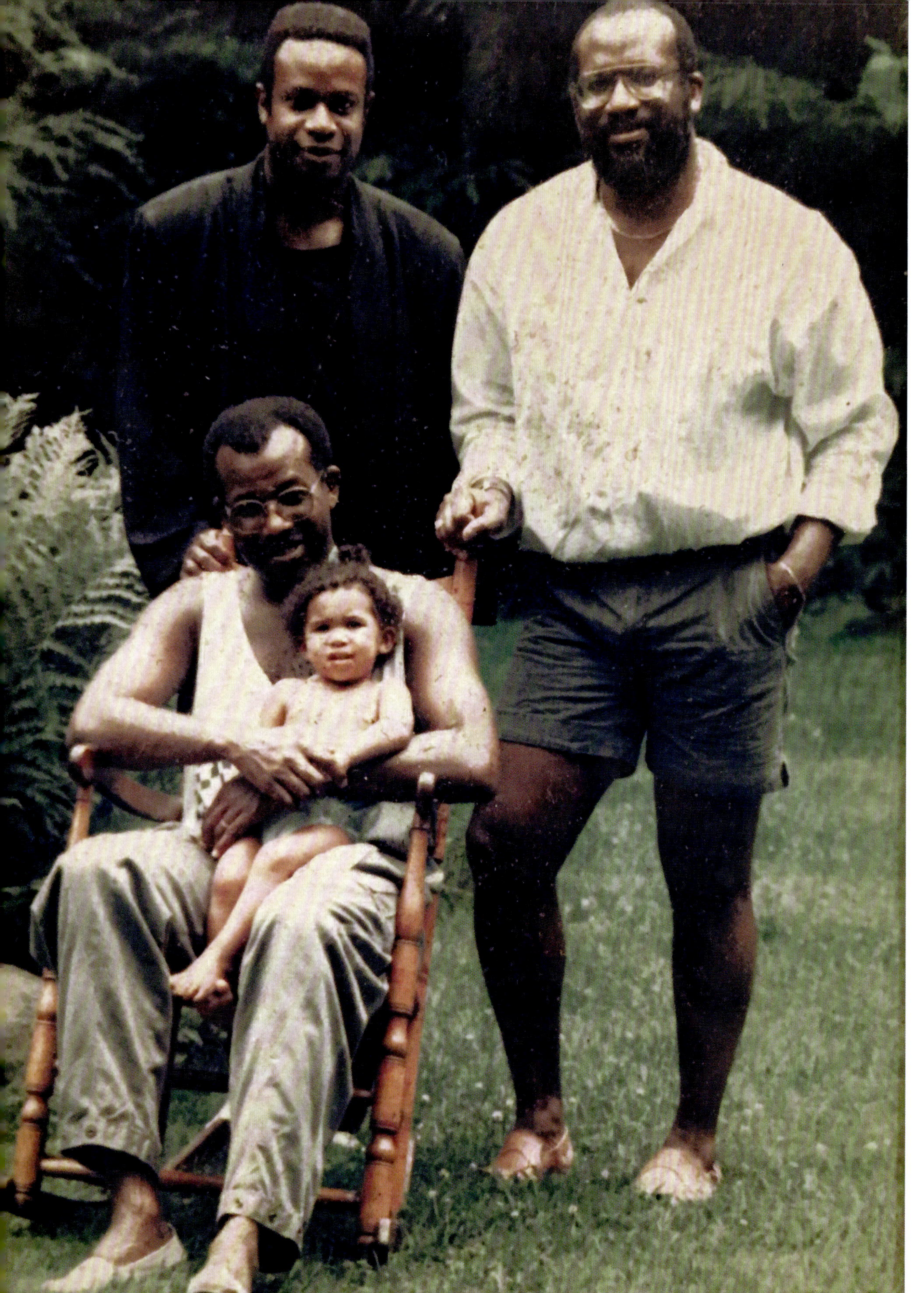

1980S

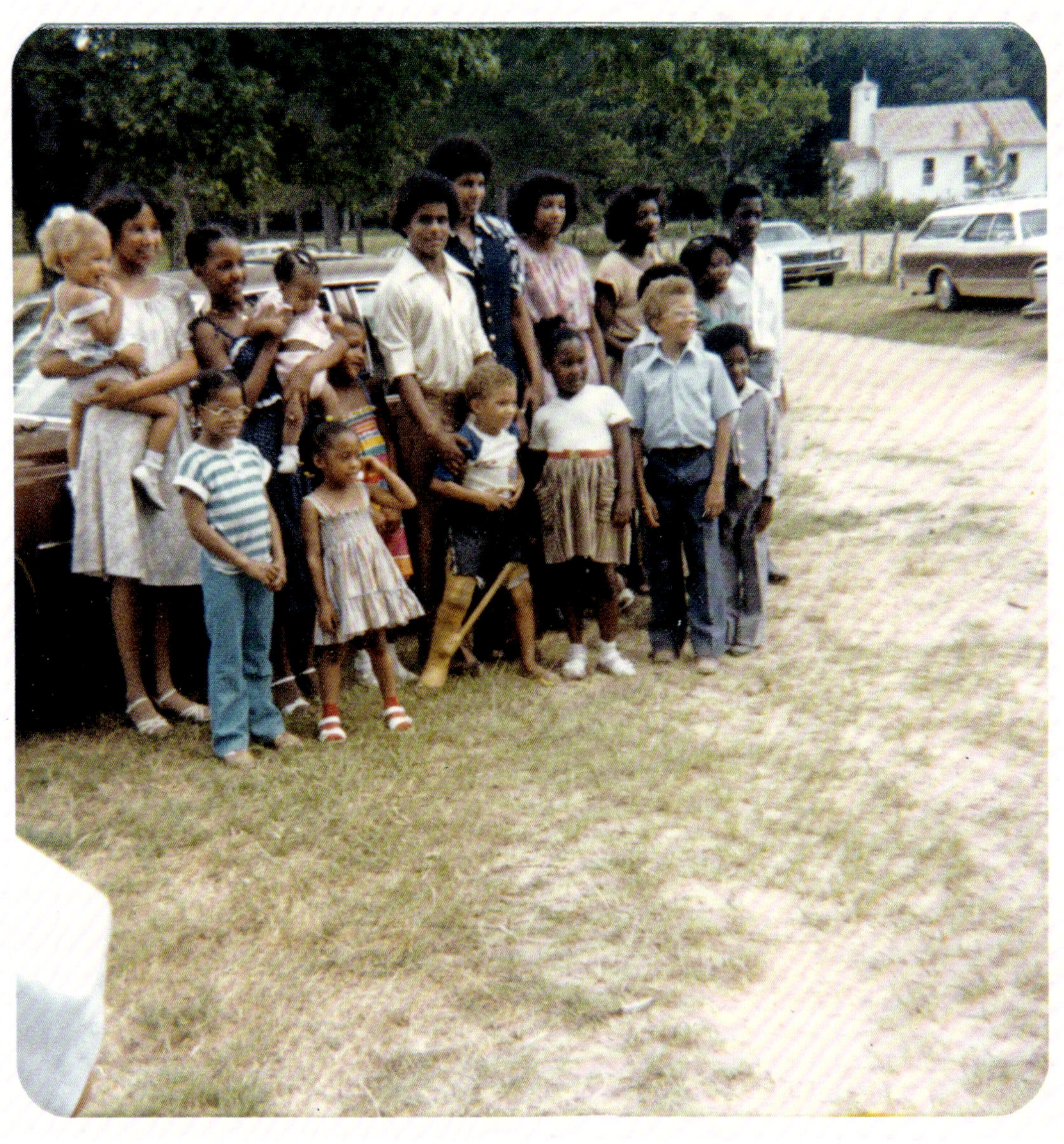

The Odom family

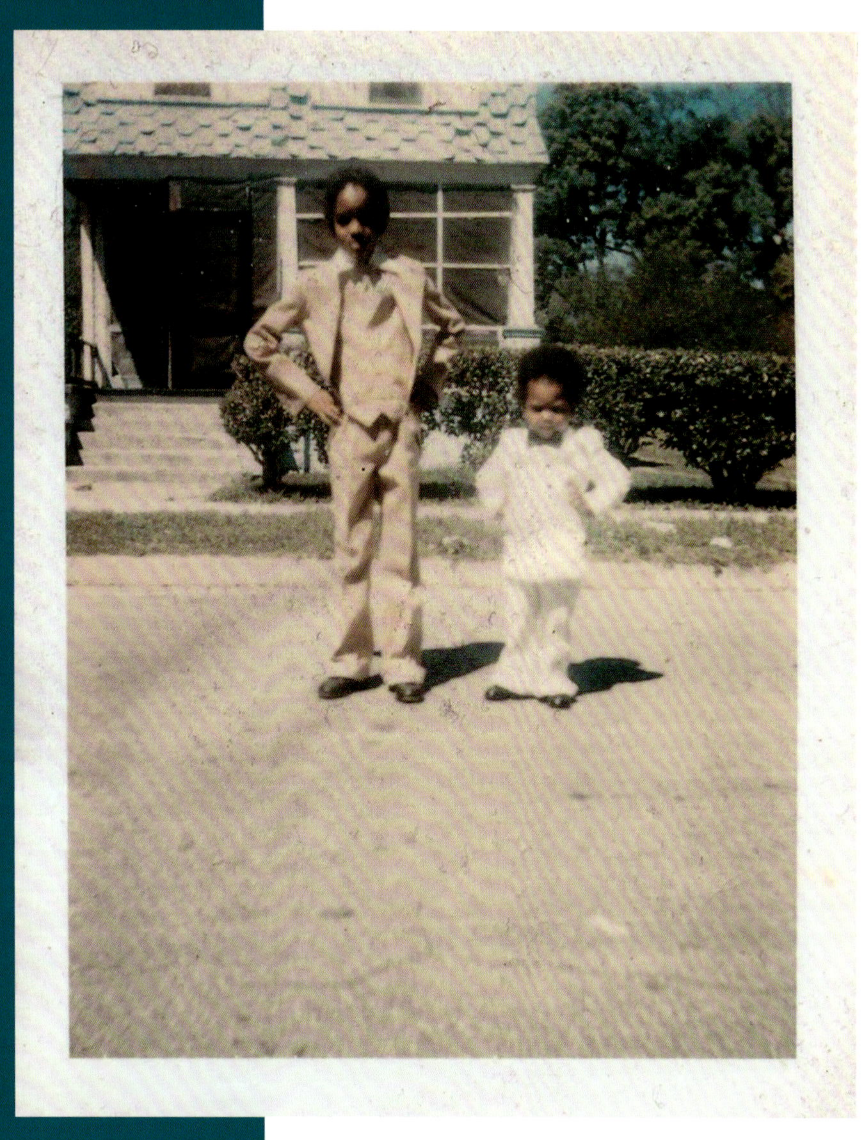

The author's uncle and cousin on Easter Sunday
JACKSONVILLE, FL
1979

SPIRITUALITY

When growing up in the South, there is nothing more influential in our lives than the church. My mother's side of the family revealed to me the quietness that can be found within spirituality. It was more of an interior relationship, a personal walking with God. My dad's side of the family, on the other hand, was exuberant in the way they approached worship – spirituality made its presence known and heard and was completely unapologetic in its appearance and teachings. Being able to witness both ends, I am grateful that my parents made space for my siblings and me to walk our own paths and cultivate our own relationships with God.

Spirituality can play a vital role in shaping one's sense of self and one's community, as well as connecting one's existence to their higher purpose and higher power. Both religion and spirituality have a significant impact on the Black experience, and their practices and rituals stretch back through the generations to our ancestors, and even well before their arrival in this realm. This series explores the depths of Black spirituality.

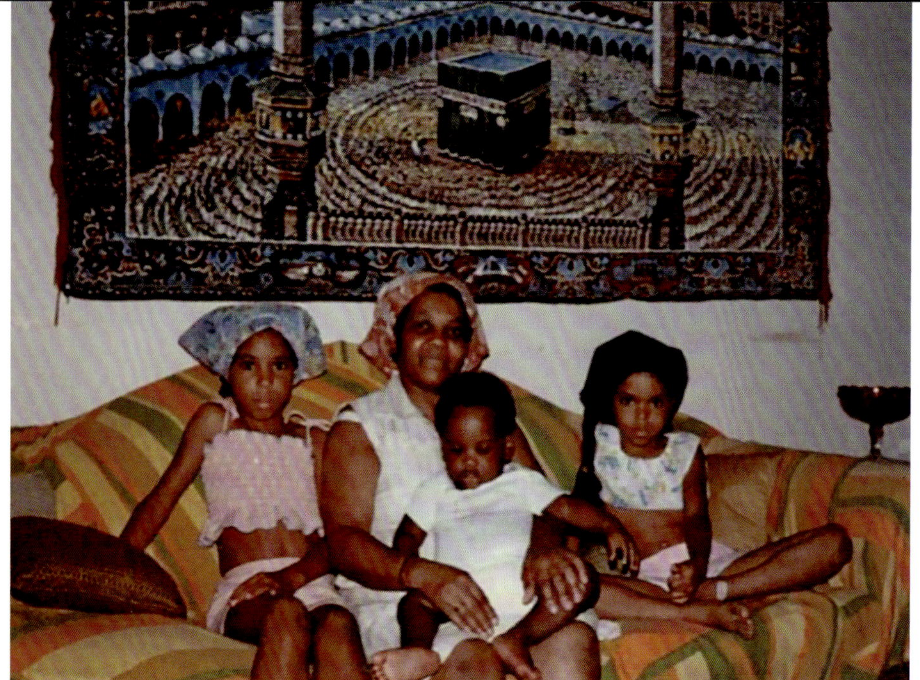

BATON ROUGE, LA

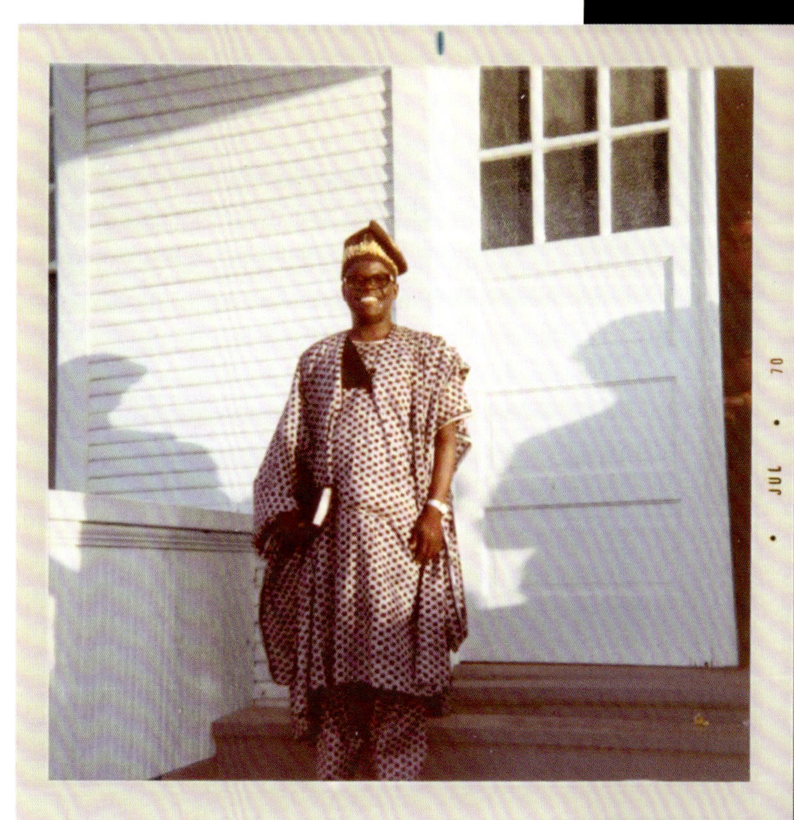

Murphy Baptist Church
1970

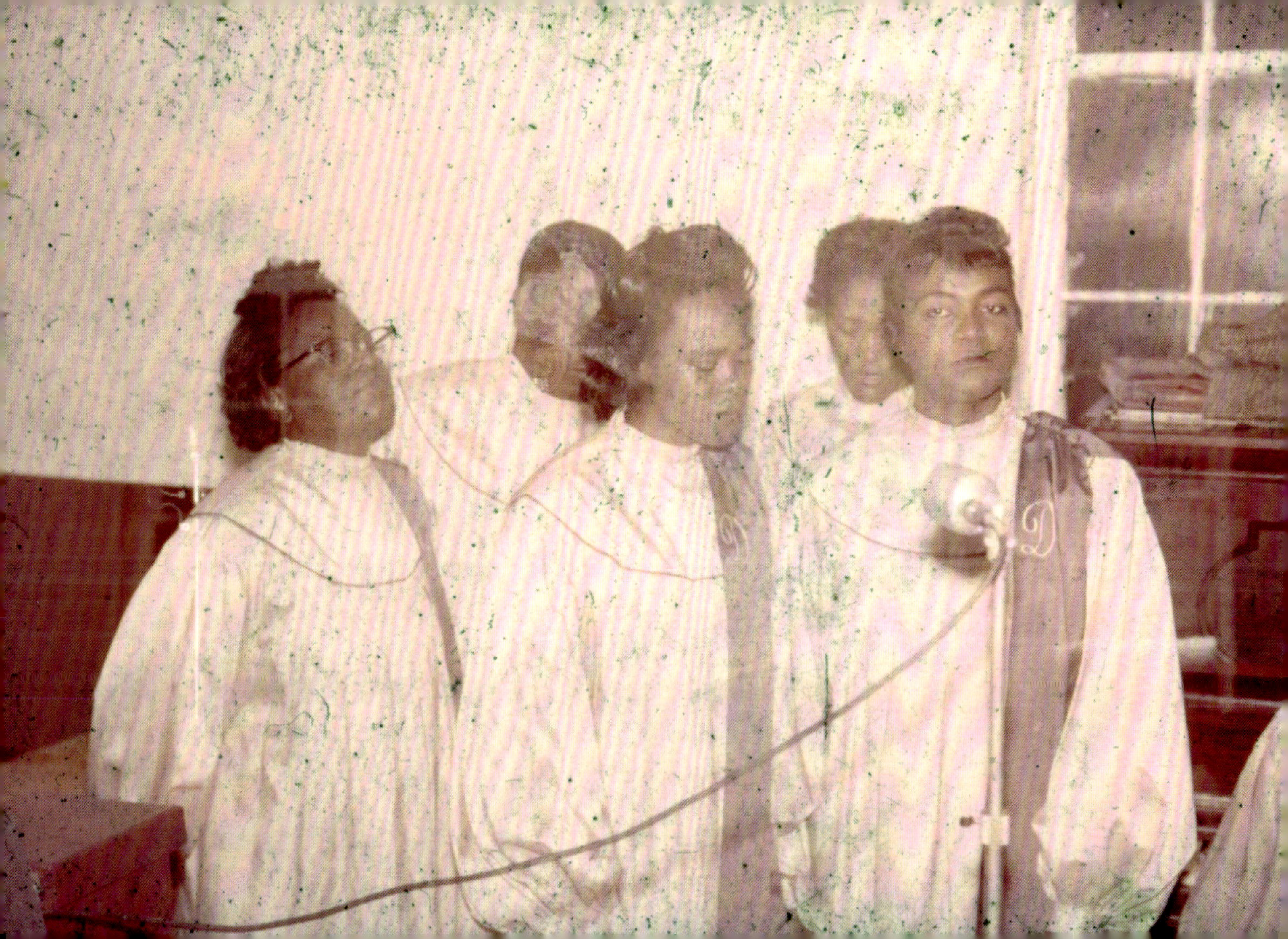

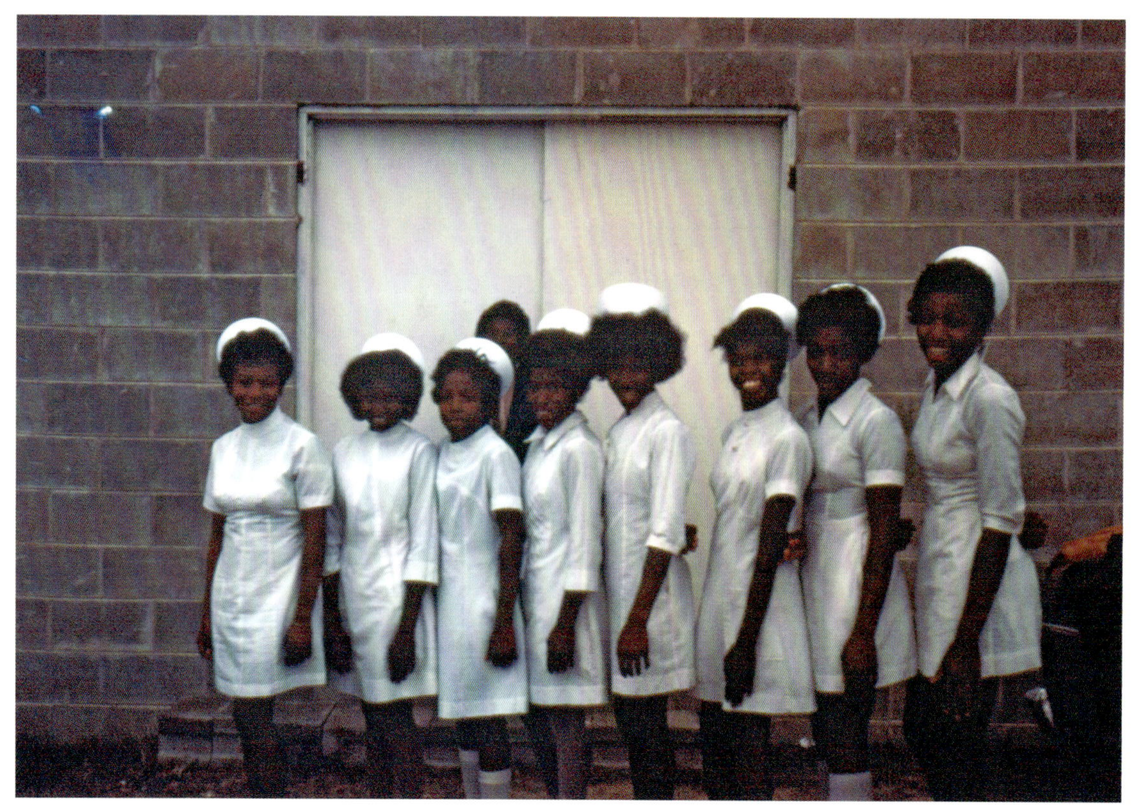

CIRCA 1975

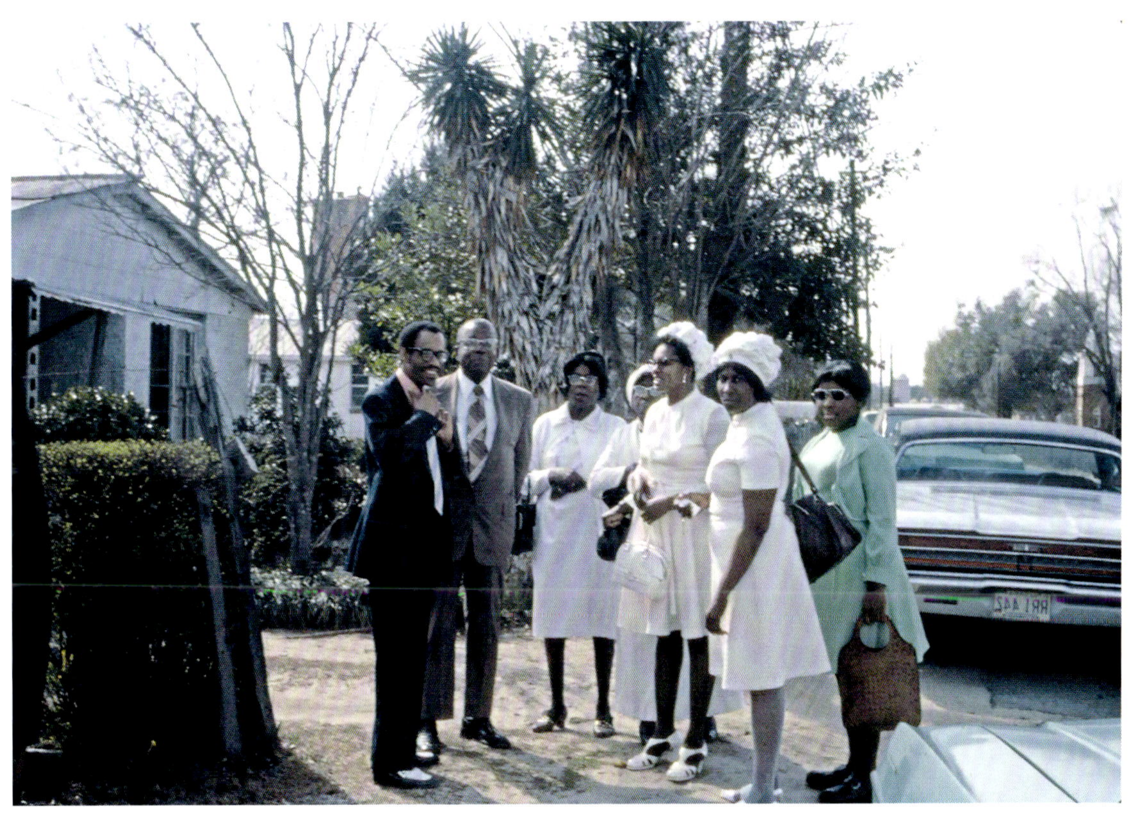

CIRCA 1980

CIRCA 1975

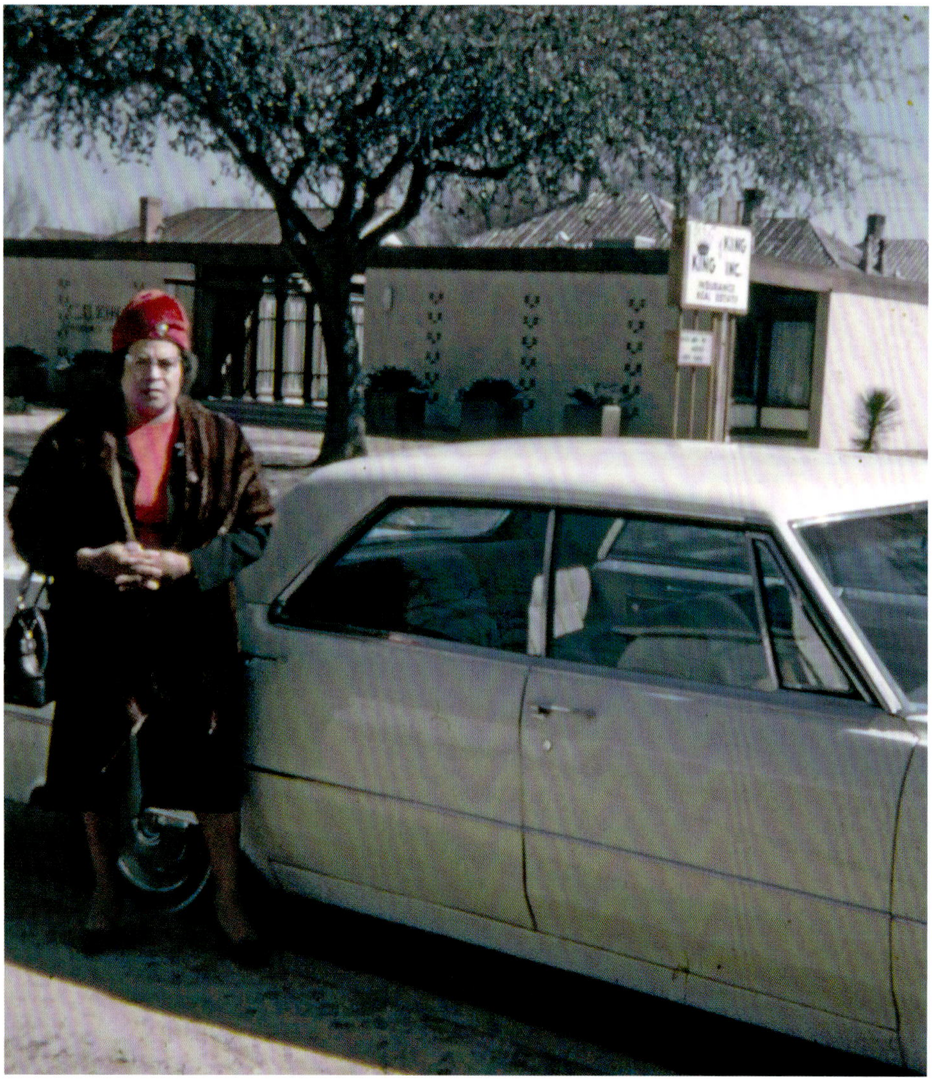

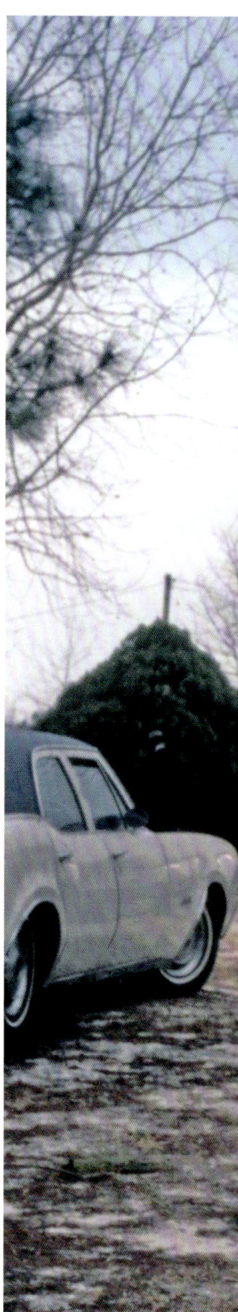

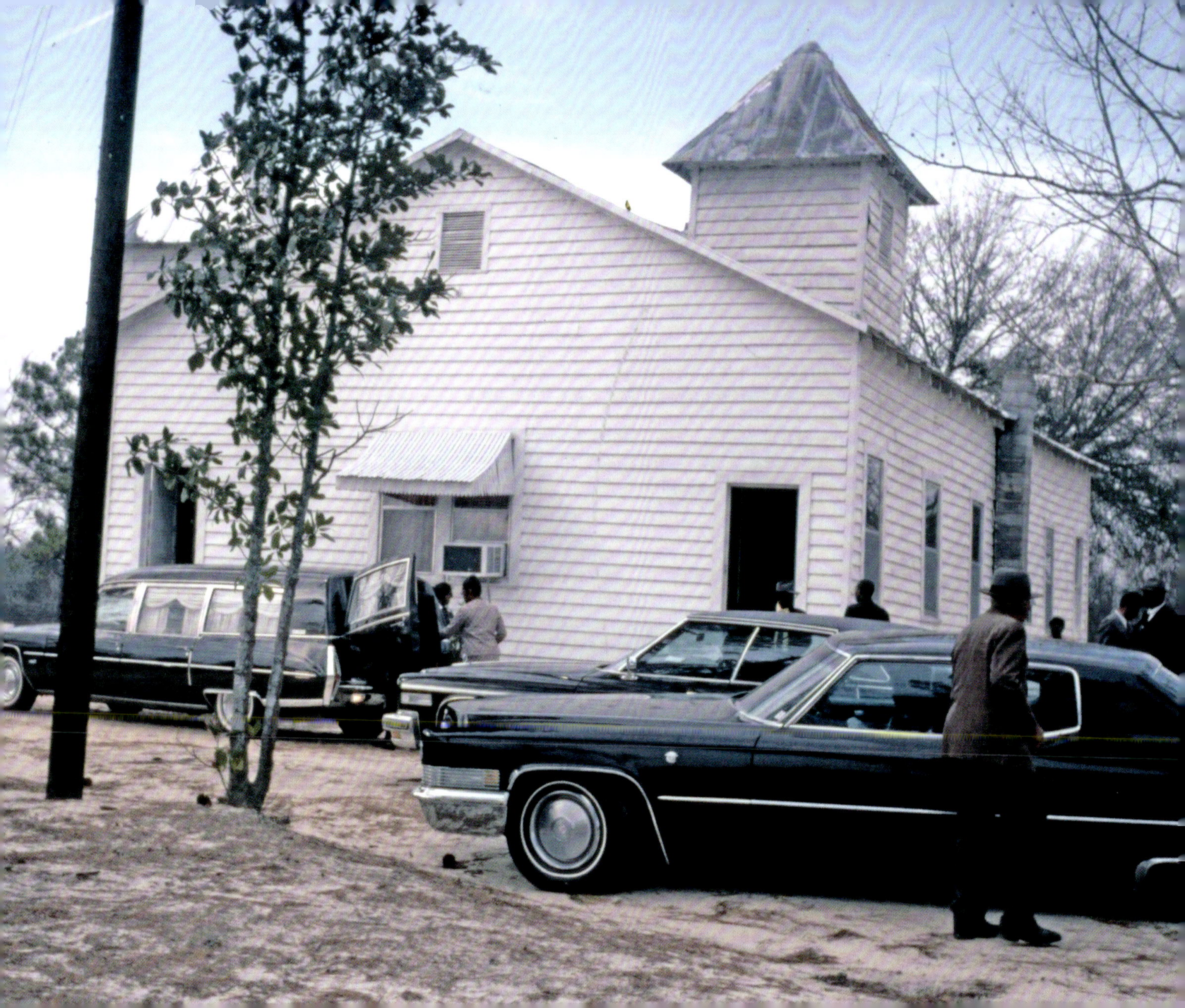

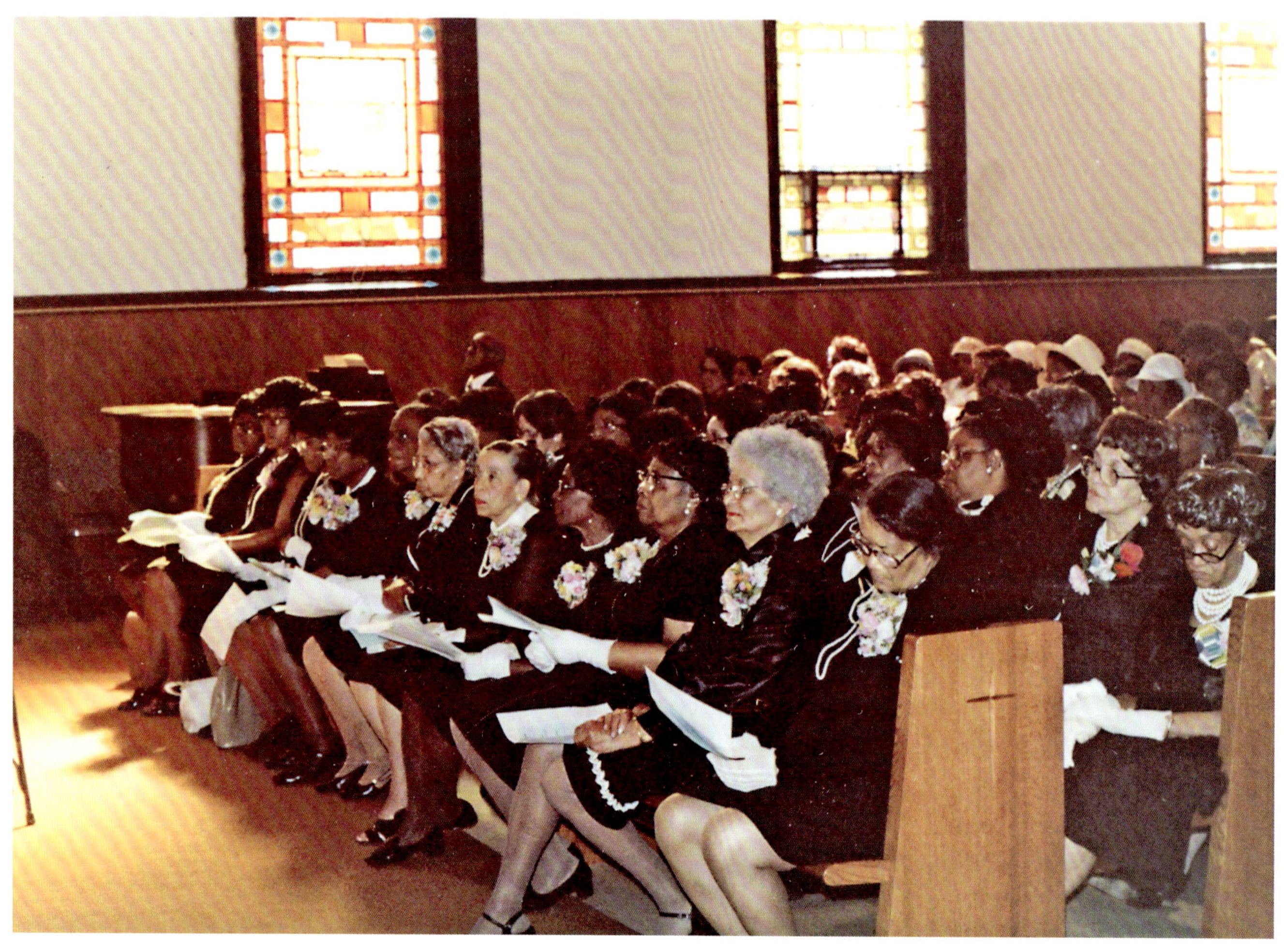

Members of Christ Temple Church
BOSTON, MA
CIRCA 1970

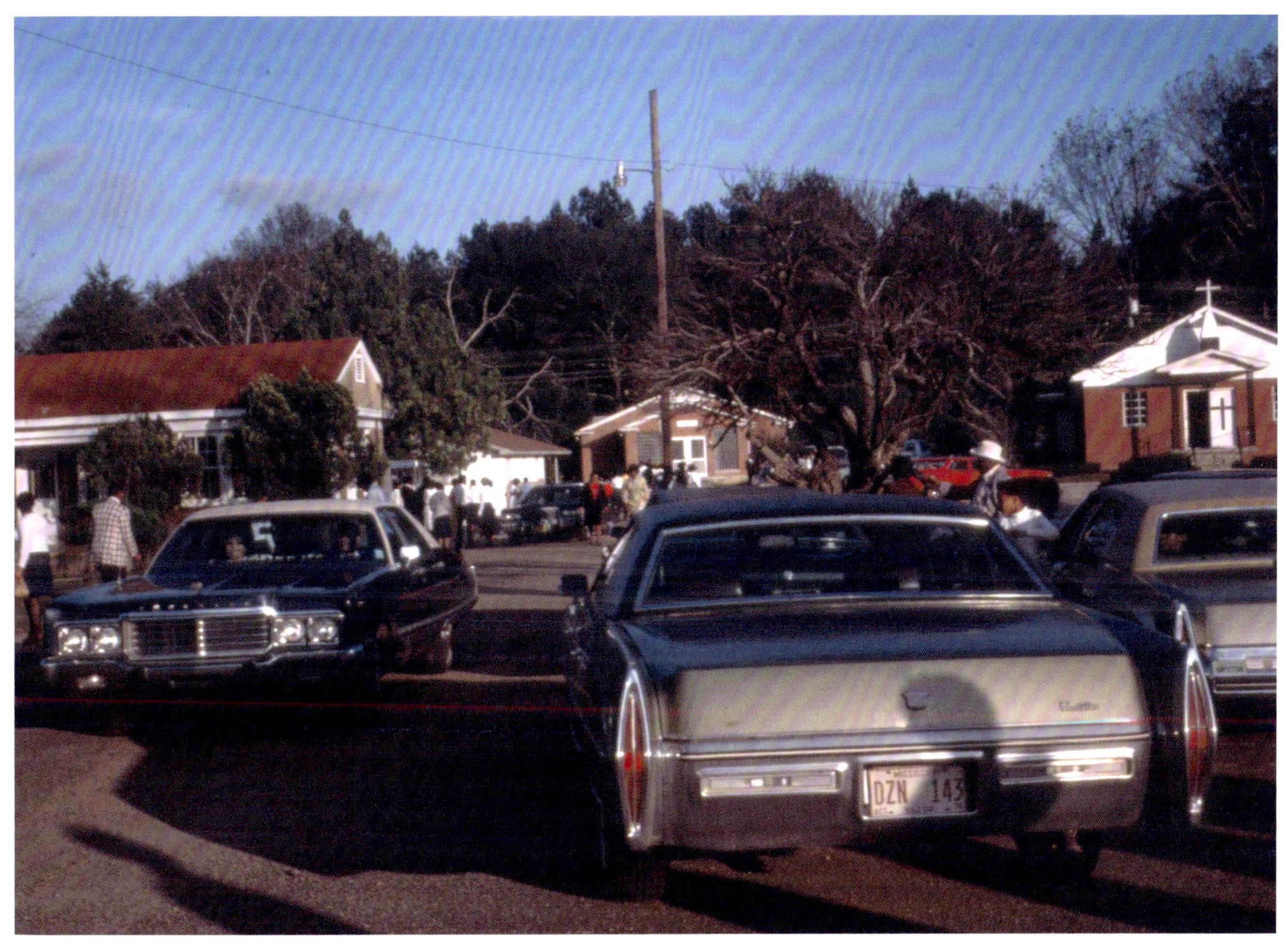

CIRCA 1980

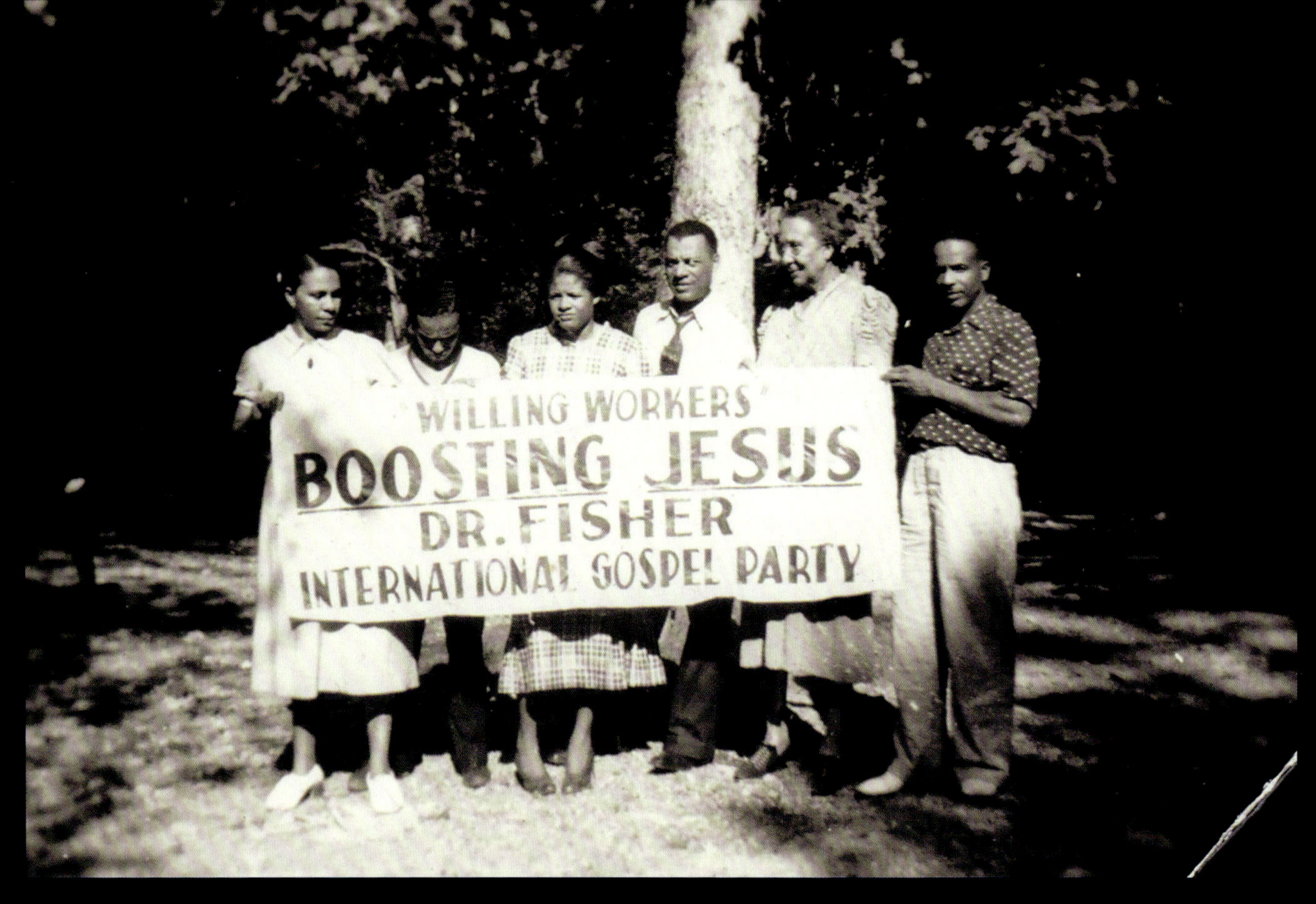

International Gospel Party

CIRCA 1945

Pageant for Christ Temple Church of Personal Experience

CIRCA 1955

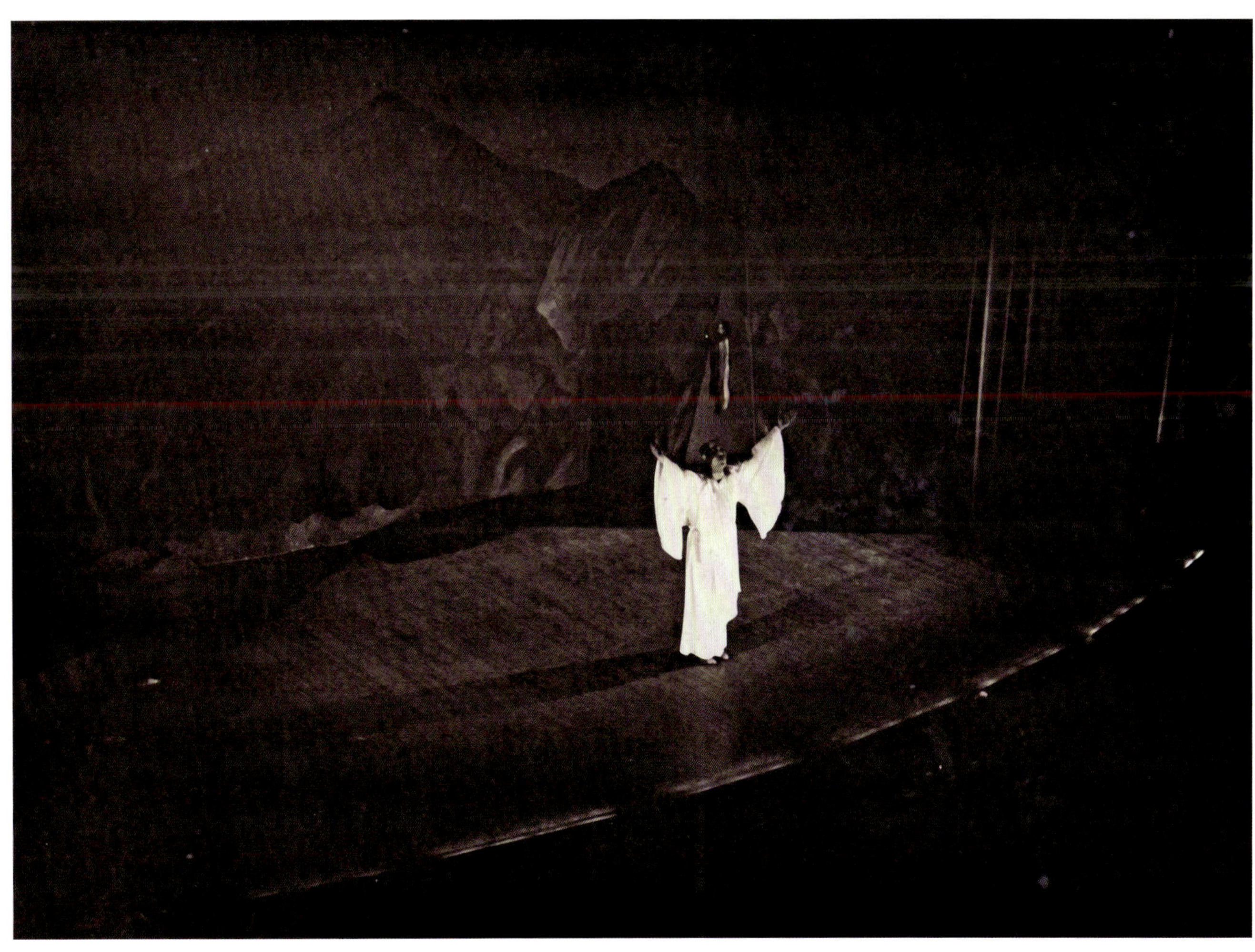

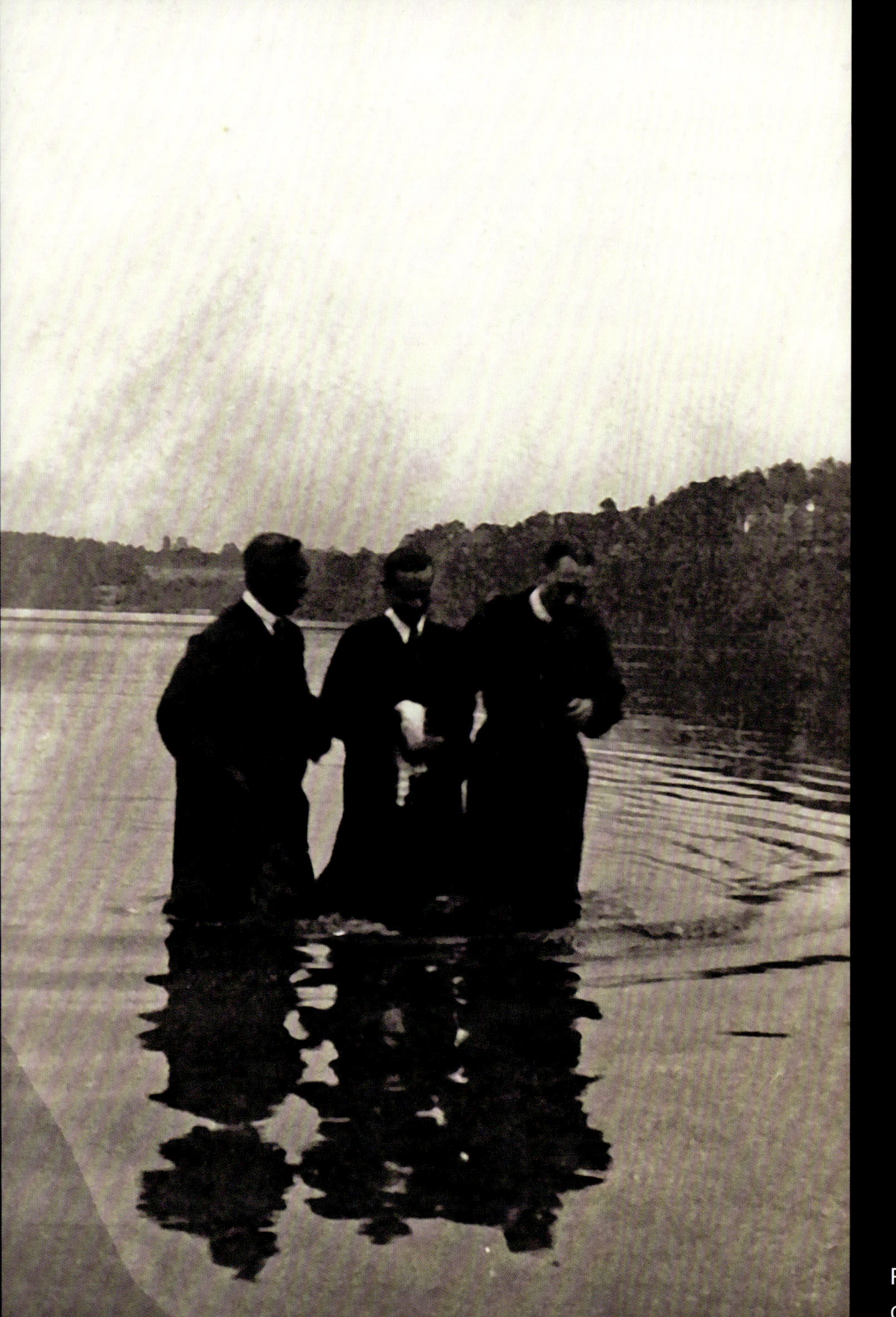

River baptism
CIRCA 1945

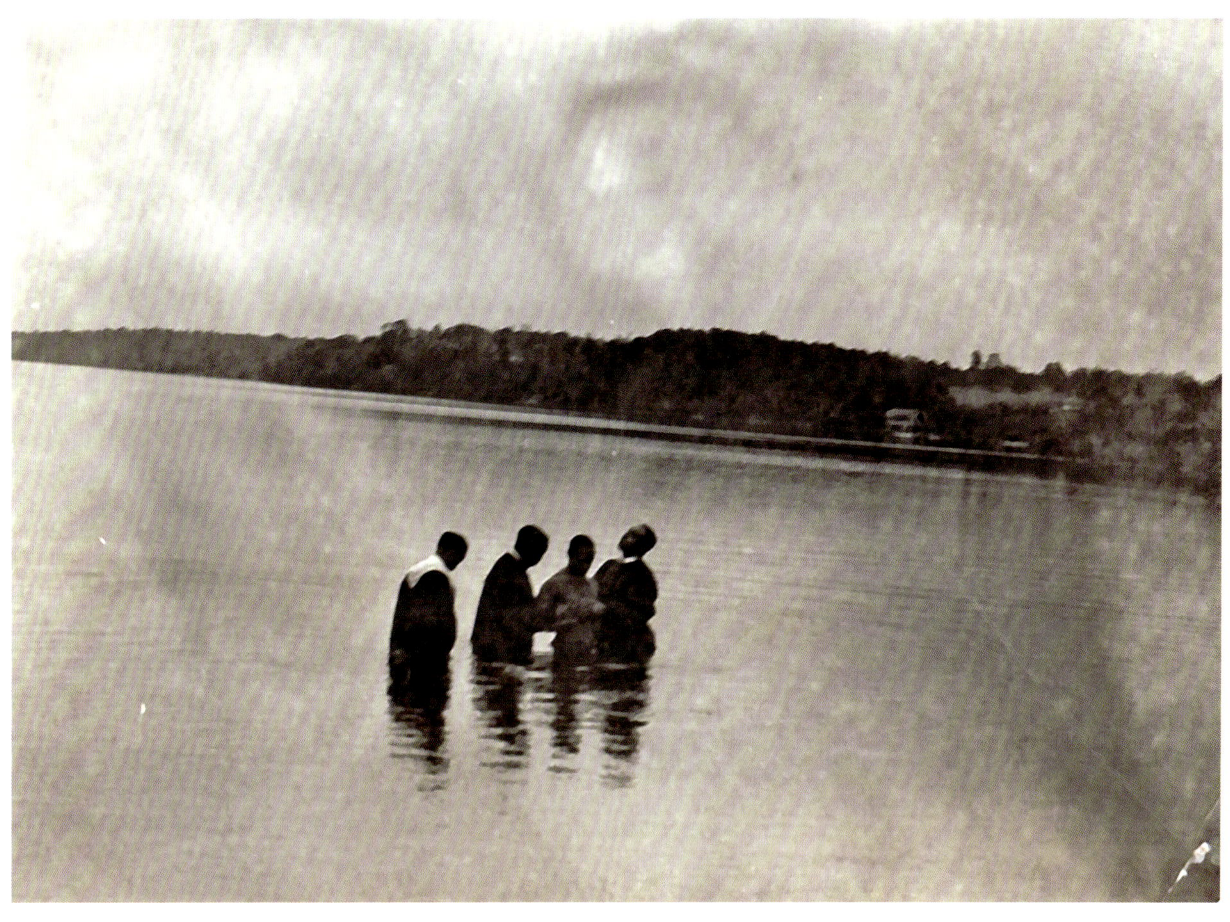

River baptism

CIRCA 1945

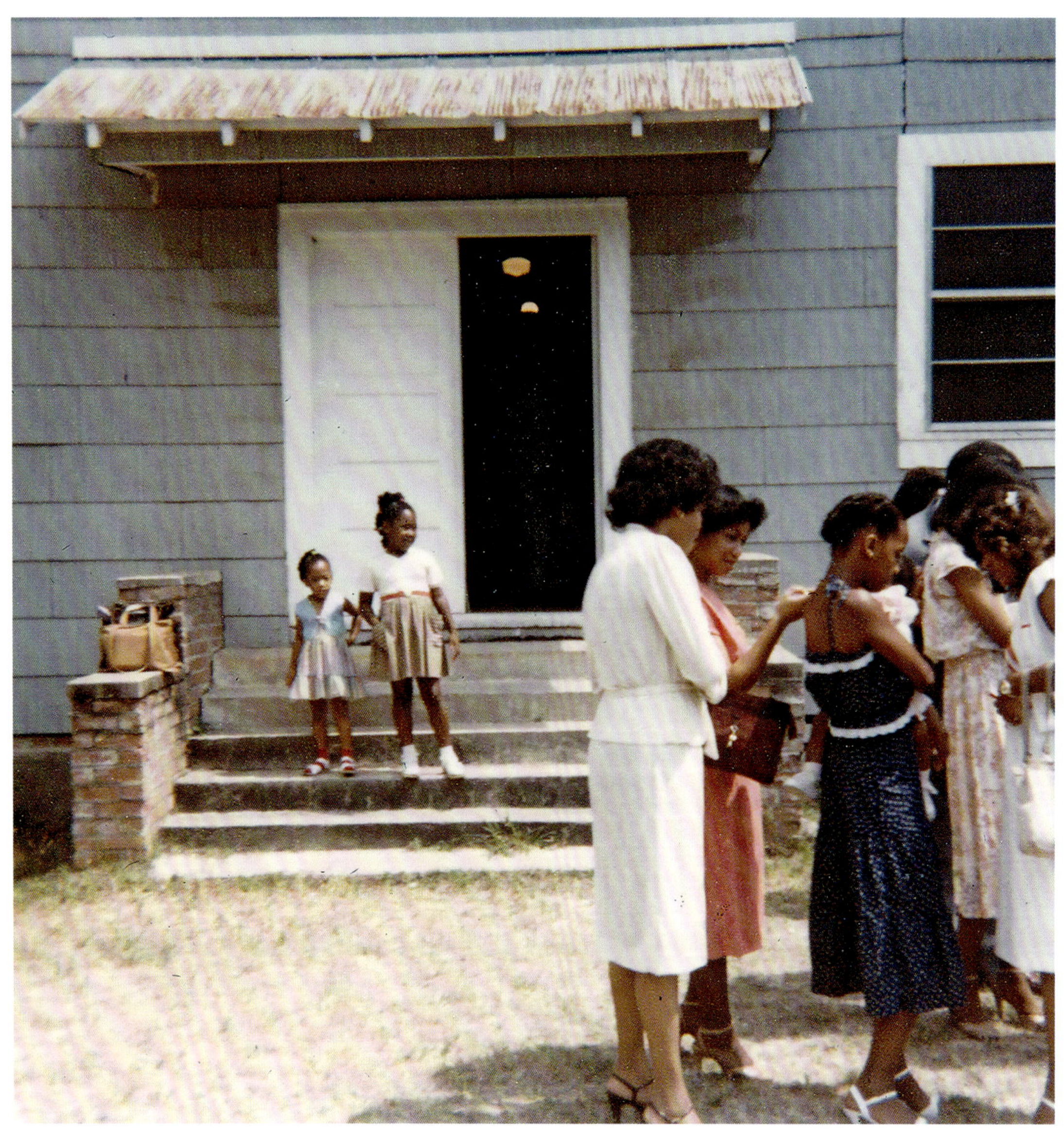

The Odom family at Mt. Hope Baptist Church

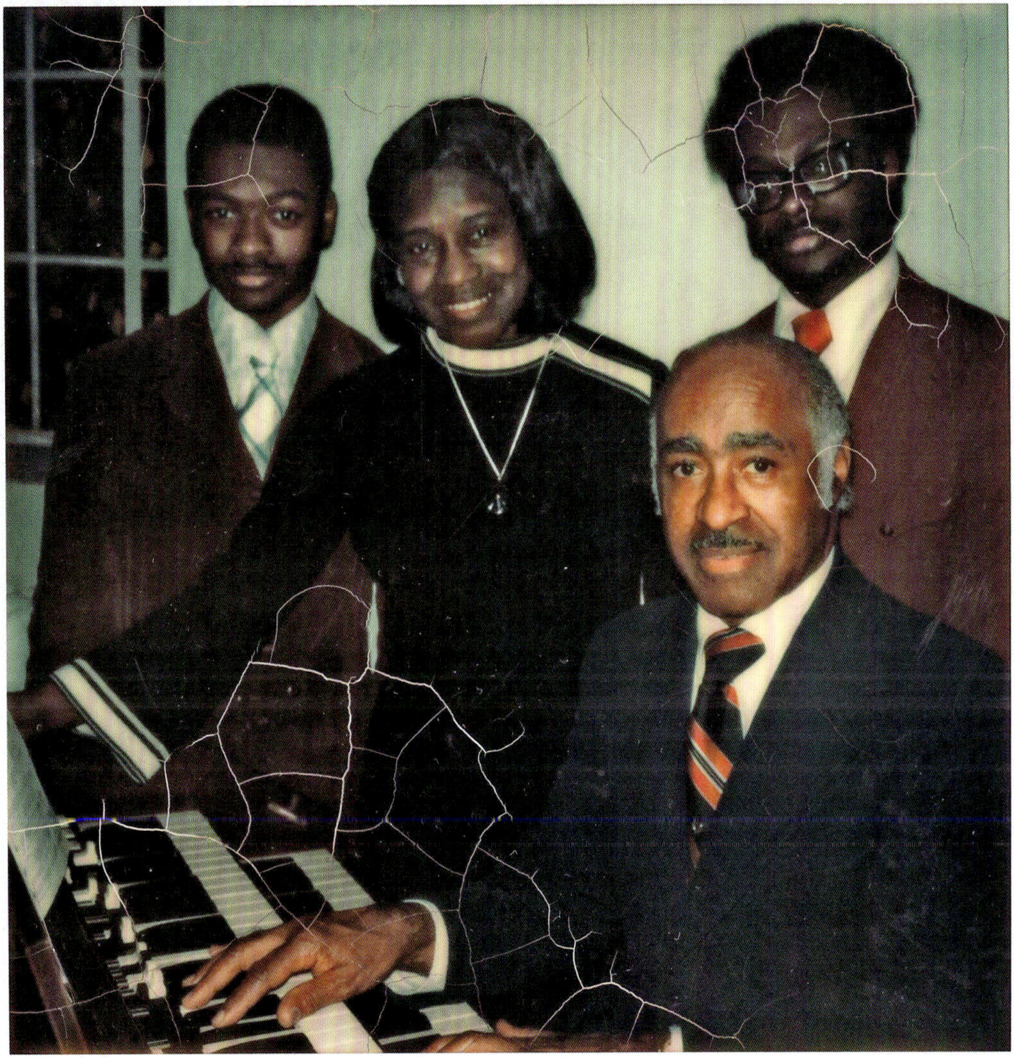

The Hunter family in front of a Hammond organ

CIRCA 1965

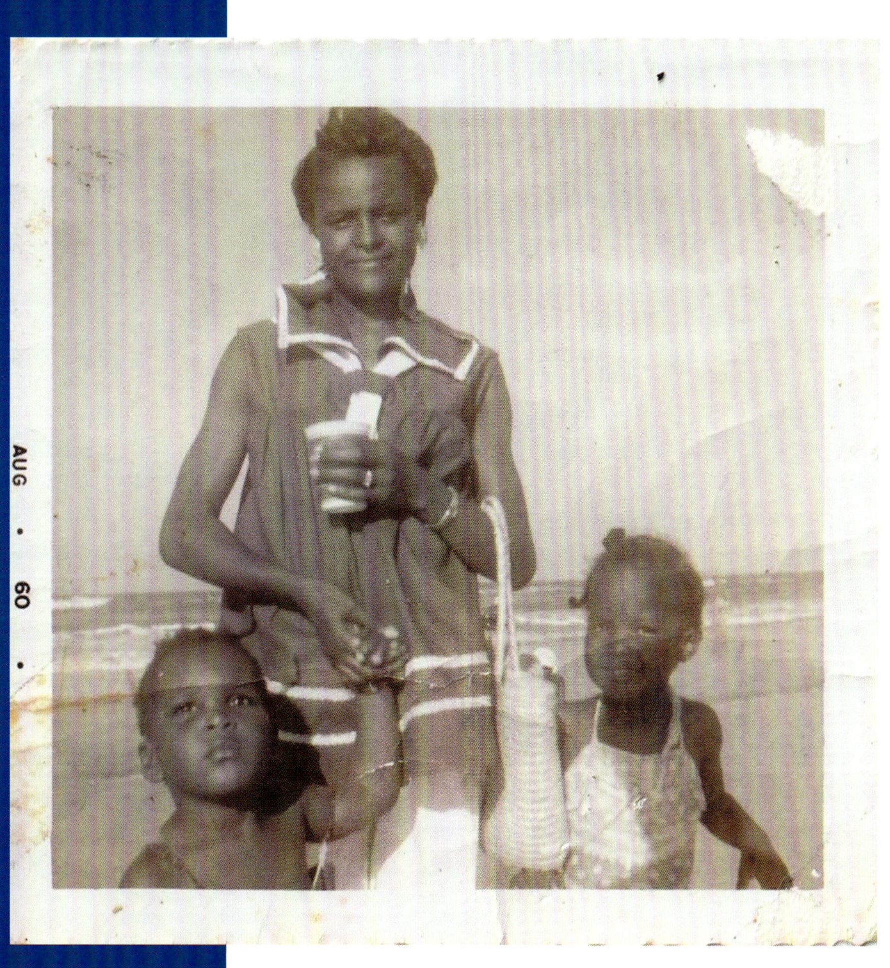

The author's aunt as a child (right)
with a family friend and child
1960

MOMENTS OF REST AND LEISURE

For Black folks to partake in rest and leisure without the burden of guilt is radical in and of itself. Throughout history, images of Black people were, more often than not, focused on our elders' and ancestors' work as laborers. Rarely did we see them at rest and yet, we know they rested. Rarely did we see them enjoy moments of leisure and yet, we also know they knew how to be in the moment with one another and oneself. Rest and leisure are often viewed as living life outside of the margins, and only after the work is done. But in this series, we center them and celebrate not only how rest and leisure help us get through the work, but how they get us back to ourselves. These moments highlight the full dimensionality of Black lives, that multitude of things that can be true at once: Black people can work, play, and make time for rest.

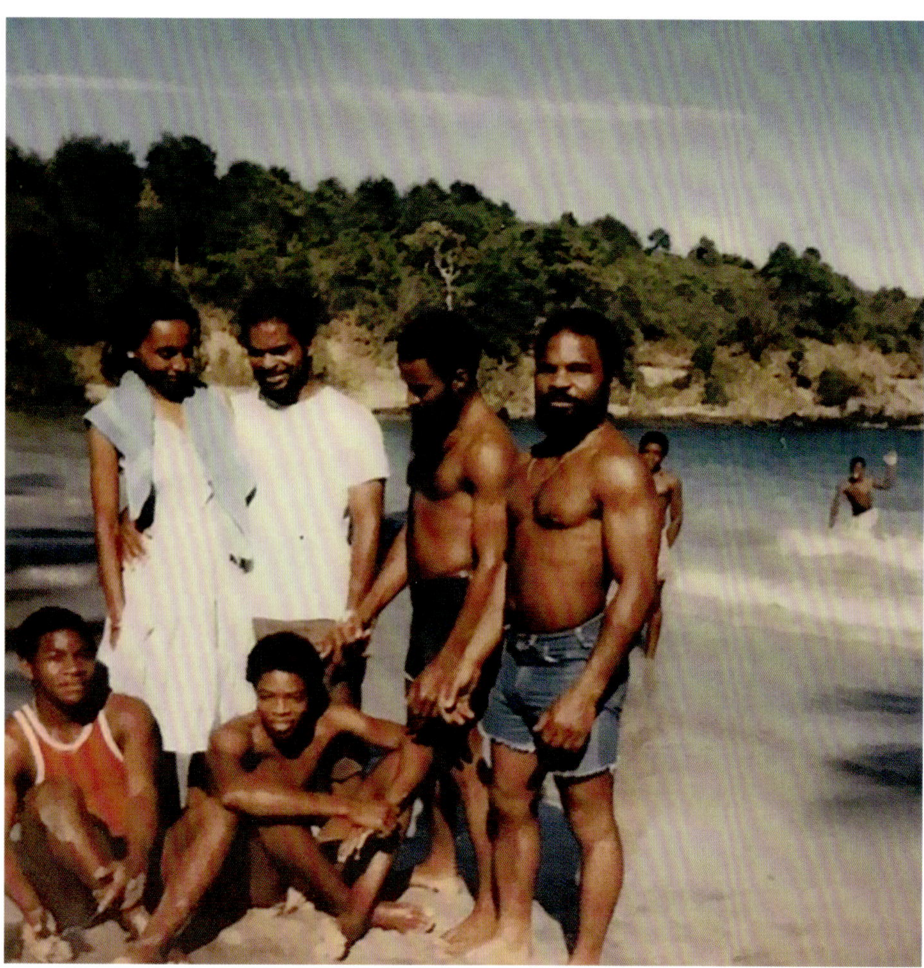

GRENADA

1981

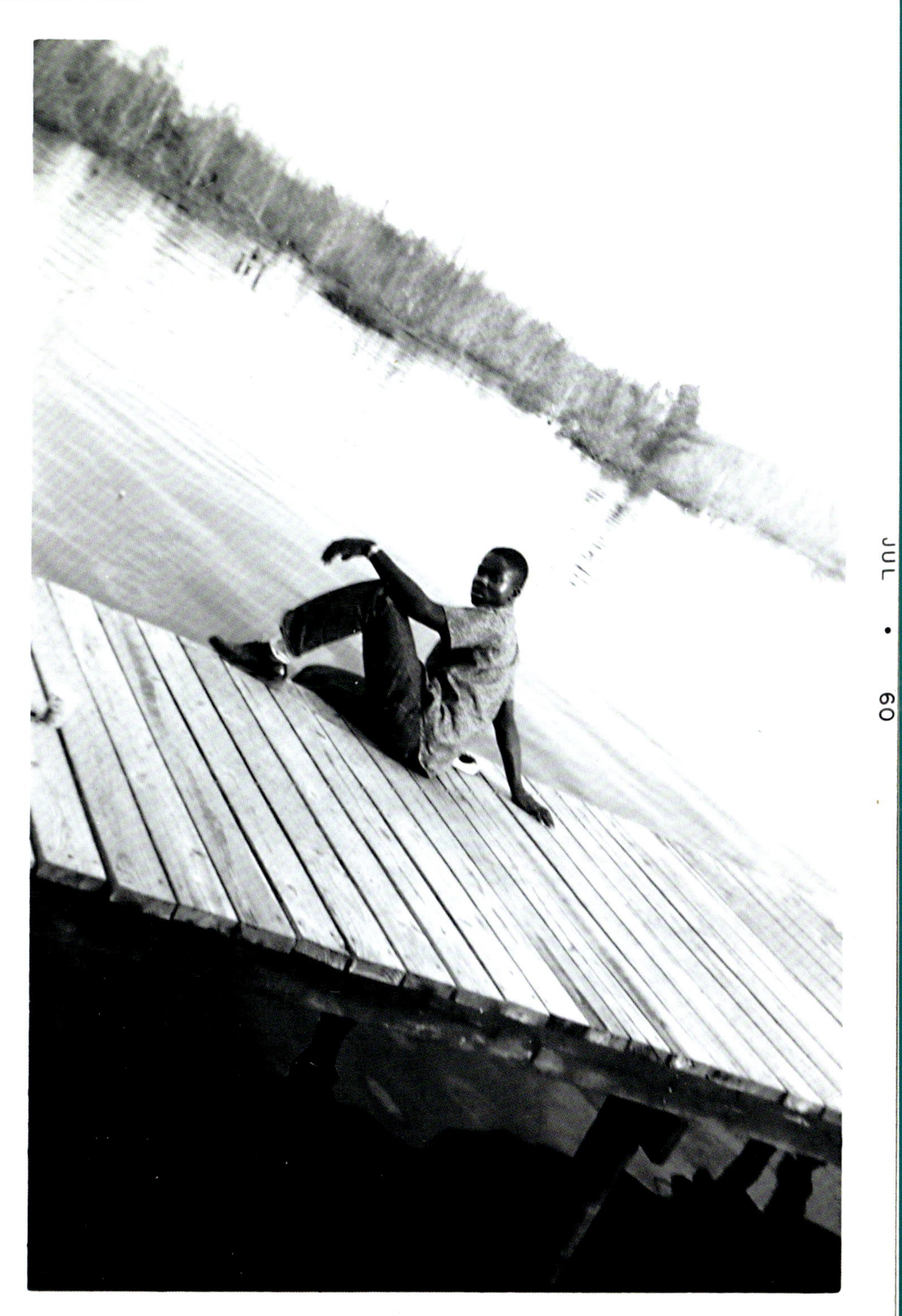

Feodie Powers
sitting on the dock
NACOGDOCHES
COUNTY, TEXAS
1960

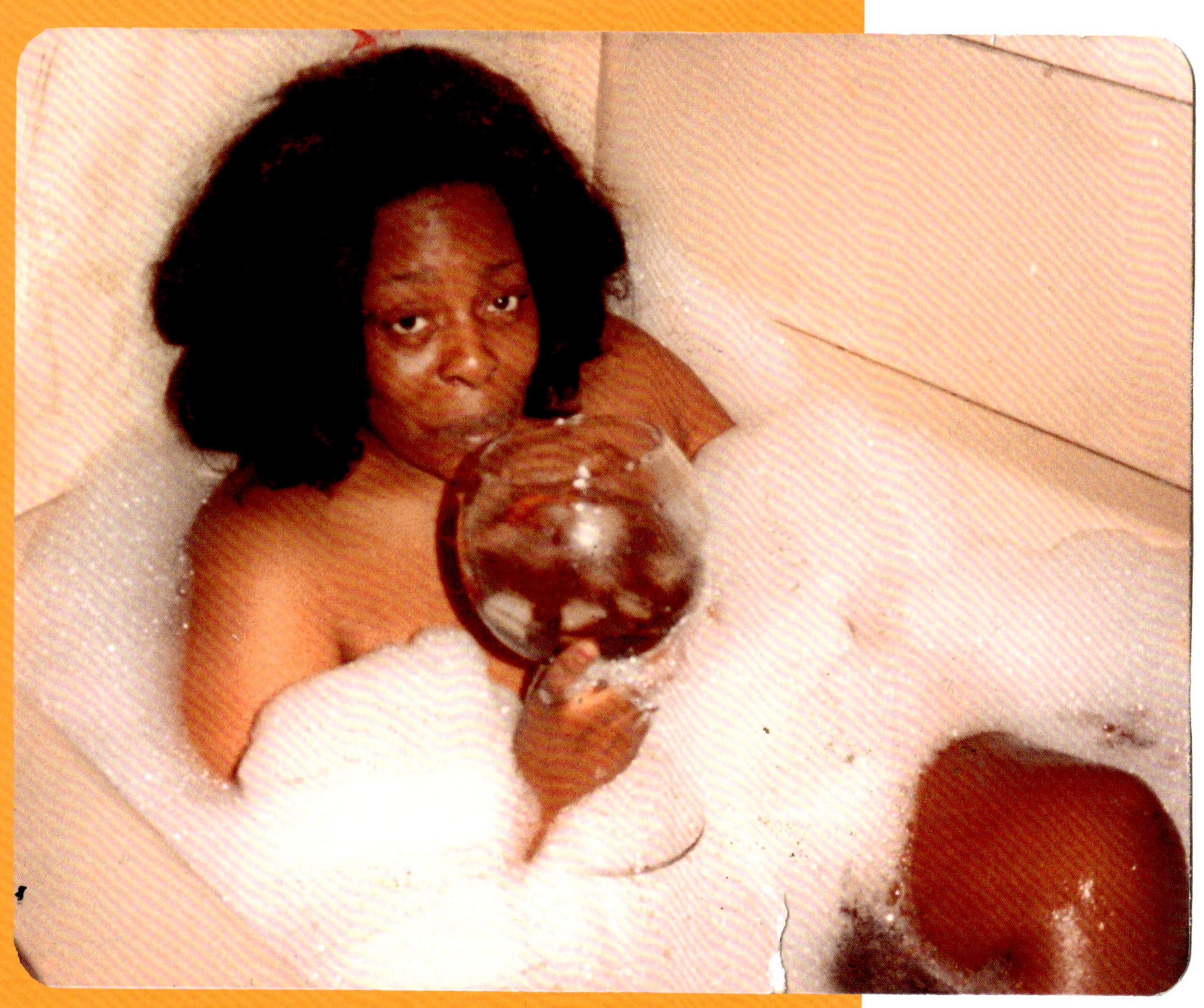

Bubble bath
1980S

Agnus Marie Miller

YOUNGSVILLE, LA

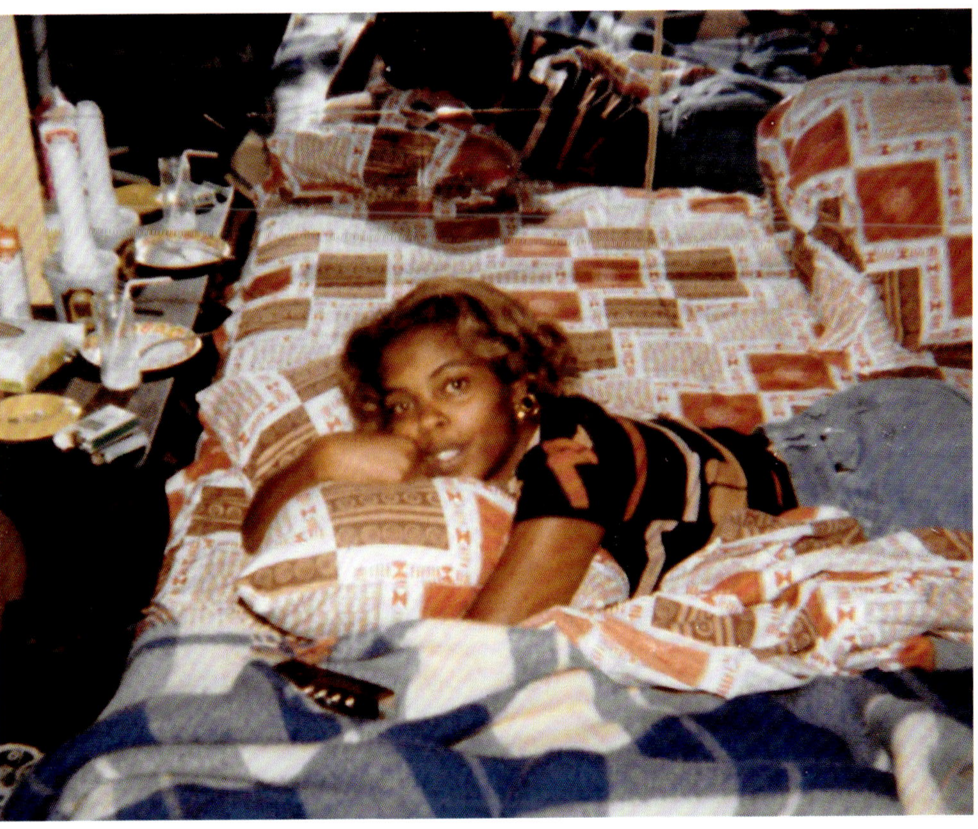

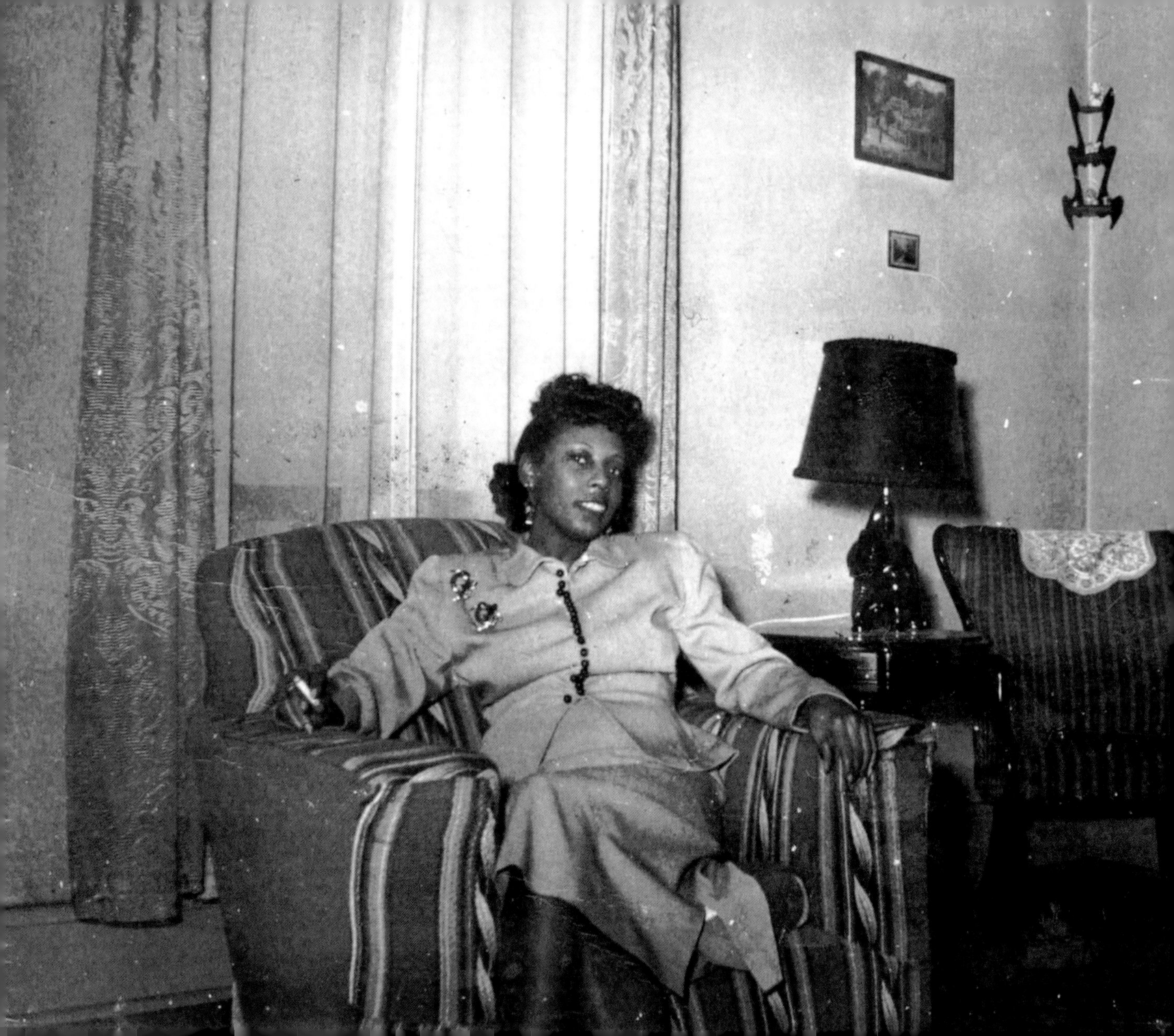

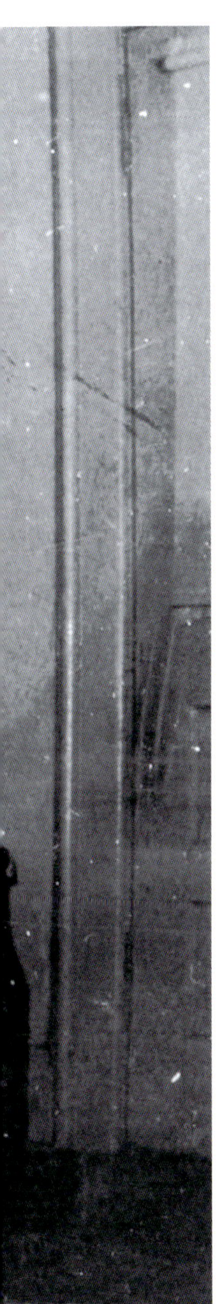

Taking a nap after Thanksgiving dinner
1980S

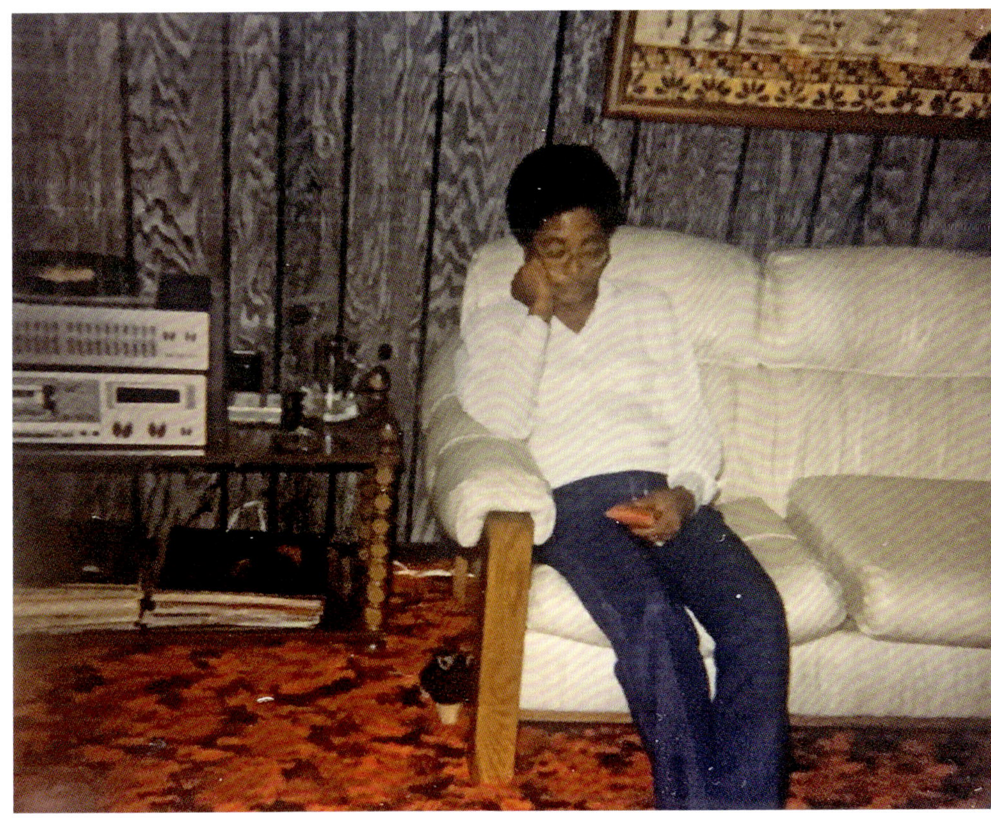

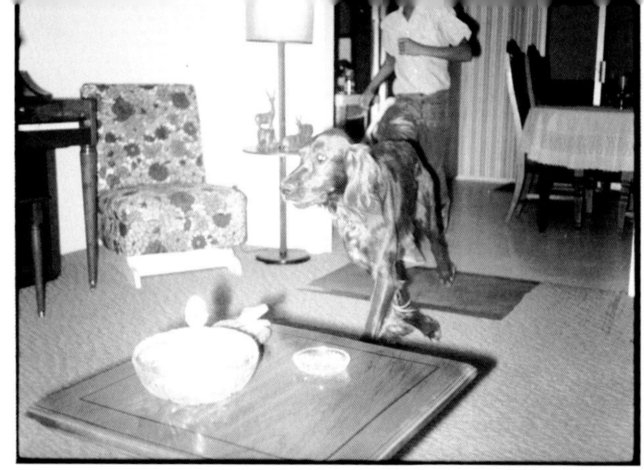

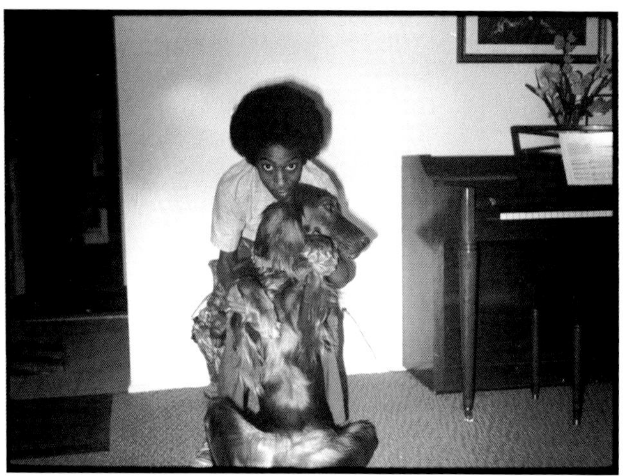

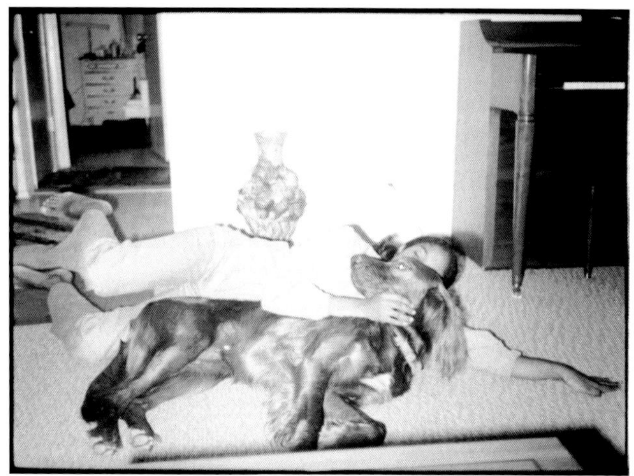

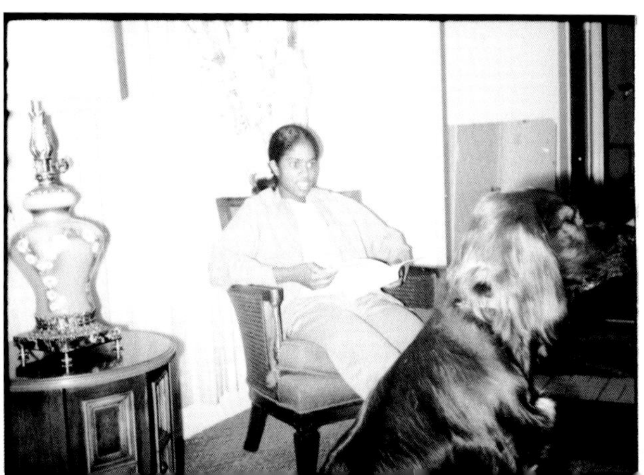

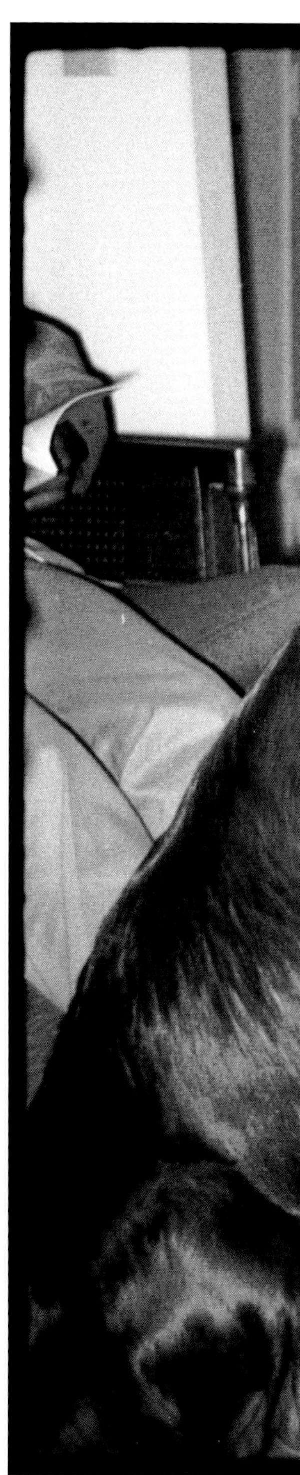

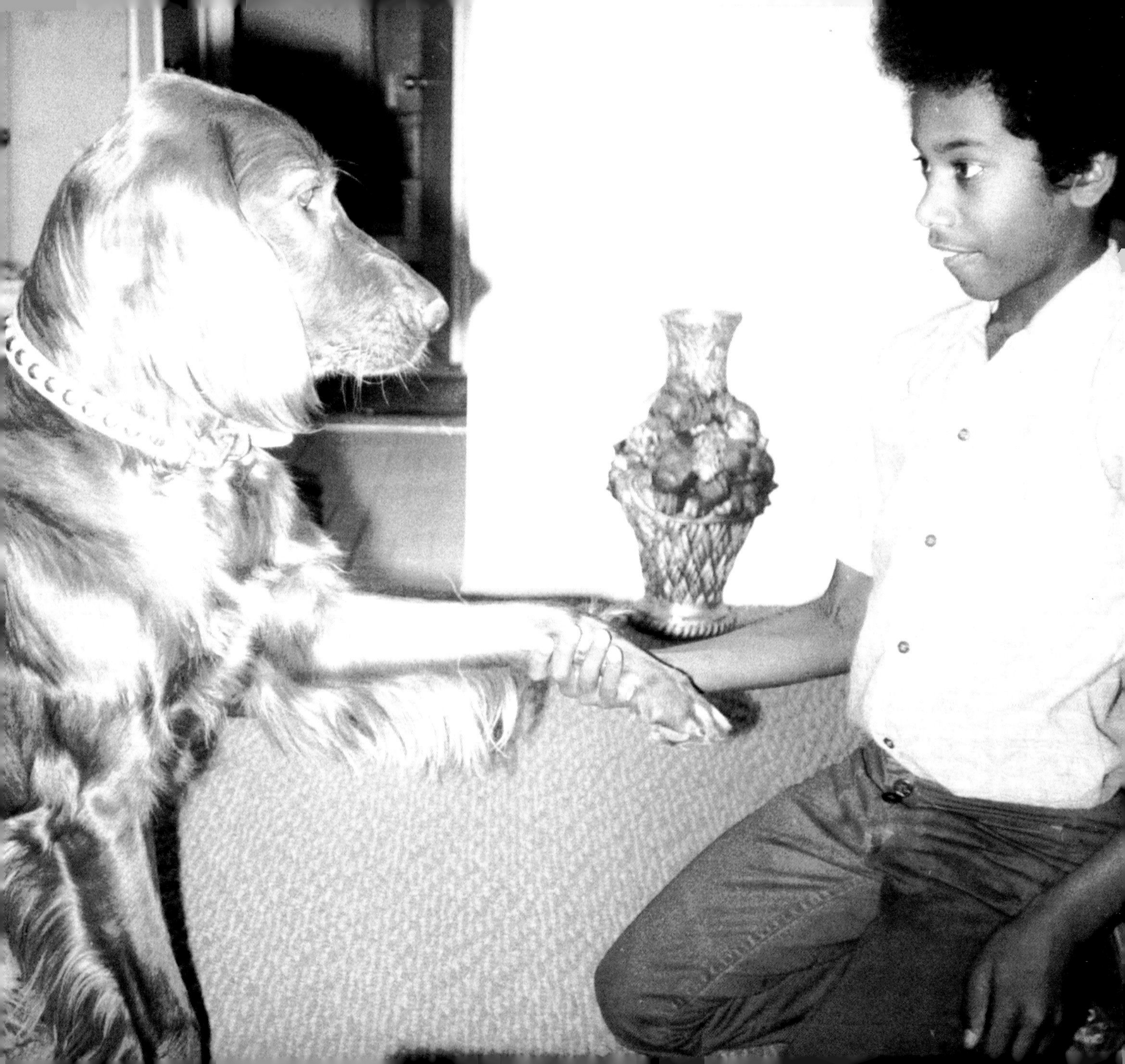

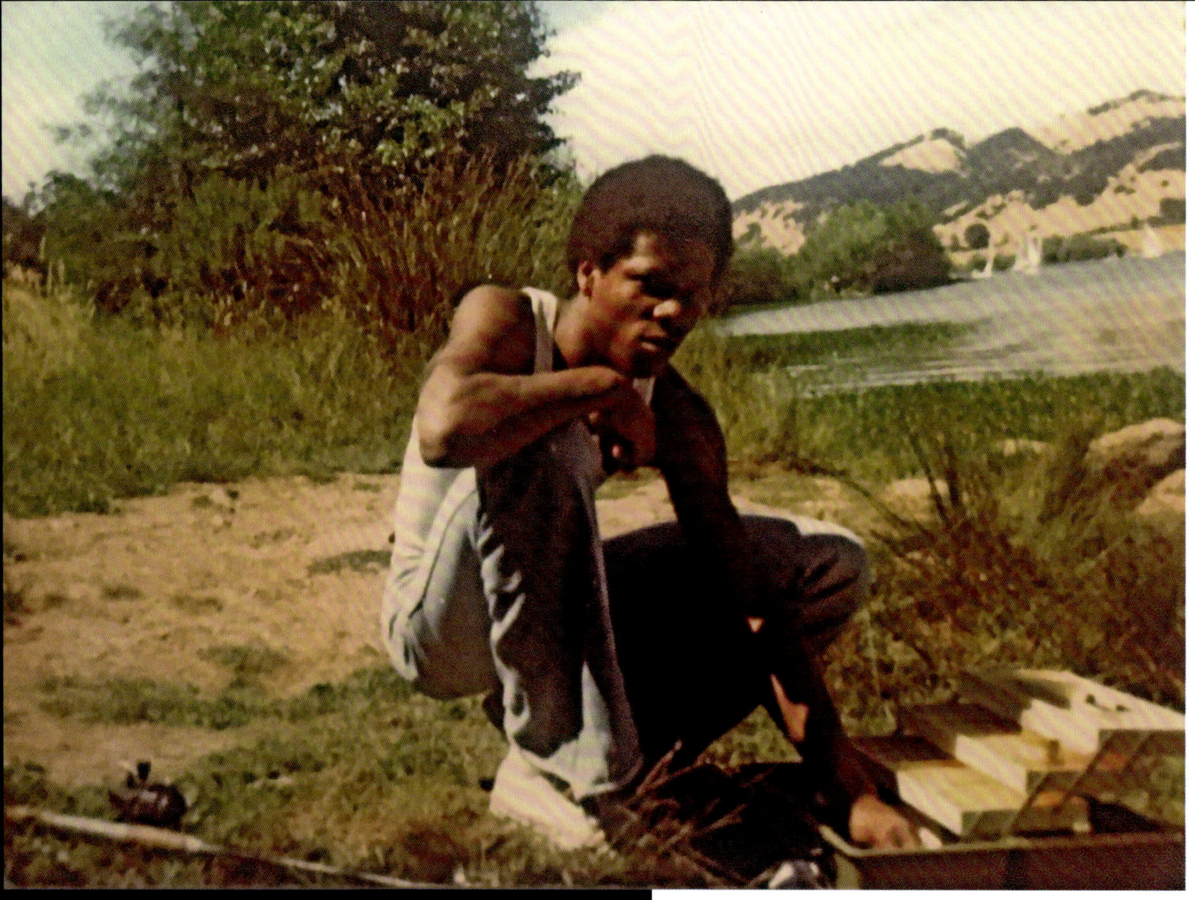

Fishing at Lake Ralphine
SANTA ROSA, CA
1980

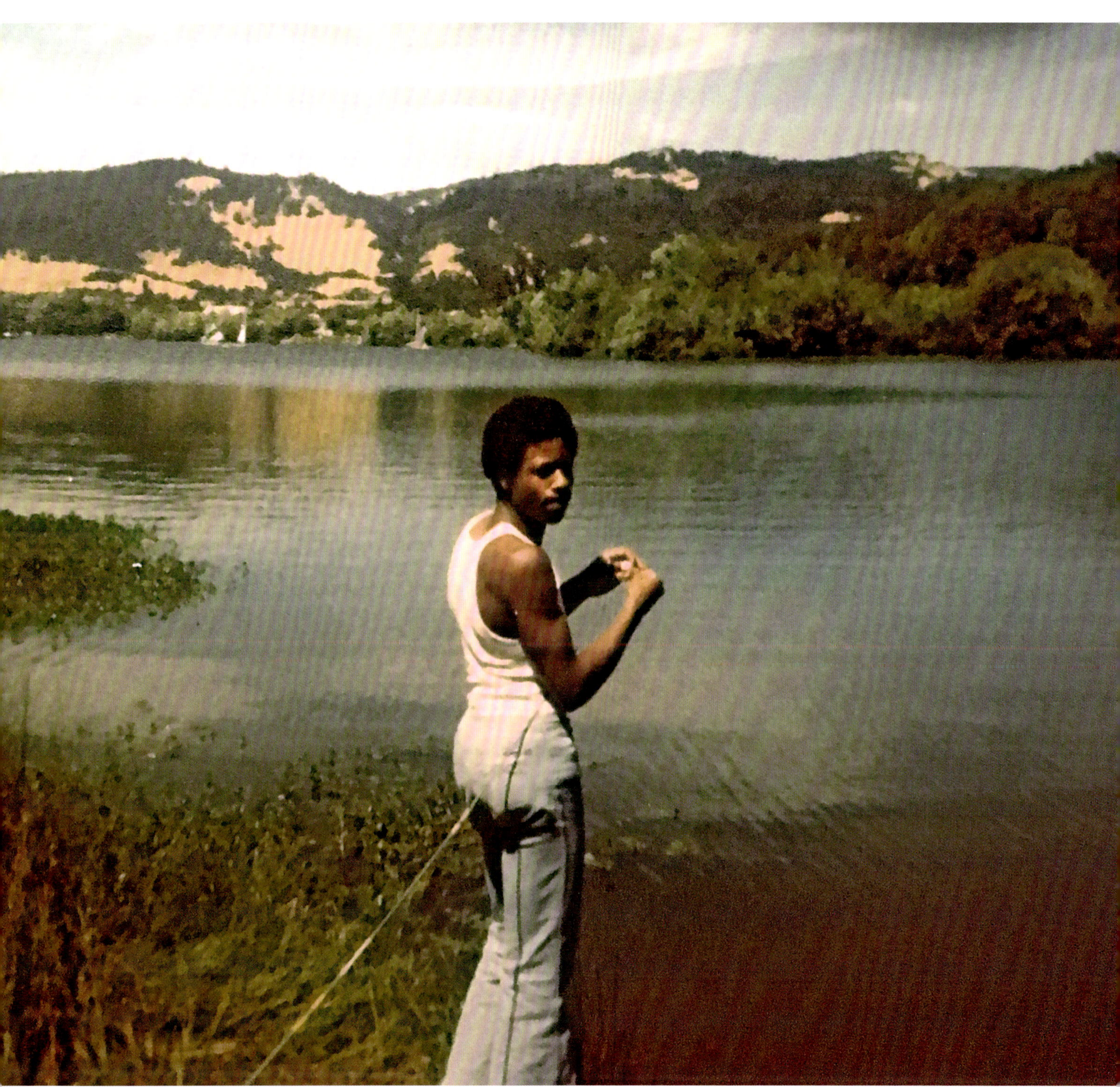

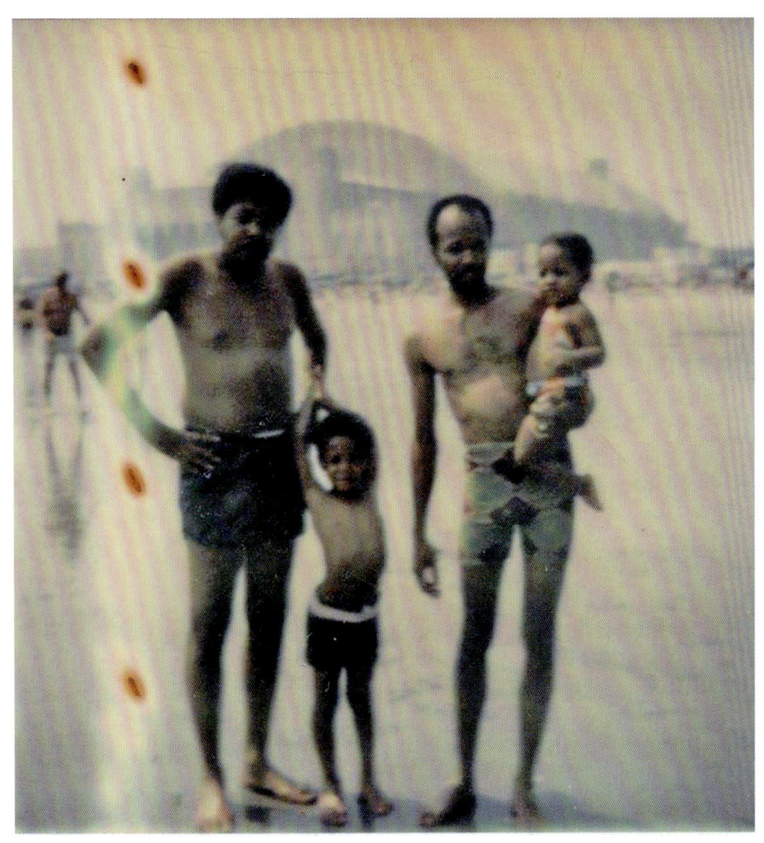

ATLANTIC CITY, NJ
1977

→ Bayshore Beach, which was the "colored side" of Buckroe Beach
HAMPTON, VA
1960

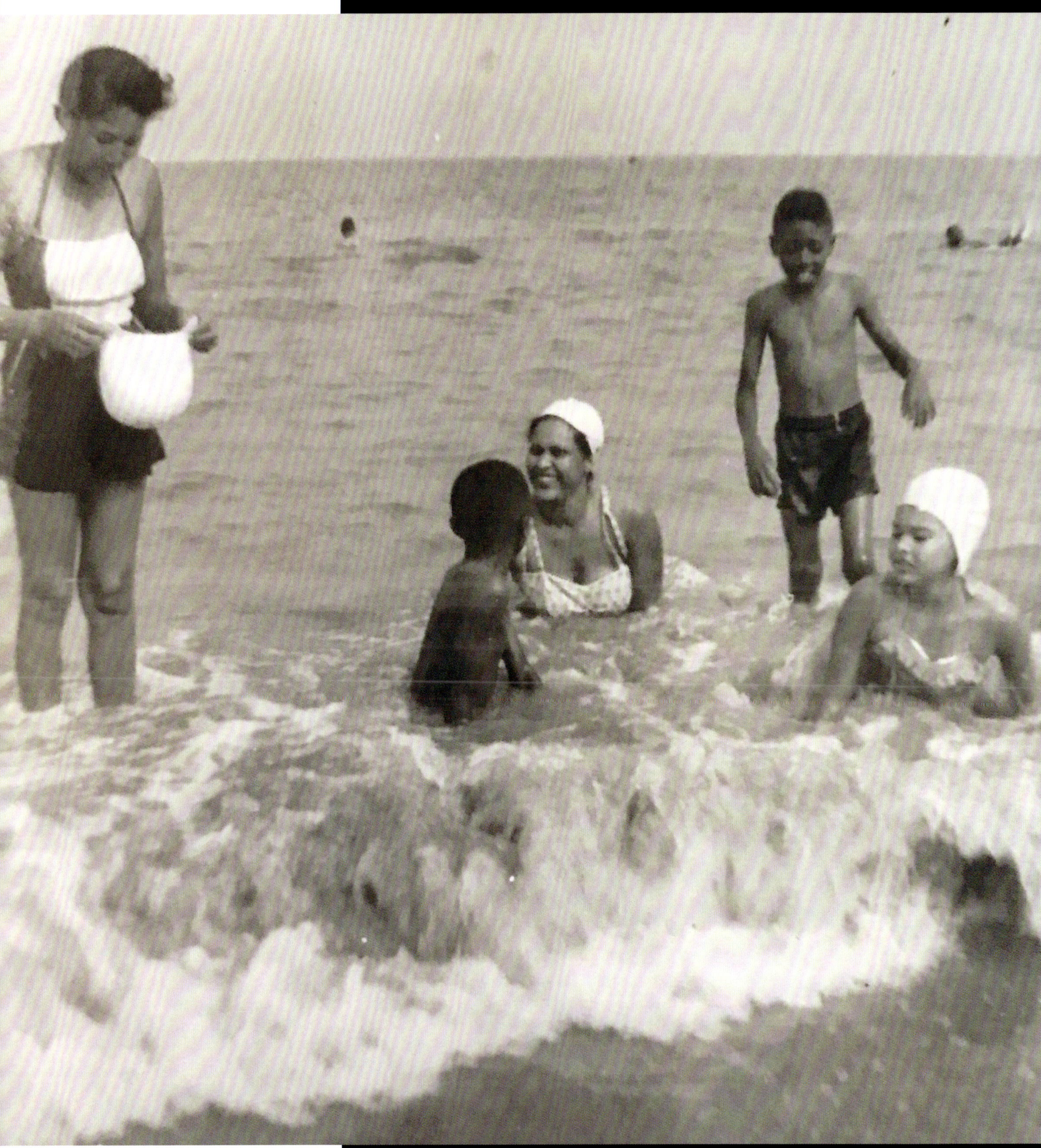

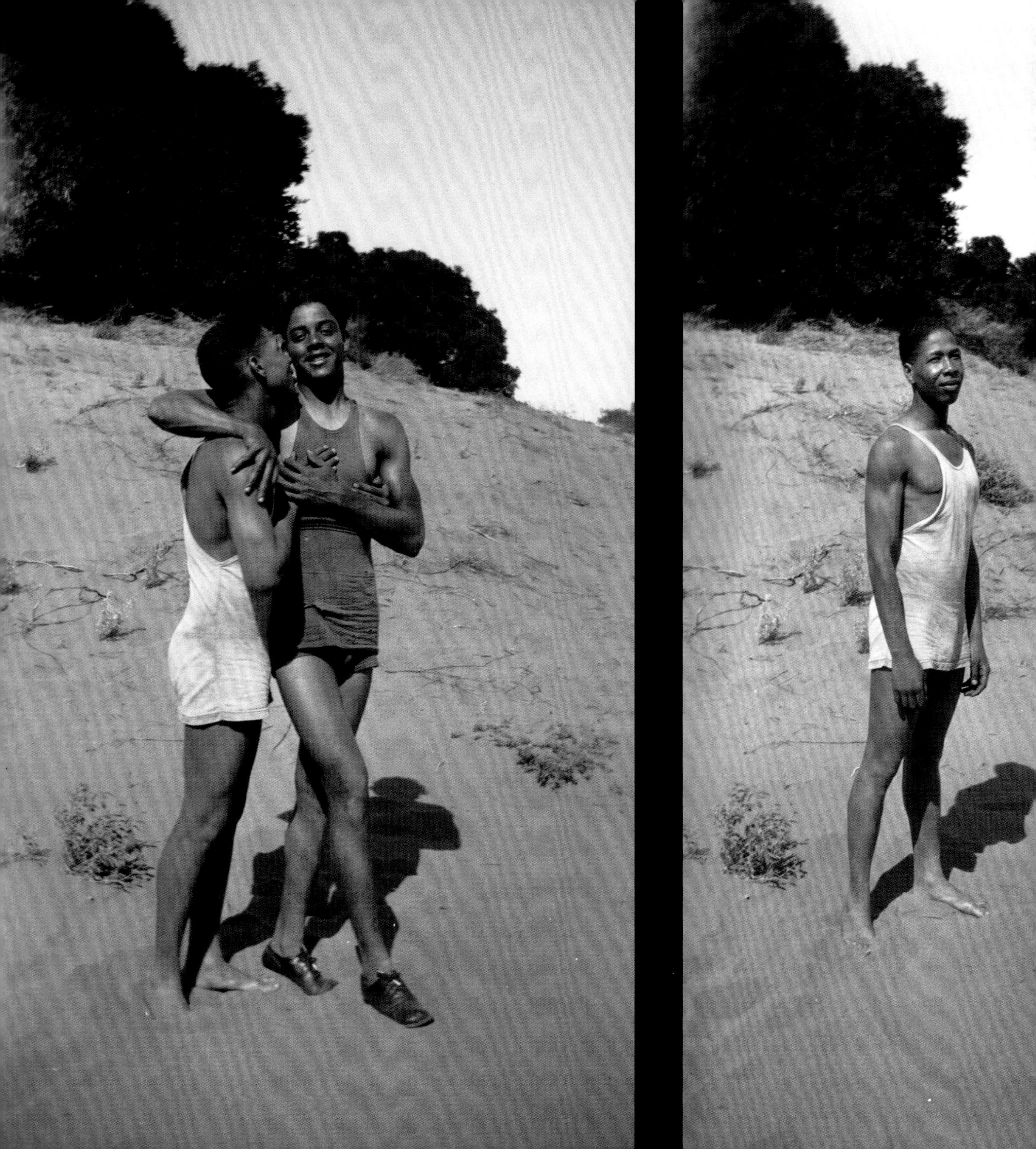

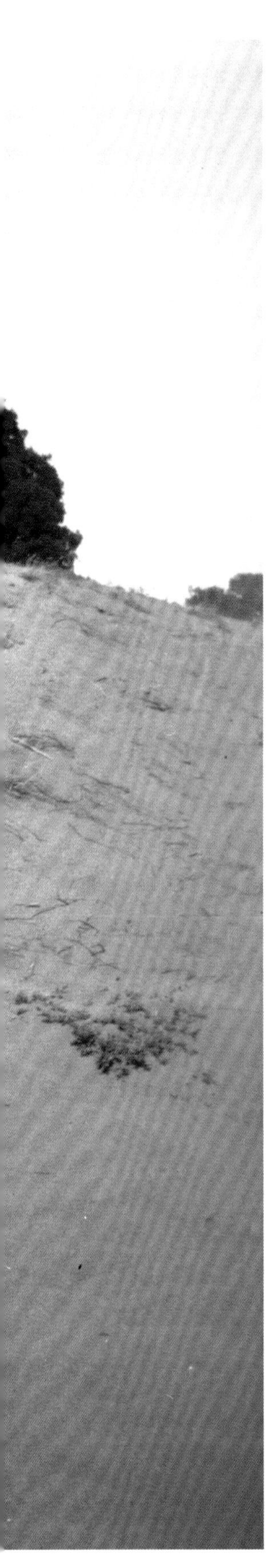

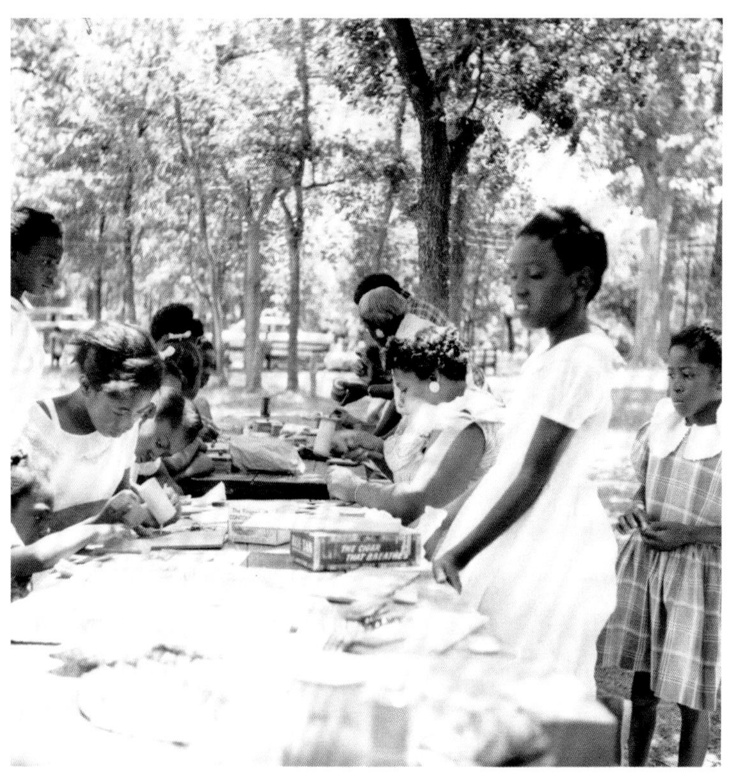

TEXAS
1958

BAY AREA, CA
CIRCA 1920S

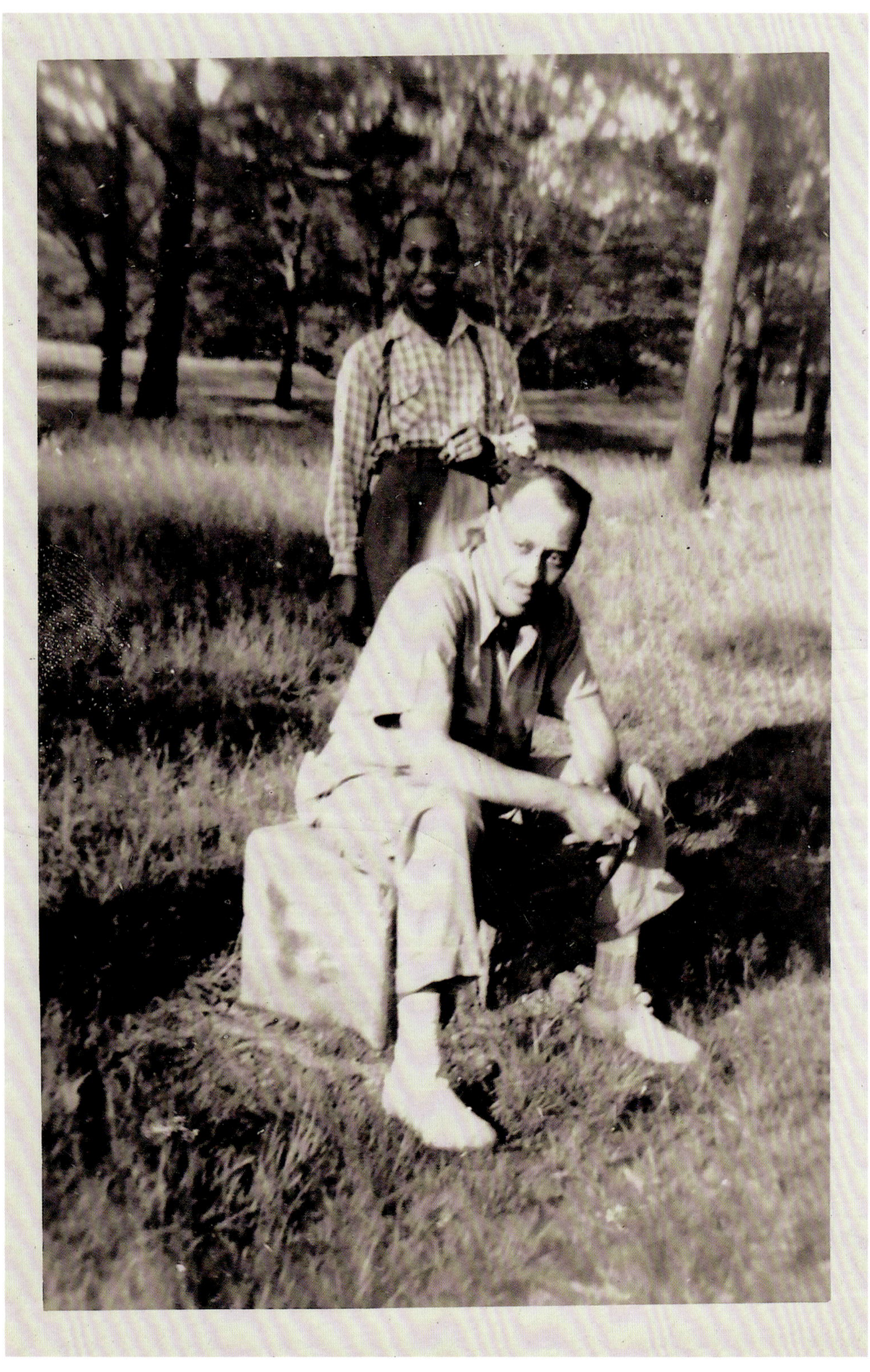

CIRCA 1945

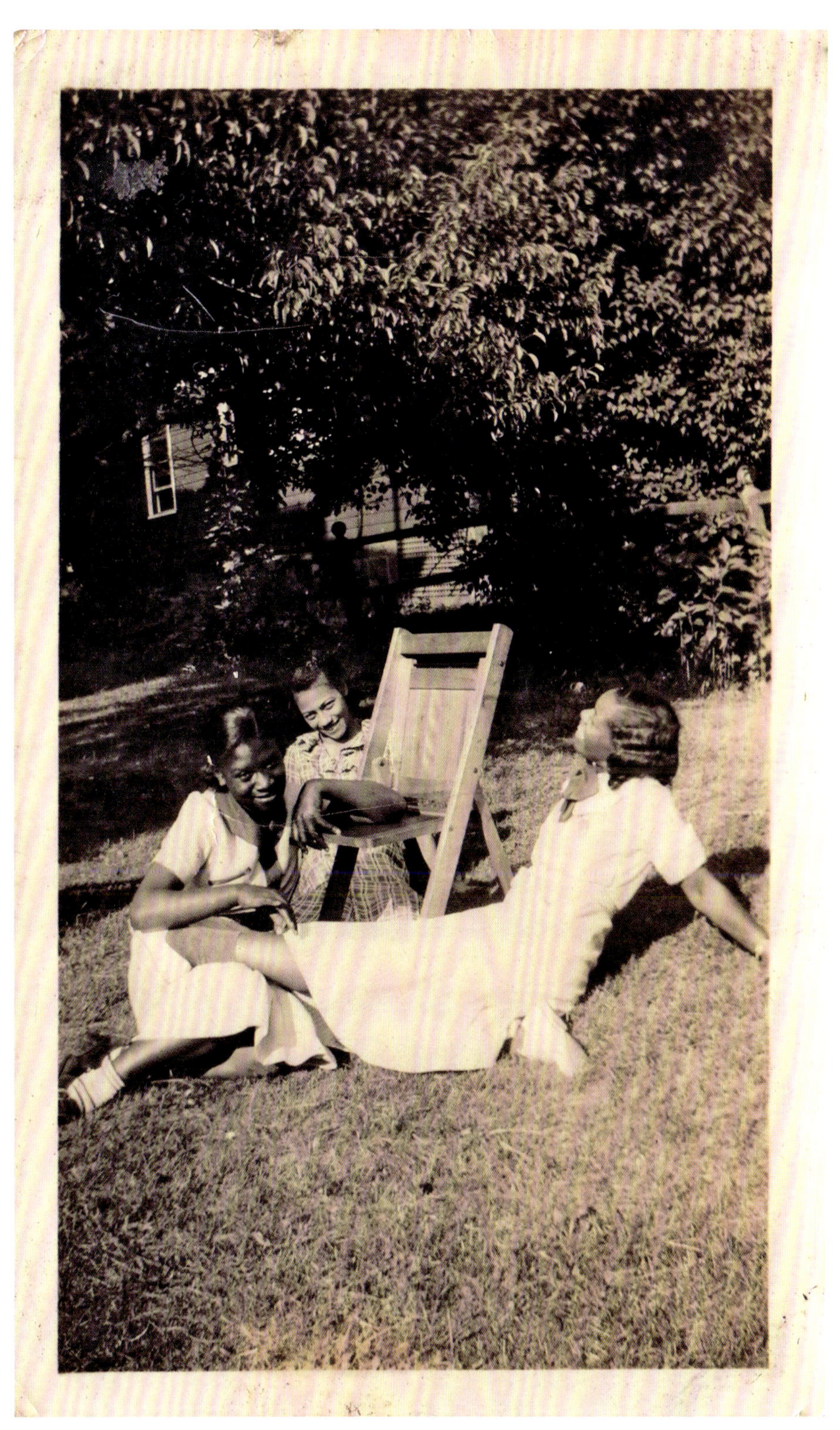

Inez Hunter
BOSTON, MA
CIRCA 1935

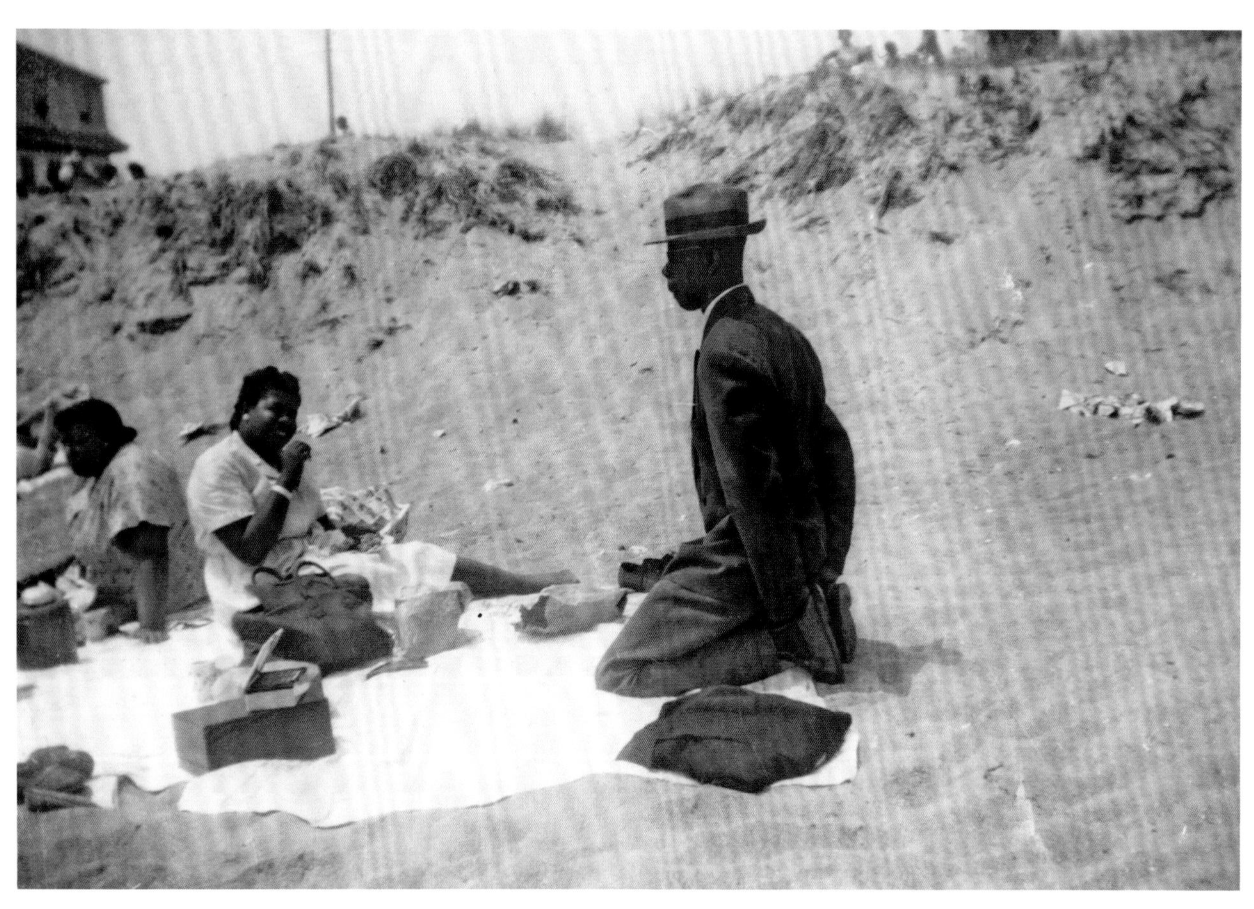

MASSACHUSETTS
CIRCA 1940

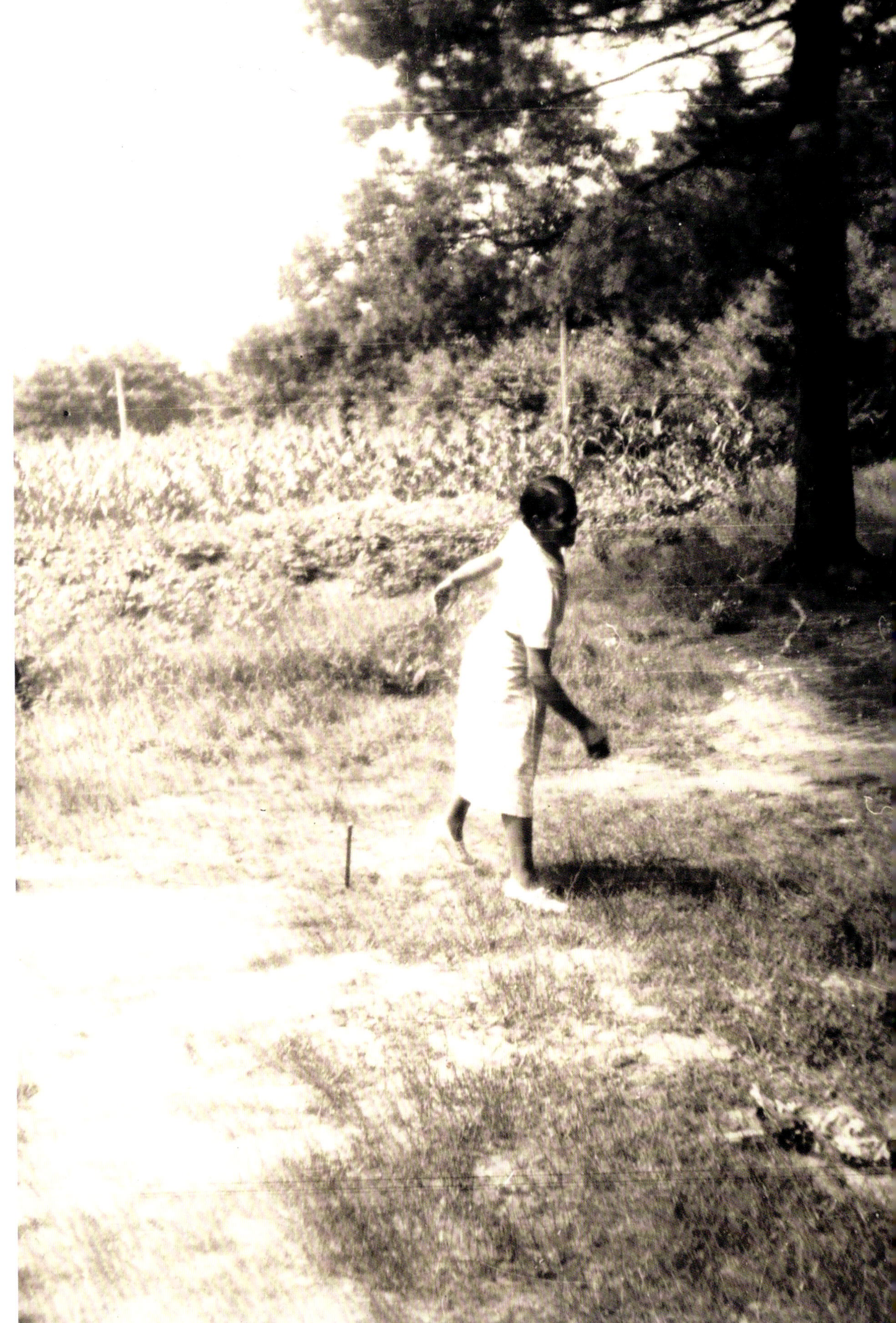

Horseshoes

CIRCA 1945

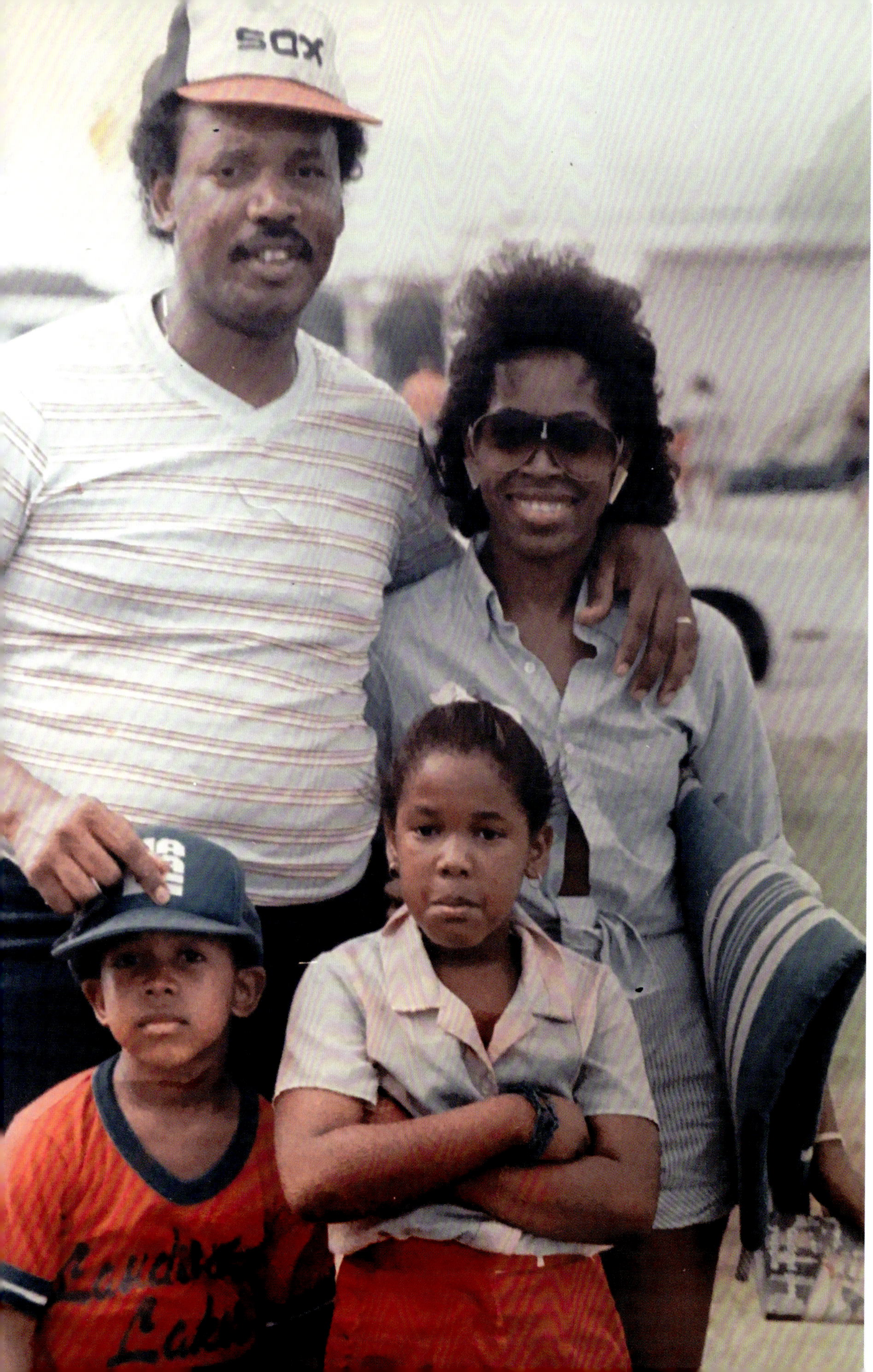

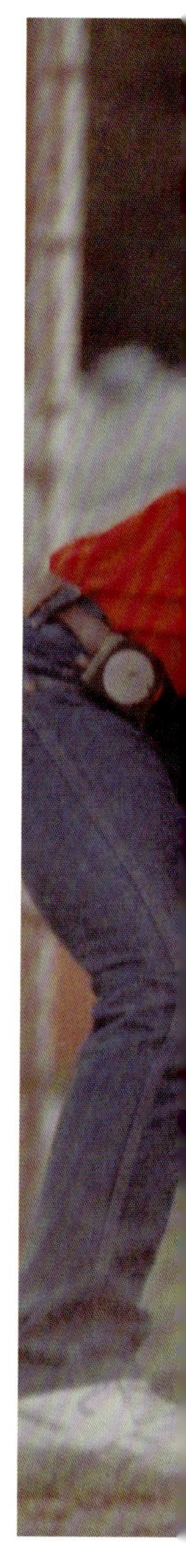

1980S

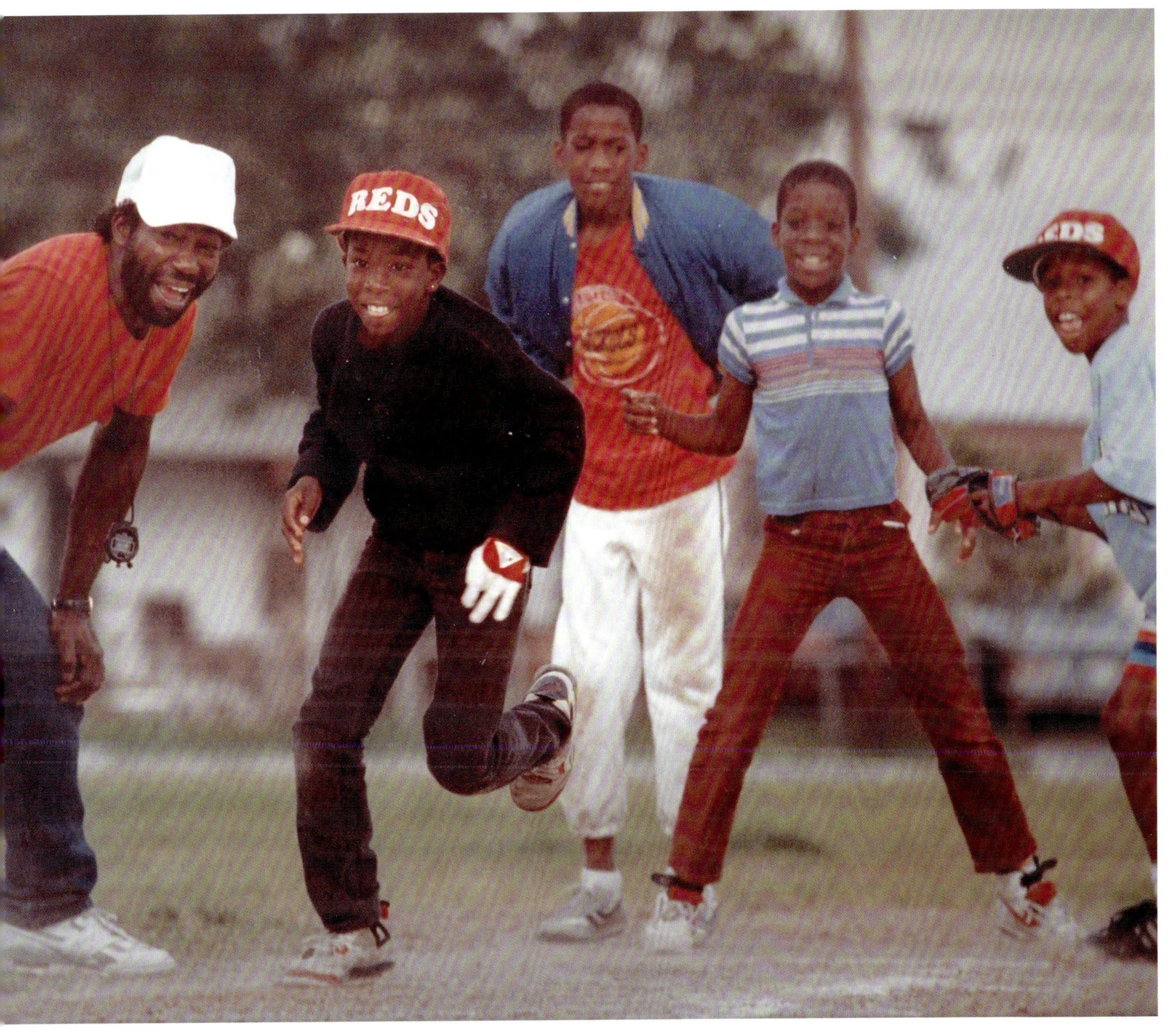

1980S

PART III

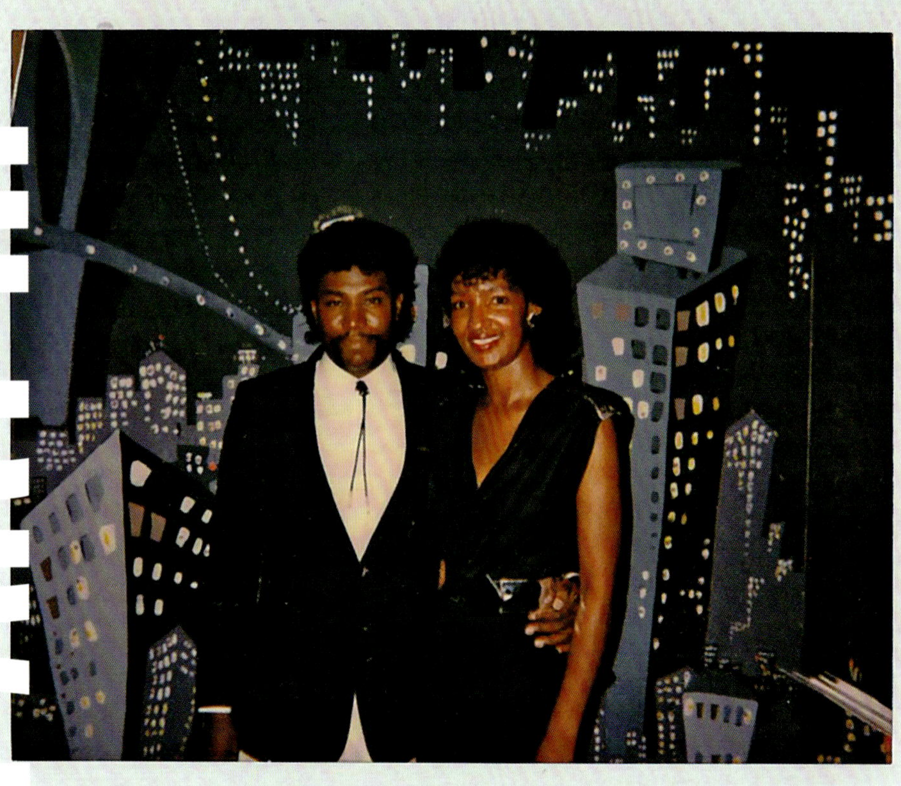

EXTERIORS

TO BE WITNESSED

Black folks are going to step out. When I was growing up, my parents went to various night clubs and social events around town weekly, taking great pride in their appearance. In coordinating fashion, their outfits announced their arrival, greeting everyone before they could even open their mouths or hand out hugs and daps. And while the act of "steppin' out" itself was a sight to behold, watching my parents prepare to leave the house for the evening became an event on its own. My siblings and I were part of my dad's "steppin' out" process, filling in as a last-minute shoe-shiner or being entrusted with his hair clippers for a quick line-up to hold him over between trips to the barbershop. The mood was always electric and vibrant when my parents were getting ready for a night out on the town.

As for mom, she always came out of their room ready to take on the world. We watched the bedroom door, waiting to marvel at her beauty. One time she was even awarded a cash prize after winning "best dressed" at the club that night. Her outfit was fly to no end for the time, but by today's standard, she looked as if she had just left her corporate job. When she showed me a photo of the outfit I jokingly asked, "You mean, this outfit wasn't what you wore to work that day? You didn't leave work and go straight to the club?"

But my parents weren't the only folks who dressed to impress. I've come to learn that style is inherently within us – a part of our genetic makeup, as far as I'm concerned. Flipping through photographs from the past is the perfect way to reveal the truth about fashion in Black culture. In the early 1900s and moving through the 1960s; '70s; '80s; and '90s we get an opportunity to bear witness to the trends and statements that inform our present-day style and appearance. Picture-ready for every occasion – from inside the home to the outside world and from photo studios to moments of everyday life – impeccable style is deeply embedded into the Black narrative.

← Previous: Polaroid of the author's parents during a night out
1985

The author’s parents at various night clubs and outings around Jacksonville, Florida

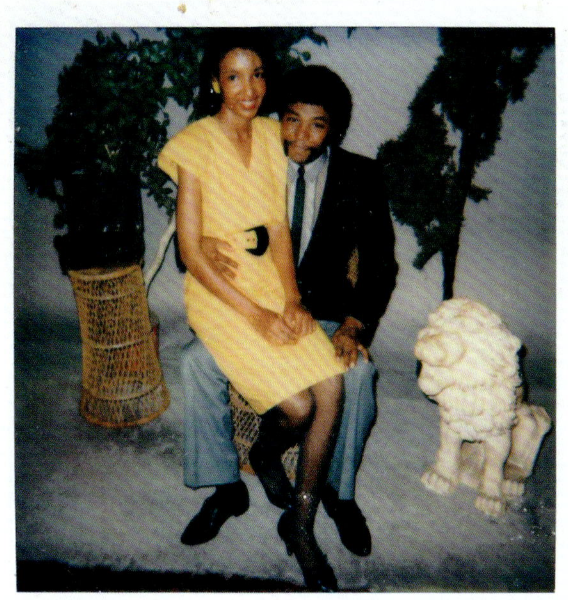

1986

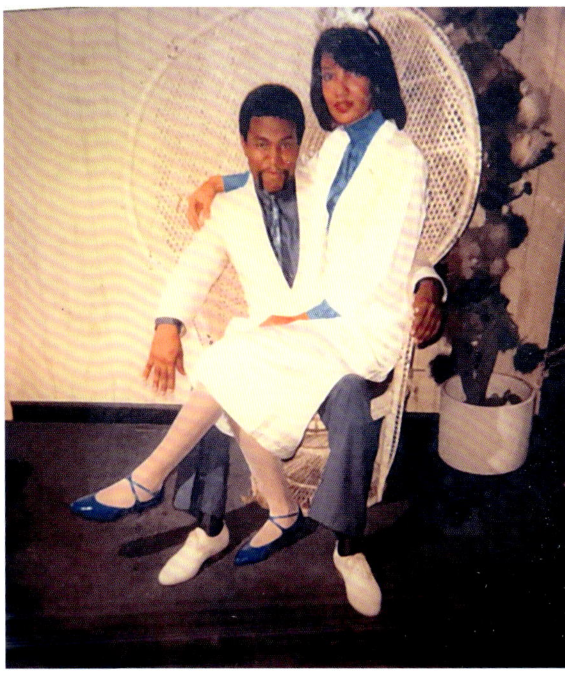

1987

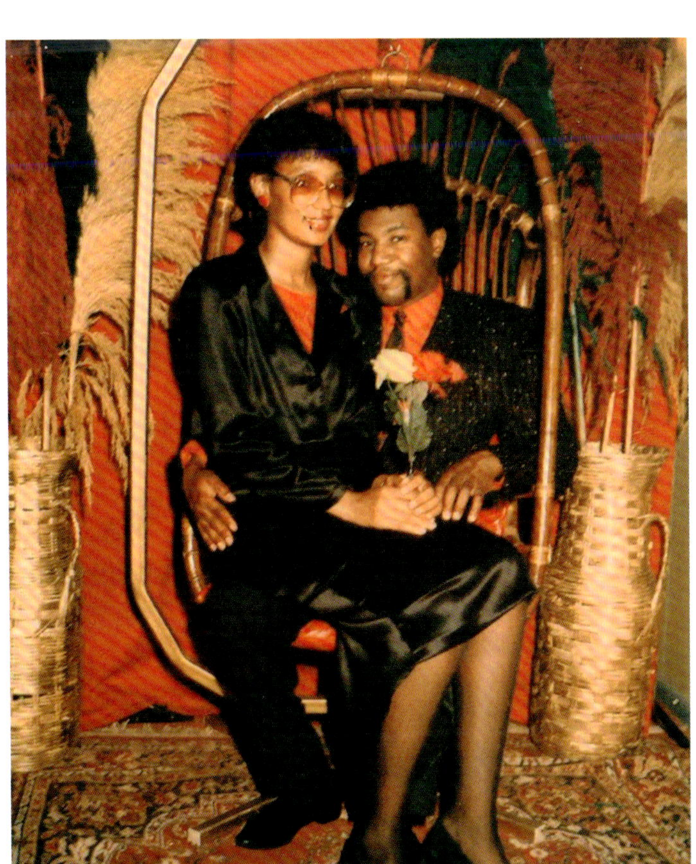

1990

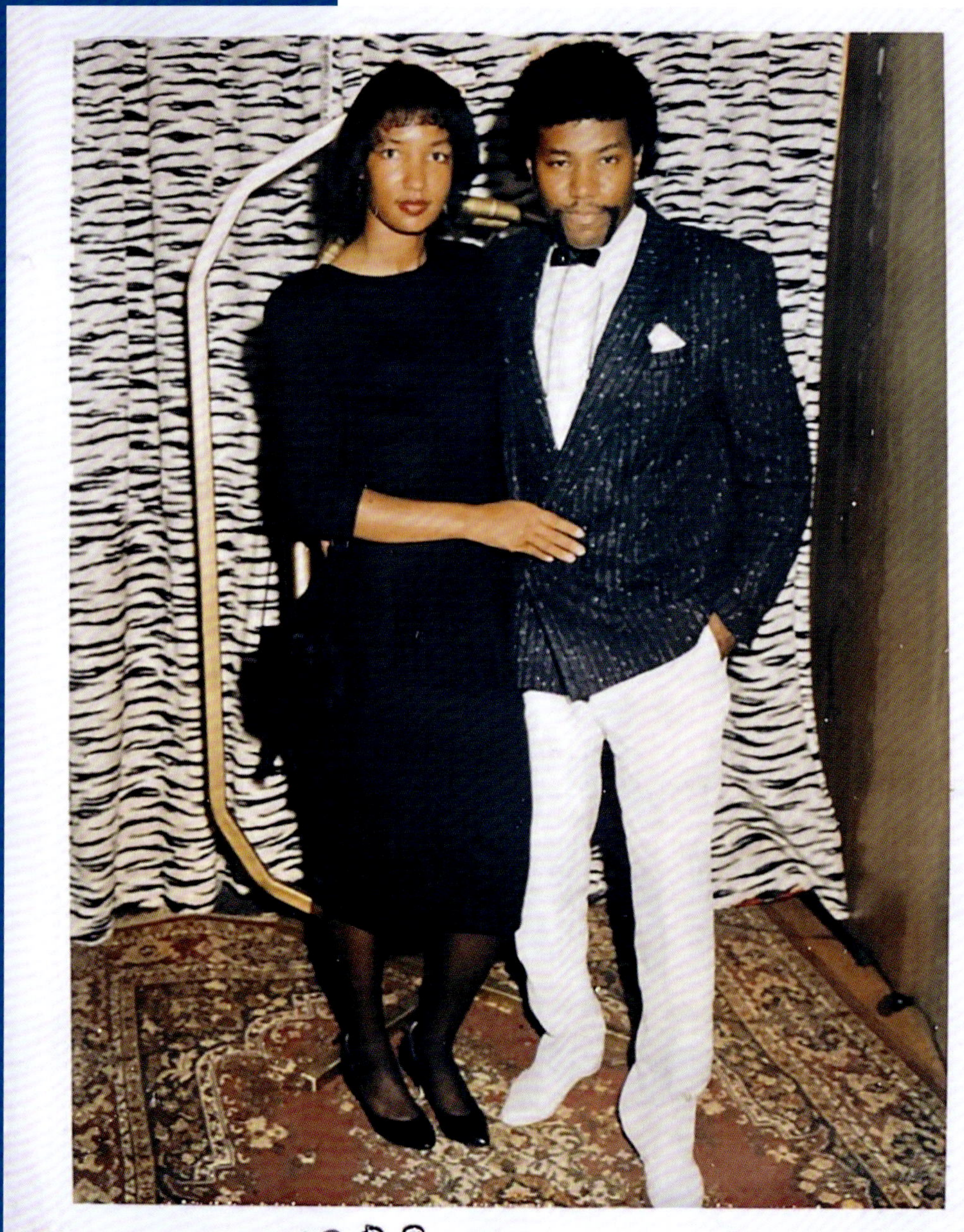

JACKSONVILLE, FL

1989

STYLE

One of the things that I love most about style is that it encompasses a bit of both interior and exterior Blackness. Style is a form of self-expression and exploration through the wearing and pairing of clothes, hairstyles, and accessories. Looking good can help one to feel good and through that, style becomes a celebration and affirmation of oneself.

Style makes a statement. It says something about you as a first impression and can become known as a consistent attribute that's synonymous with your reputation. Whether personal, political, or an act of rebellion, style can also just be what it is for its own sake. This series uncovers the meaning of being a witness to Black folks and how we recognize one another by way of fashion.

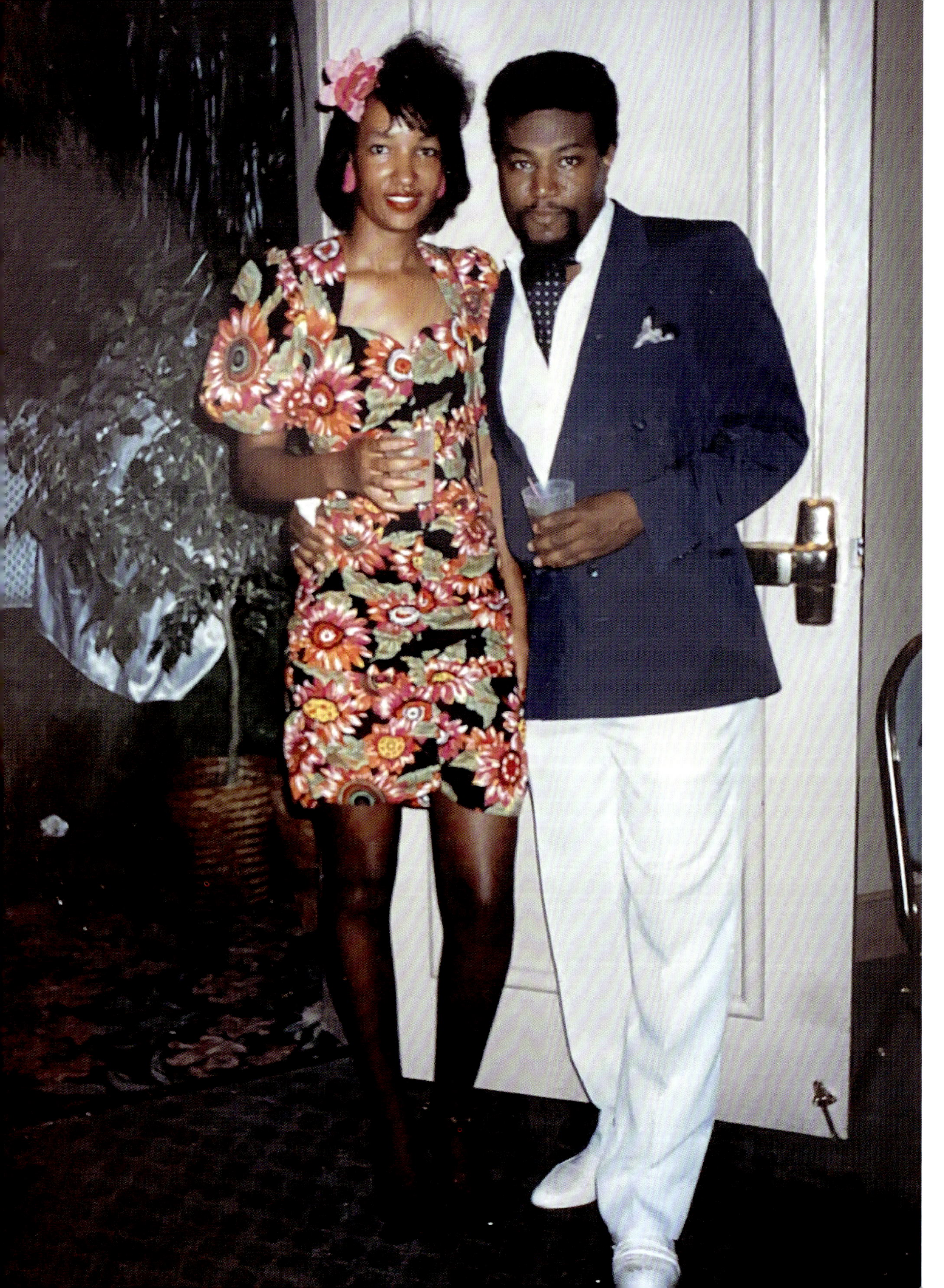

← 1994

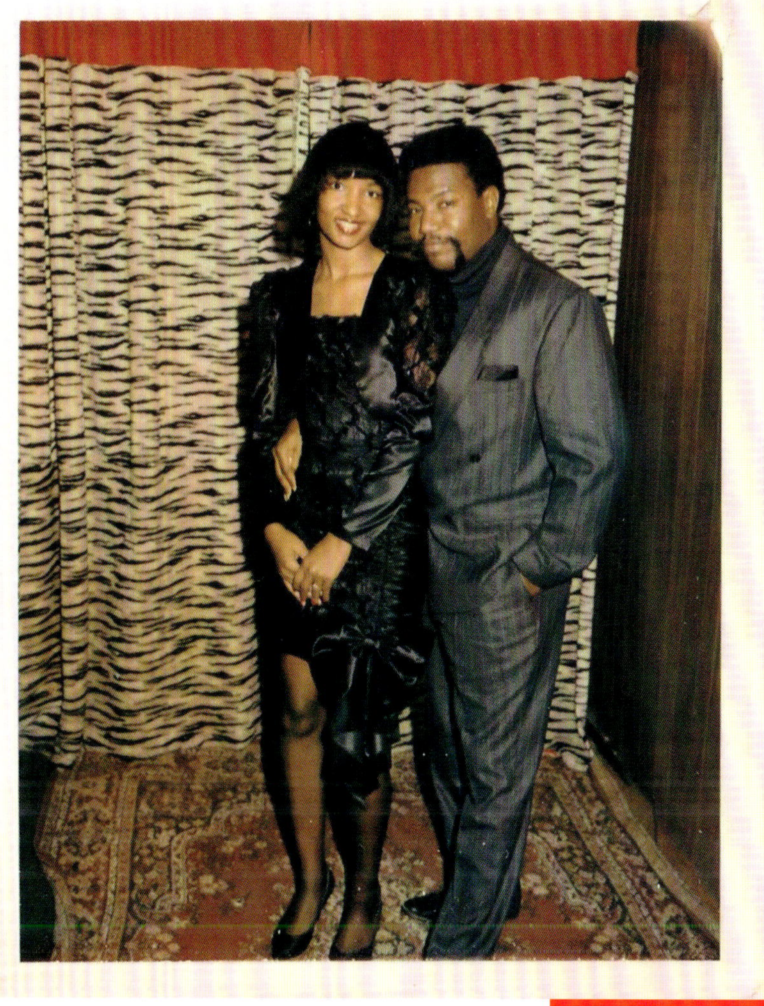

1990

Posing in front of the Golden Gate Bridge

MARIN COUNTY, CA

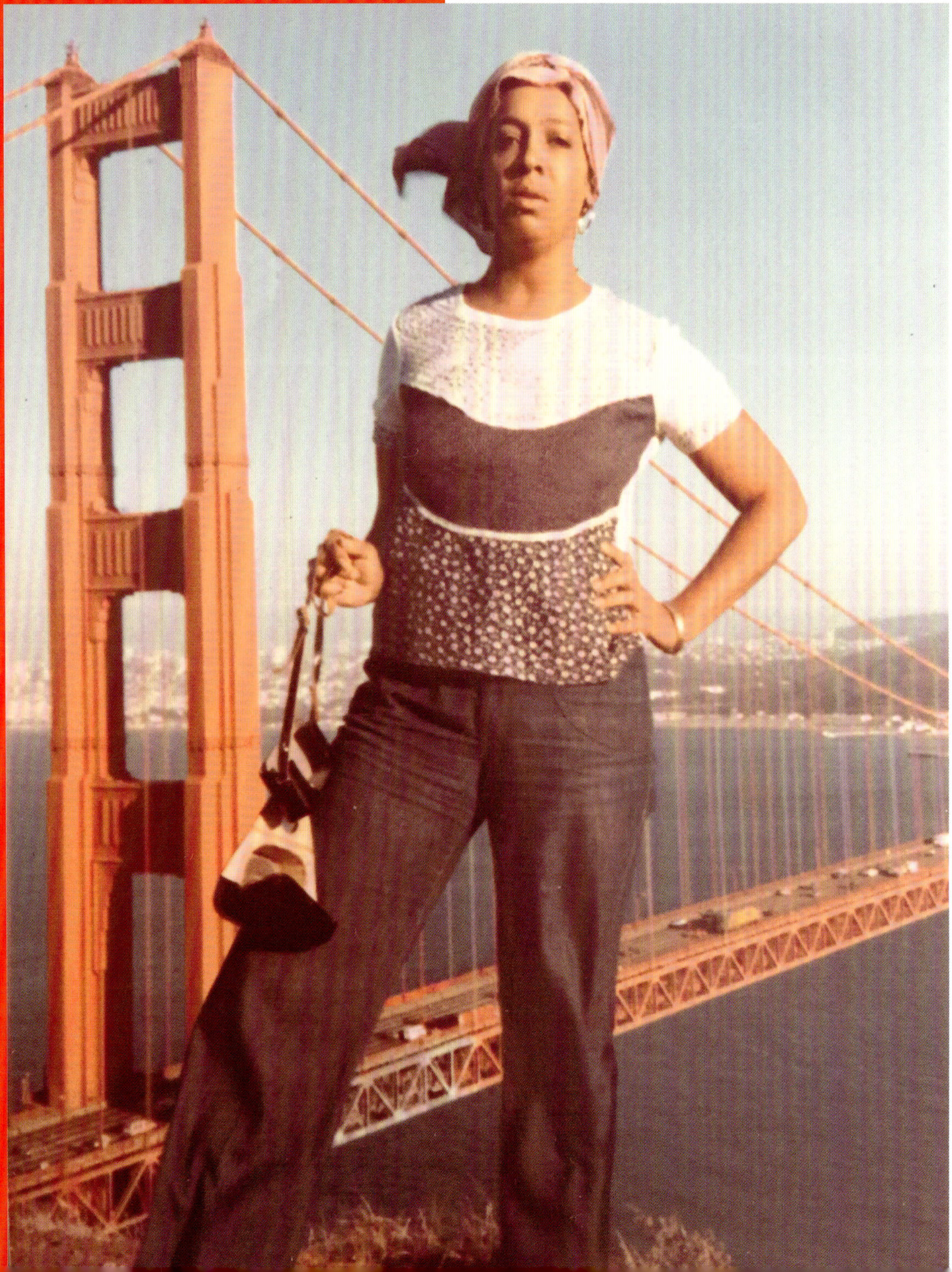

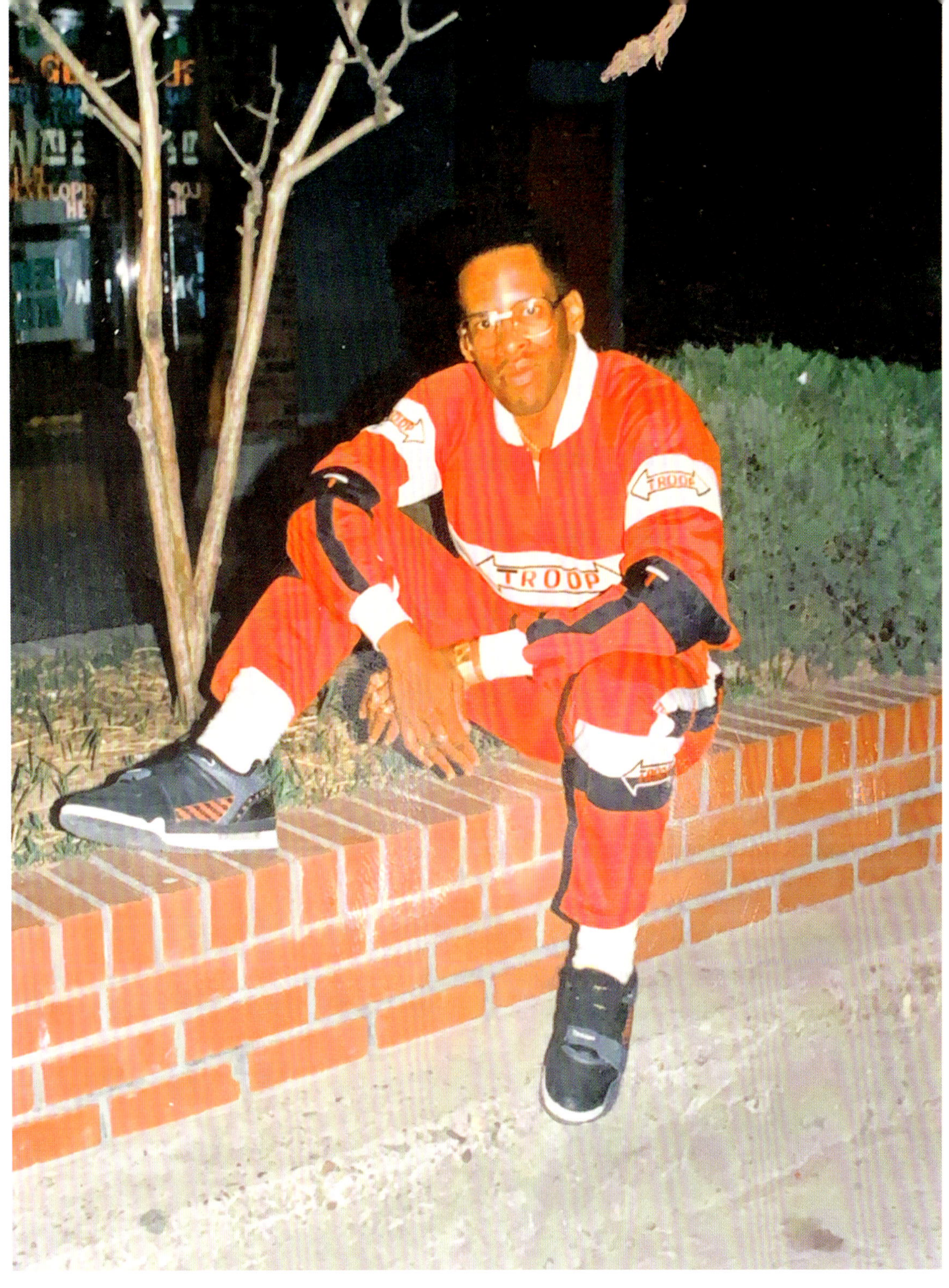

James Lewis during the Summer Olympics

SEOUL, SOUTH KOREA

1988

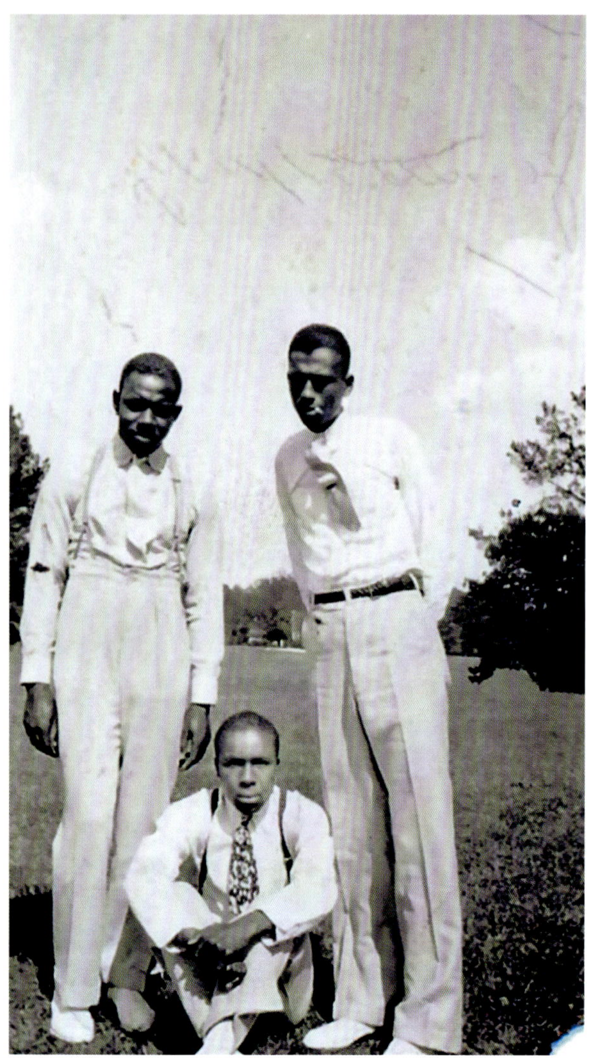

James Murry and friends

CAMDEN, SC

CIRCA 1933

→ WEST VIRGINIA

CIRCA 1942

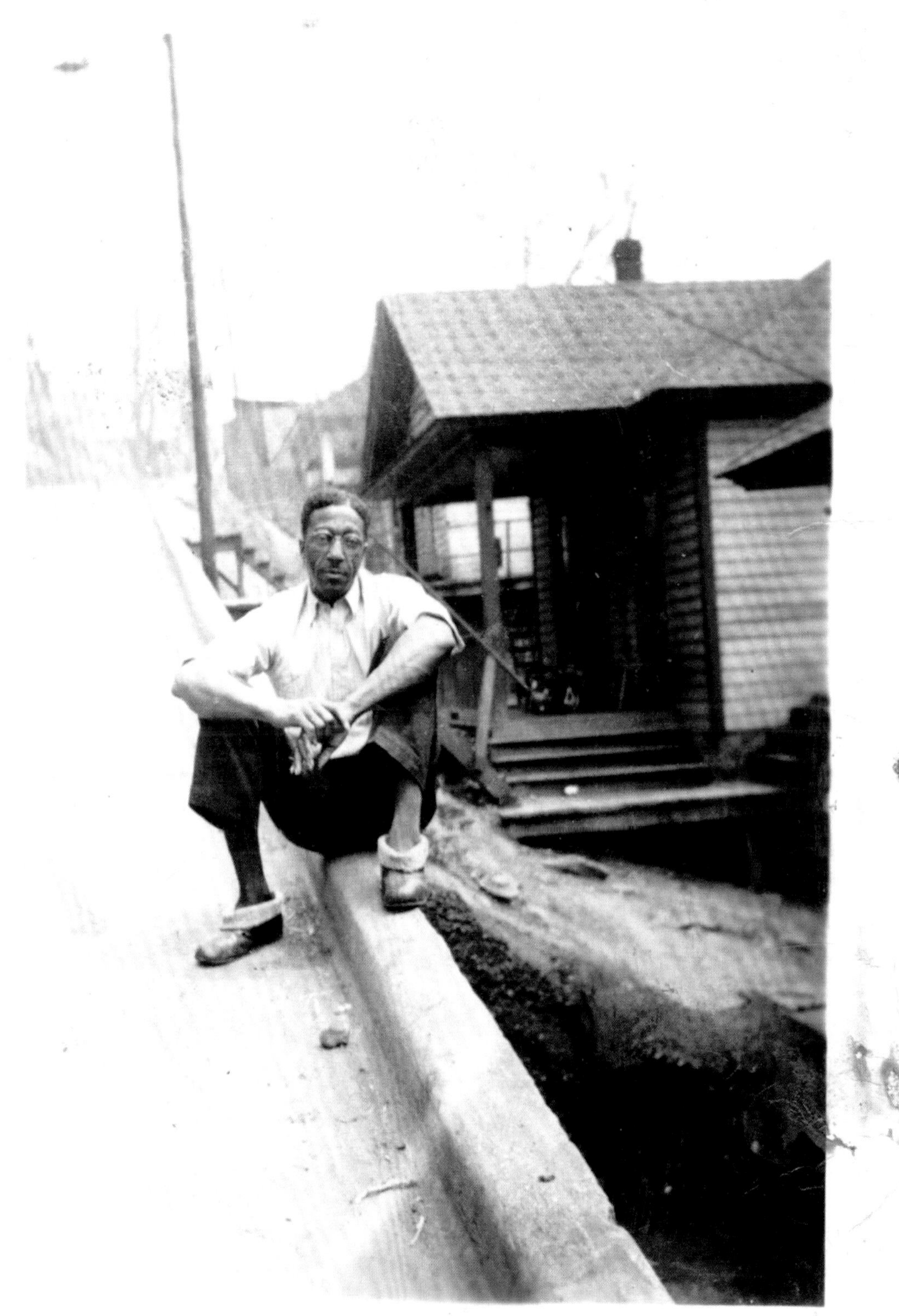

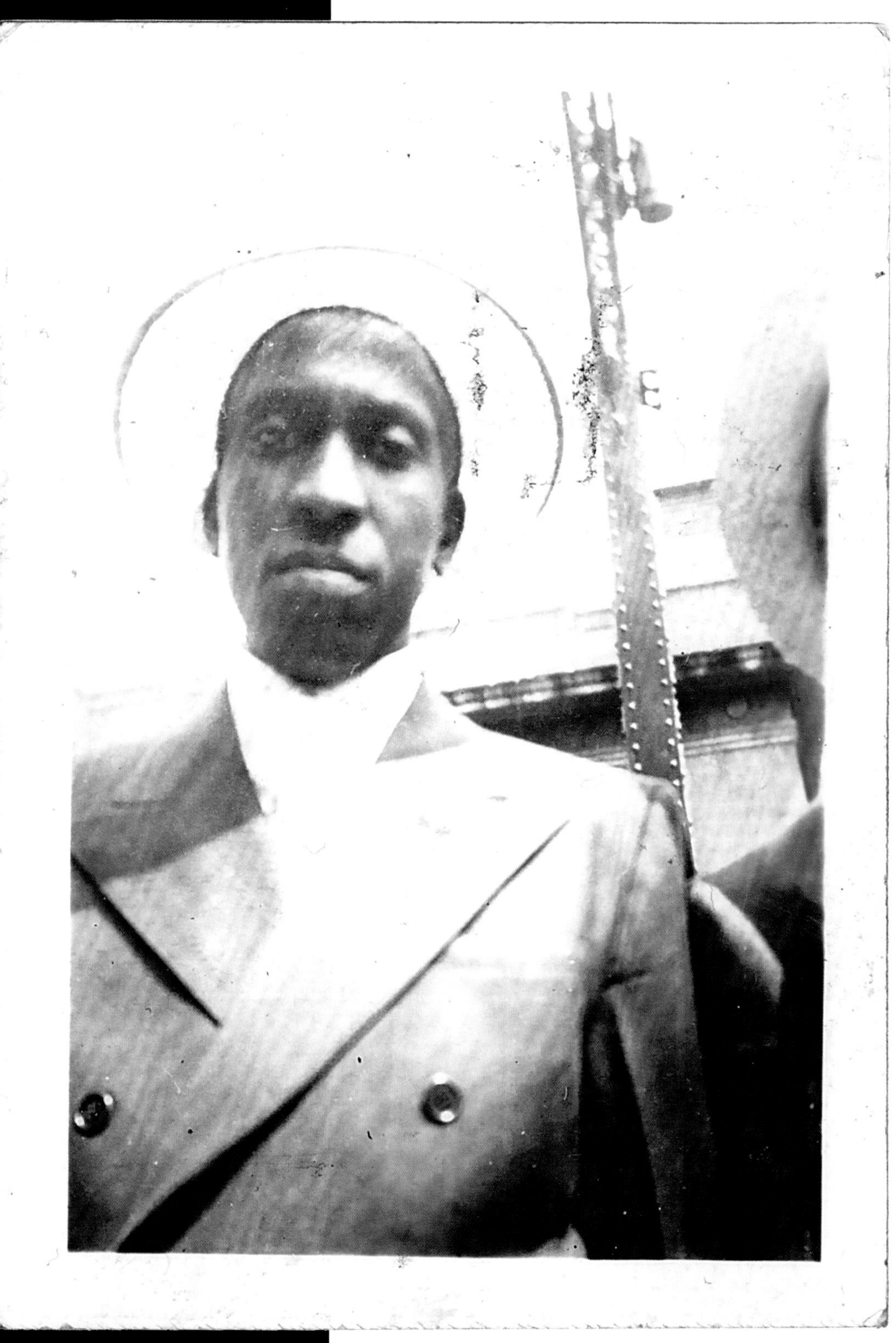

WEST VIRGINIA
CIRCA 1942

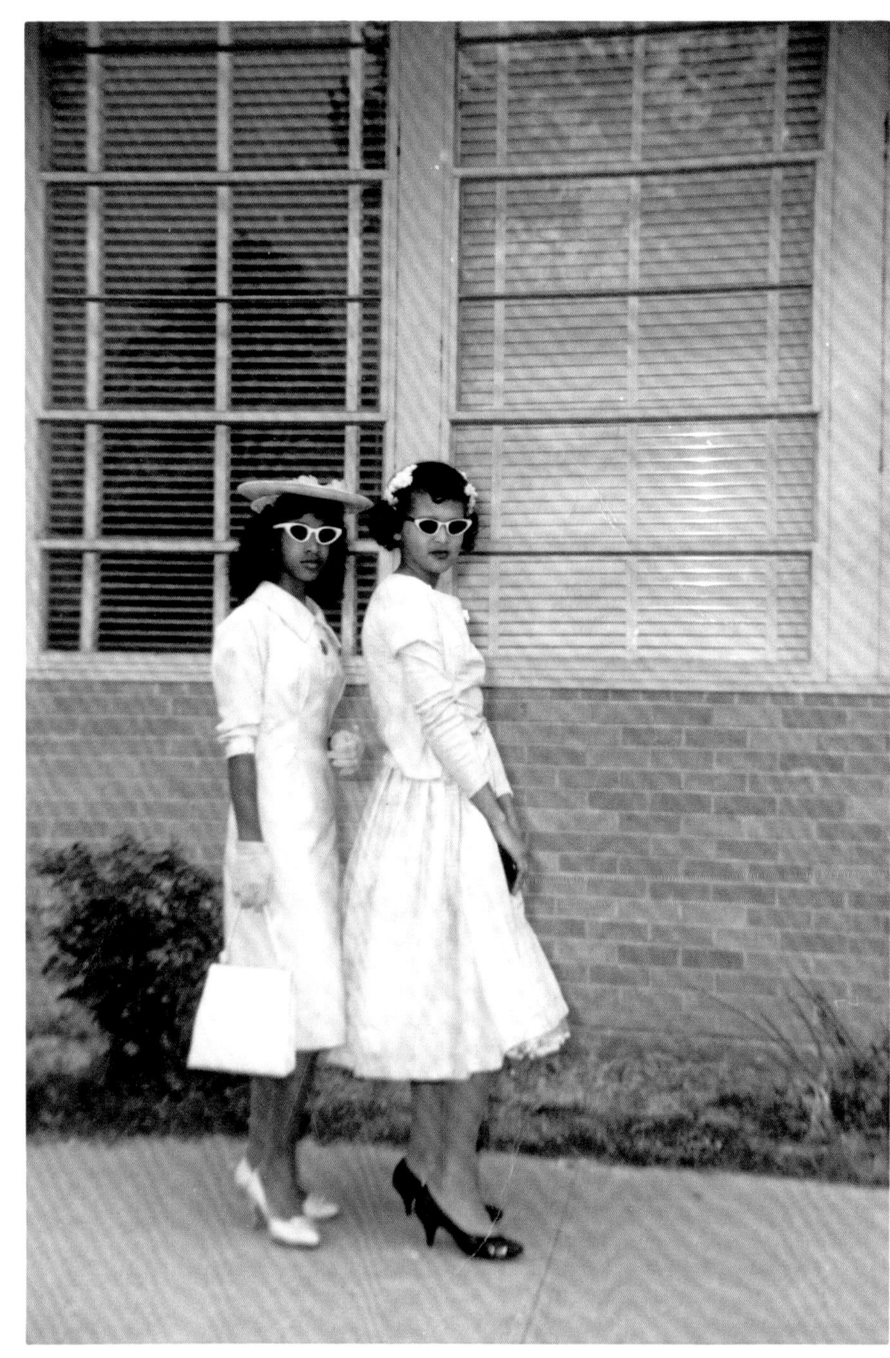

Ladies from Louisiana posing in front of E. J. Campbell High School
NACOGDOCHES COUNTY, TX
1958

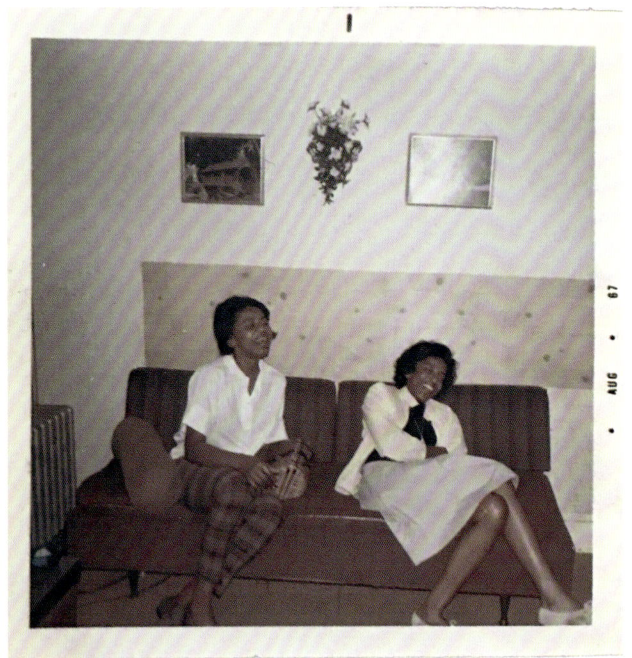

Annetta Taylor and Irene Freeman
1967

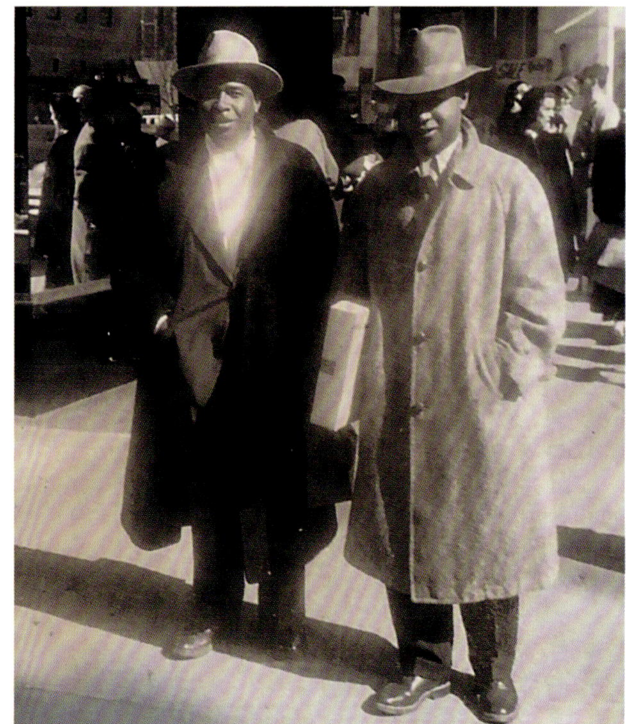

Freshman at Amherst College and his father
AMHERST, MA
1952

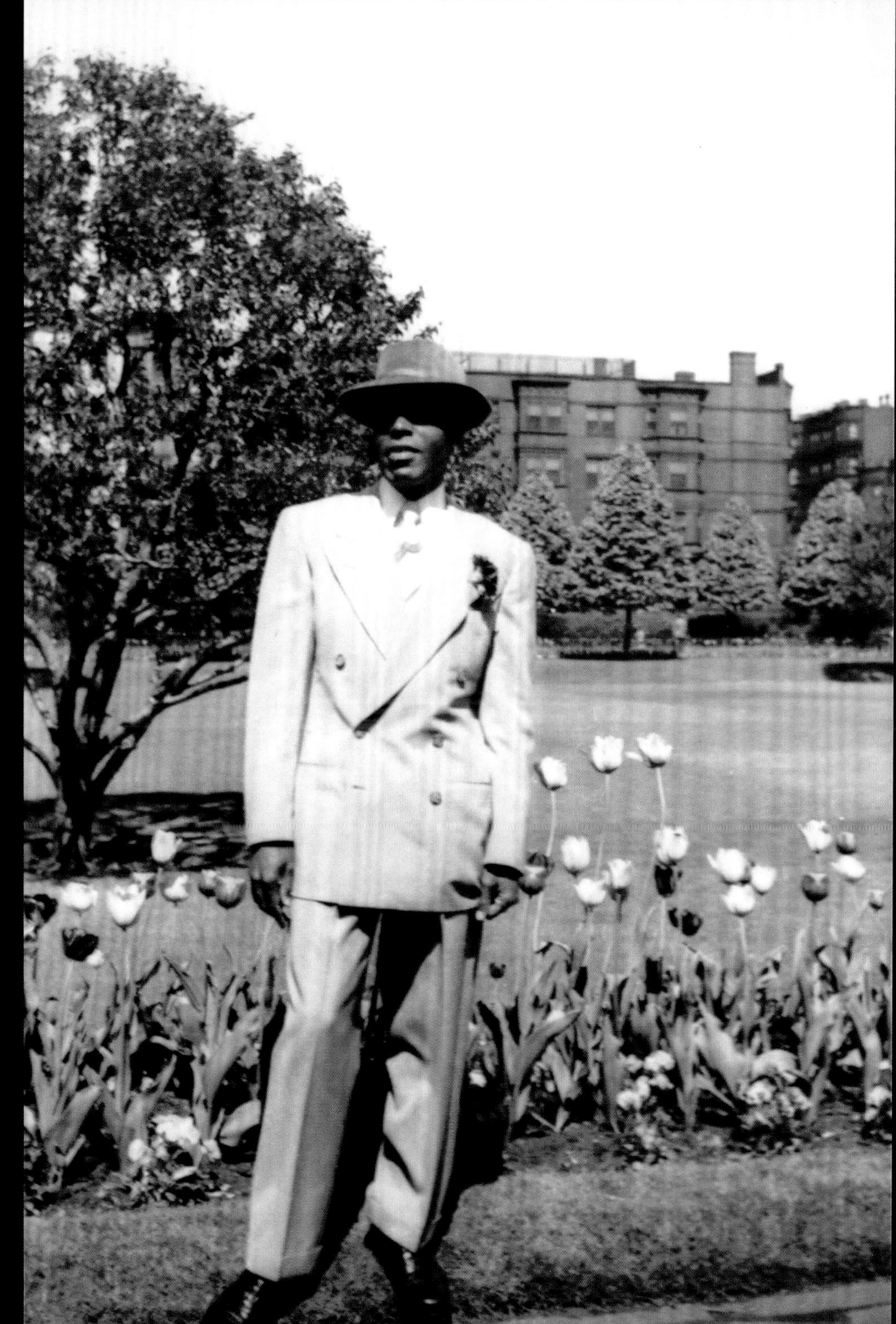

1945

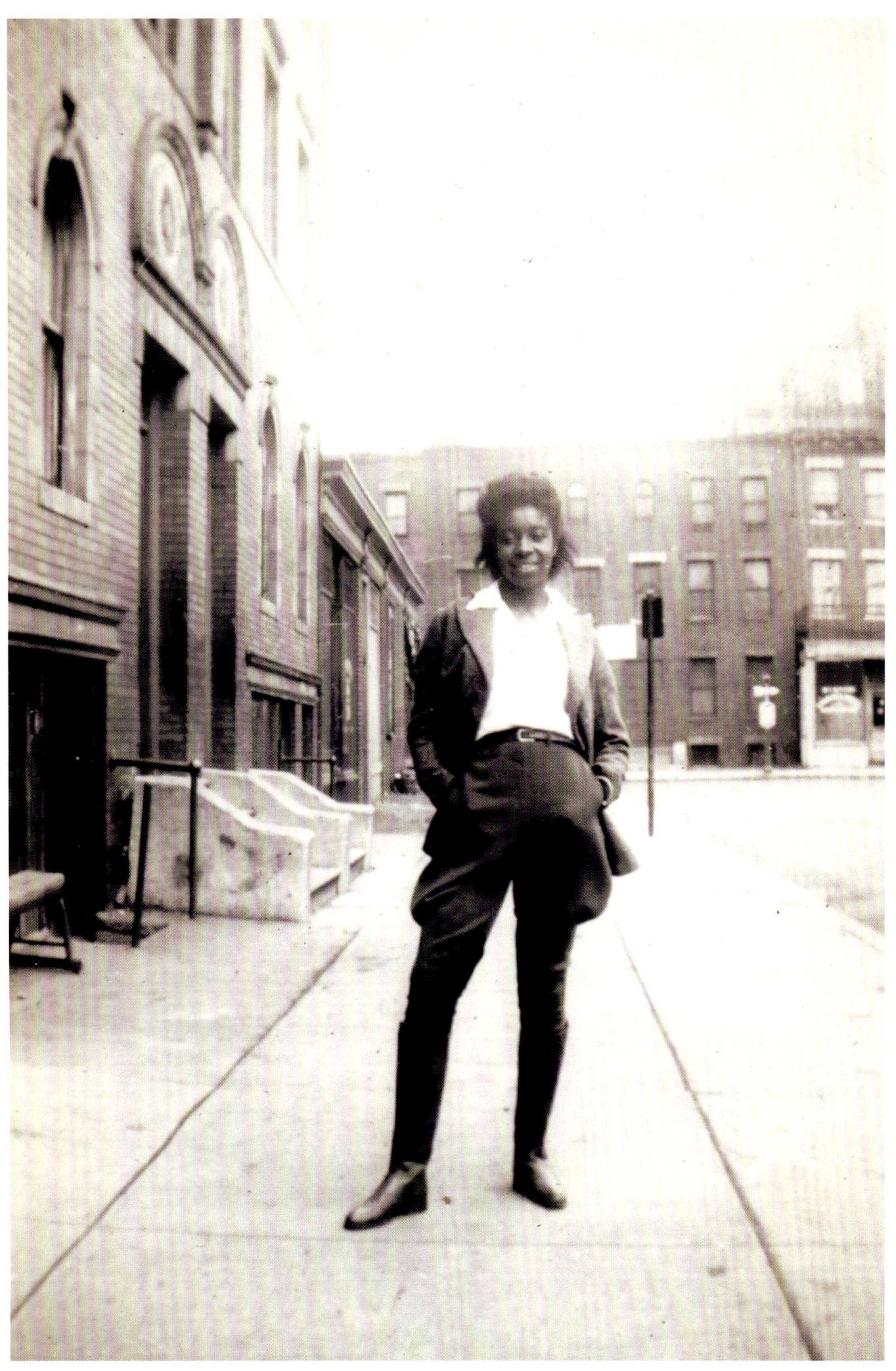

Winnie Irish
returns from riding
in Forest Hills
CIRCA 1940

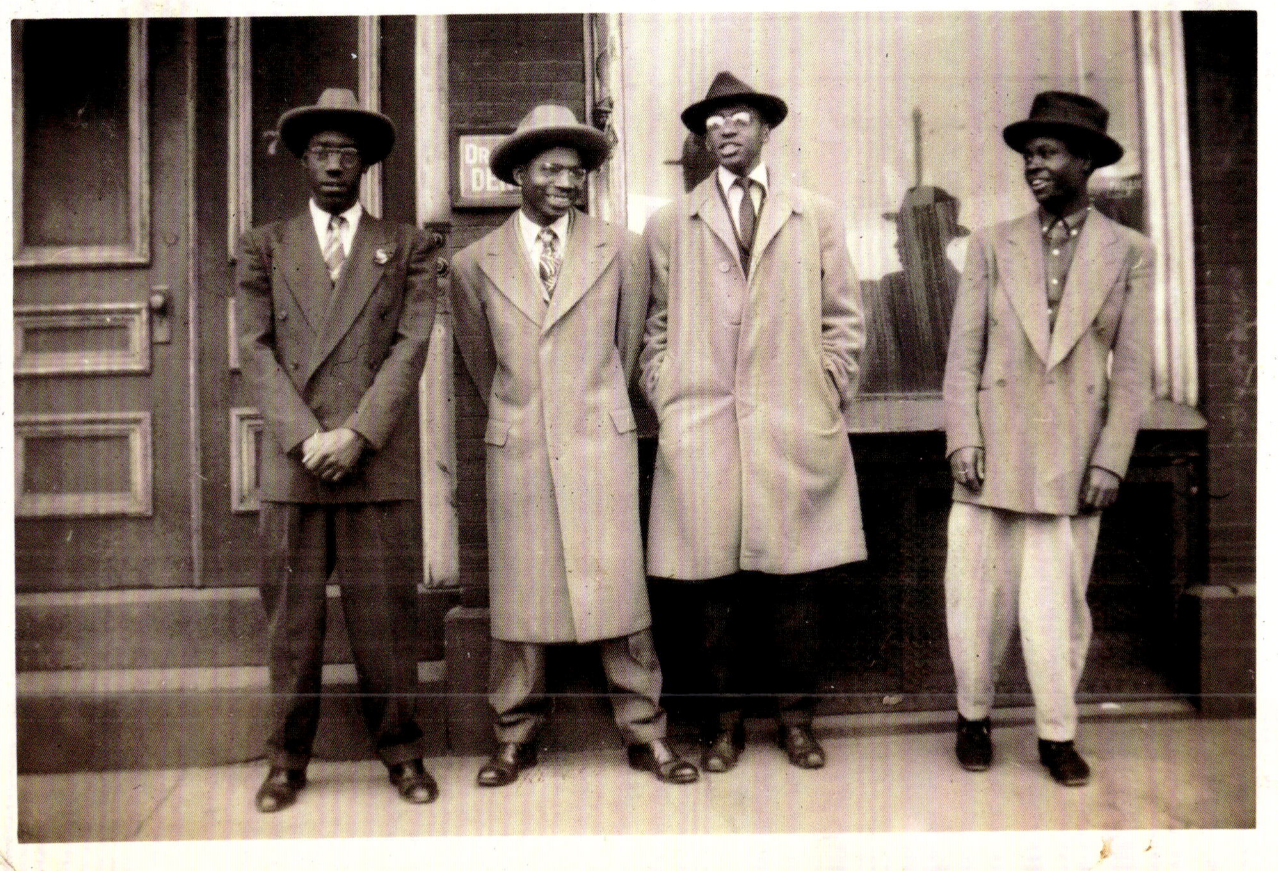

Tremont Street

BOSTON, MA

CIRCA 1940

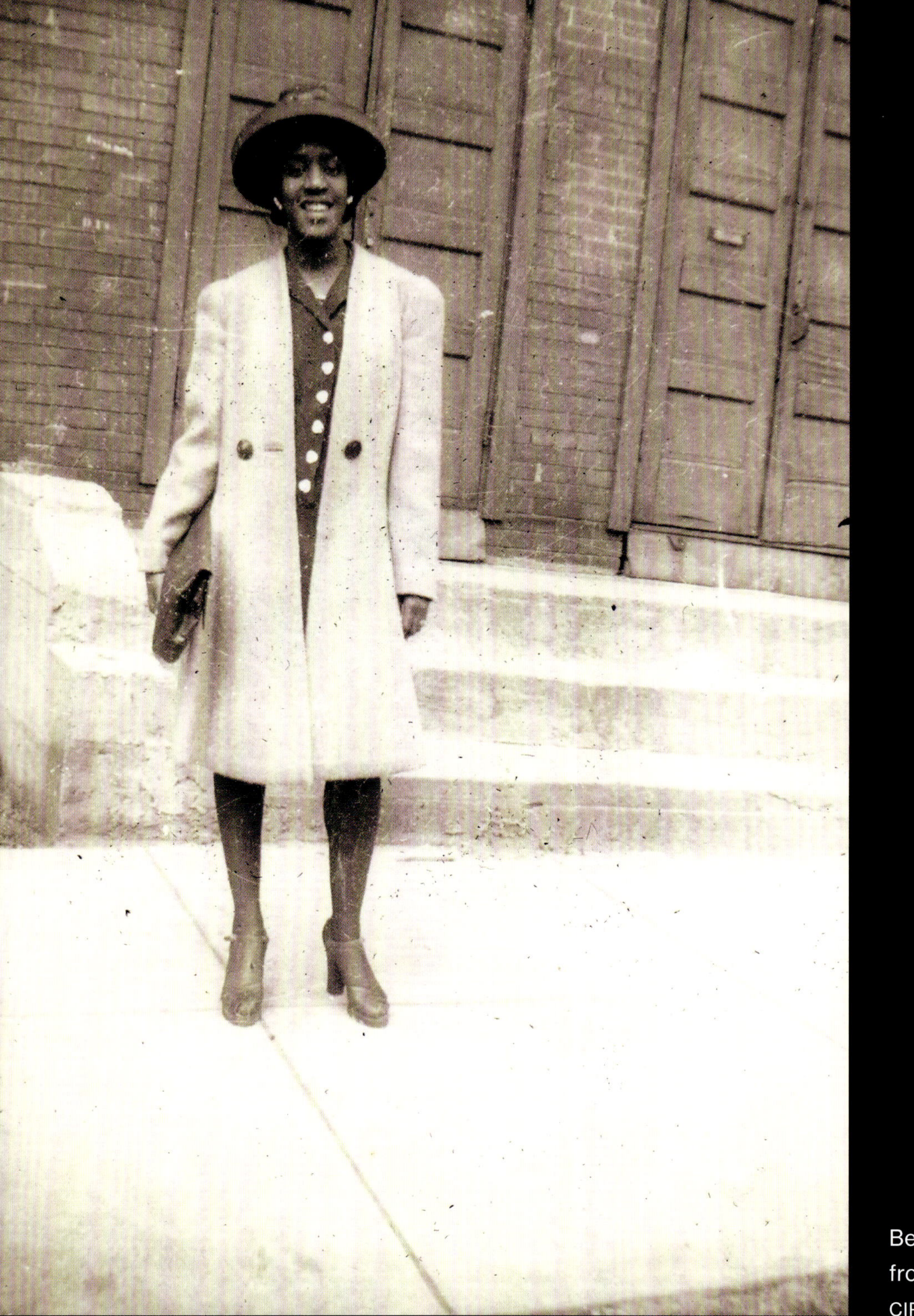

Belle Rotch in
front of churc
CIRCA 1940

Samuel Johnson Sr. and Sammy the Doberman in Hunters Point
SAN FRANCISCO, CA
1972

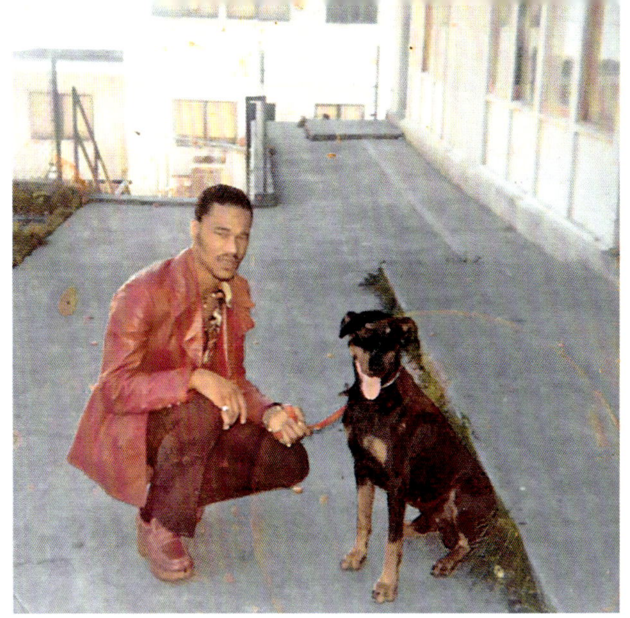

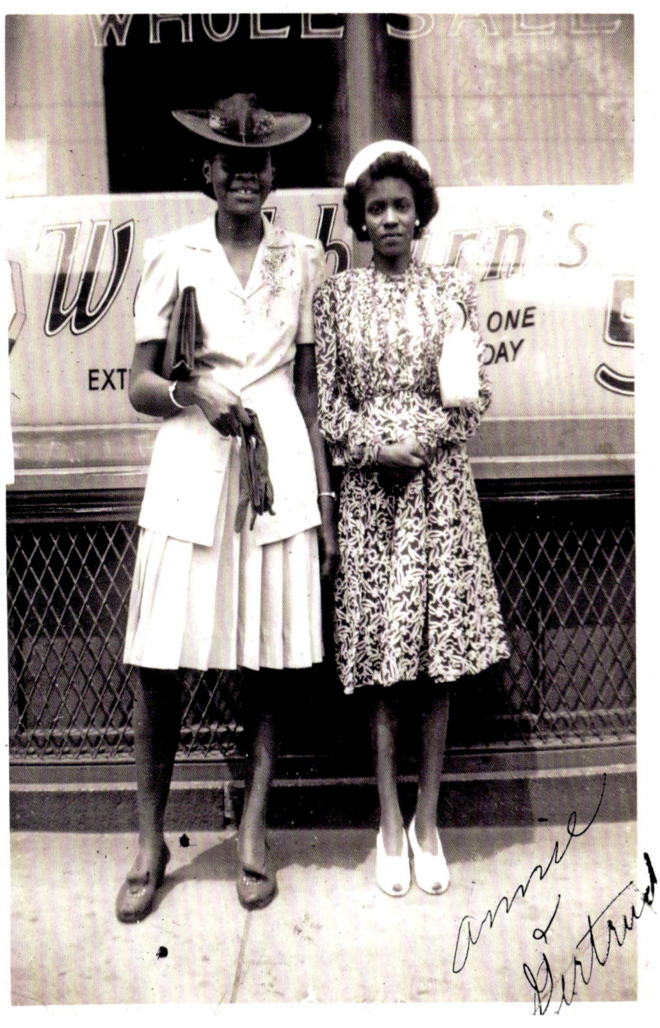

Annie and Gertude on Tremont Street
BOSTON, MA
CIRCA 1945

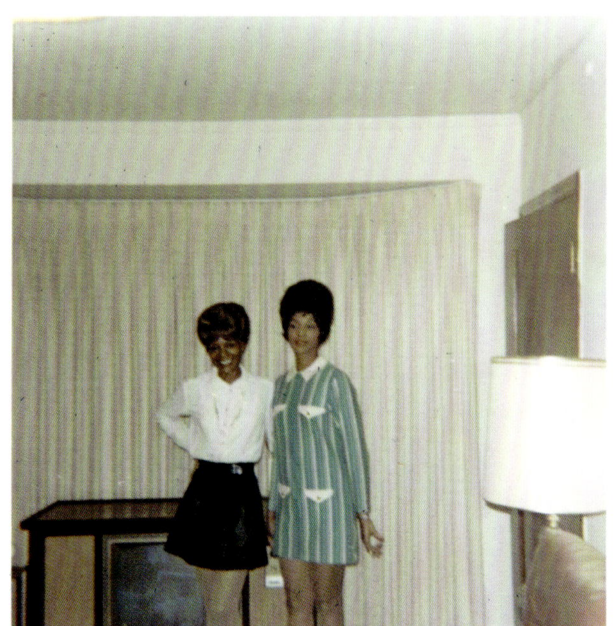

The Odom family home

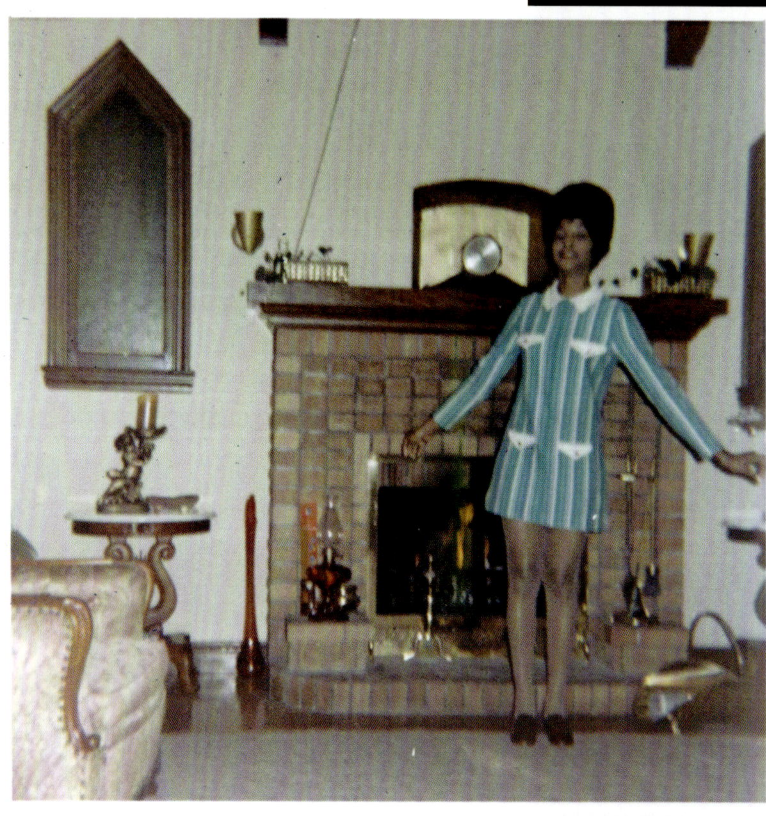

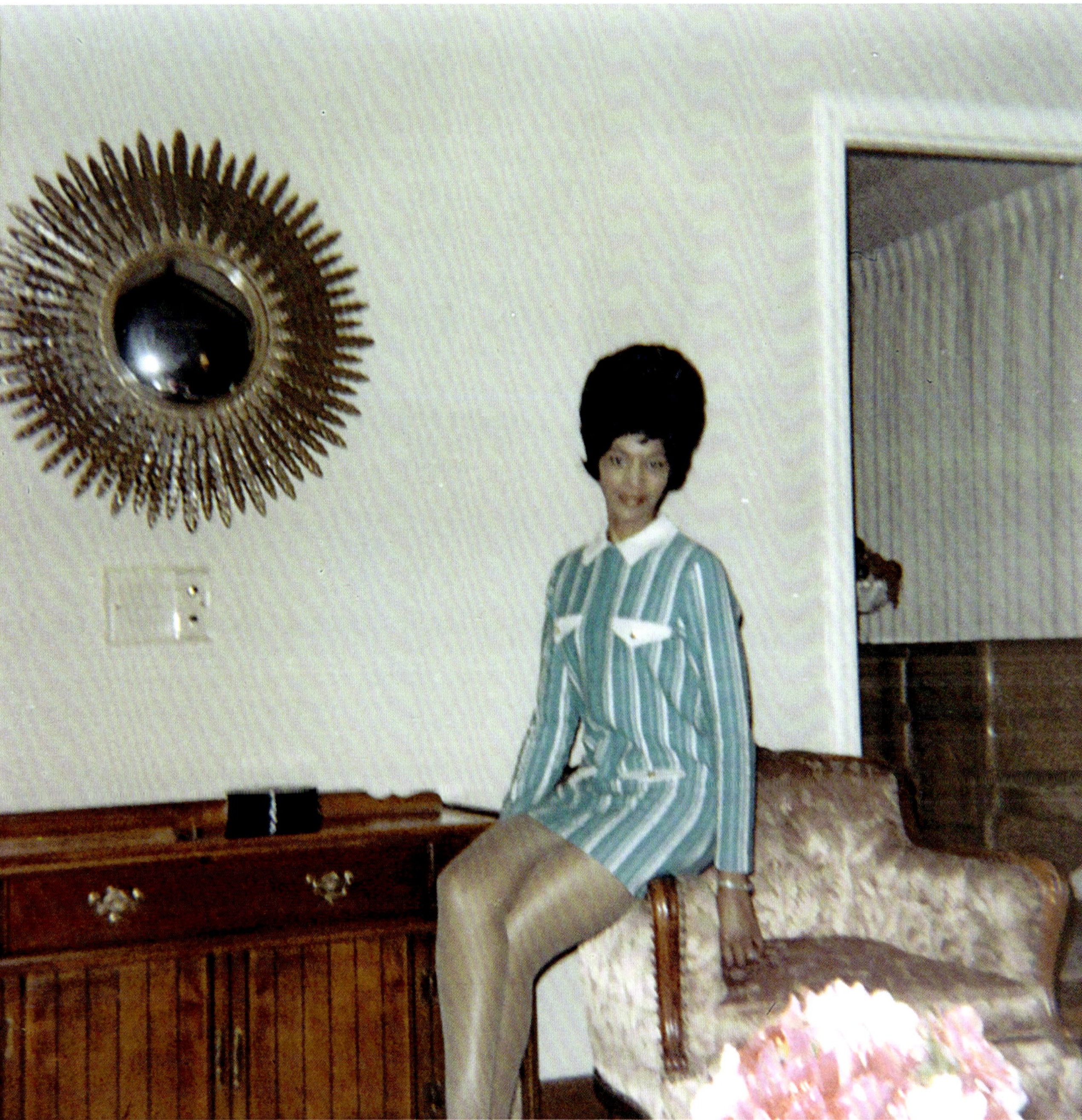

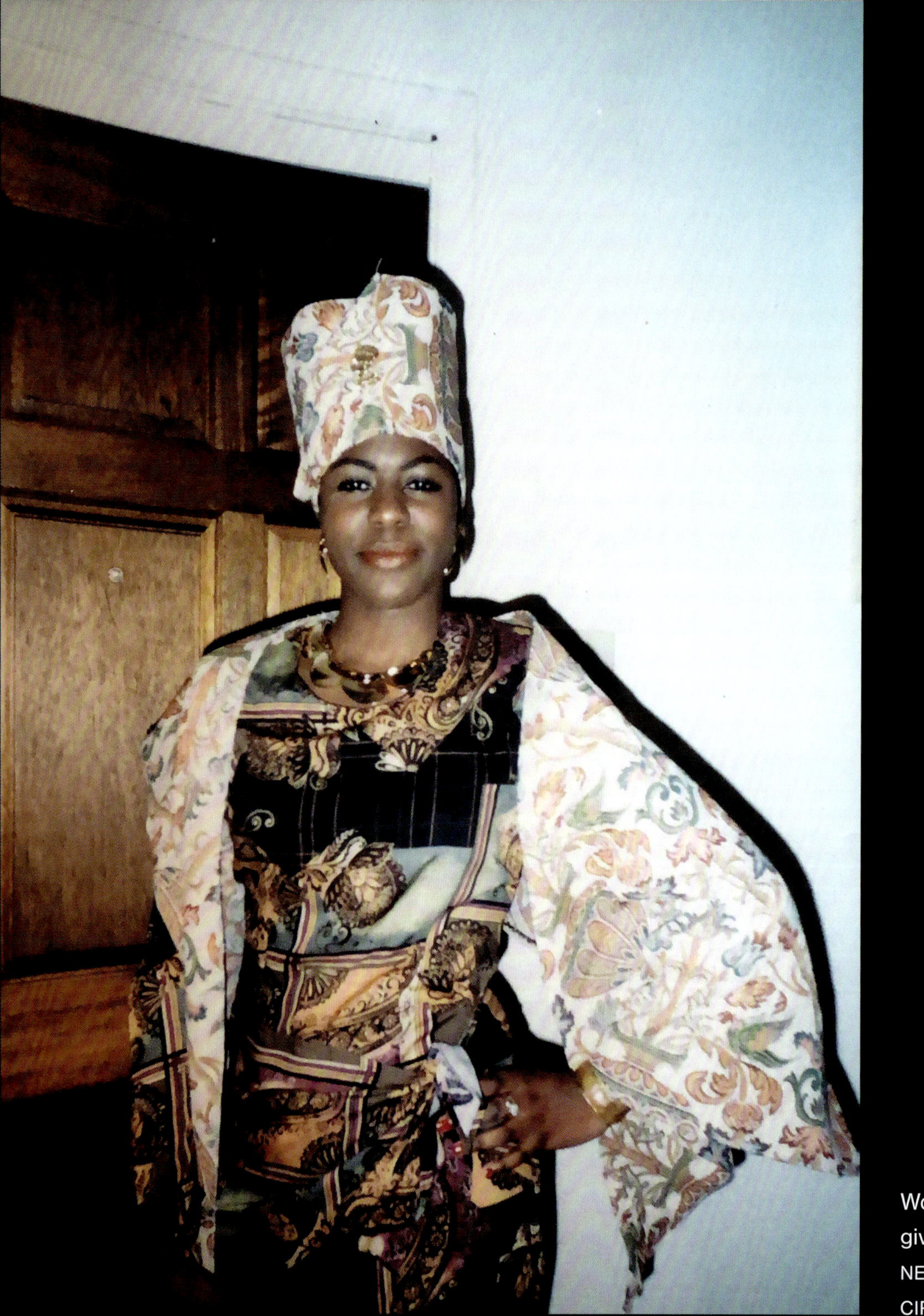

Woman wearing a dress given to her by a relative
NEW ORLEANS, LA
CIRCA 1996

HOUSE PHONE ONLY
George V - Paris
Hotel Des Bergues-Switzerland

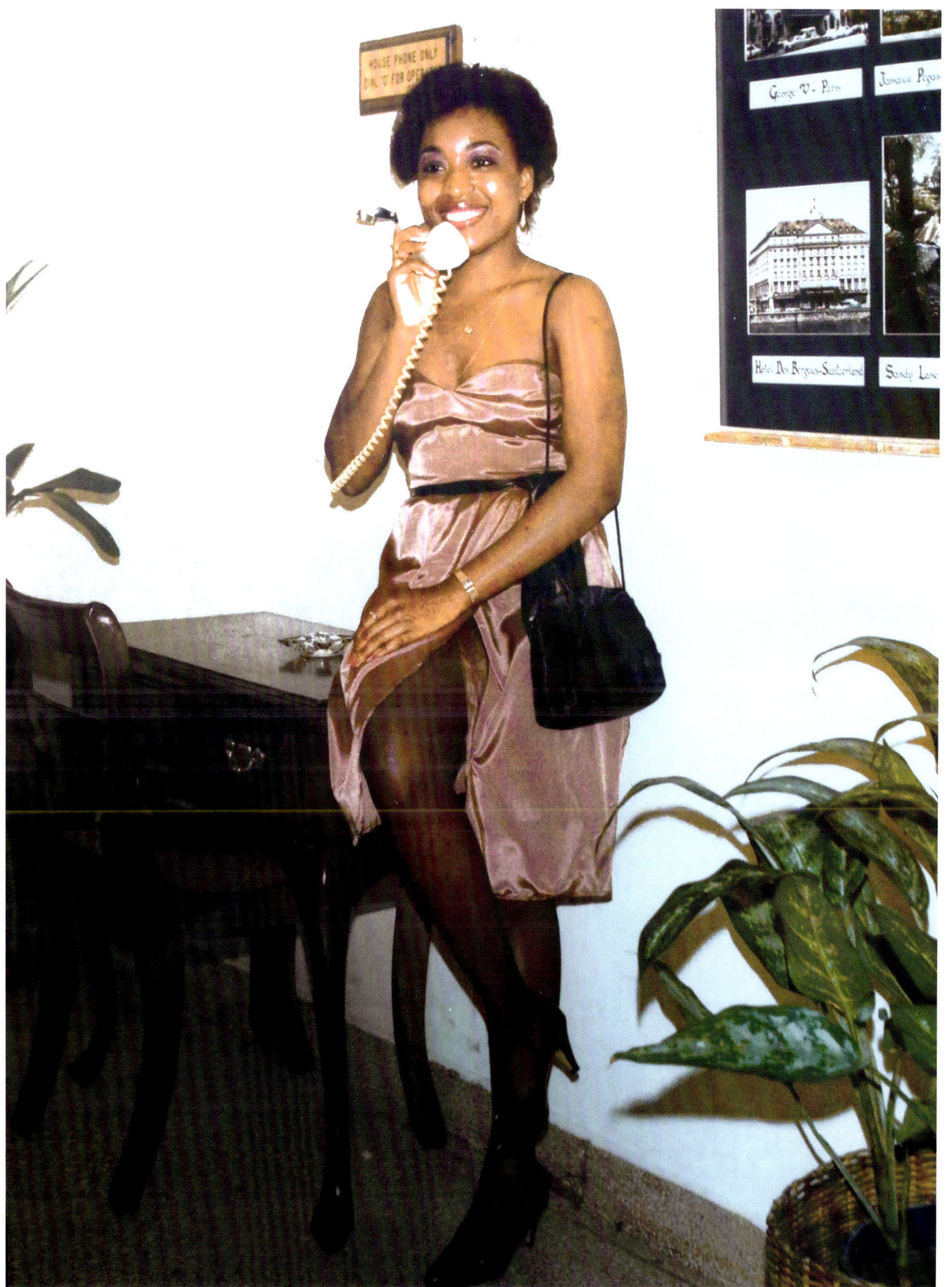

JAMAICA

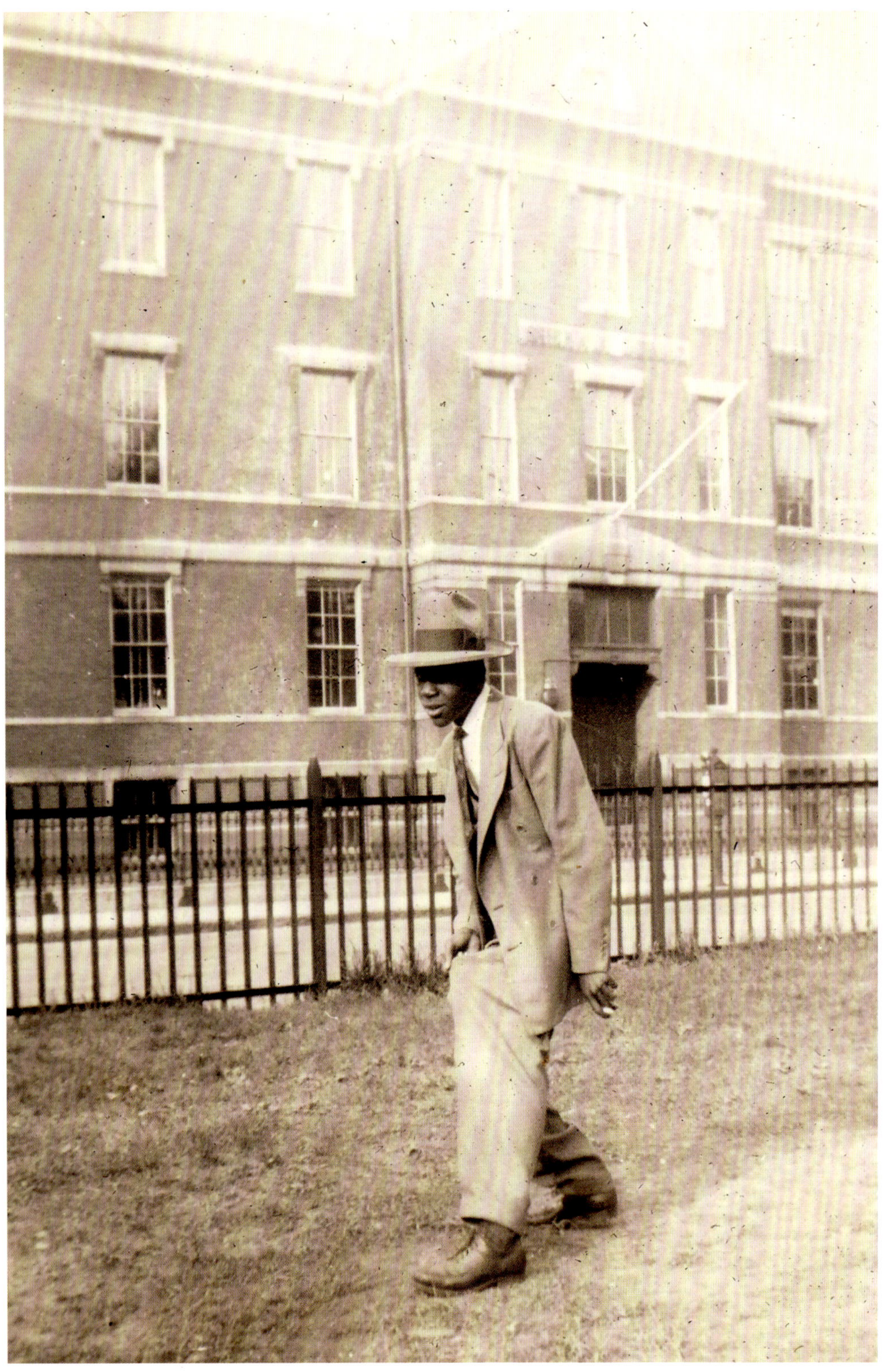

Sherwin School on Sterling Street
BOSTON, MA
CIRCA 1945

→ BALTIMORE, MD
1970S

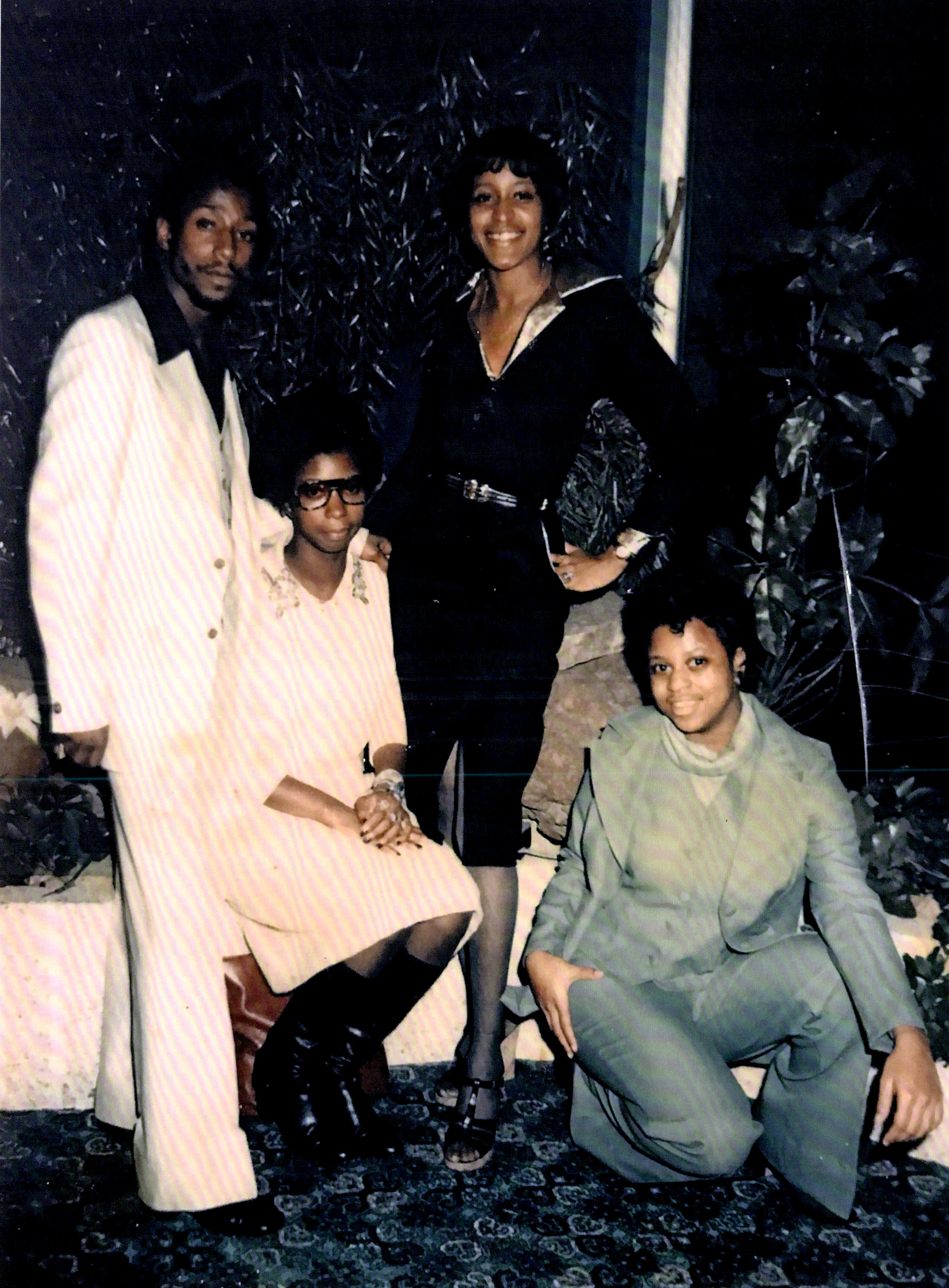

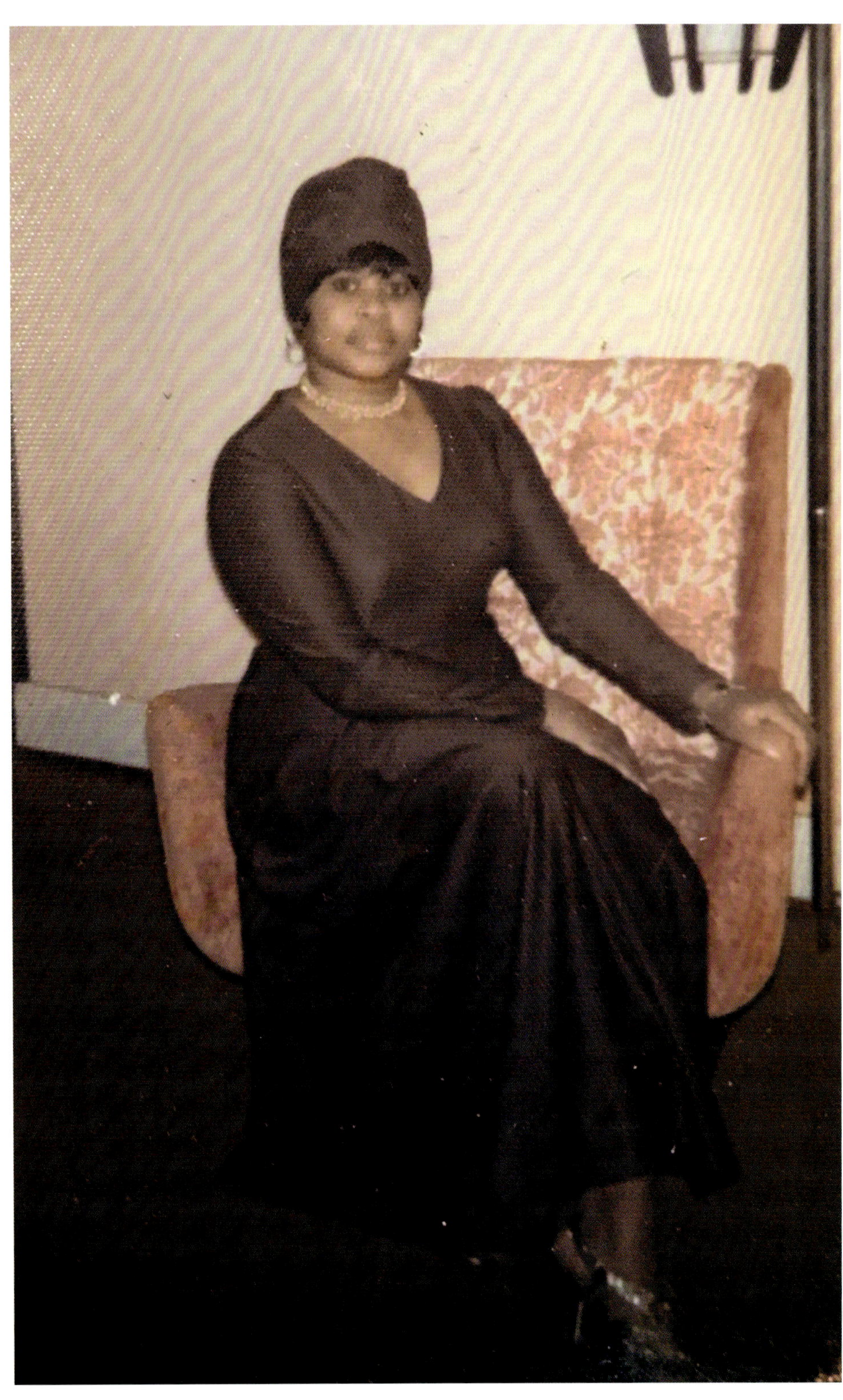

A night out
NEWPORT NEWS, VA
1970S

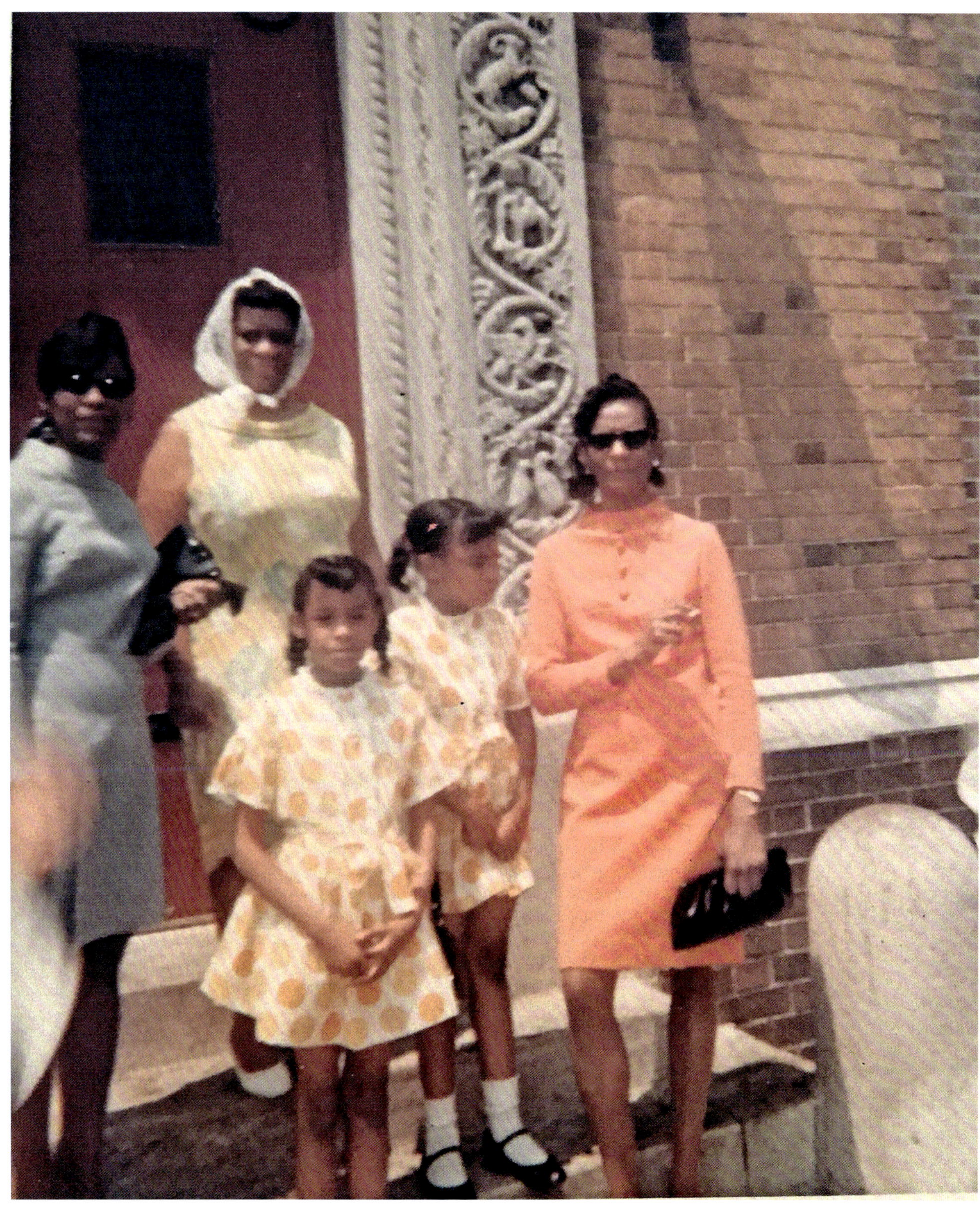

1960S

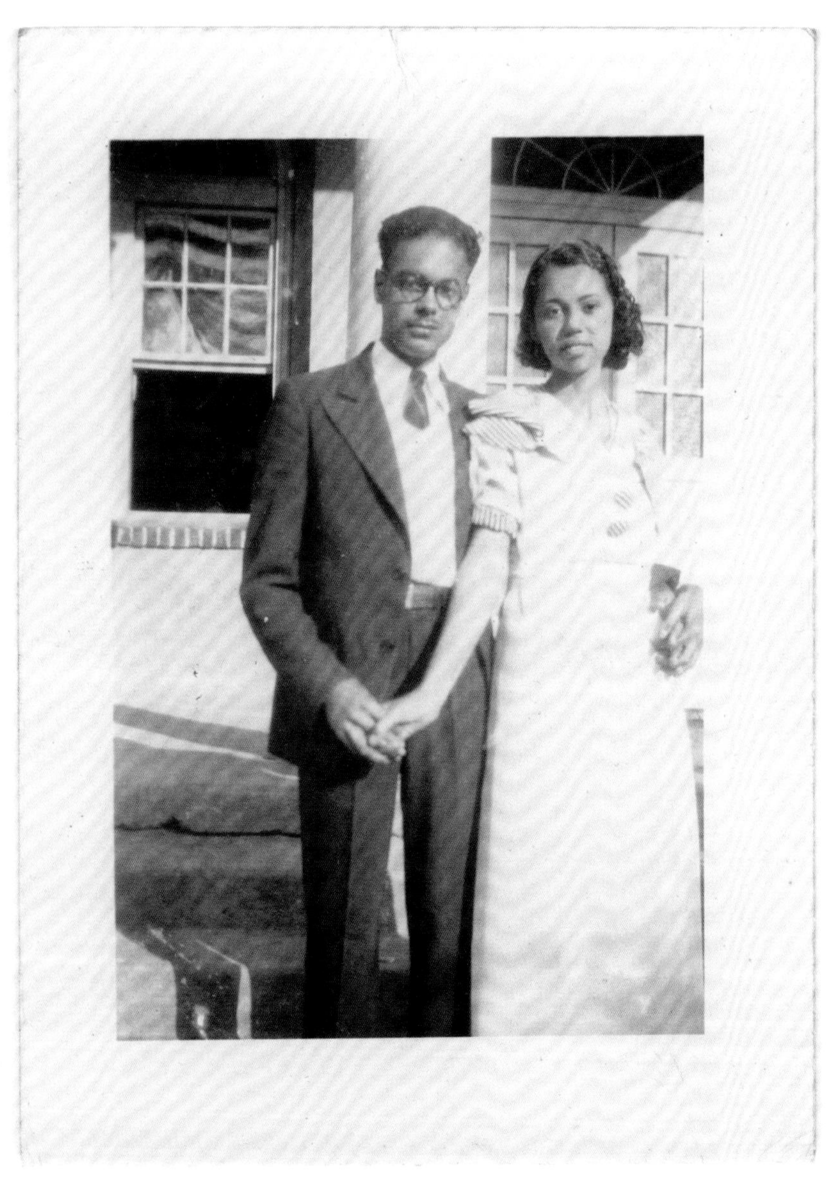

CIRCA 1934

→ Folsom State Prison

FOLSOM, CA

1991

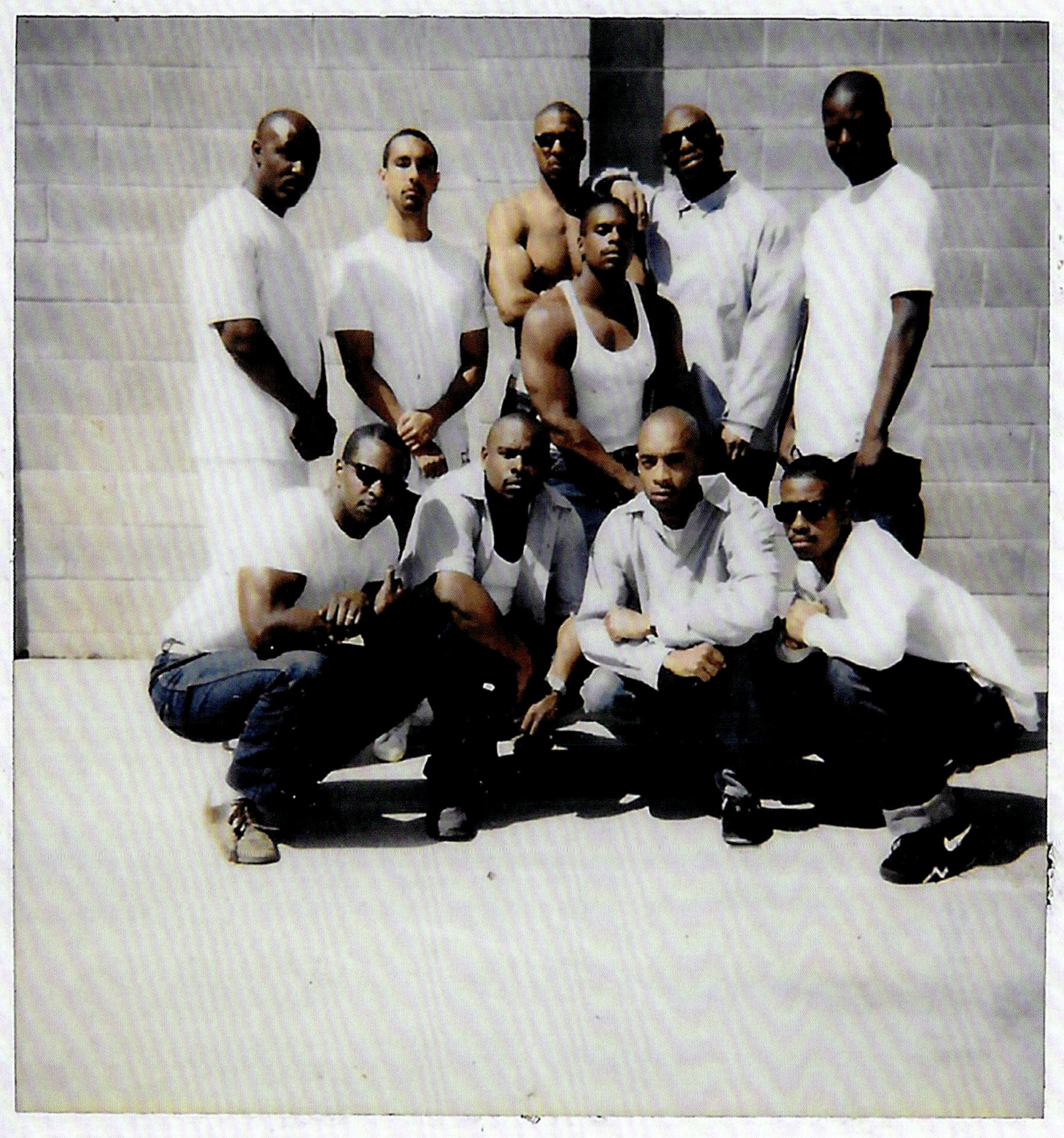

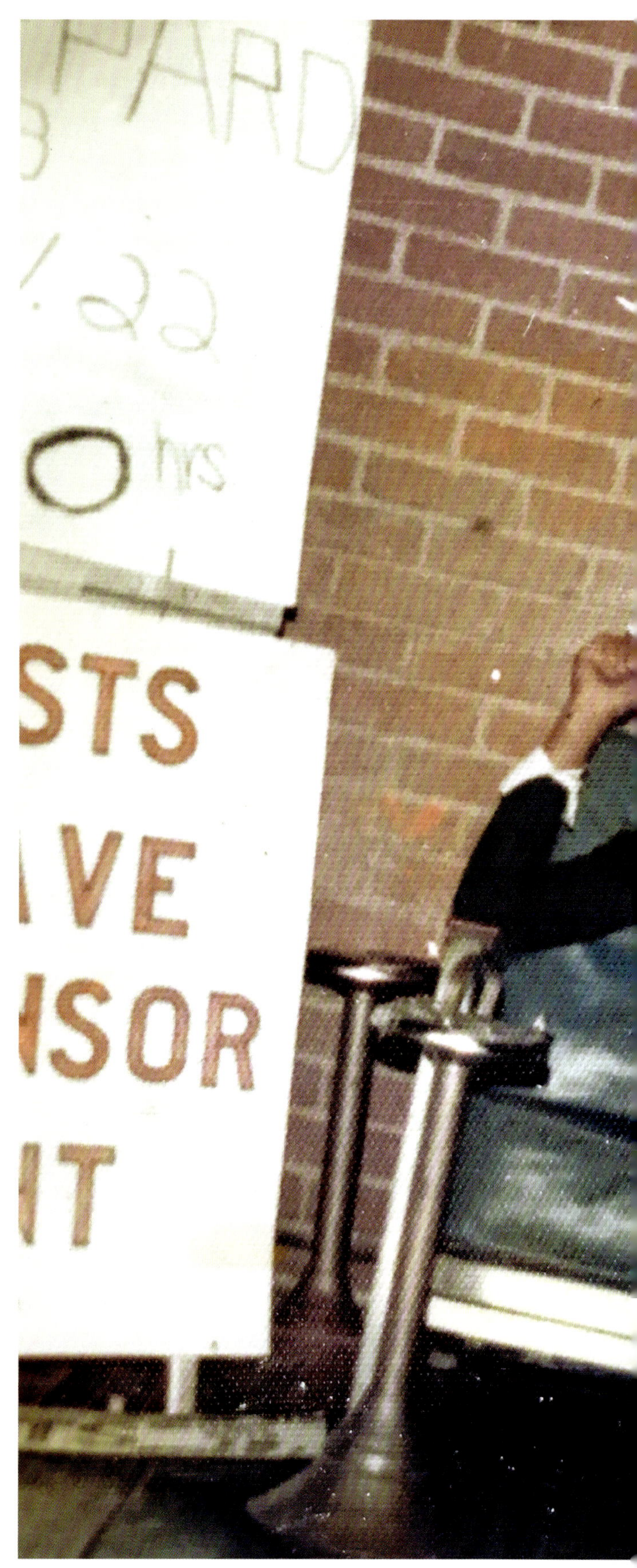
PARD
22
hrs
STS
AVE
NSOR

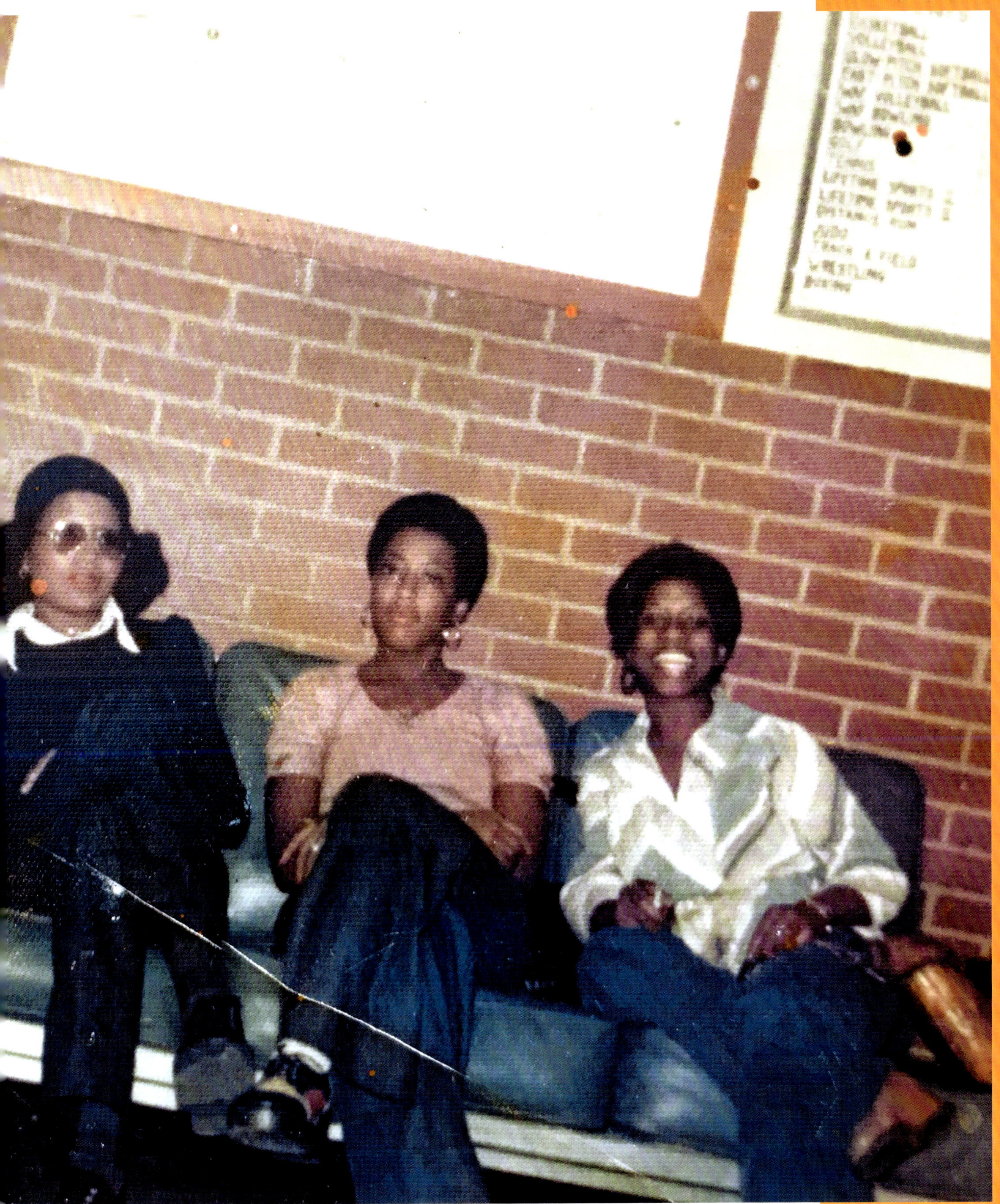

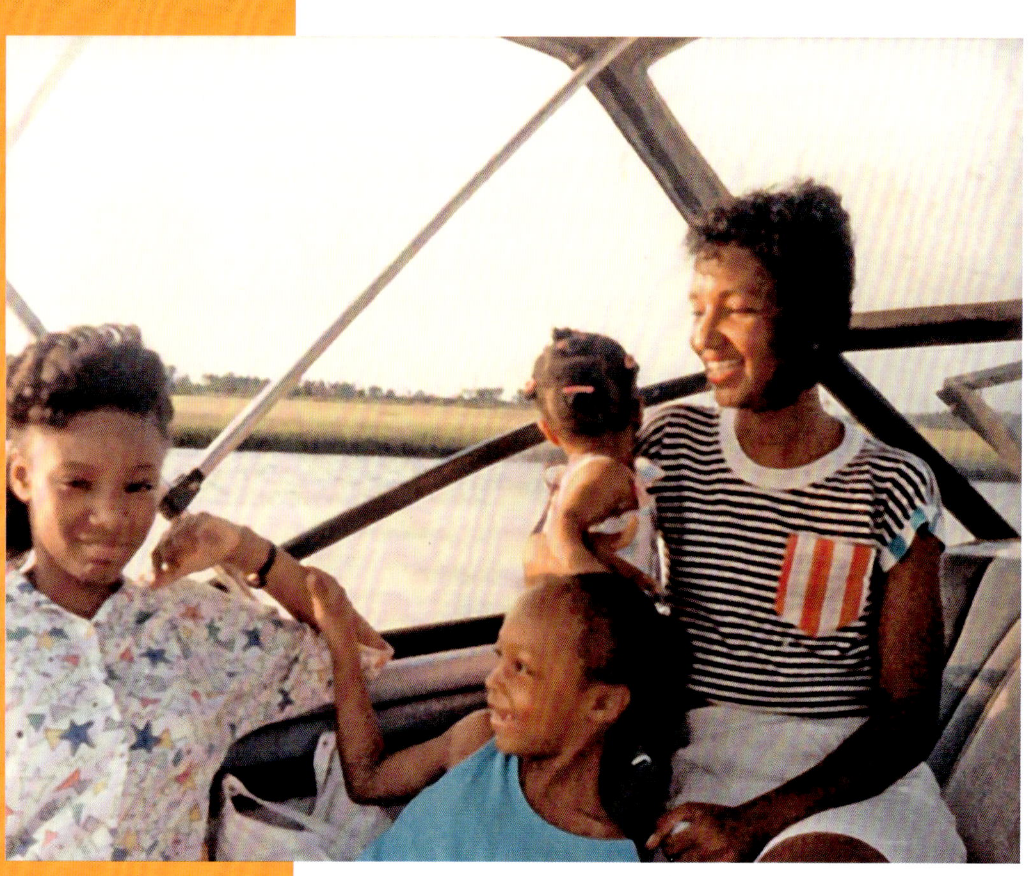

The author and her family out on a boat
JACKSONVILLE, FL
1988

LANDSCAPES AND OUTDOORS

Being outside is one of my favorite pastimes. I spent nearly all my childhood and adolescence outdoors playing by myself or with friends, or spending time with family. And in a coastal southern city such as Jacksonville, the heat makes you want to seek out a breeze and be on or near the water. From hanging out at the beach and pool to fishing and crabbing in the St. Johns River to taking boat rides through the local marshes and wetlands, the water has always been my home away from home.

But being outside and experiencing the outdoors as Black folks is more than just the act of connecting with the land and its resources. It can be therapeutic and liberating, enabling our thoughts to roam while also giving us the space to be together, and to connect with ourselves, our bodies, and our minds.

This series takes us along the scenic route while immersing us in various outdoor spaces as experienced and occupied by Black people.

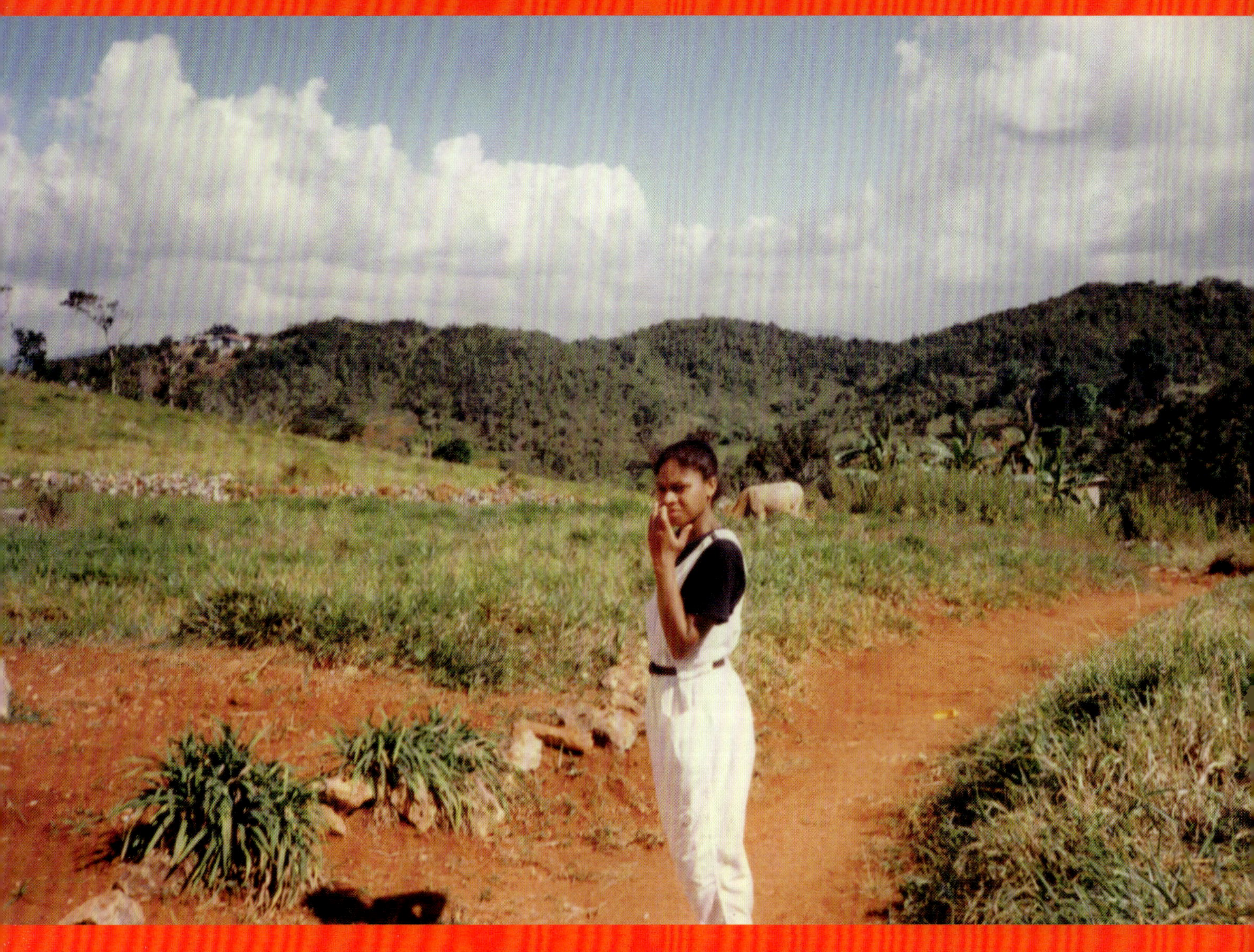

JAMAICA
1980S

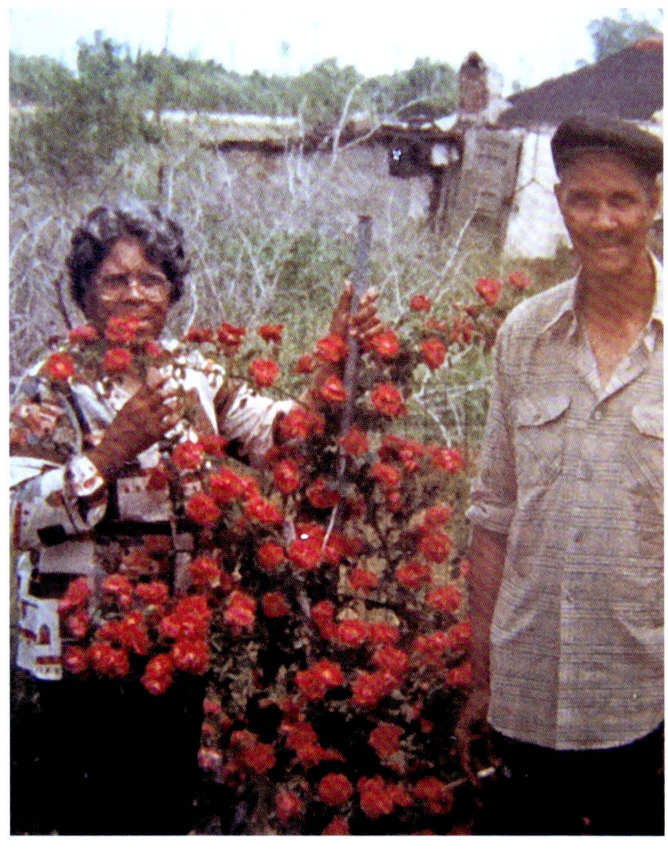

GARY, IN
1983

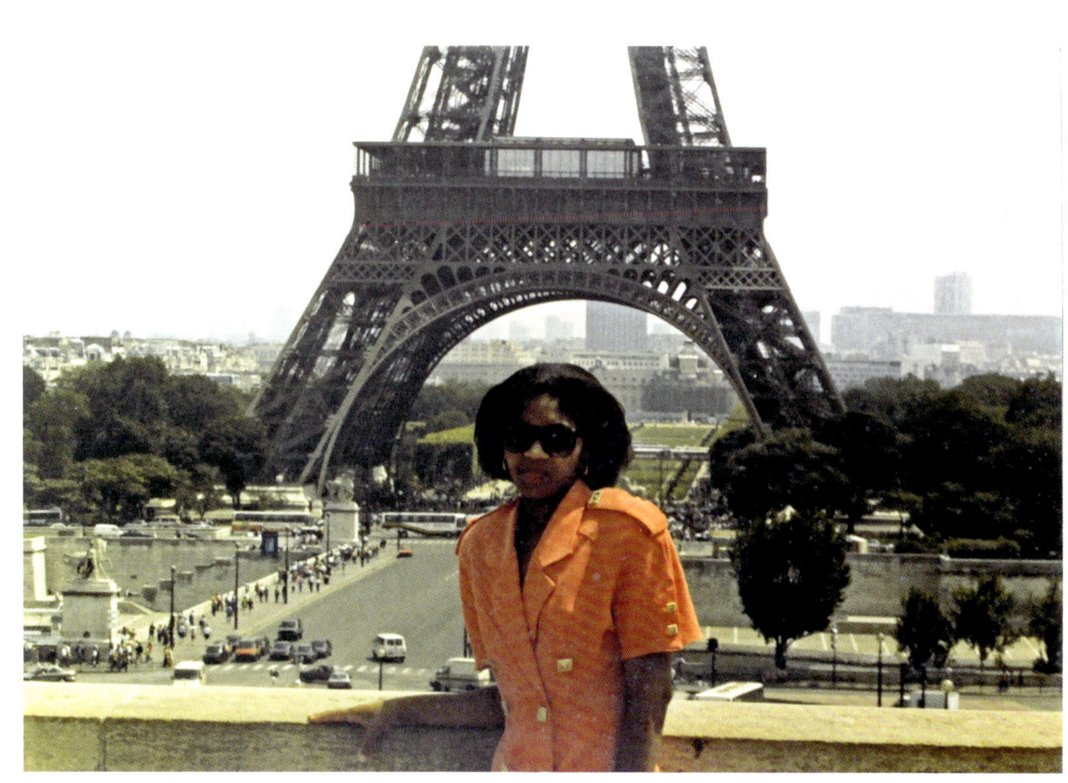

PARIS, FRANCE
1980S

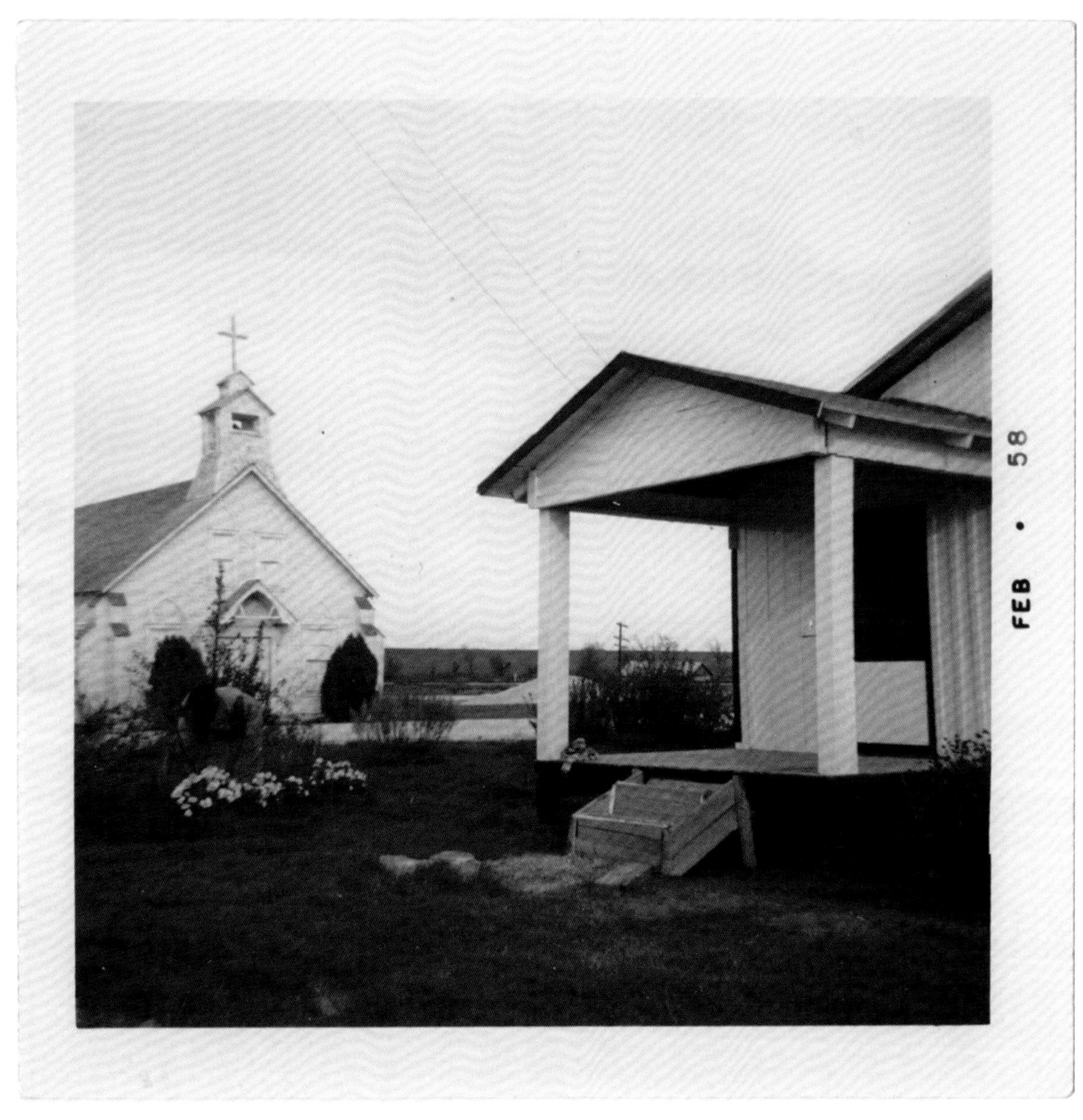

TEXAS
1958

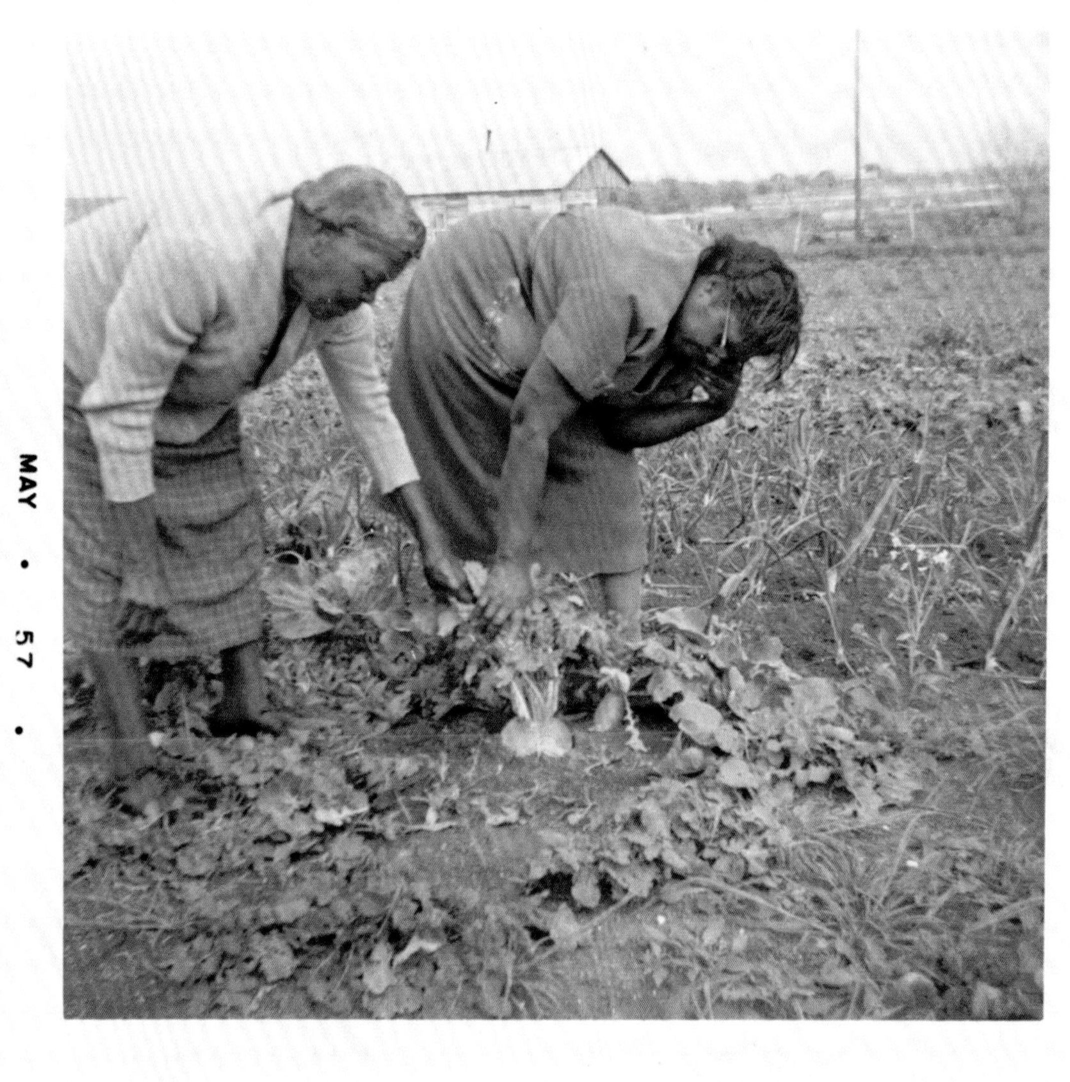

TEXAS
1957

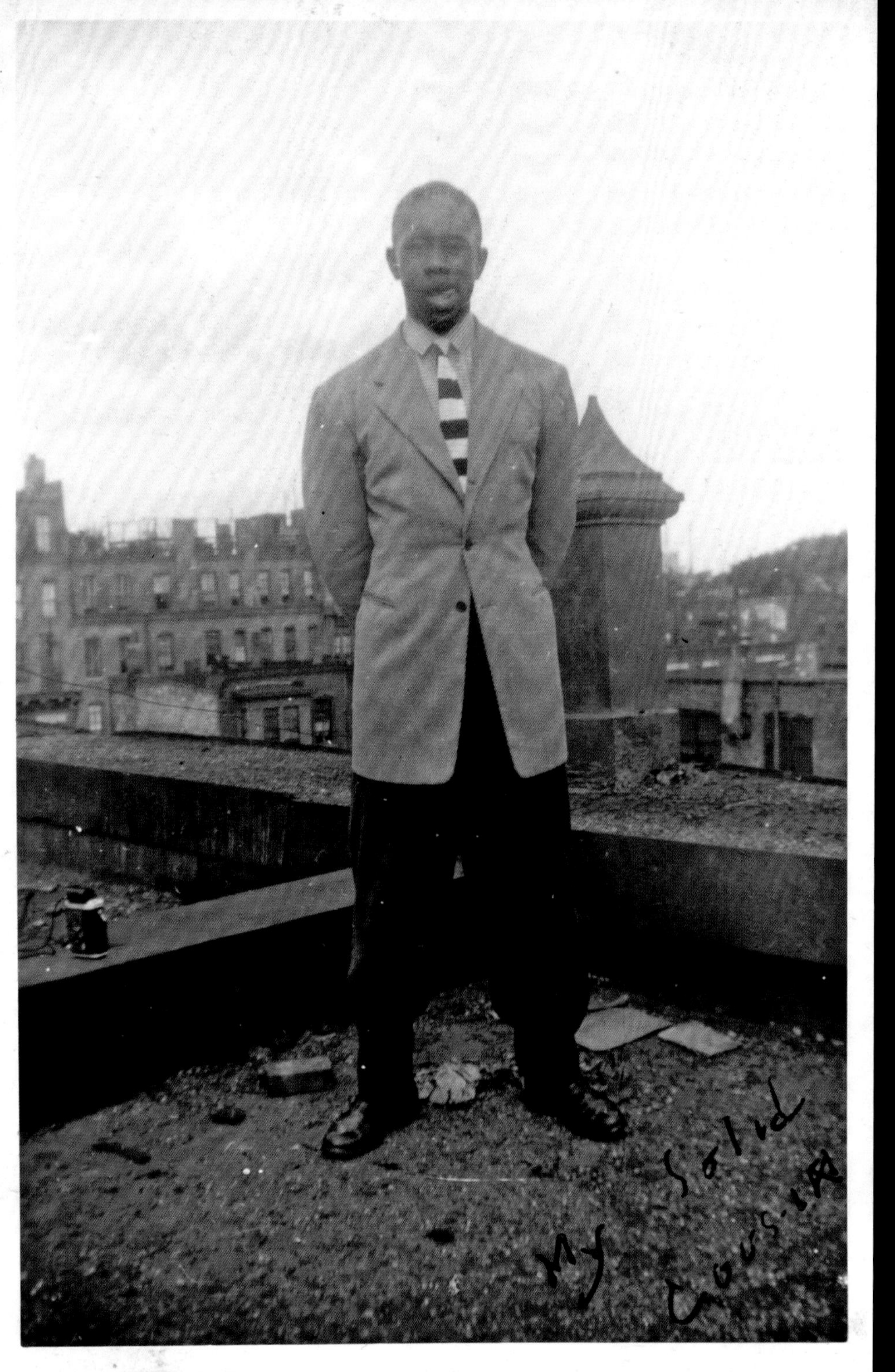

Overlooking Haskins Street in Roxbury
BOSTON, MA
CIRCA 1940

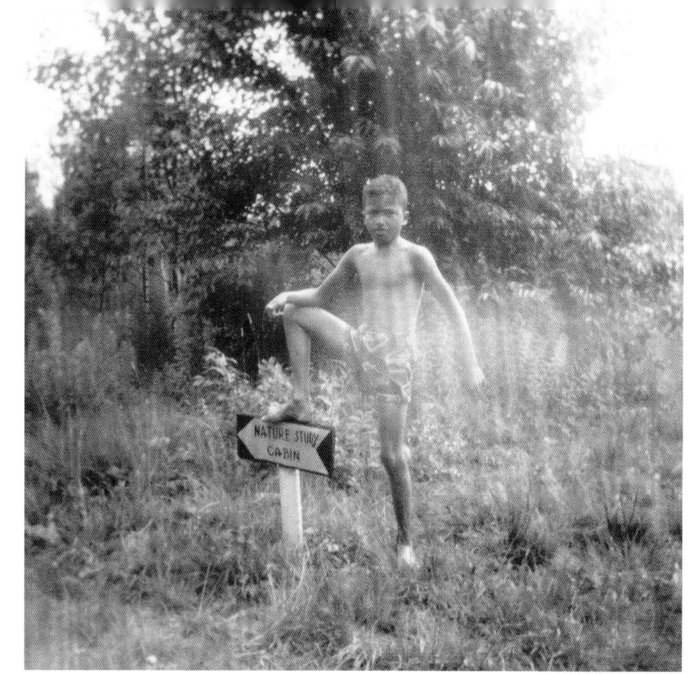

MASSACHUSETTS
1940S

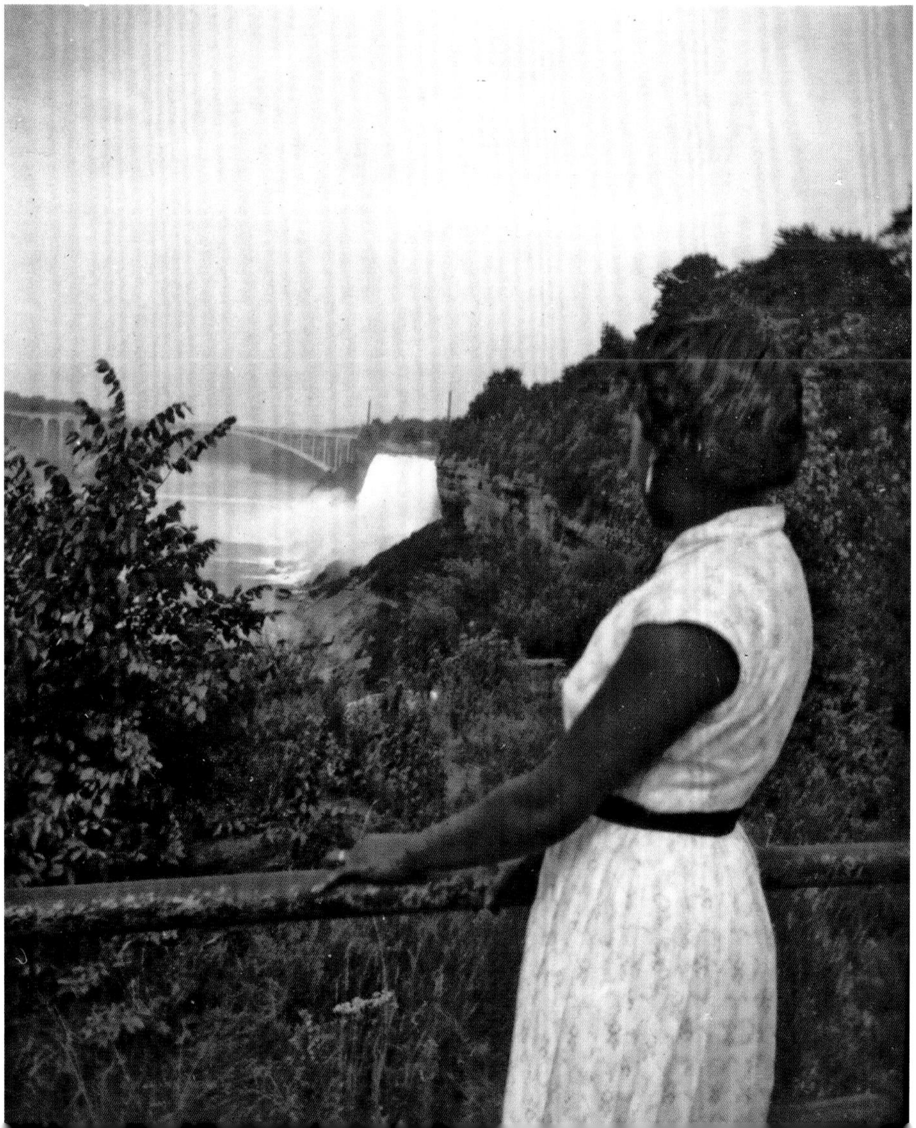

Inez Hunter
CIRCA 1945

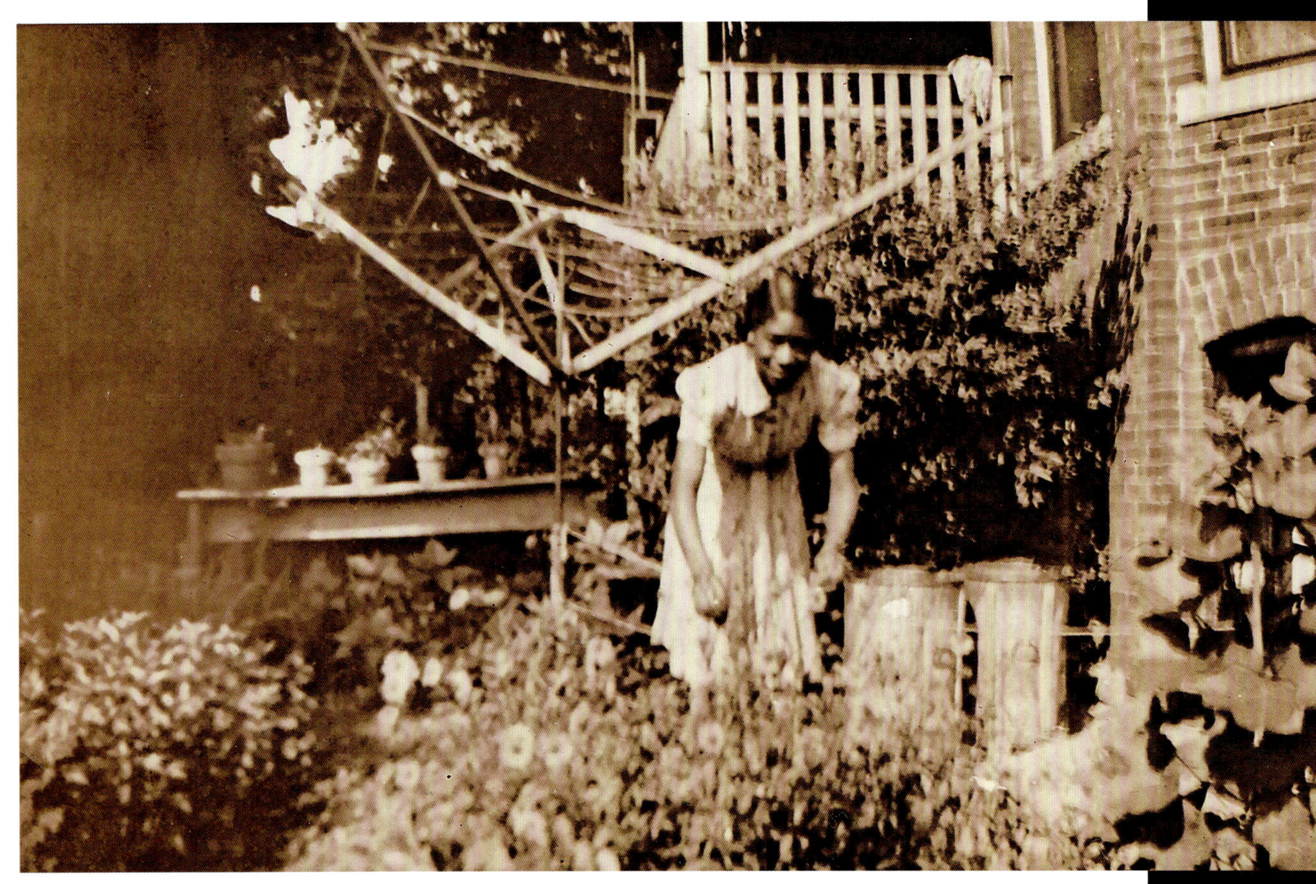

Inez Hunter in her garden

BOSTON, MA

CIRCA 1935

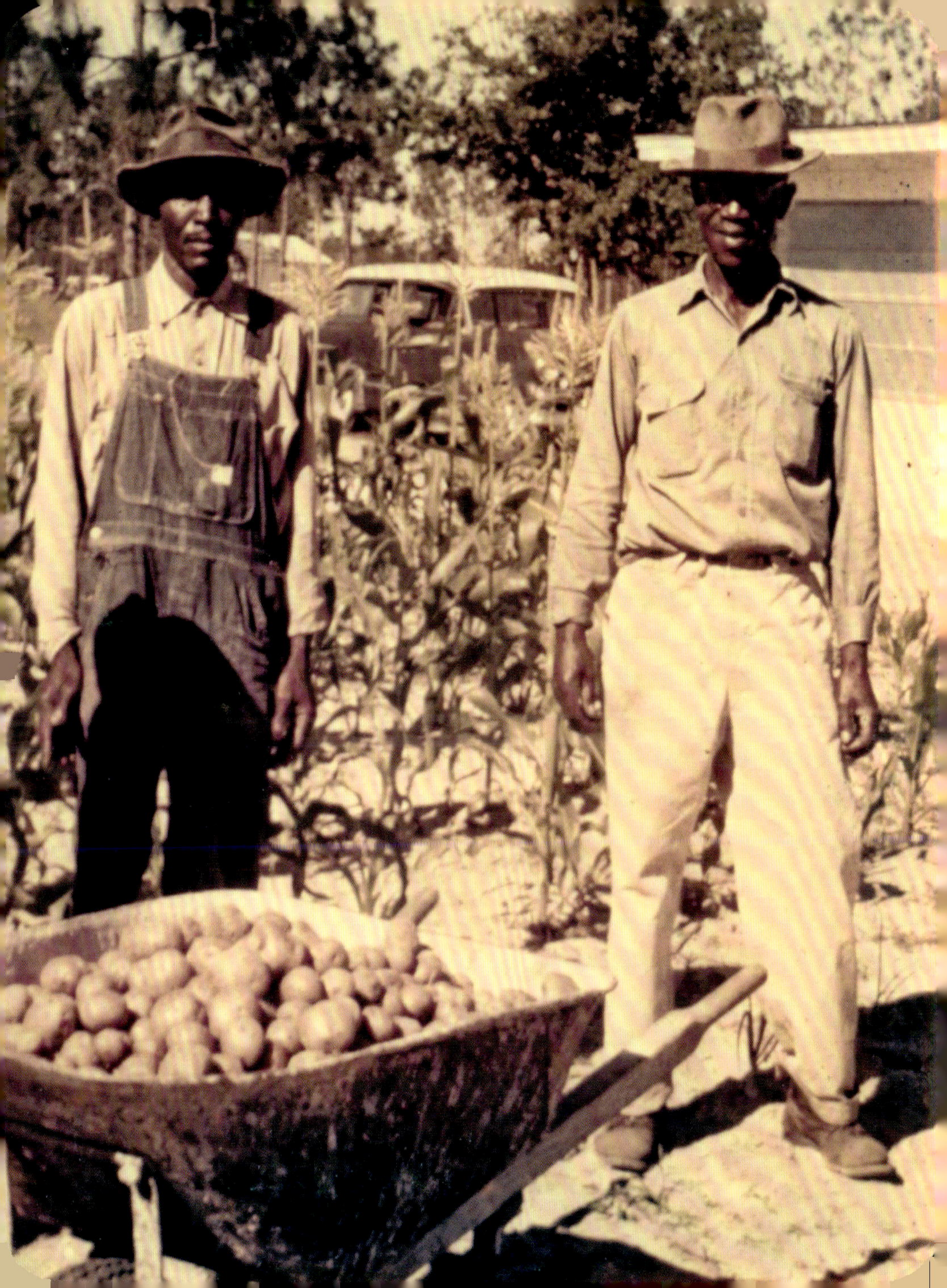

→ Marlon Lowe
climbing a palm tree
GRENADA
1986

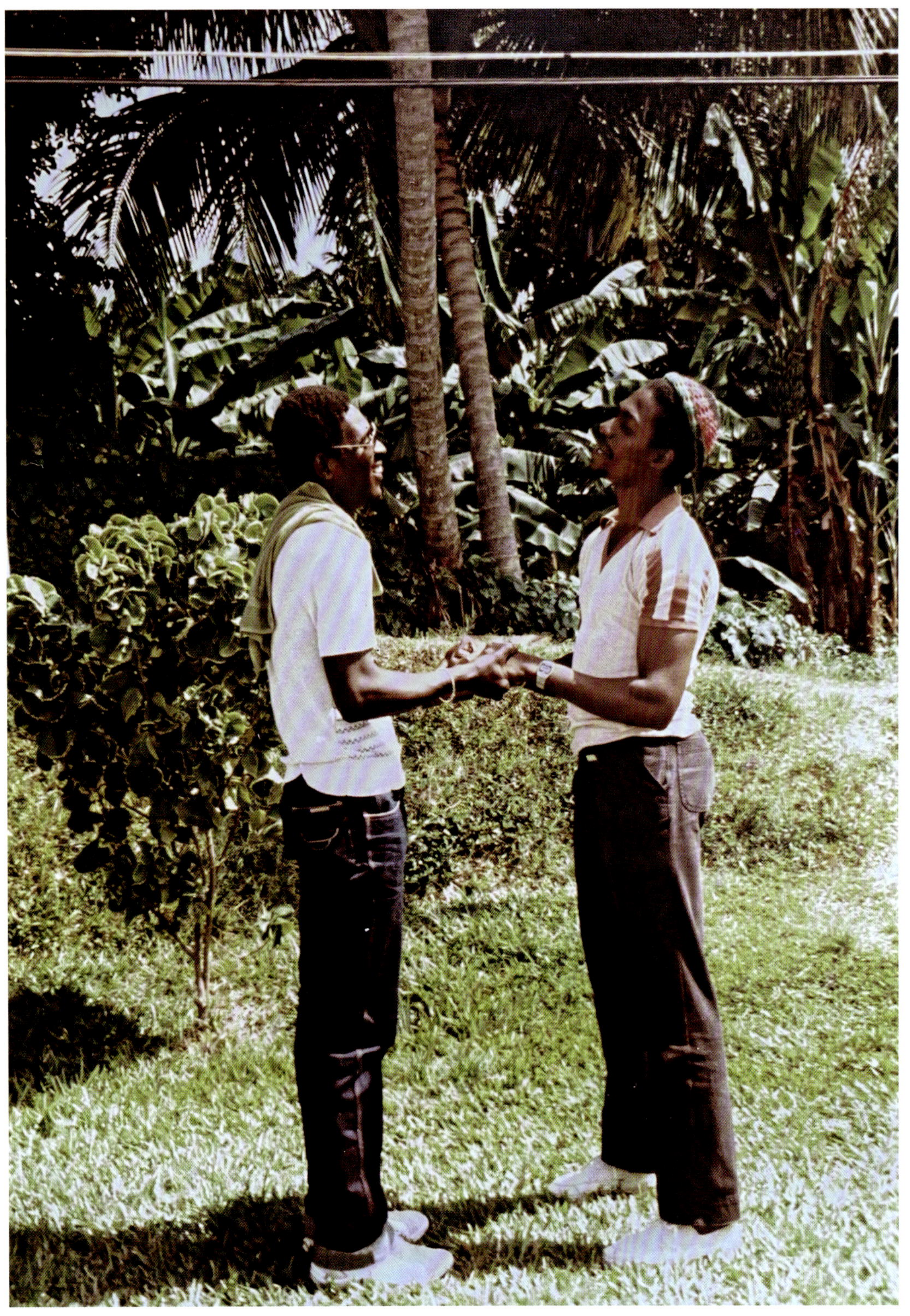

Kenneth Charles (left)
and Carlisle Julien
GRENADA
1989

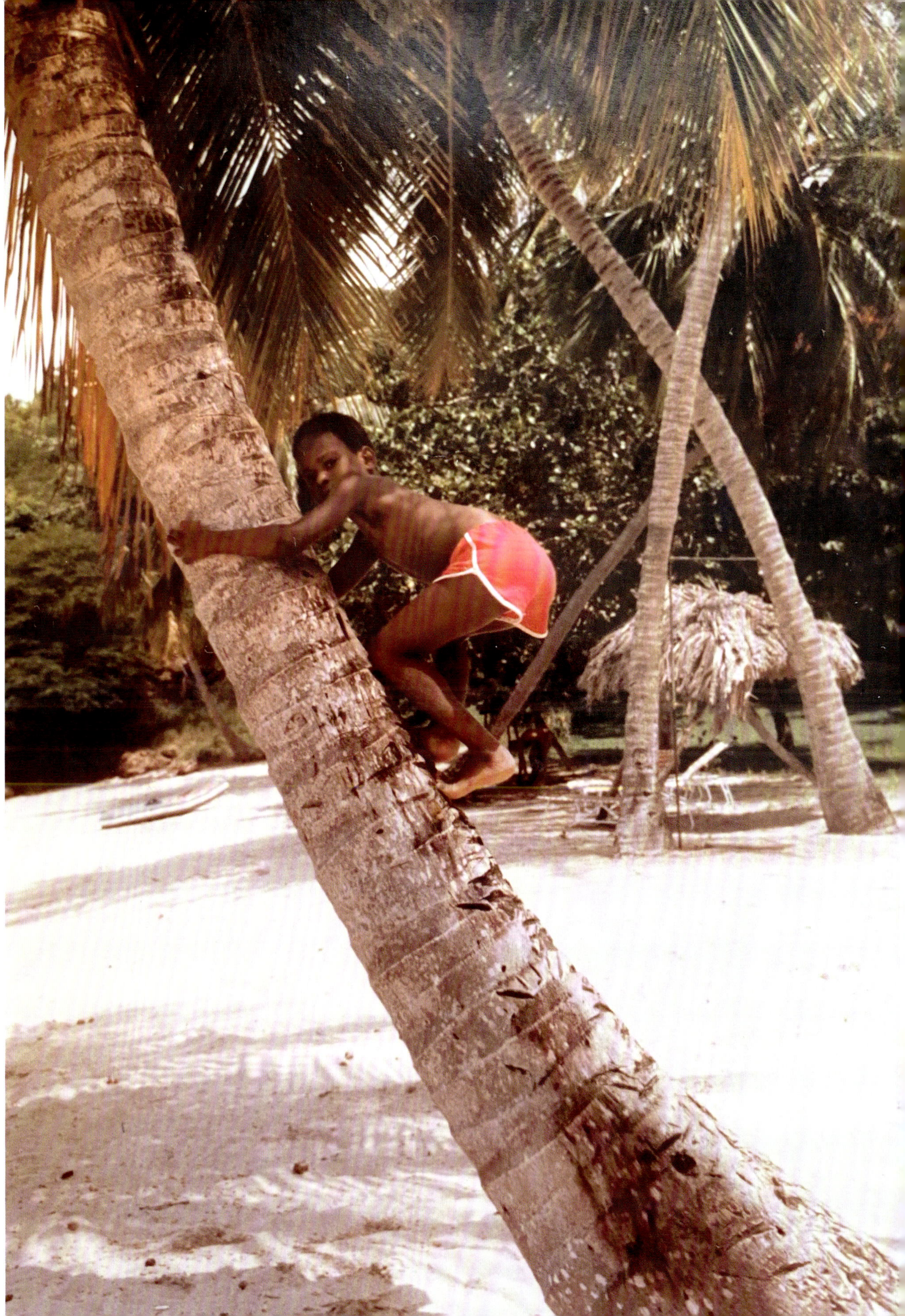

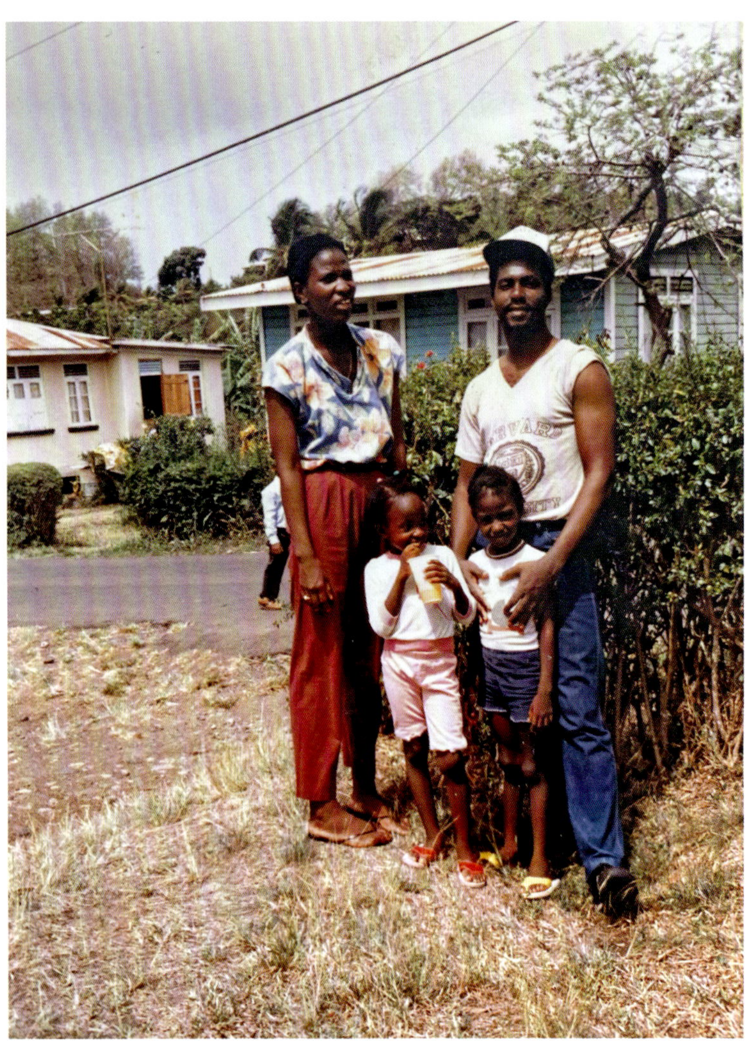

The Julien family
GRENADA
1990

Cathy Counts traveling in Mexico before she had kids
MEXICO
1980S

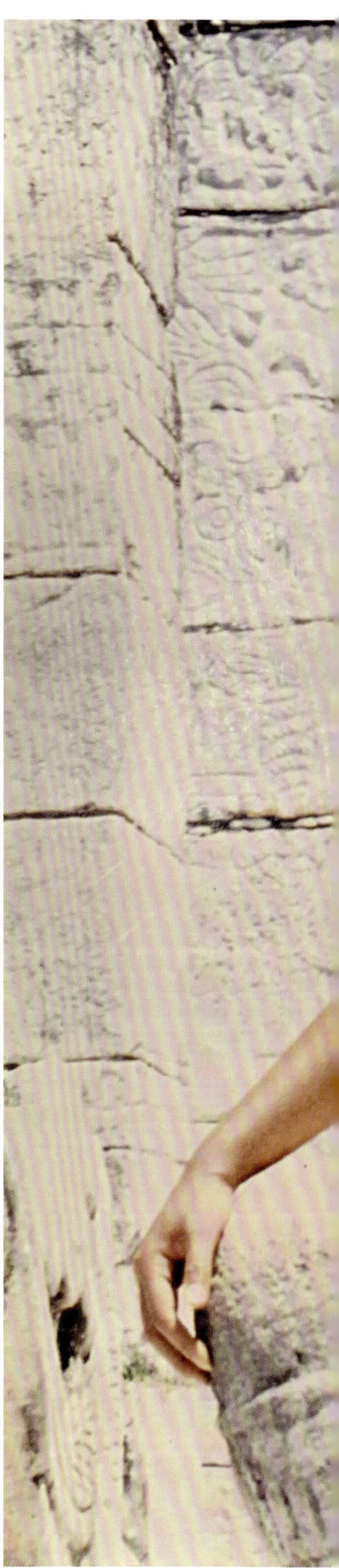

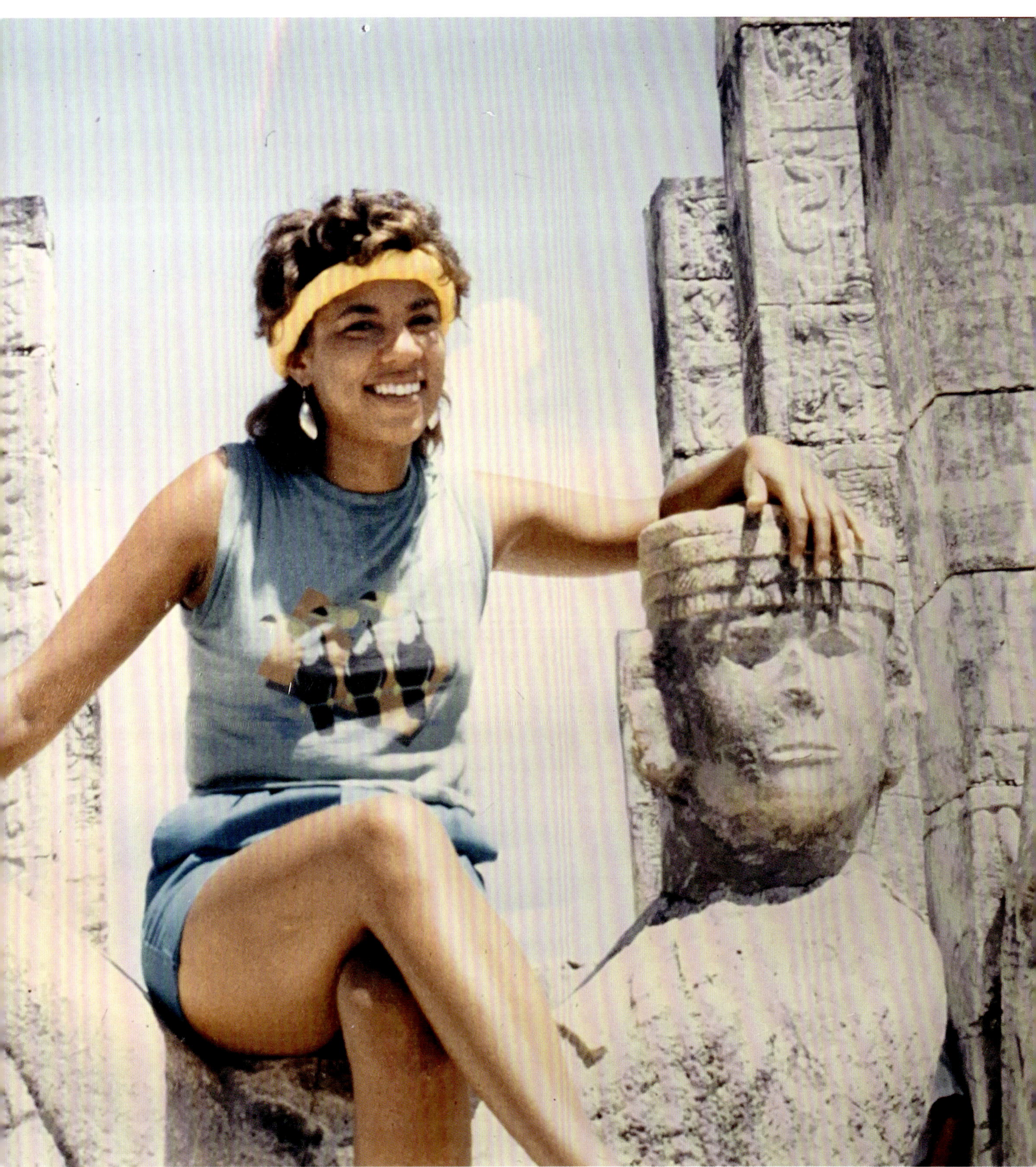

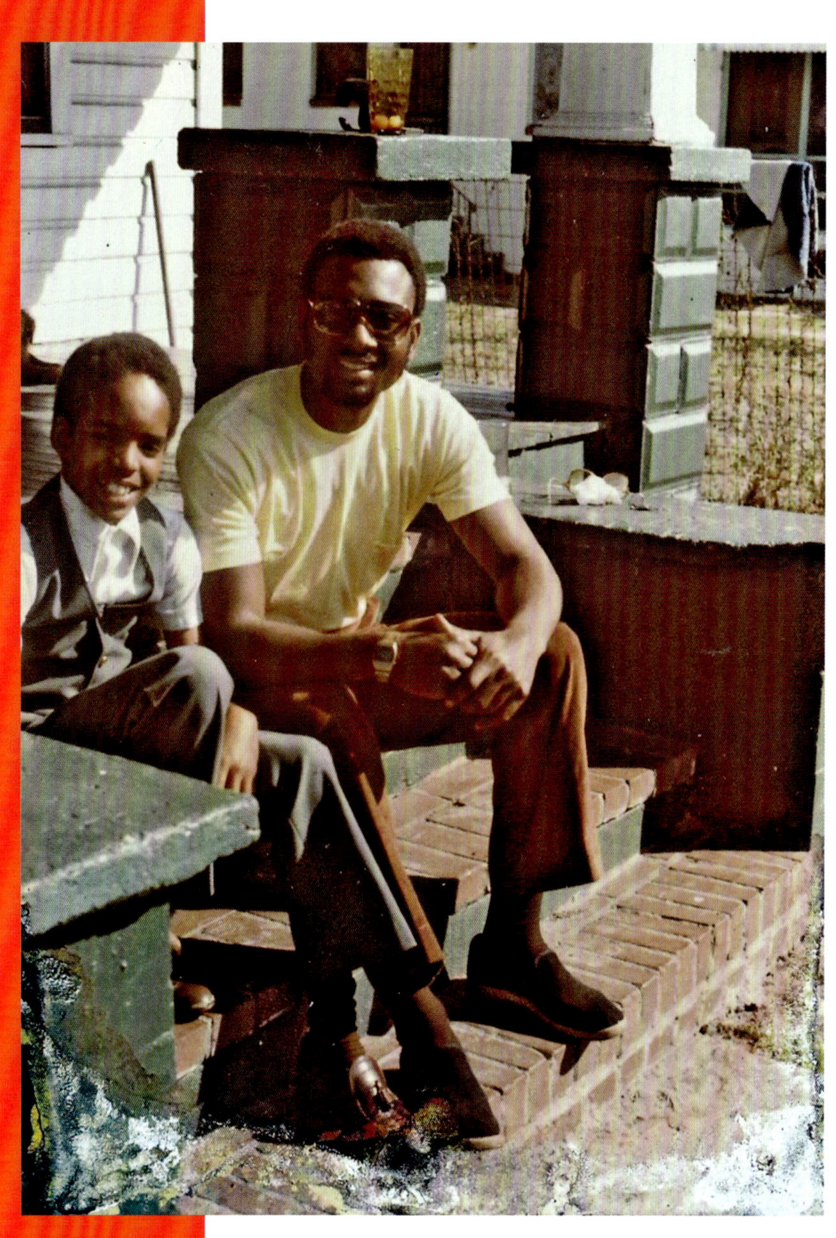

The author's uncle and a family friend
JACKSONVILLE, FL
1970S

THE FRONT PORCH

There was a long sidewalk that ran through my grandmother's housing development, with apartment buildings on either side, each of which had a front porch. Some porches had chairs and stools, others had plants, while others remained bare. I always considered that sidewalk a runway where neighbors within the community would strut down the block and greet everyone sitting or standing on their porches, making their way to and from their homes or around town.

I always marveled at the people on their porches being able to carry on a conversation while greeting the folks passing by and keeping an eye out on the neighborhood kids without missing a beat. The front porch or stoop is one of the best places just outside of the home to sit and reflect. It's also a hub for picture-taking, story-swapping, hair-braiding and haircuts, as well as a place to convene and build community, to make decisions, and imagine new worlds. This collection celebrates the front porch as a sacred place to be in community with the air and land, as well as each other.

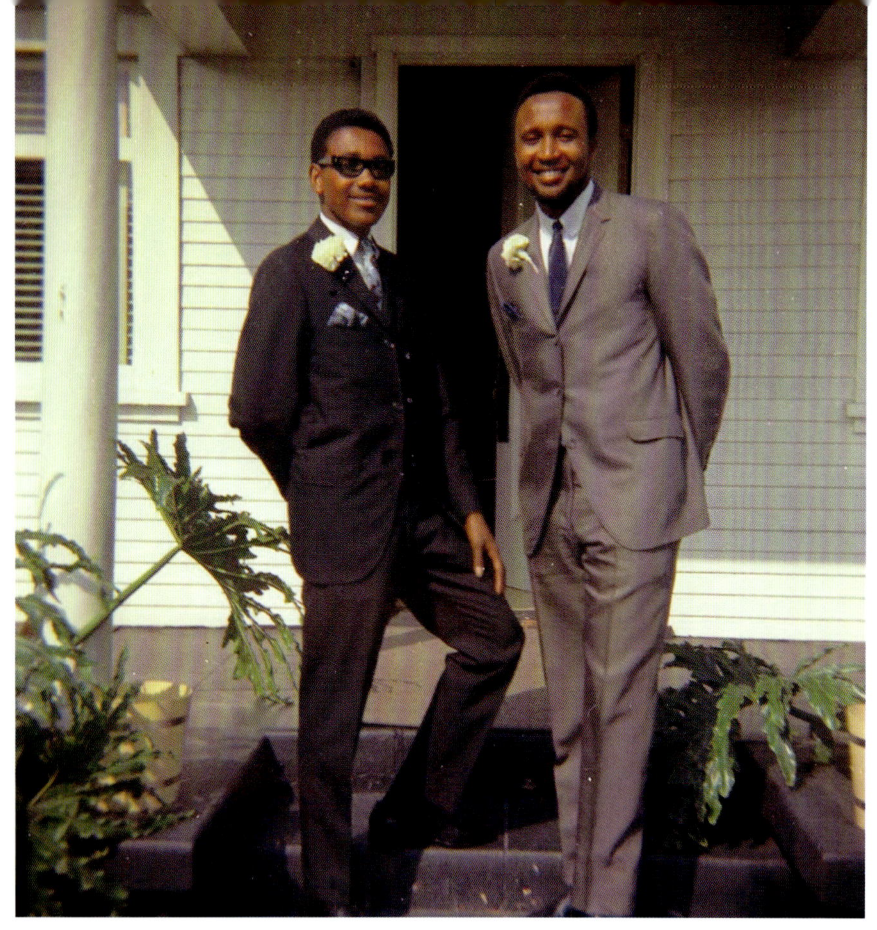

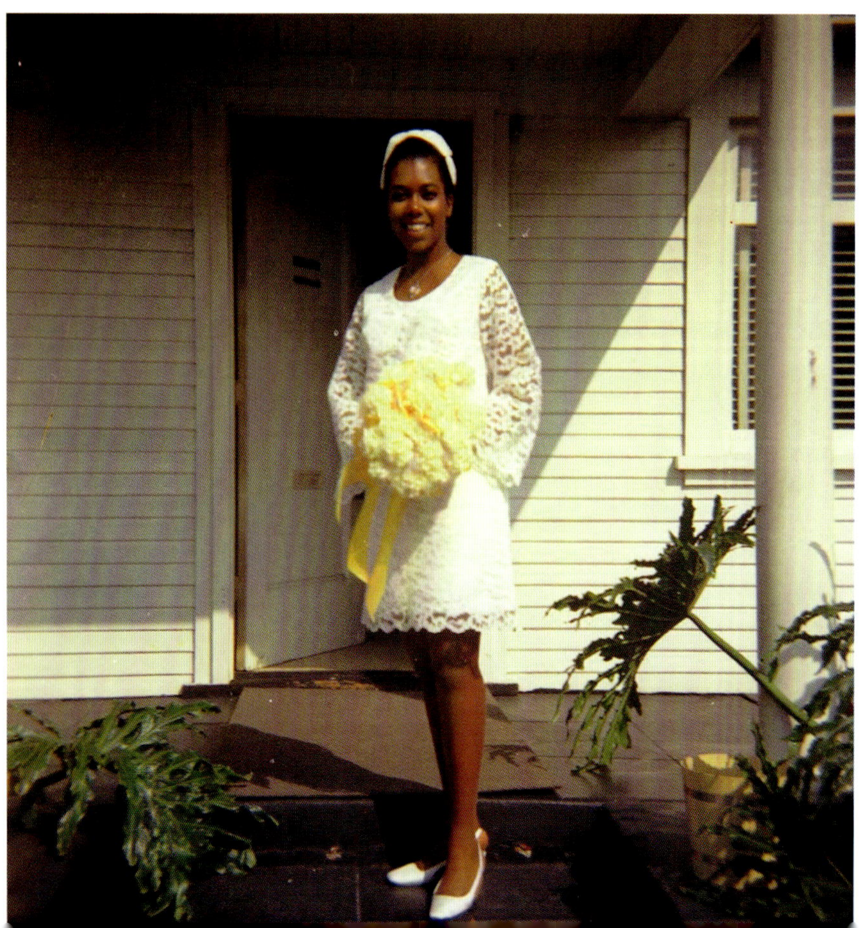

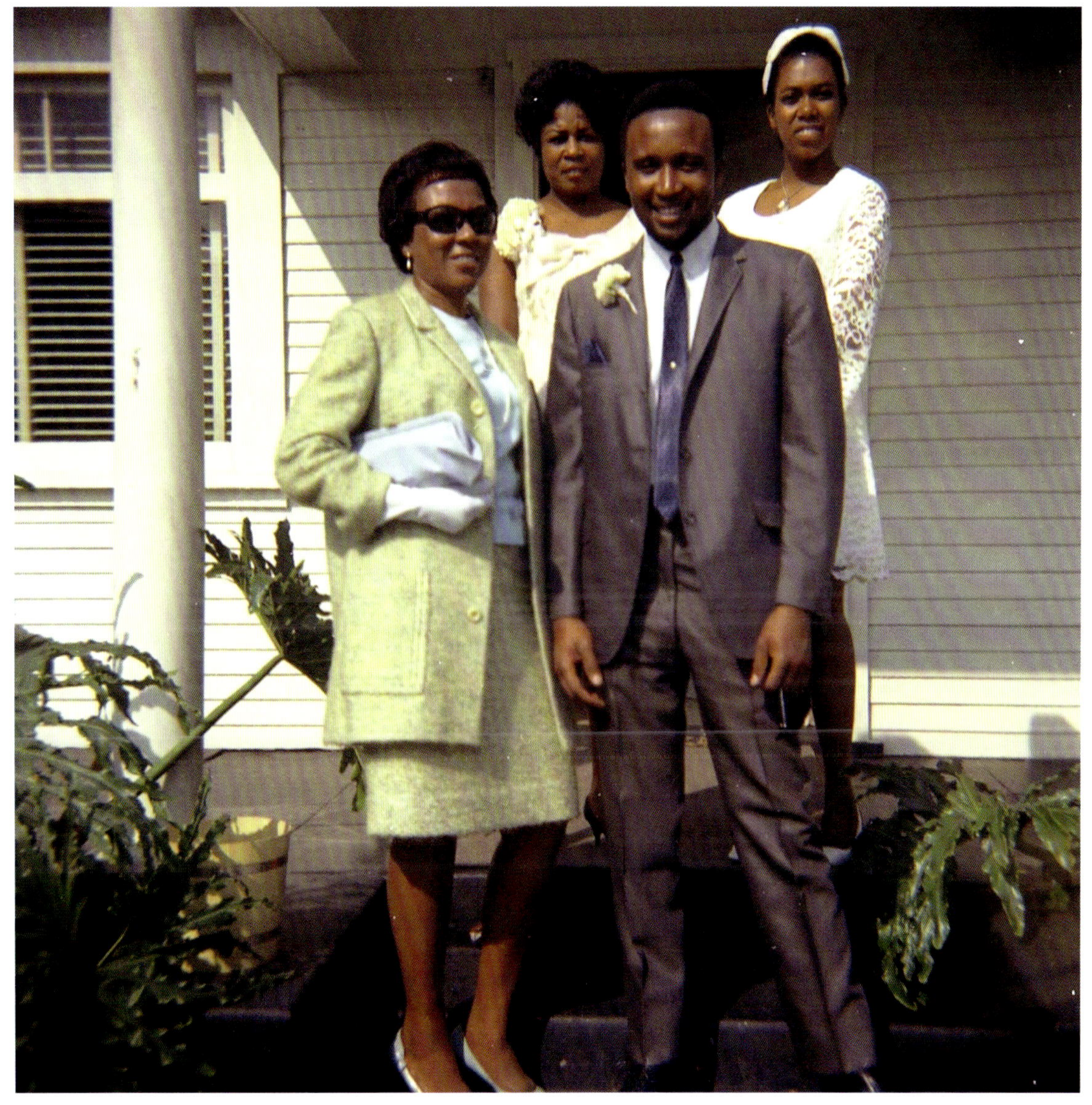

1960S

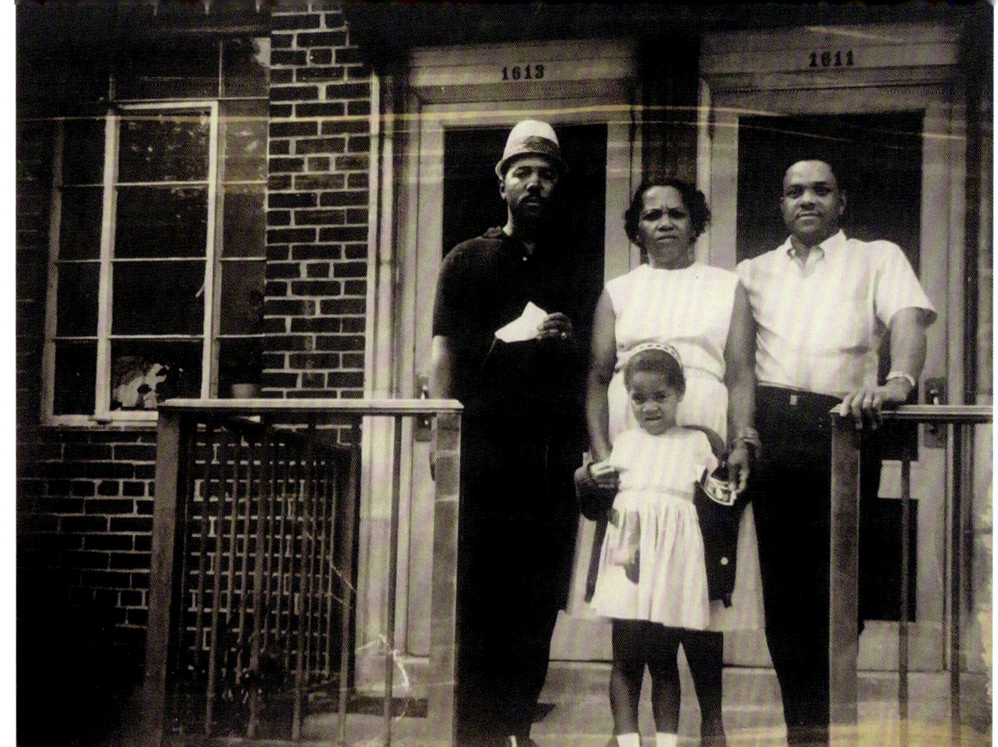

OHIO
1950S

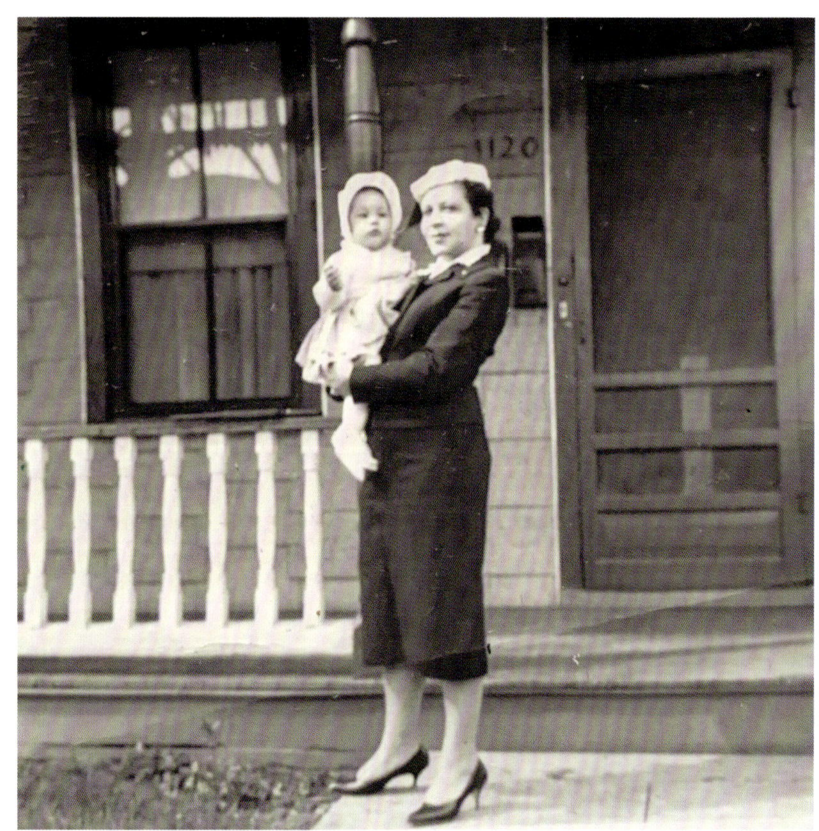

1950S

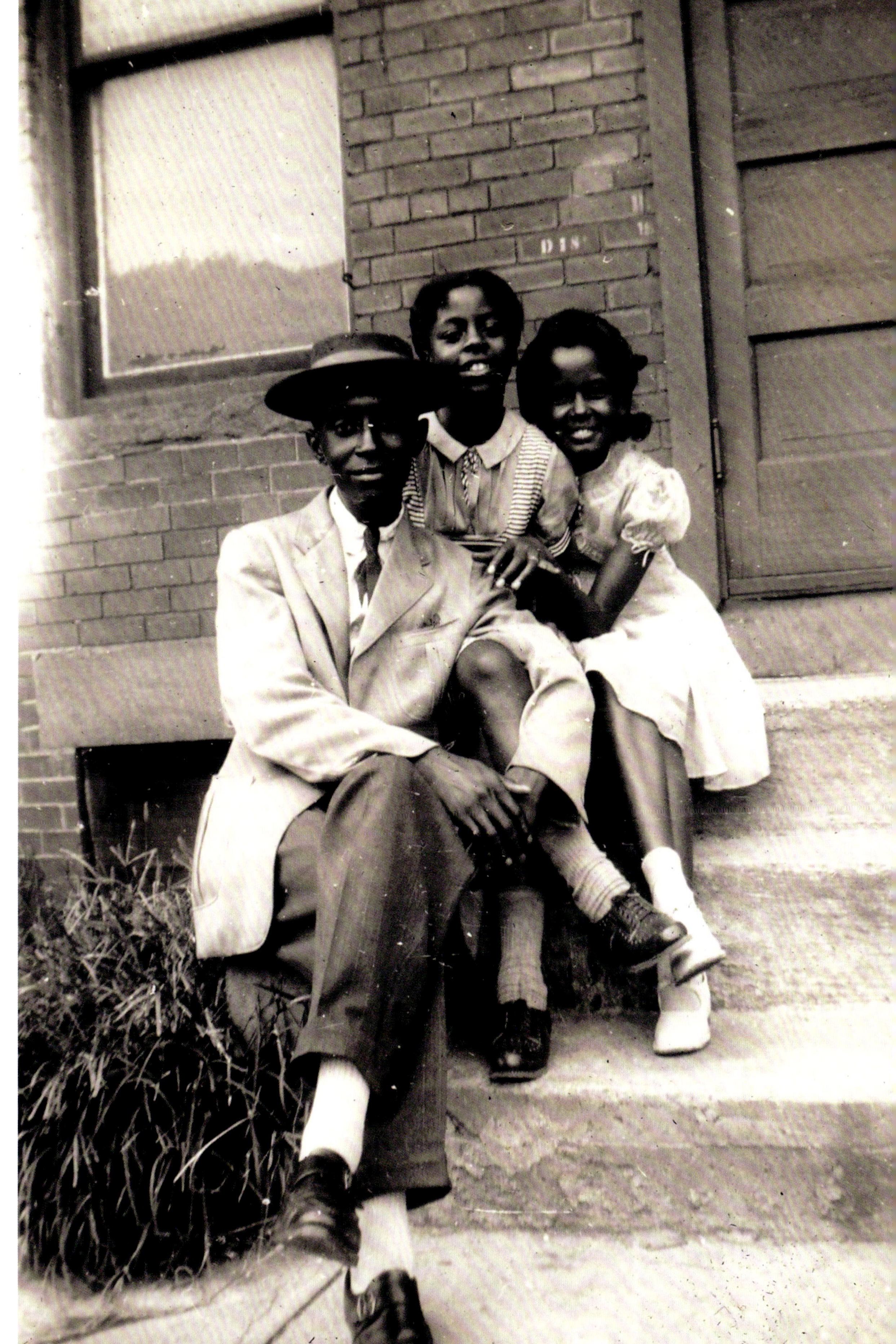

BOSTON, MA
CIRCA 1940

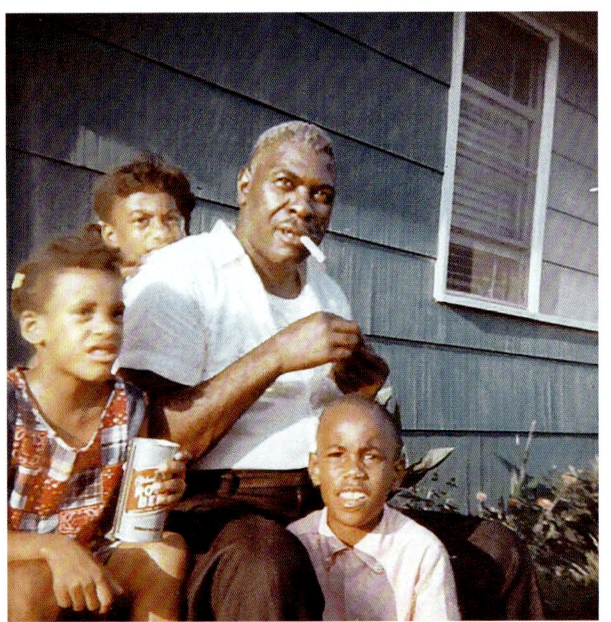

RICHMOND, VA

1966

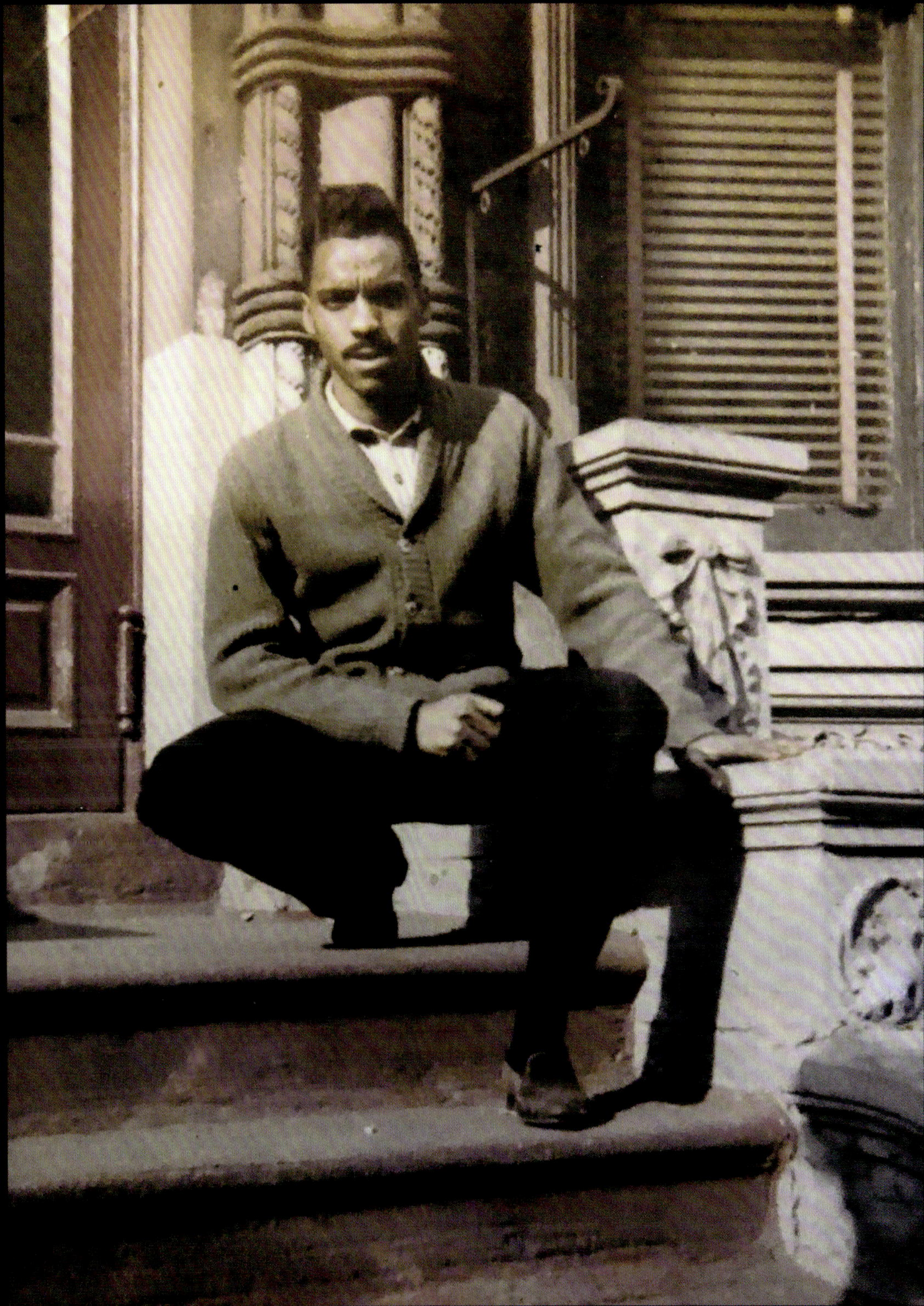

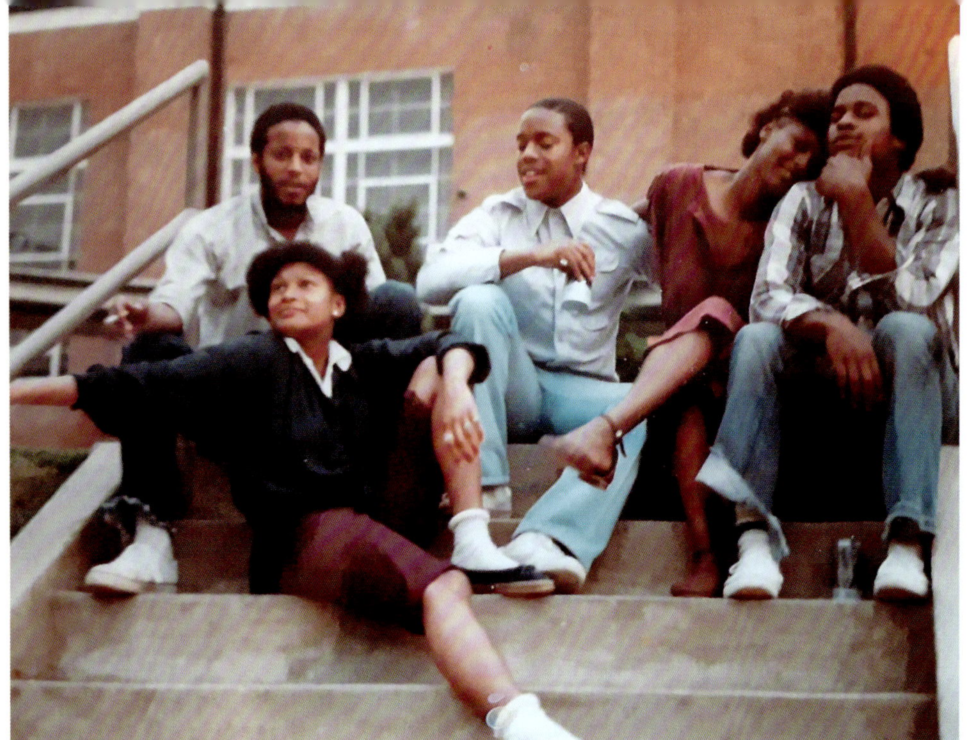

1980S

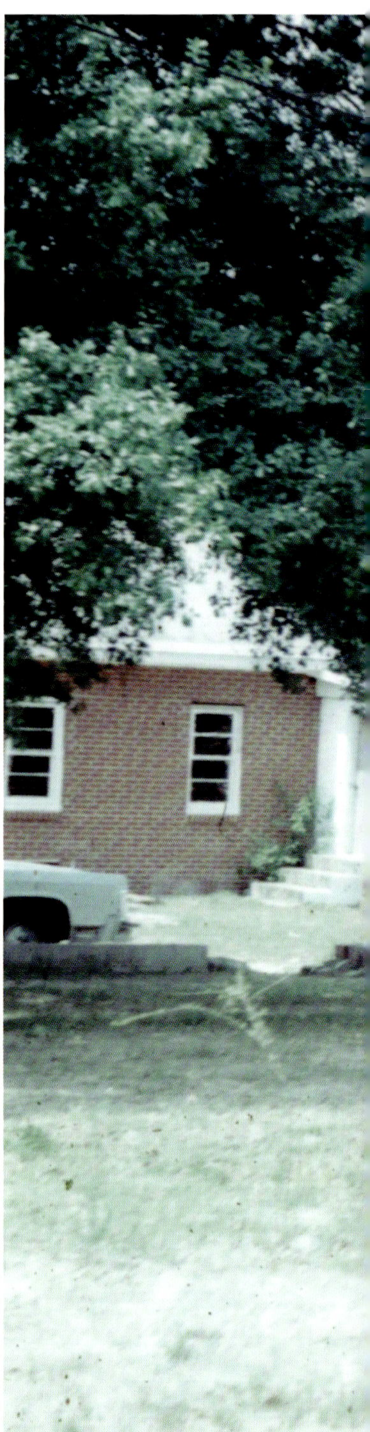

The South

CIRCA 1980

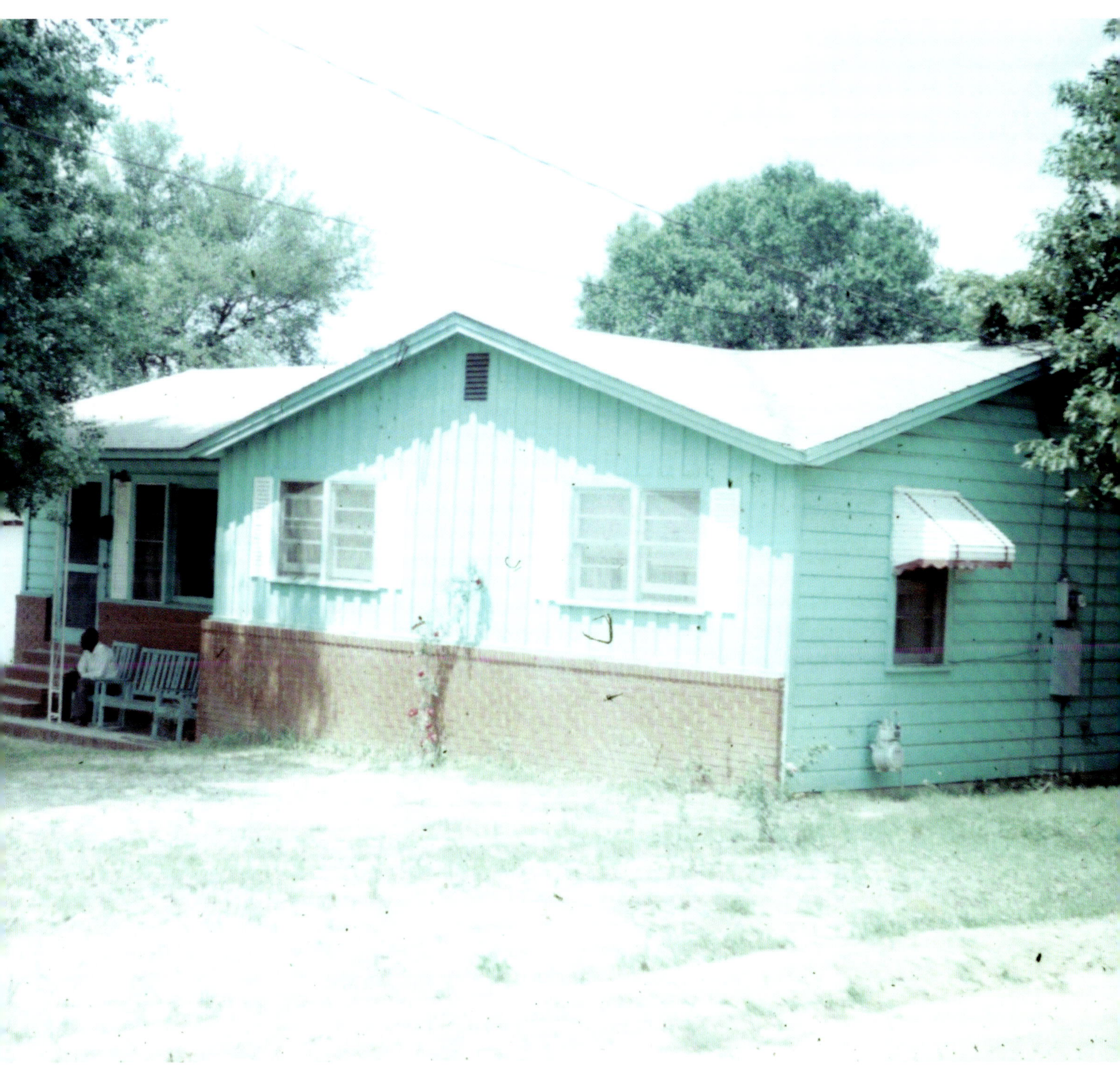

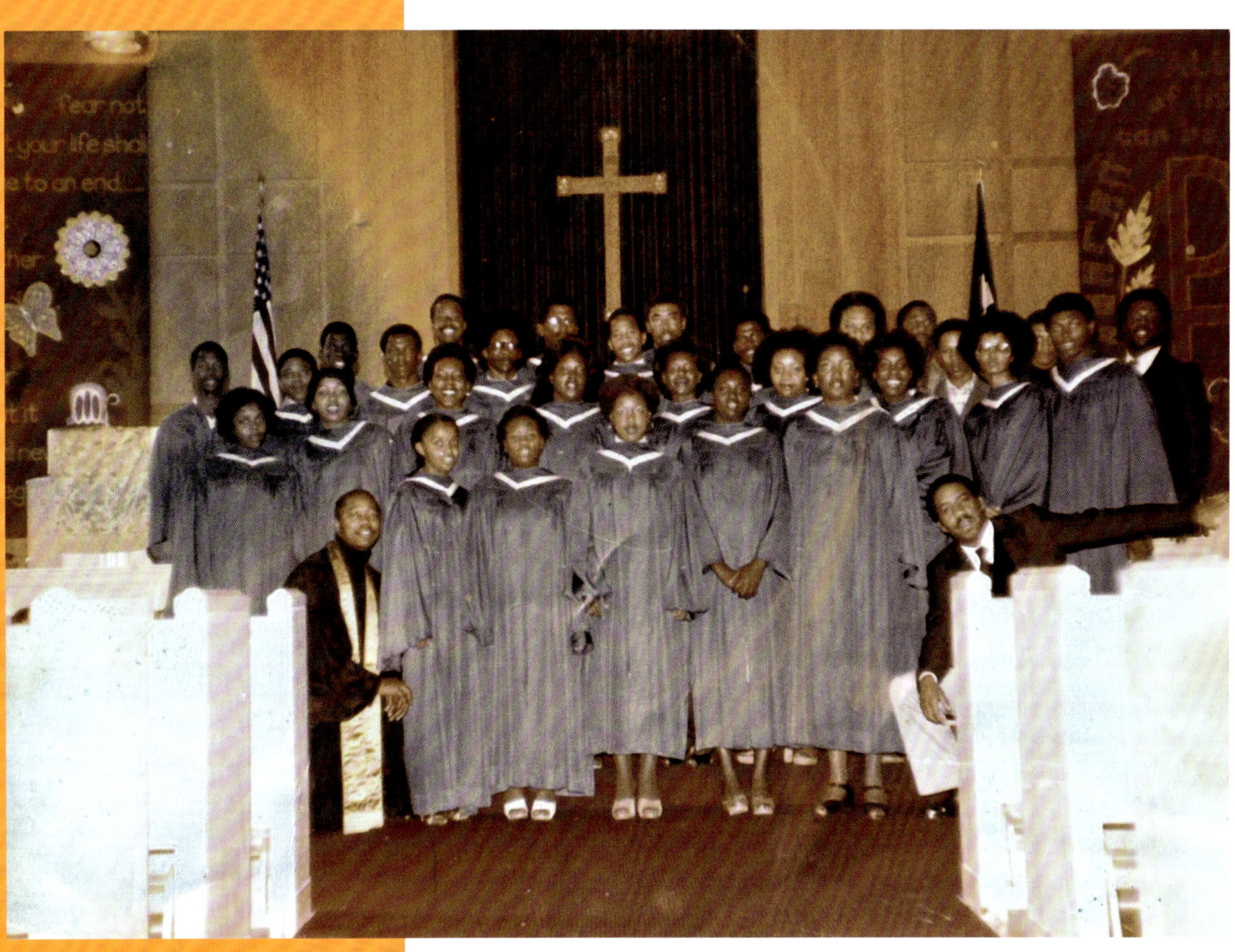

The author's mother in a choir comprised of Army members and their spouses
FORT ORD, CA
1979

IN UNIFORM

Wearing uniforms is an effective way for members within a profession, sporting team, organization, church, or military branch to identify themselves. But when Black people dress in this coordinated manner, we have a particular way of distinguishing ourselves that highlights our individuality within conformity, allowing our personalities to emerge out of unison.

This series explores the cadence of Black people. It spotlights the ways that we harmonize while leaning into our individuality.

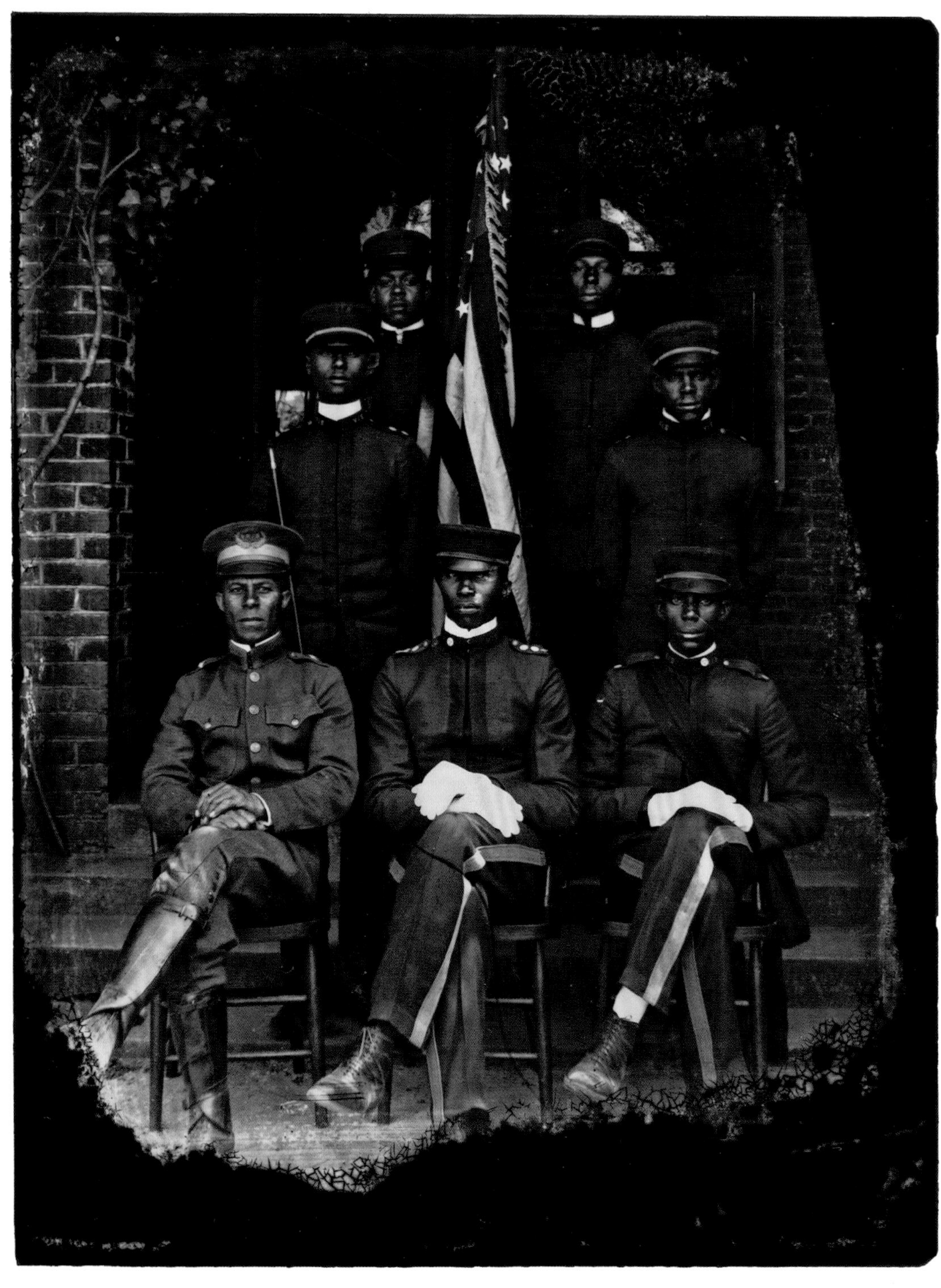

SOUTH
CAROLINA

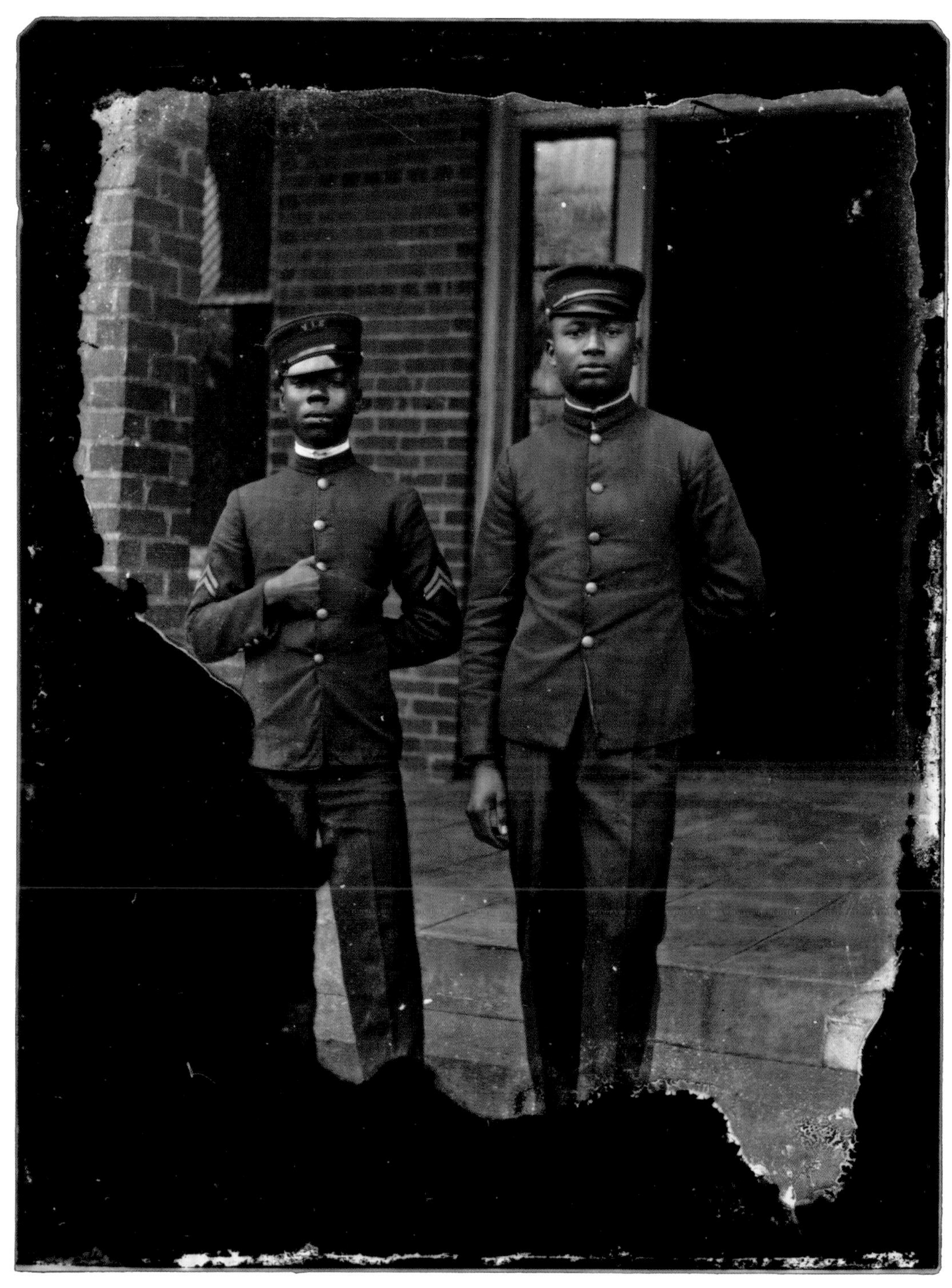

SOUTH
CAROLINA

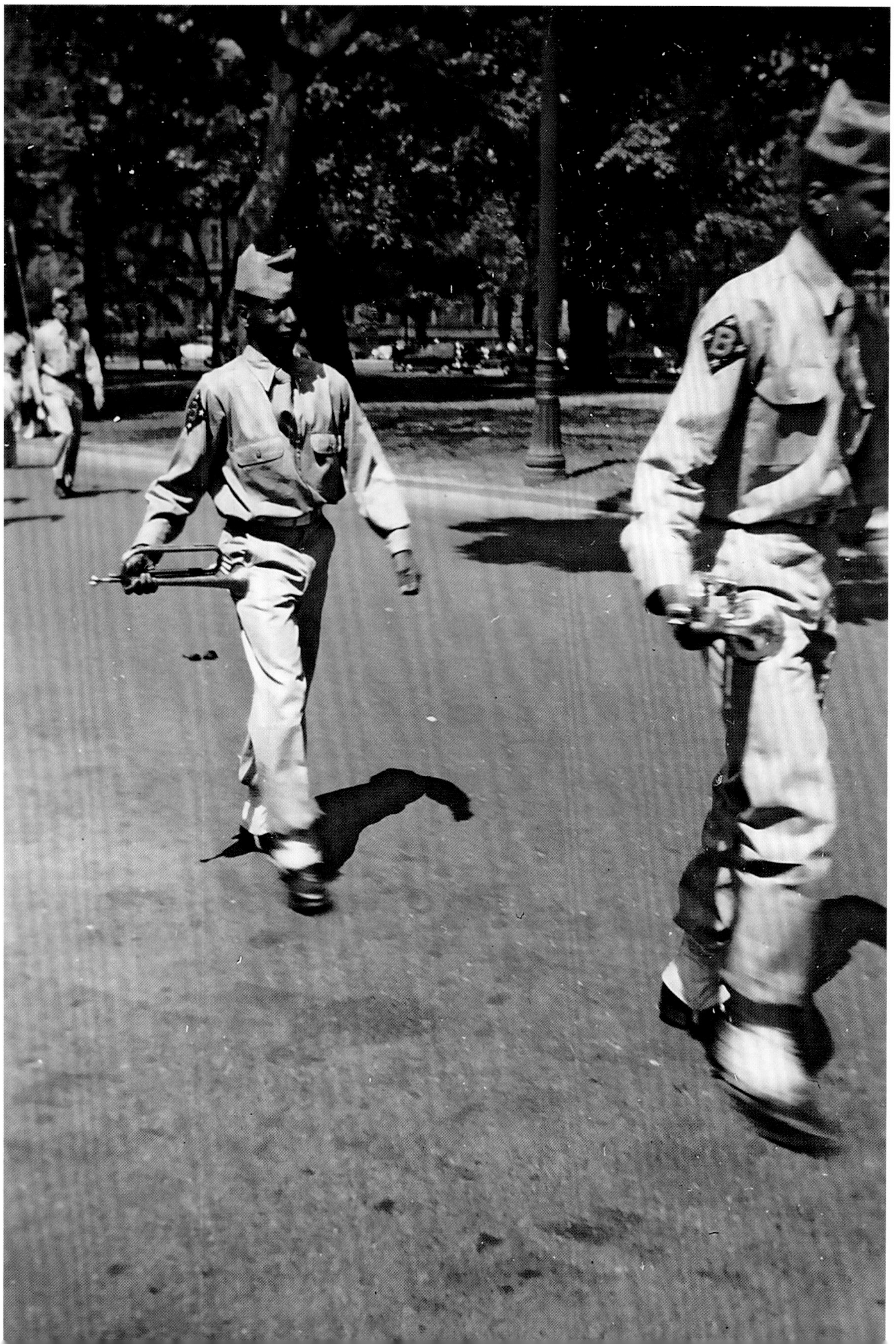

← Boston School Boy Cadets Parade
CIRCA 1945

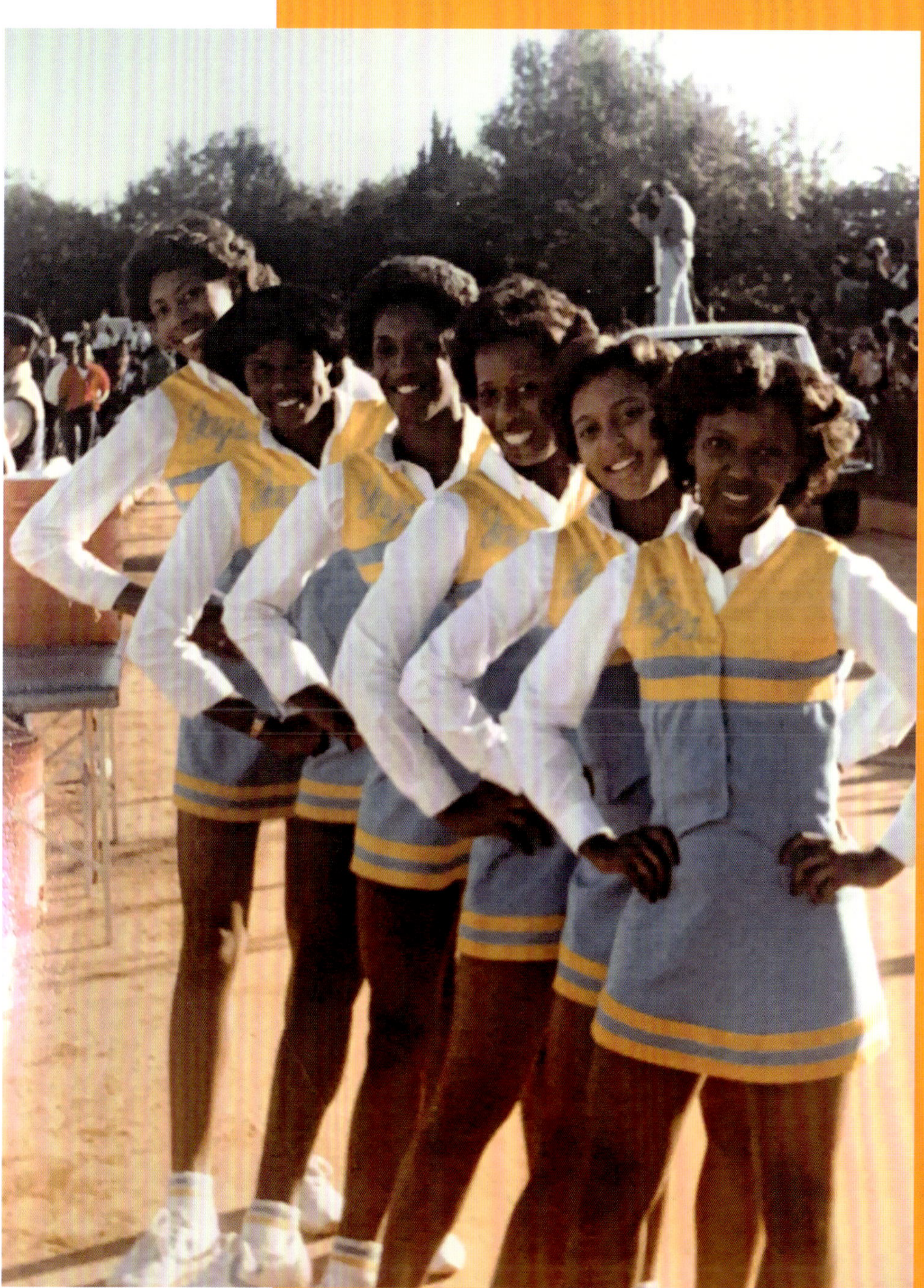

1981

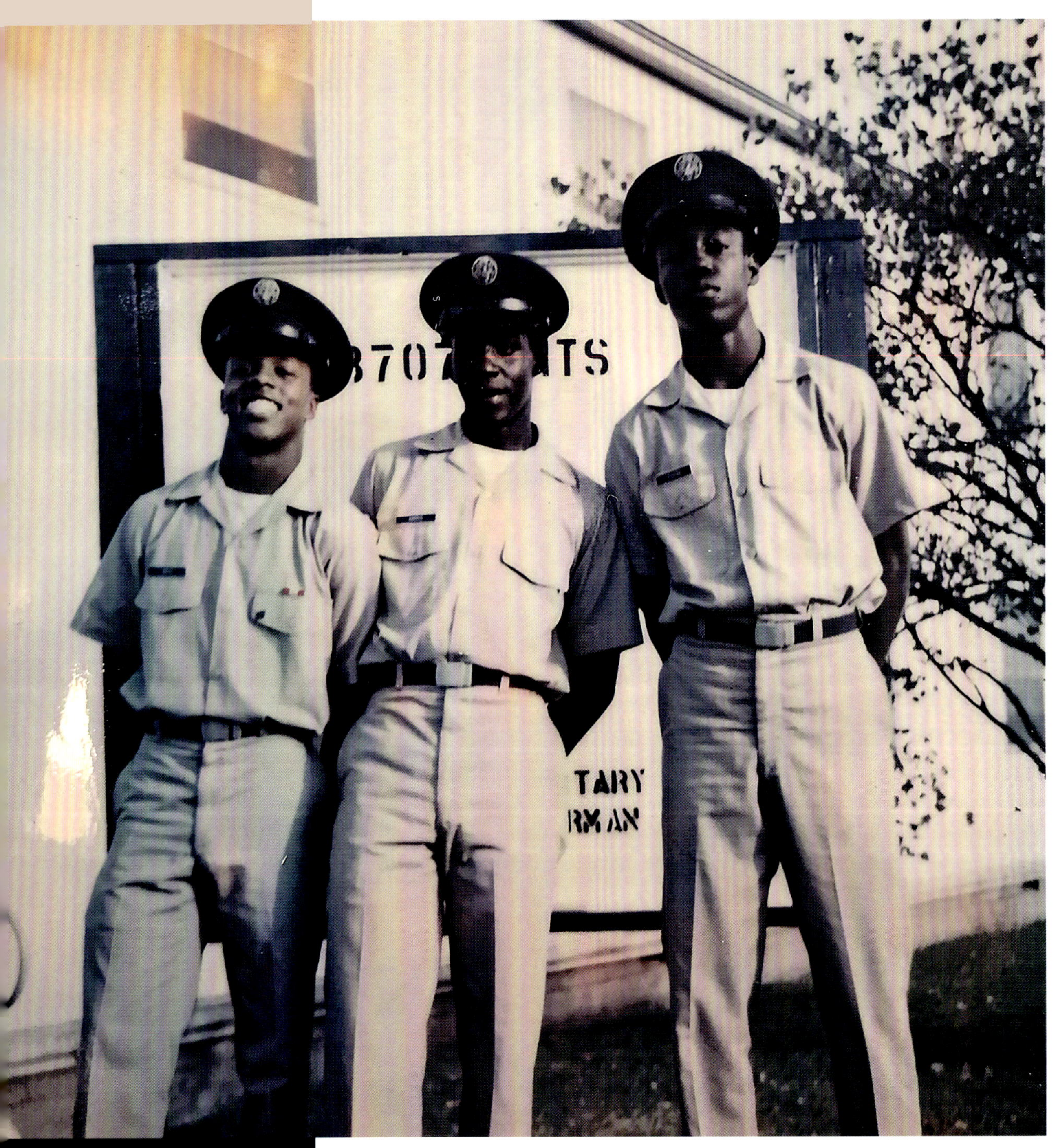

Military comrades

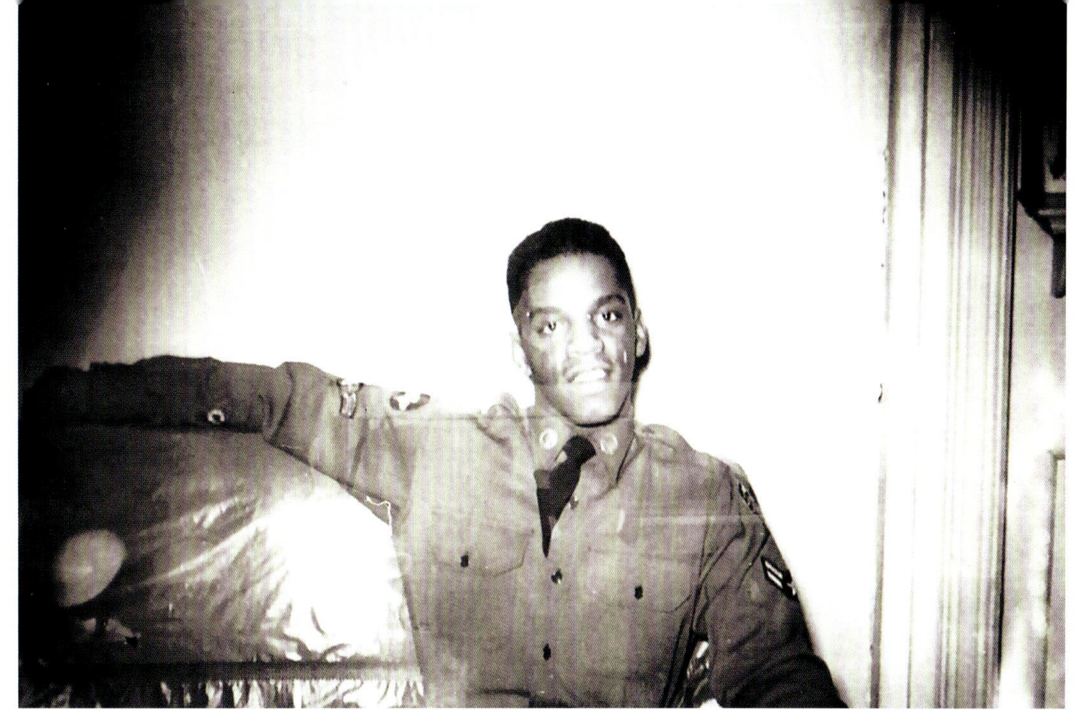

CIRCA 1945

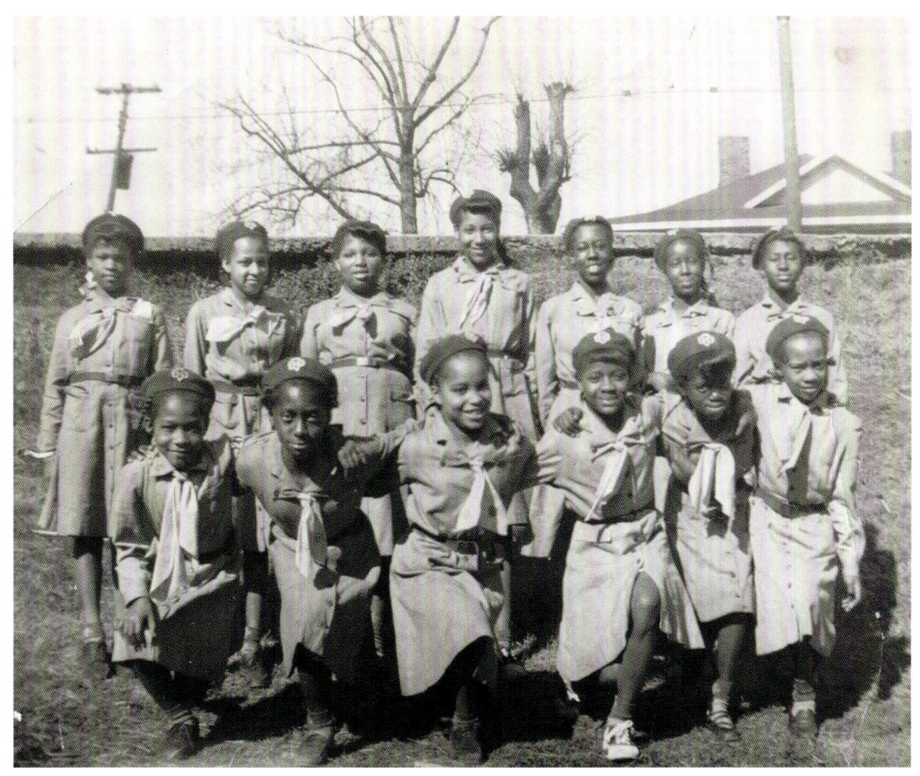

Girl Scouts

ASHEVILLE, NC

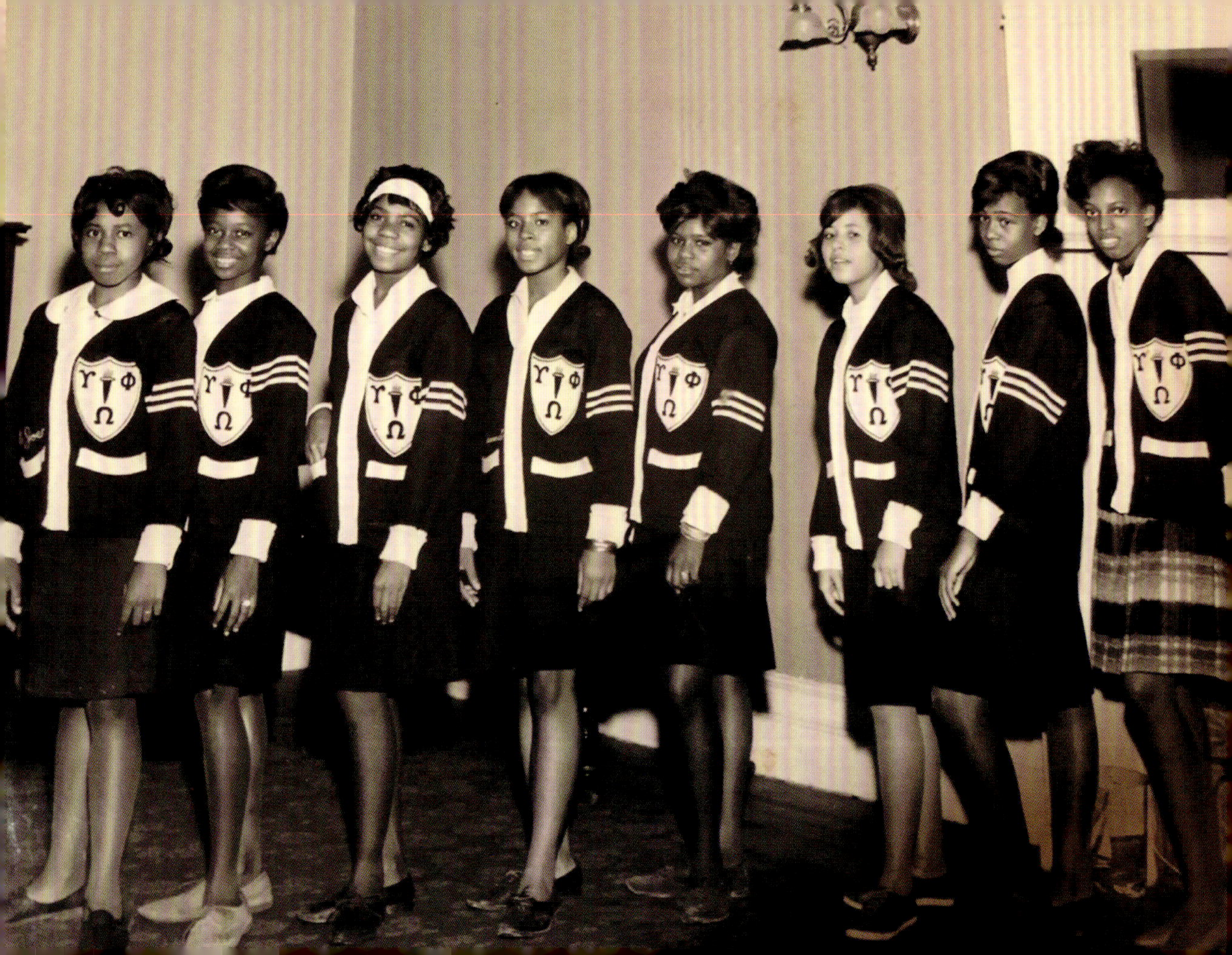

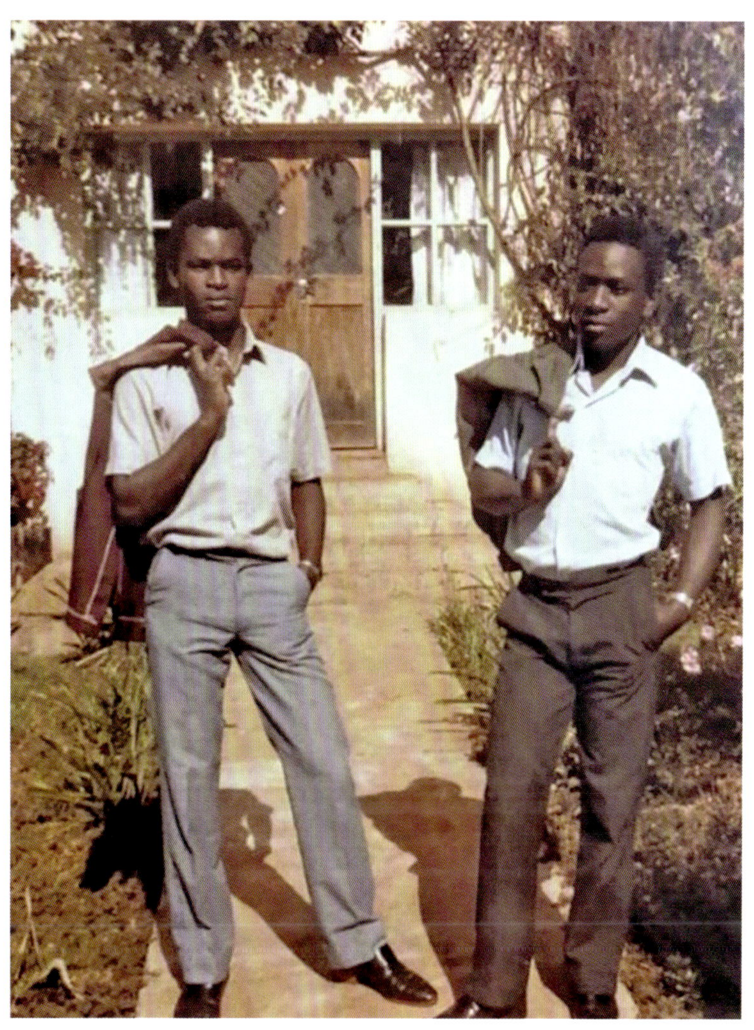

KENYA

1984

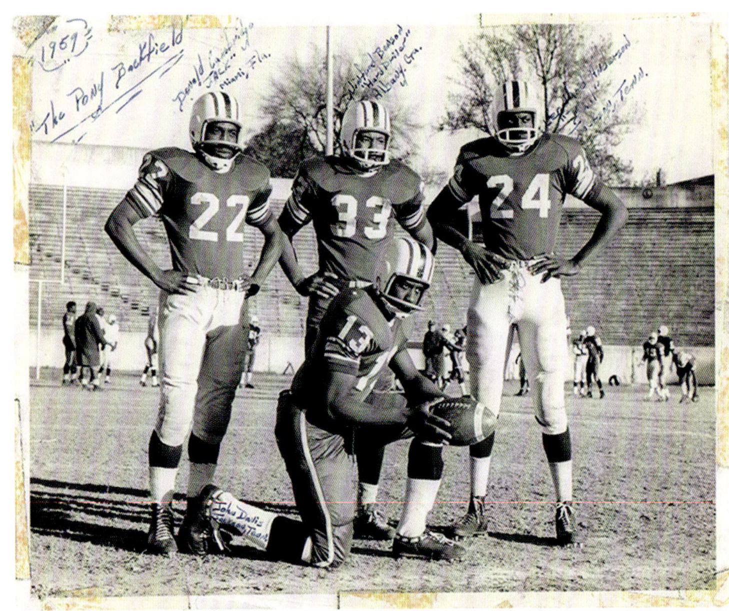

Joseph Donald Cambridge and "The Pony Express," which was the nickname for the stable of running backs on the Morris Brown football team.

ATLANTA, GA

1959

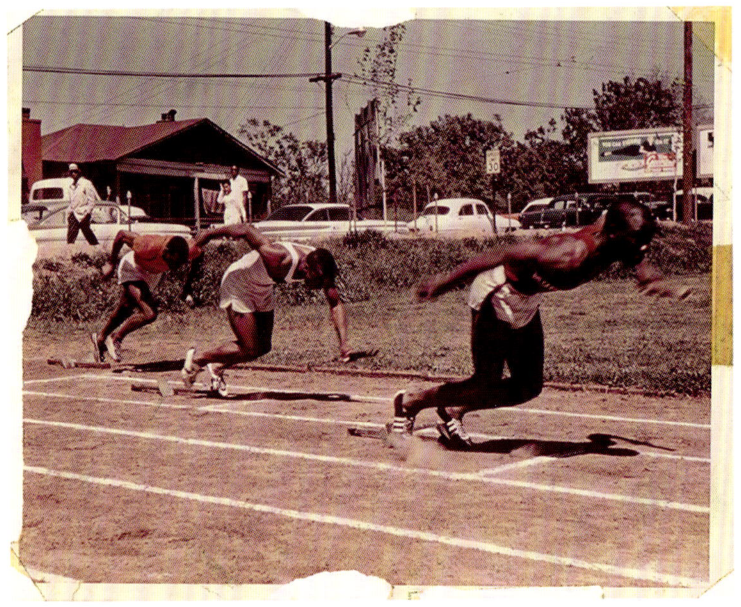

Joseph Donald Cambridge running the 100-yard dash at Morris Brown. He and his son Russell Cambridge are both in the Morris Brown Hall of Fame.

ATLANTA, GA

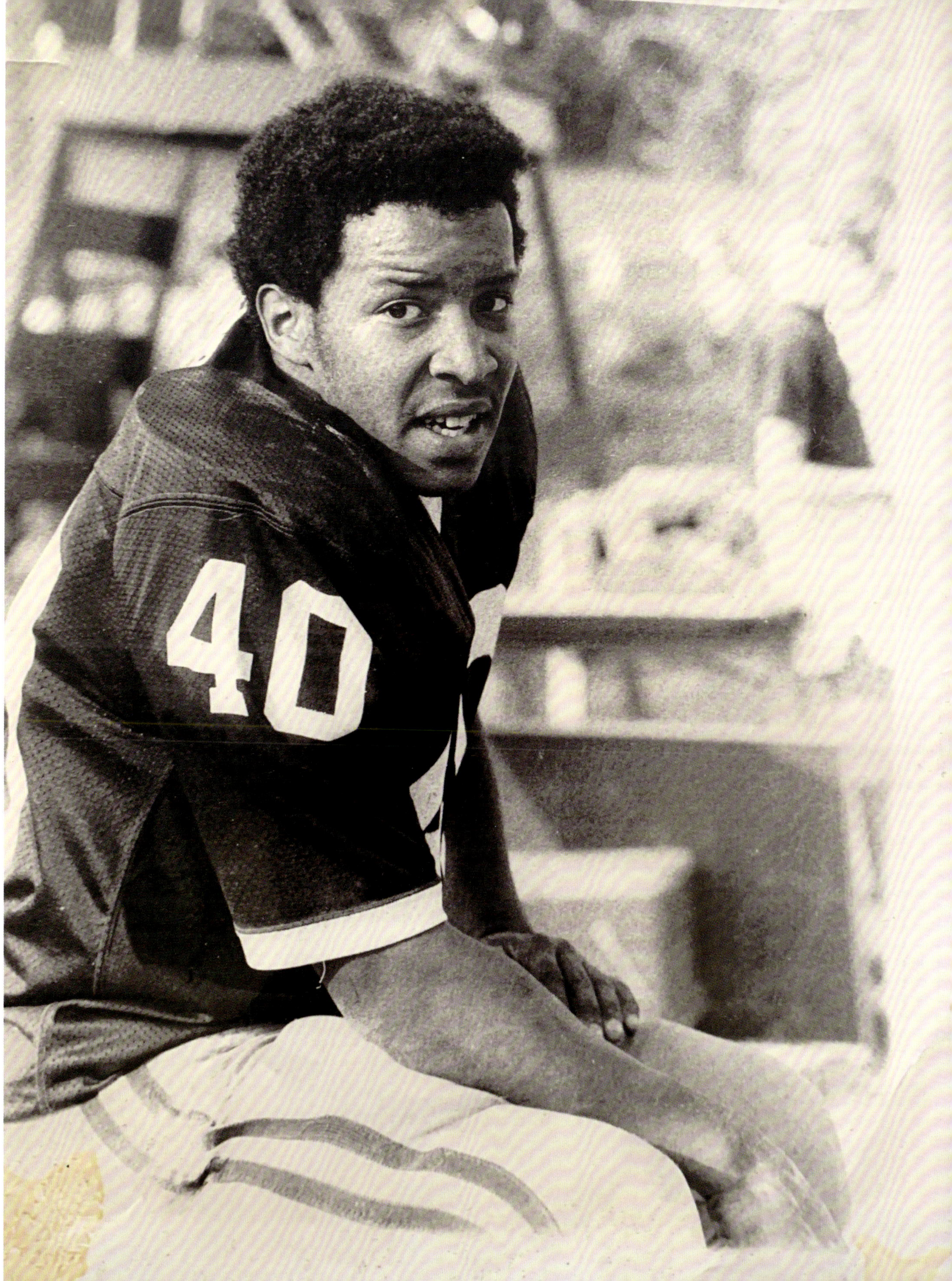
40

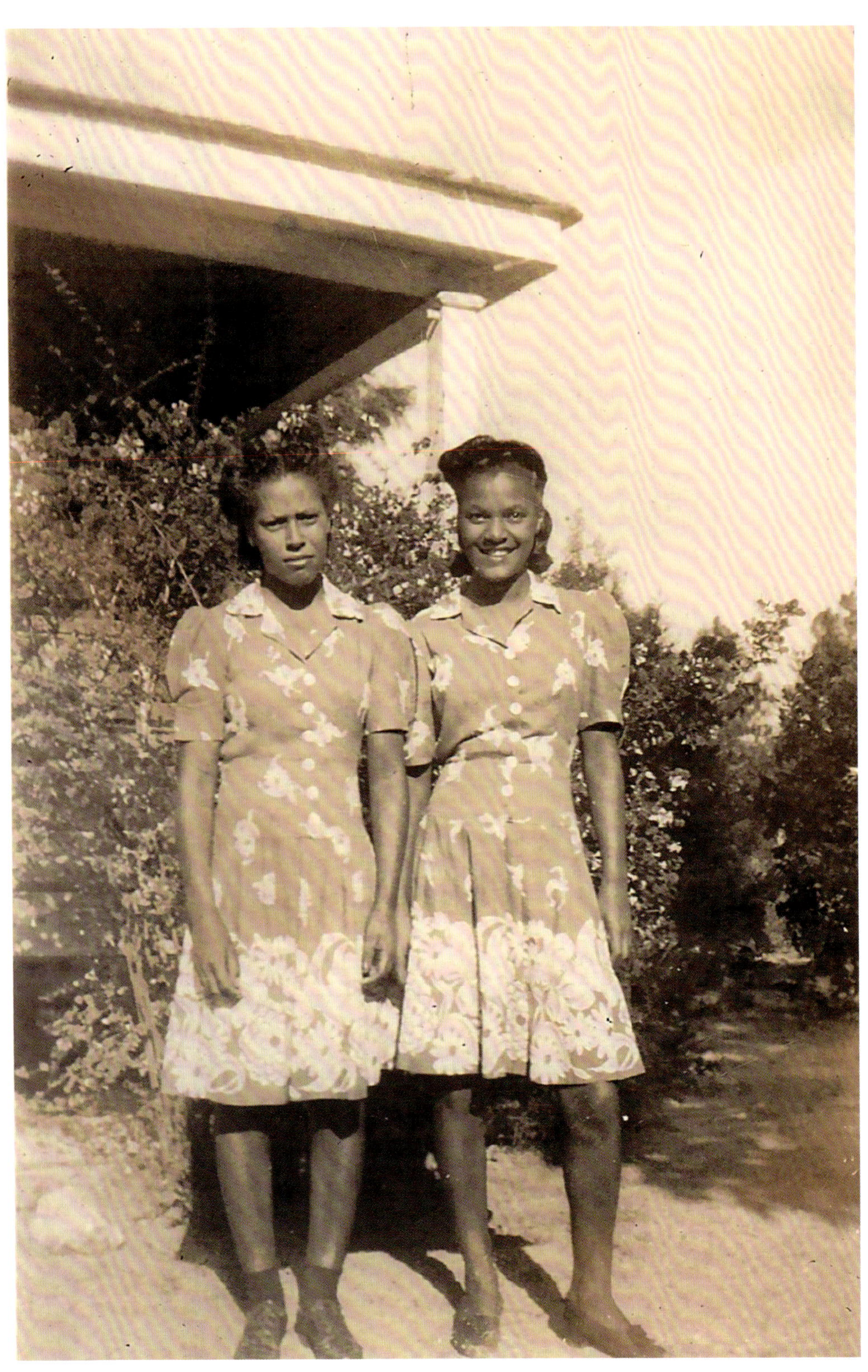

Lottie and
Mattie Brevard
at home
CAMDEN, SC
CIRCA 1940

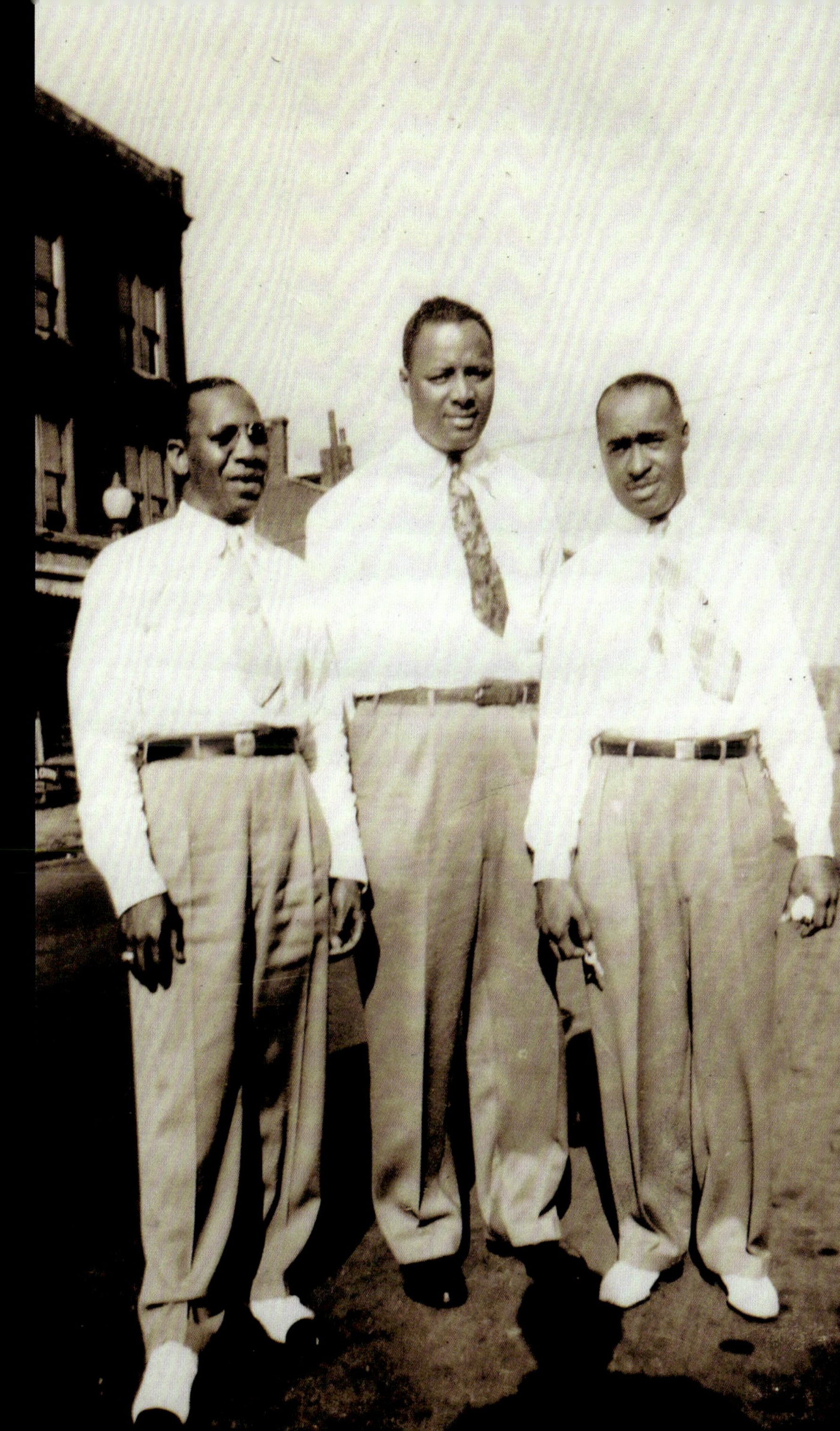

1945

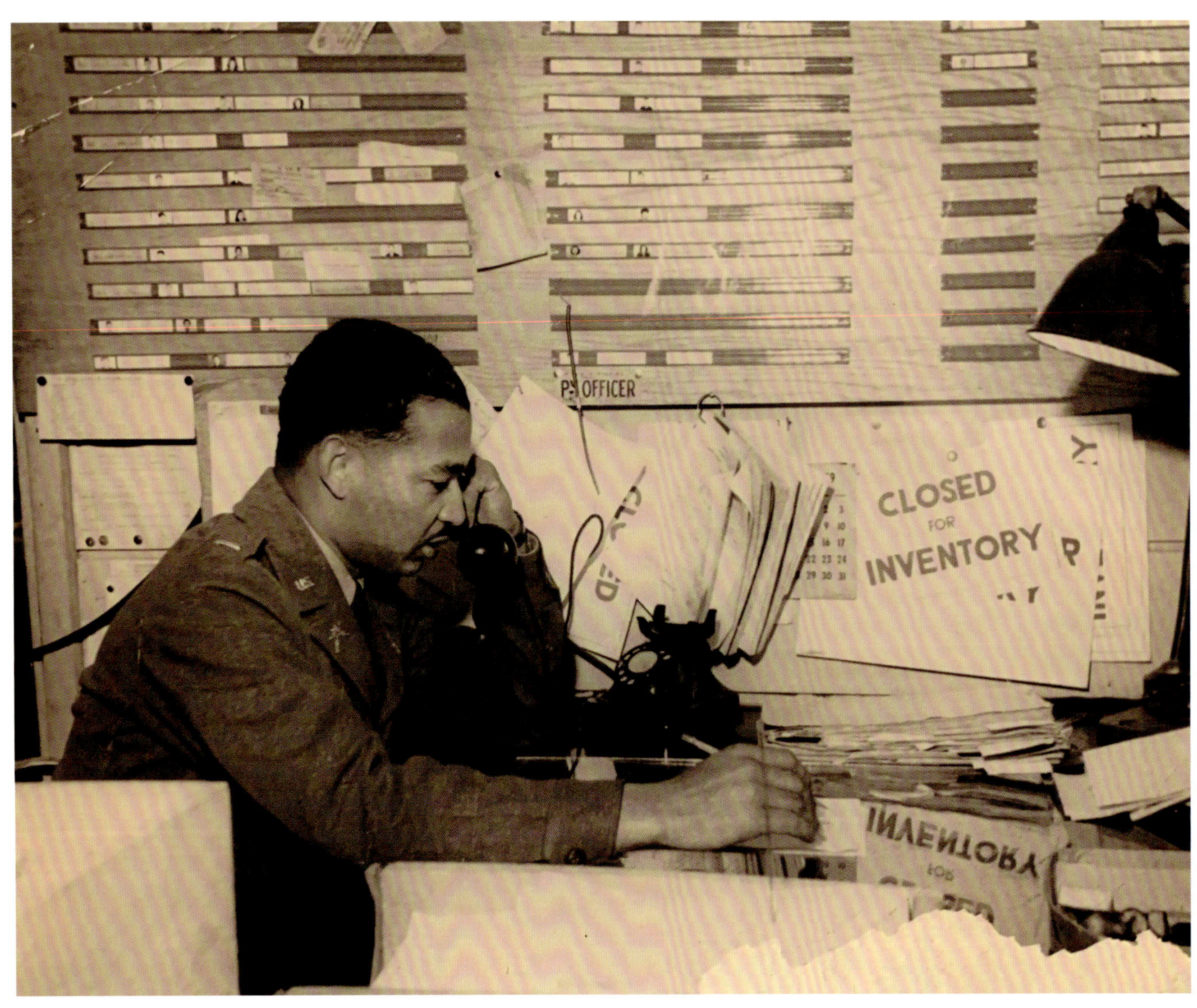

Lieutenant Colonel Price

CIRCA 1945

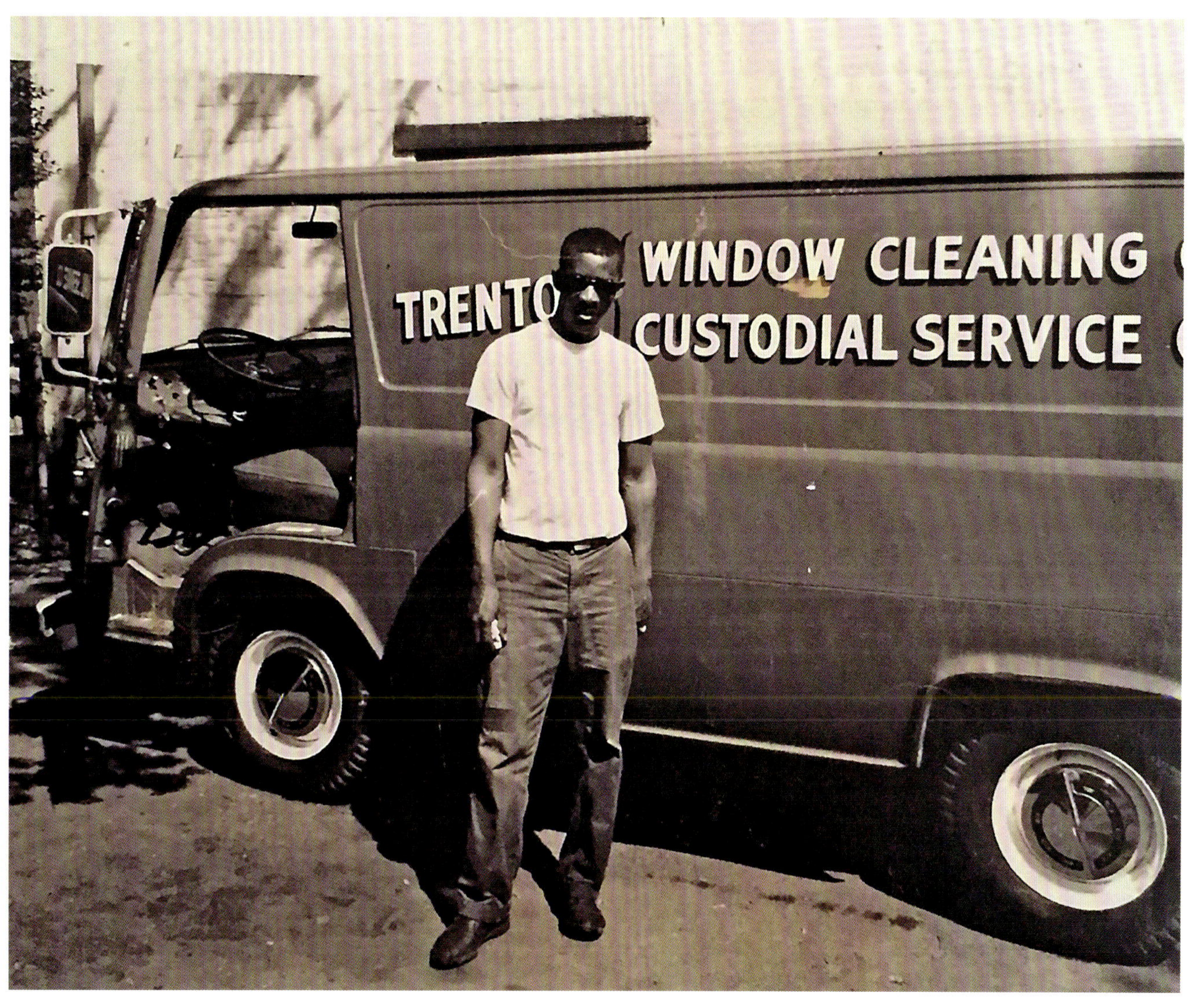

1960S

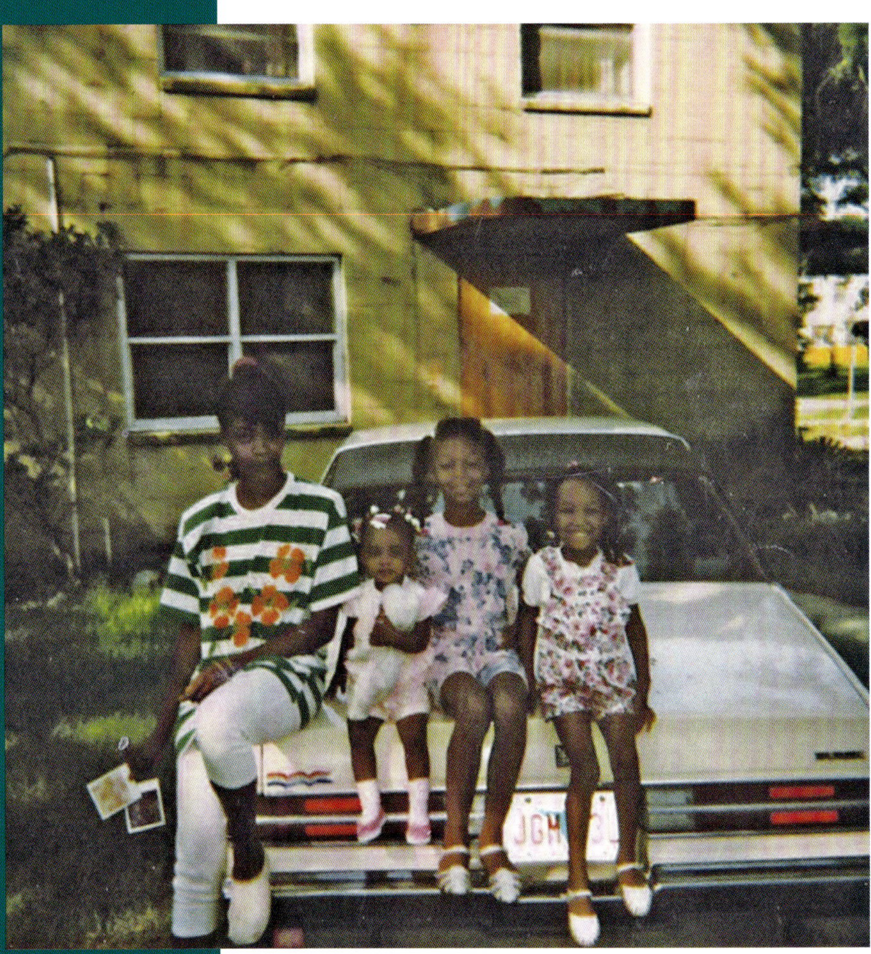

The author and her relatives sitting on the back of her grandfather's car
JACKSONVILLE, FL
1990S

POSES WITH CARS

Since the invention of motor vehicles, Black people have long played a vital role in not only their manufacturing, but also in the implementation of vehicle safety features and the creation of traveling guides such as *The Negro Motorist Green Book*. Collectively, these contributions have assisted travelers on their journey from one destination to another while also empowering them to experience the open road.

Car ownership has been and continues to be a moment of celebration for many Black people. It signifies wealth or upward mobility to some; joy or liberation to others, and the perfect way to memorialize these moments has been through the use of the camera. Dating back to the earliest snapshots of people posing with cars, it's apparent that Black people have mastered the art of capturing the moment from both sides of the camera. From the selection of the car itself to the subject placements, the act of posing with cars is style personified.

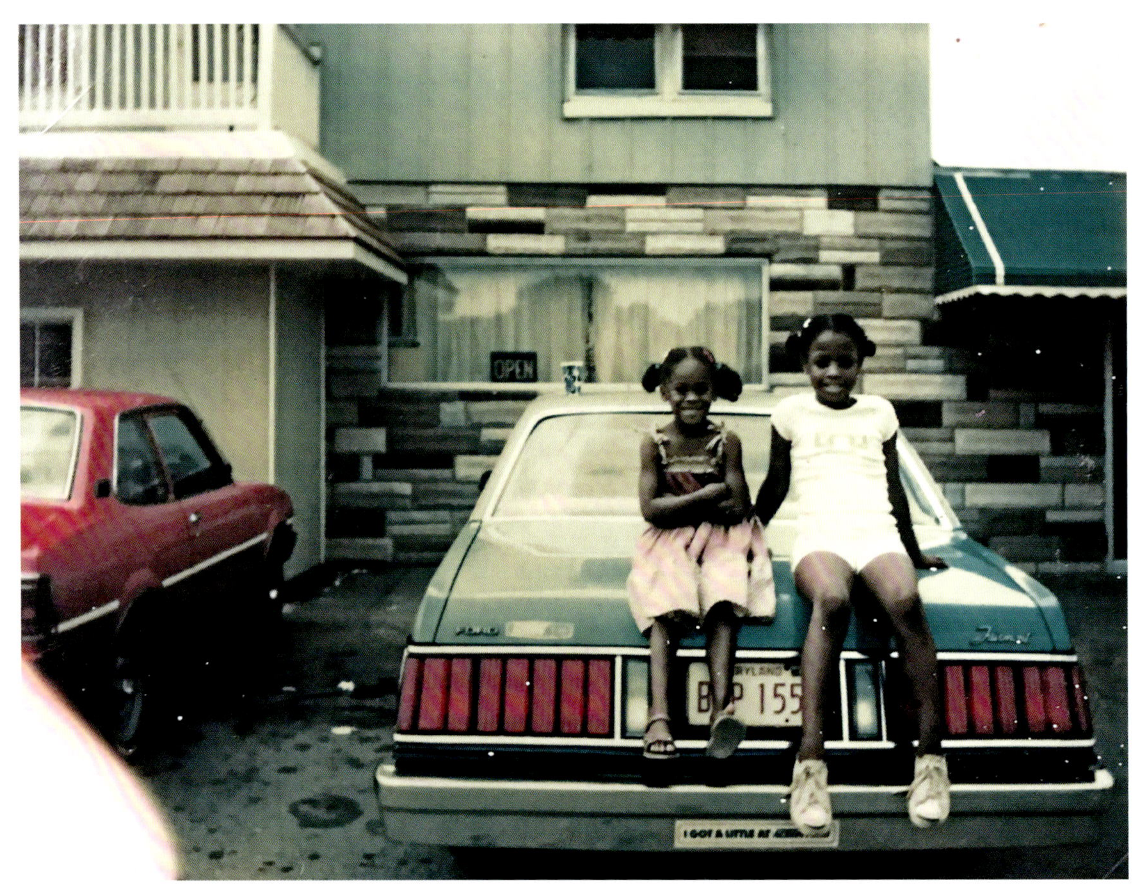

Mom and Teyonya
1978

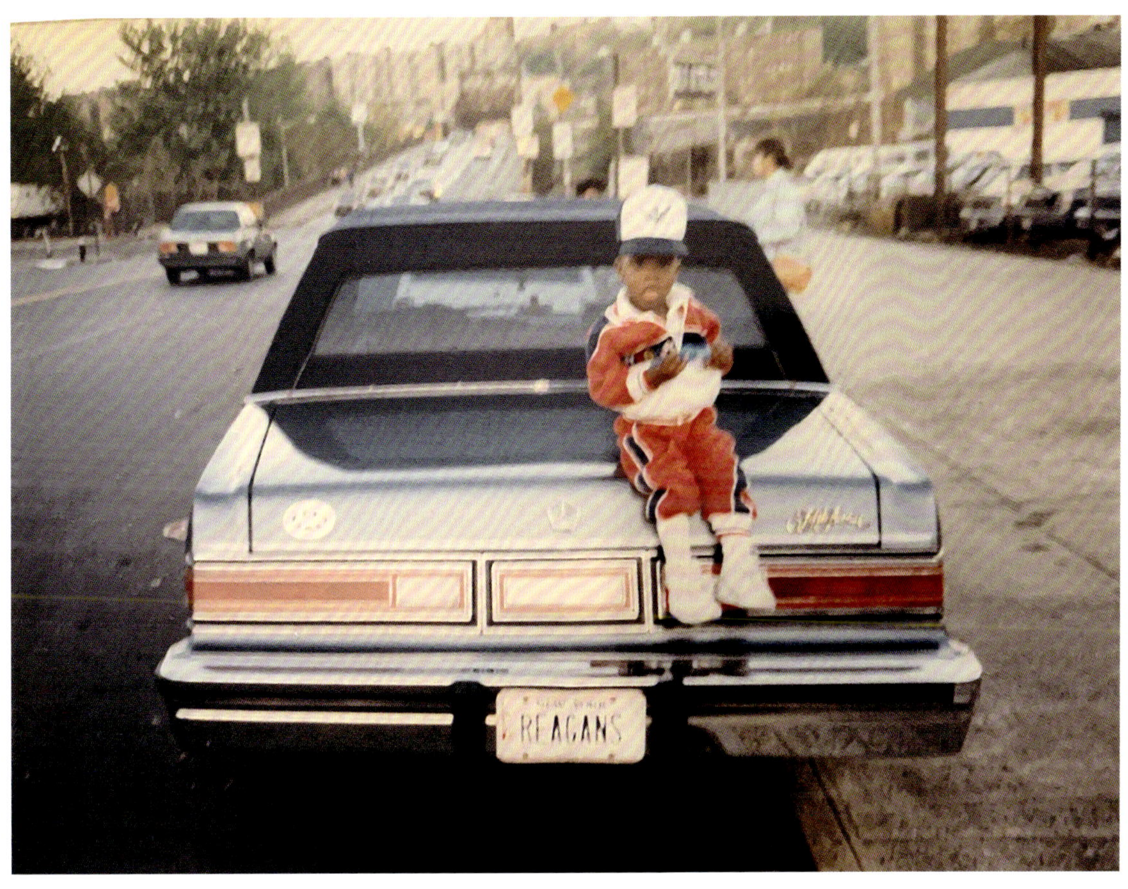

HARLEM, NY

1980S

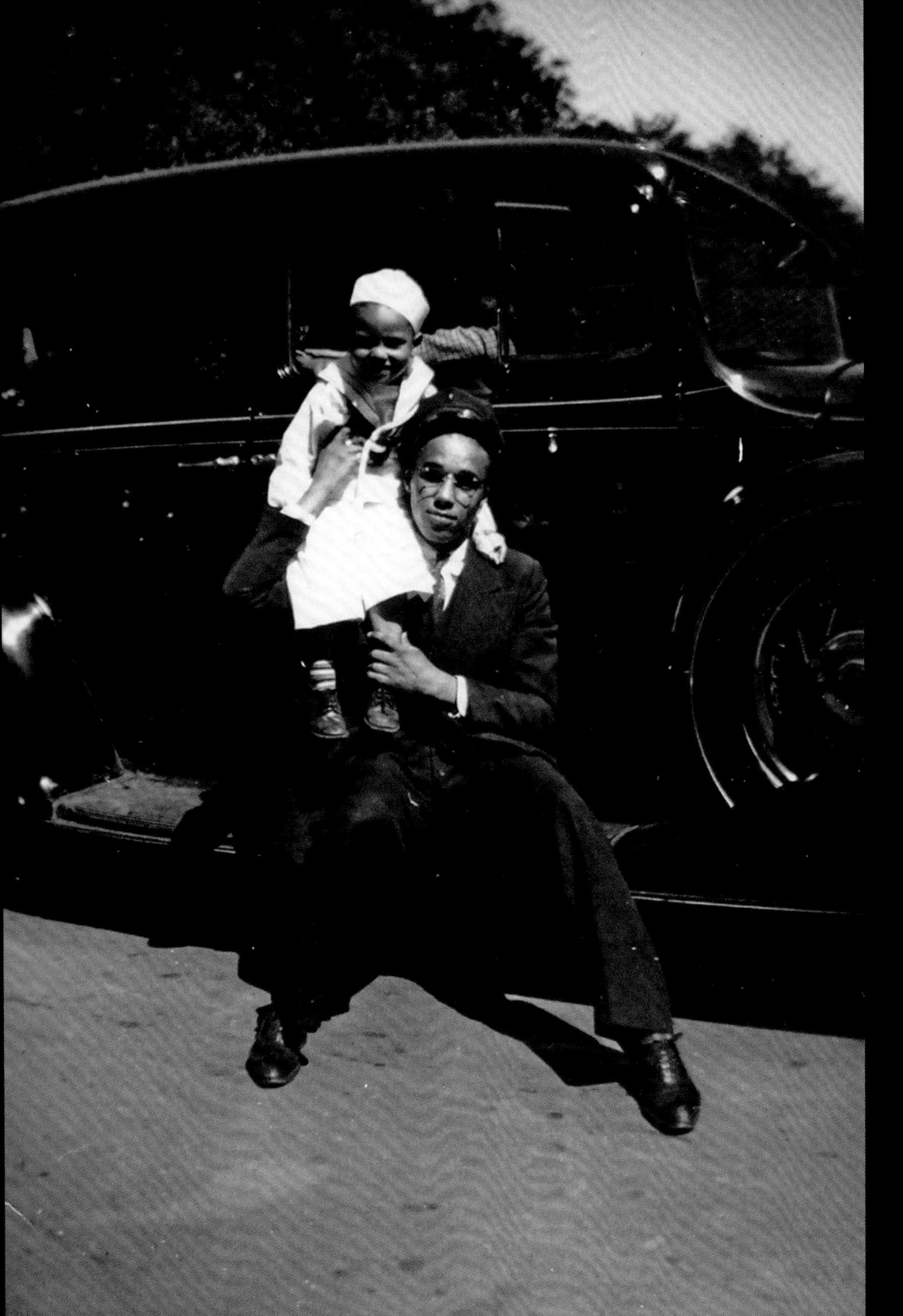

CIRCA 1940S

CIRCA 1945

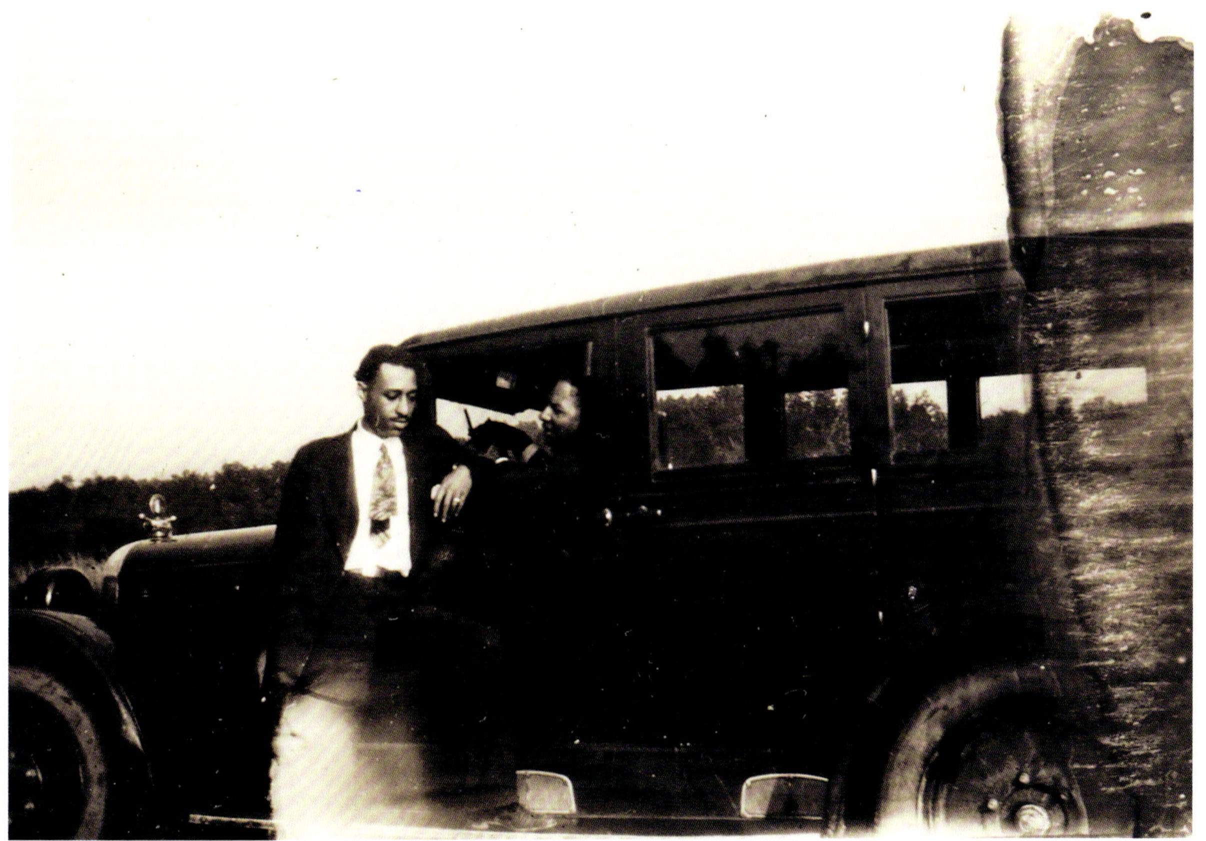

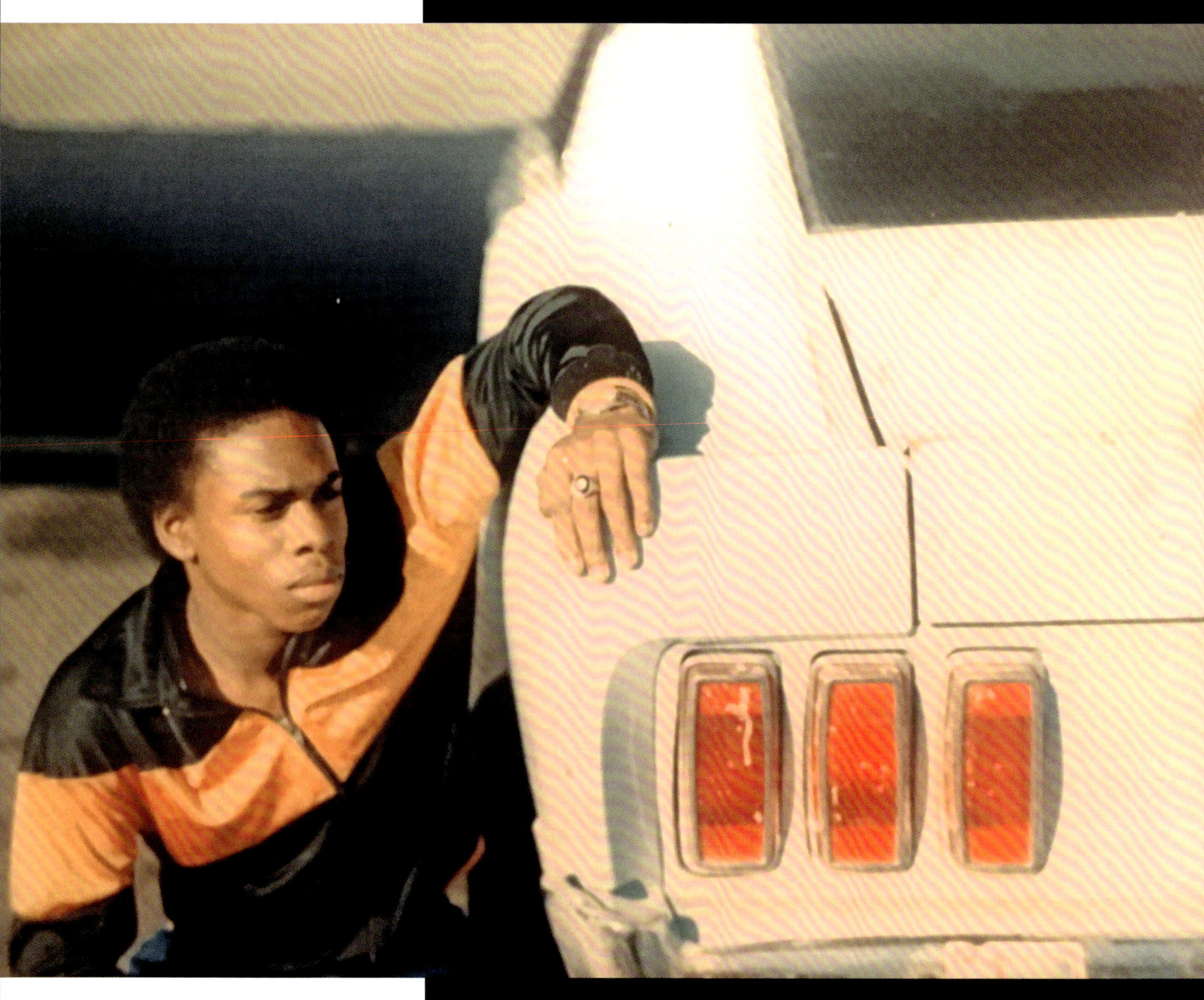

James and his car
SANTA ROSA, CA
1980S

→ JAMAICA

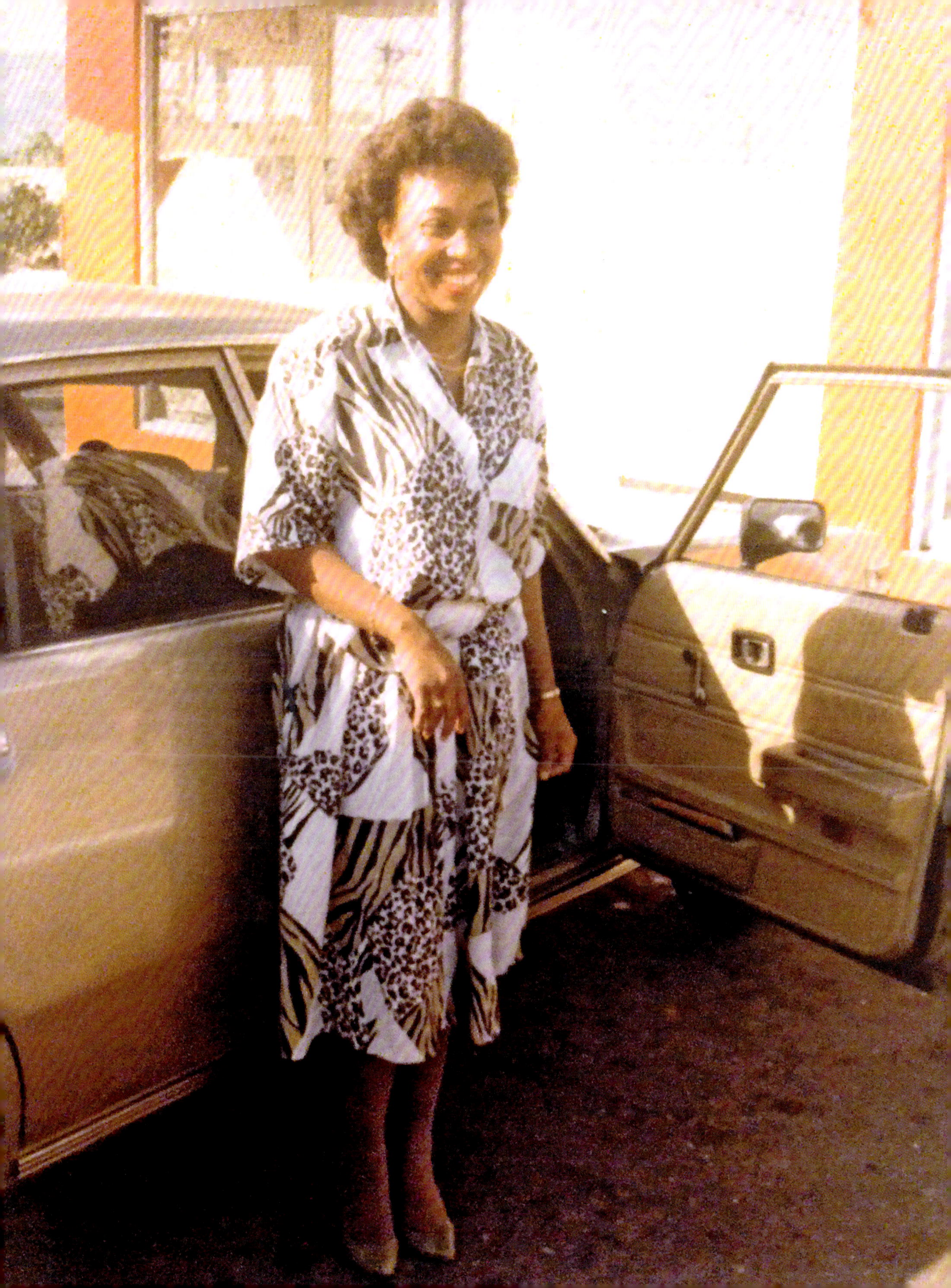

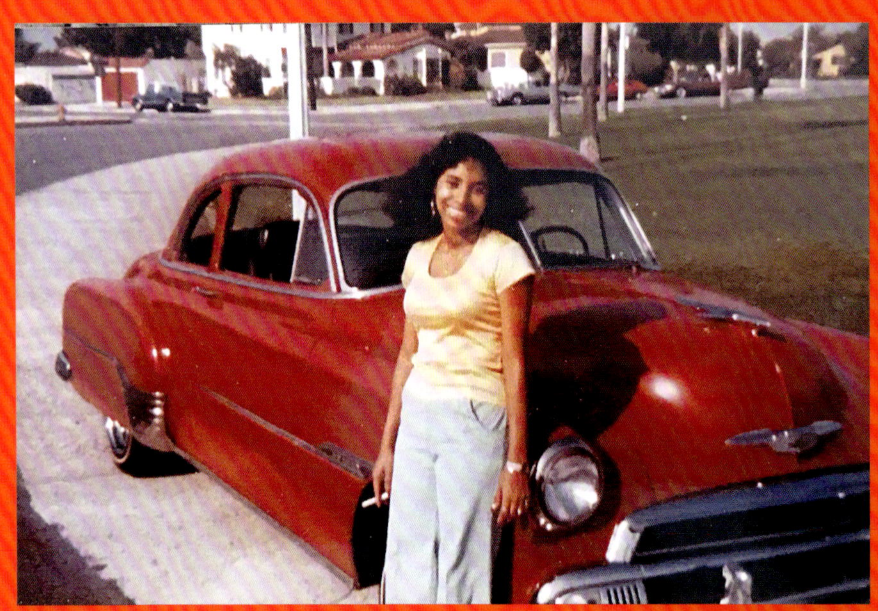

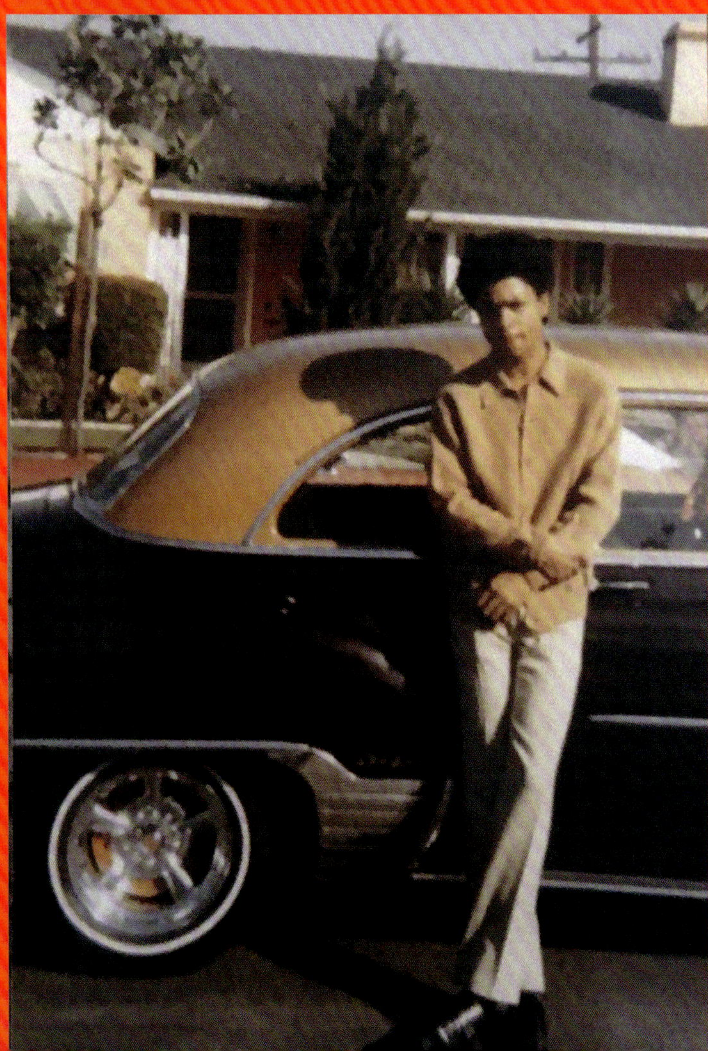

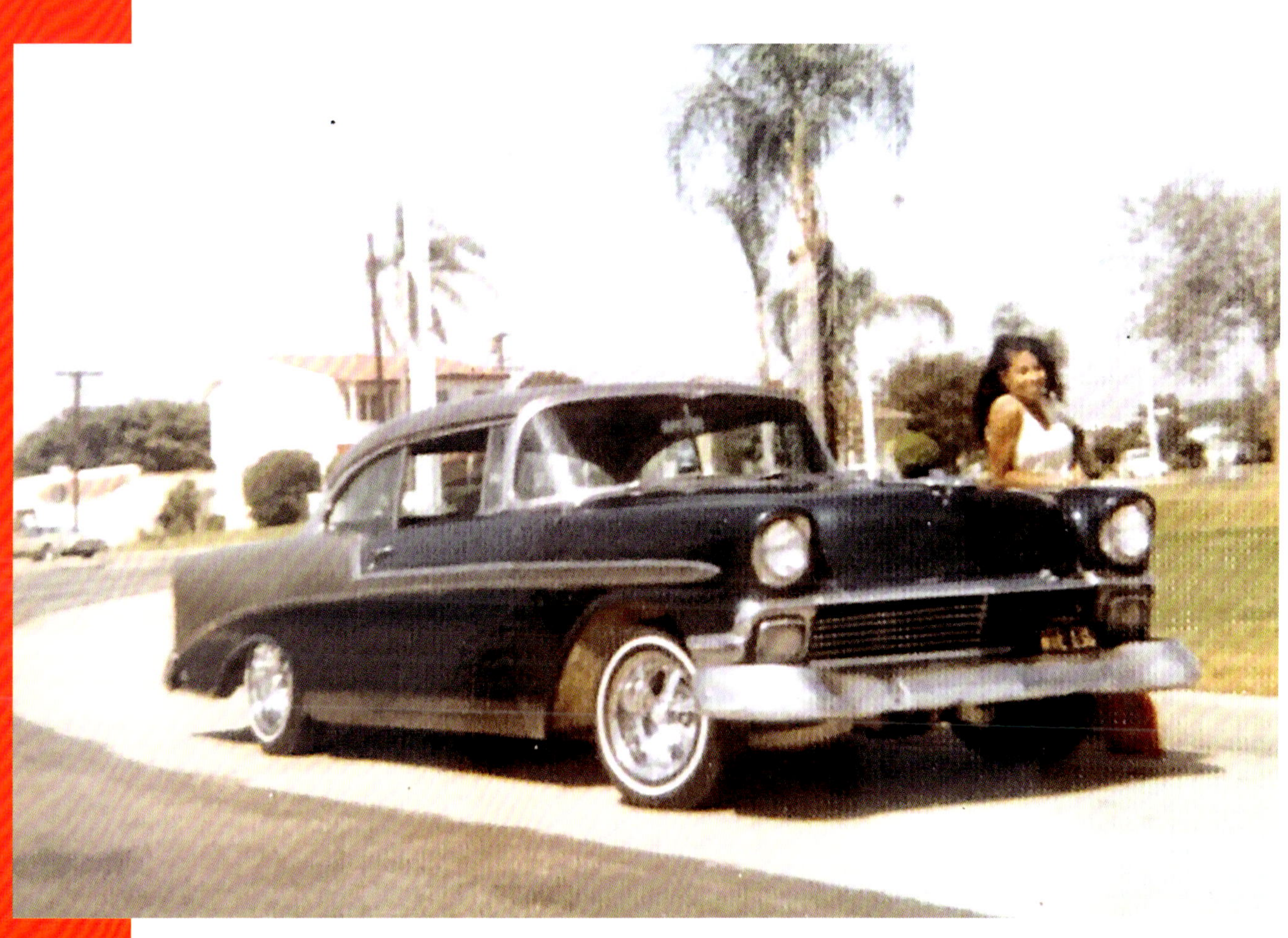

Morningside Park
INGLEWOOD, CA
1970S

Robert and Tressie Knox outside their home
DETROIT, MI
1970S

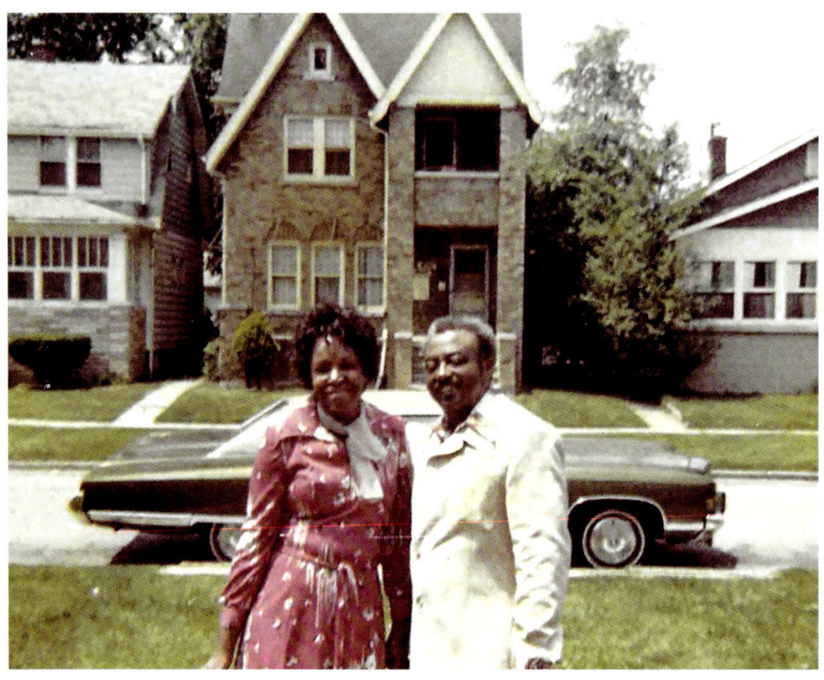

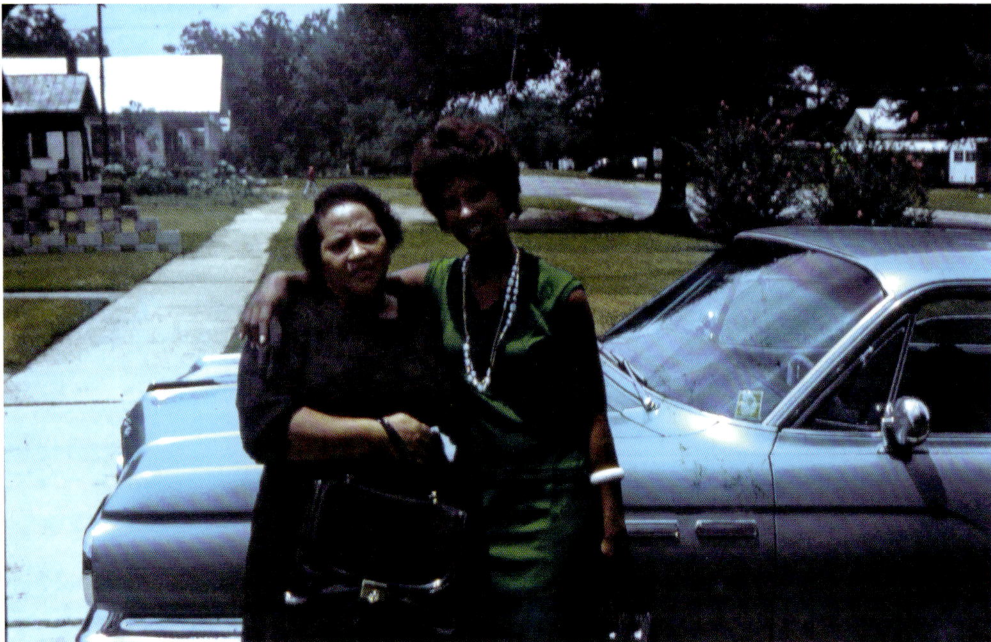

The South
CIRCA 1998

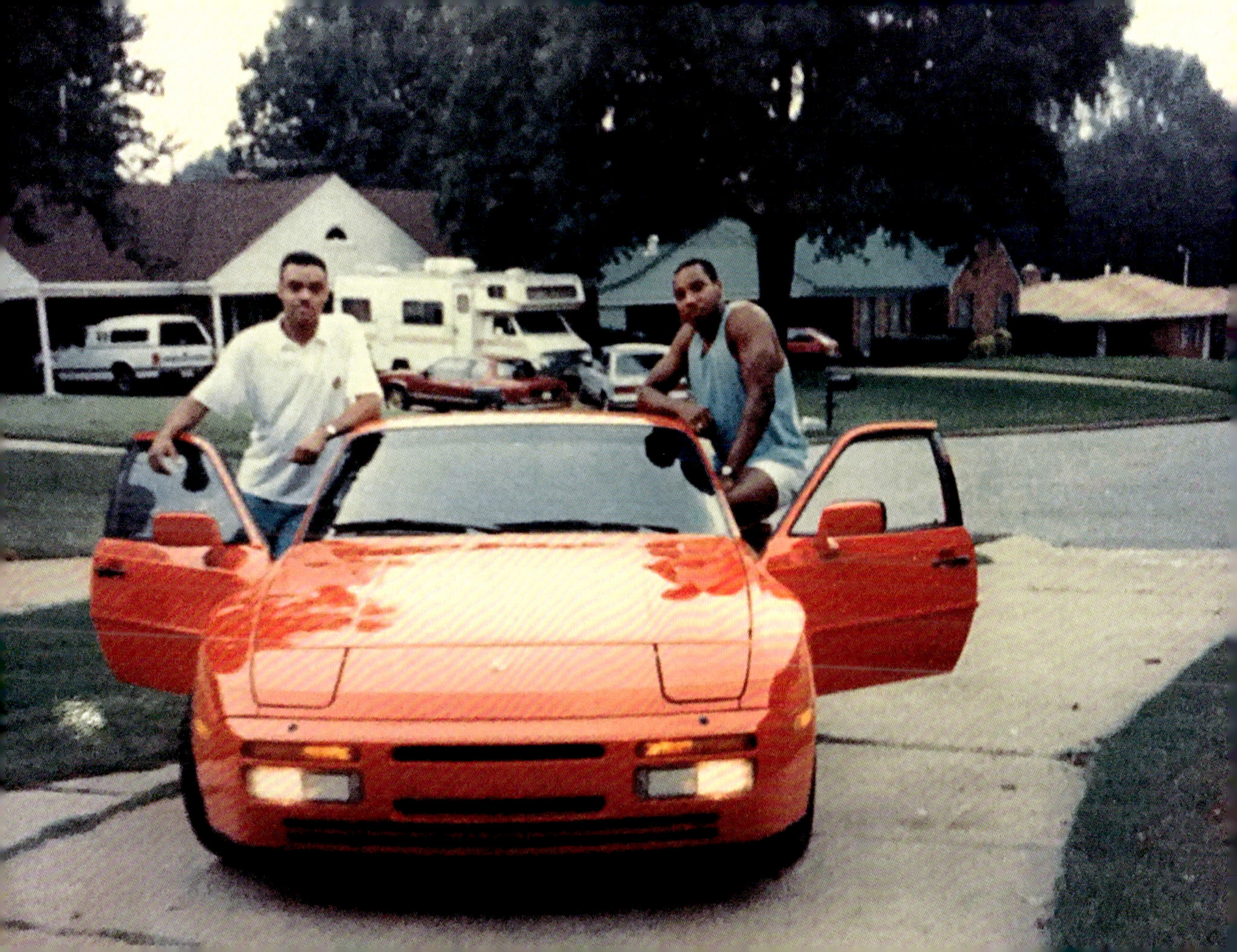

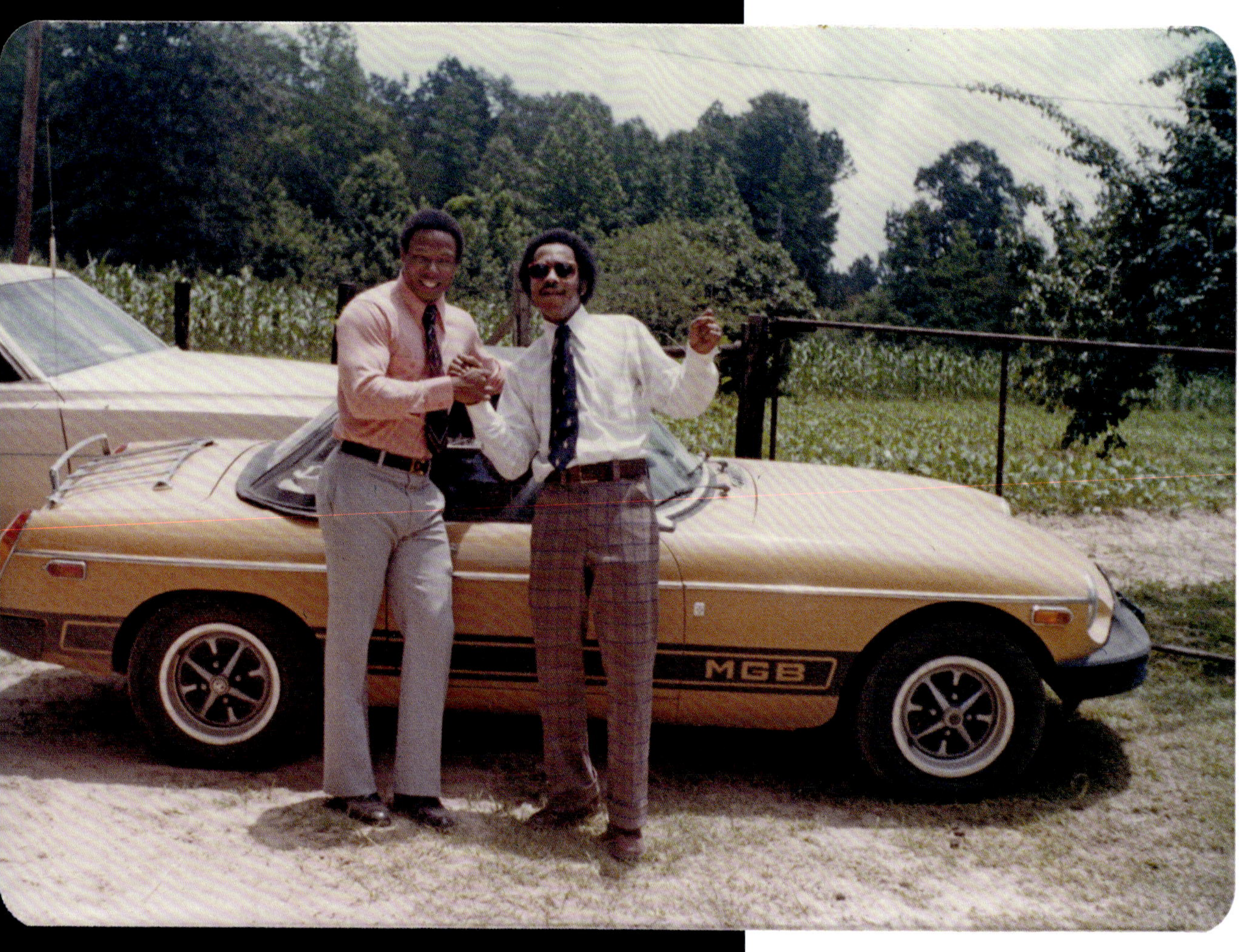

The Odom family

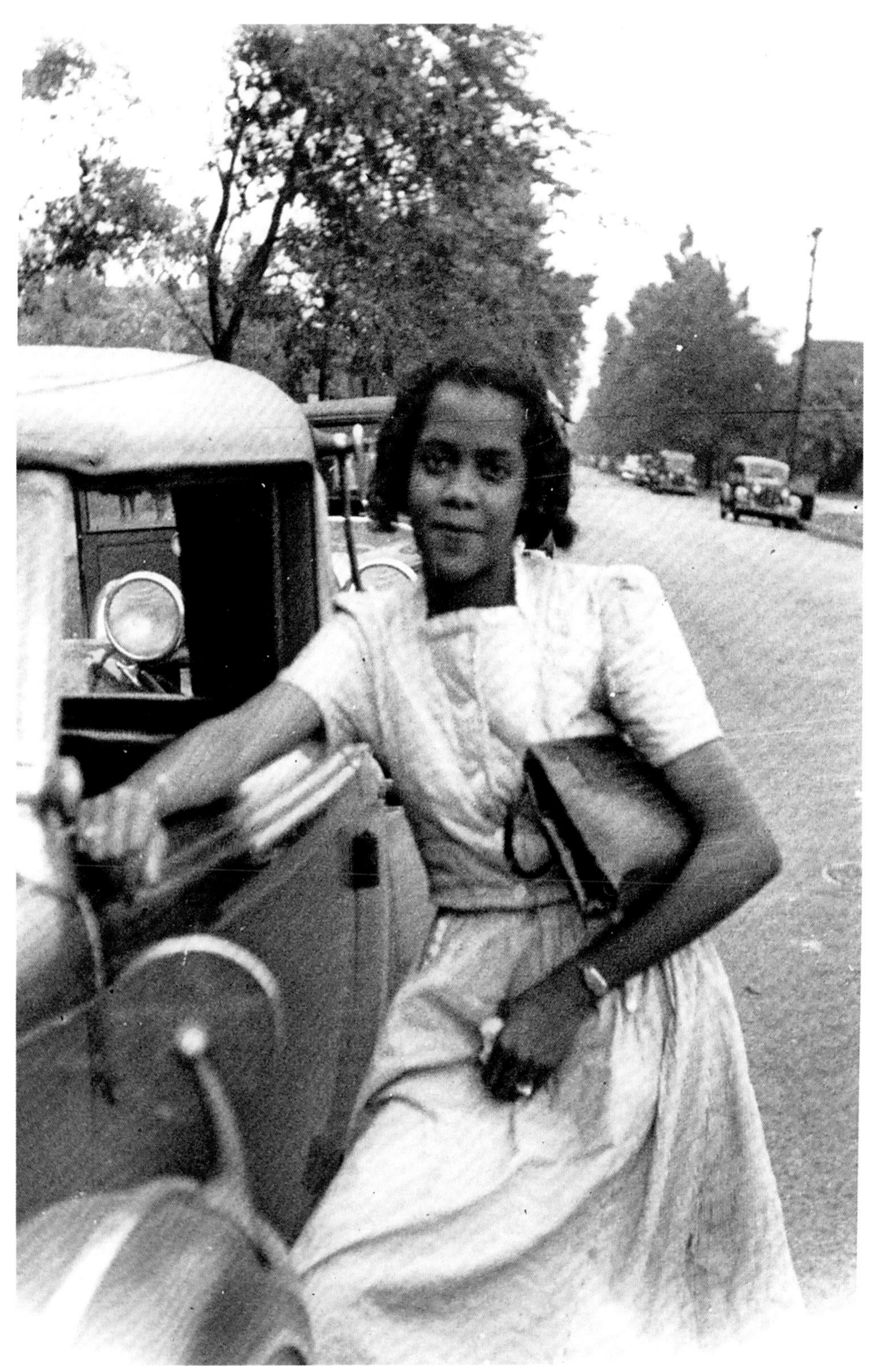

BOSTON, MA

CIRCA 1955

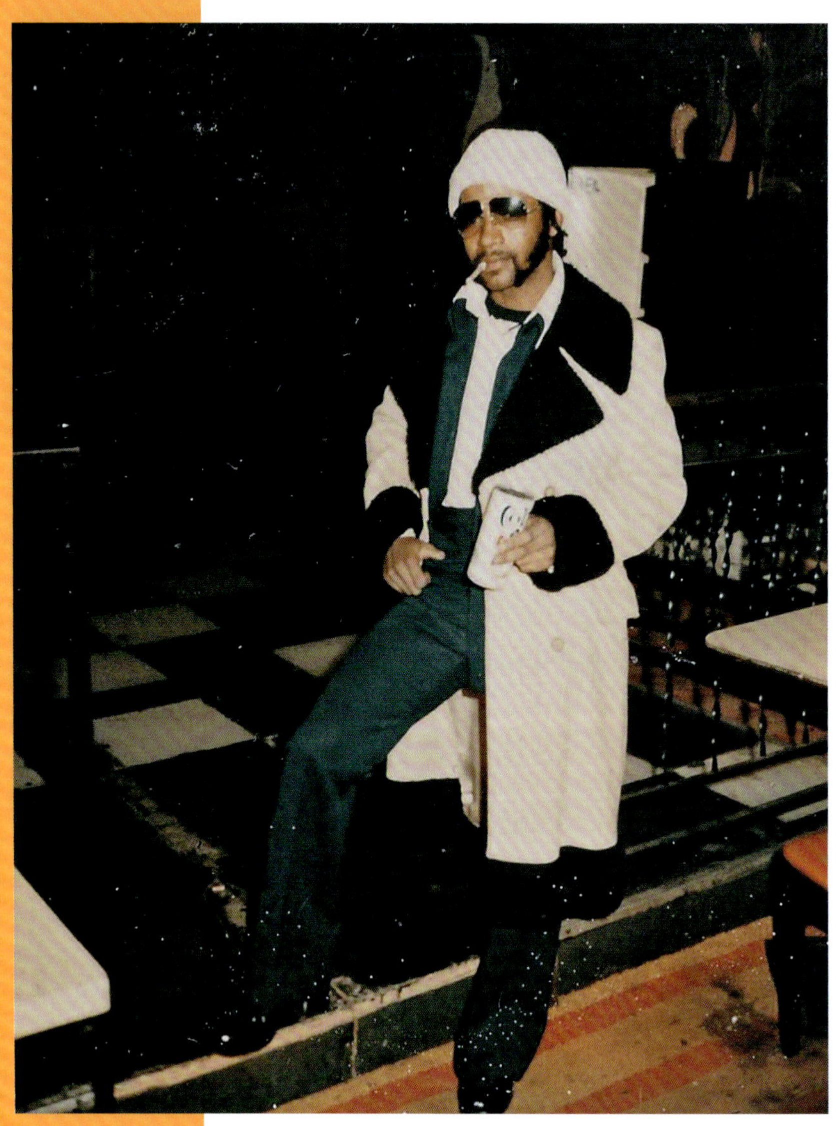

A family friend of the author's during a night out
1970S

A GOOD TIME

Black people have always found a way to have a good time. Whether it's a night out on the town with friends, a party, or a solo date night, having a good time is the joy we gift ourselves for living. And a joyous occasion doesn't always have to be under the greatest conditions – sometimes, enjoying the moment can be simply what you make of a situation, for better or worse.

Making time to celebrate ourselves and loved ones can also be about our lived experiences and the choices made in light of, or because our circumstances. It can be defined as being fully present, or the ways by which we find comfort and escape from the daily pressures of life. Even the anticipation of having a good time is necessary for our survival because in those thoughts of joy, the promise of a celebration can carry us through. This series is a celebration. It serves as a reminder to take up space in this world and preserve the moment as evidence of a life fully lived.

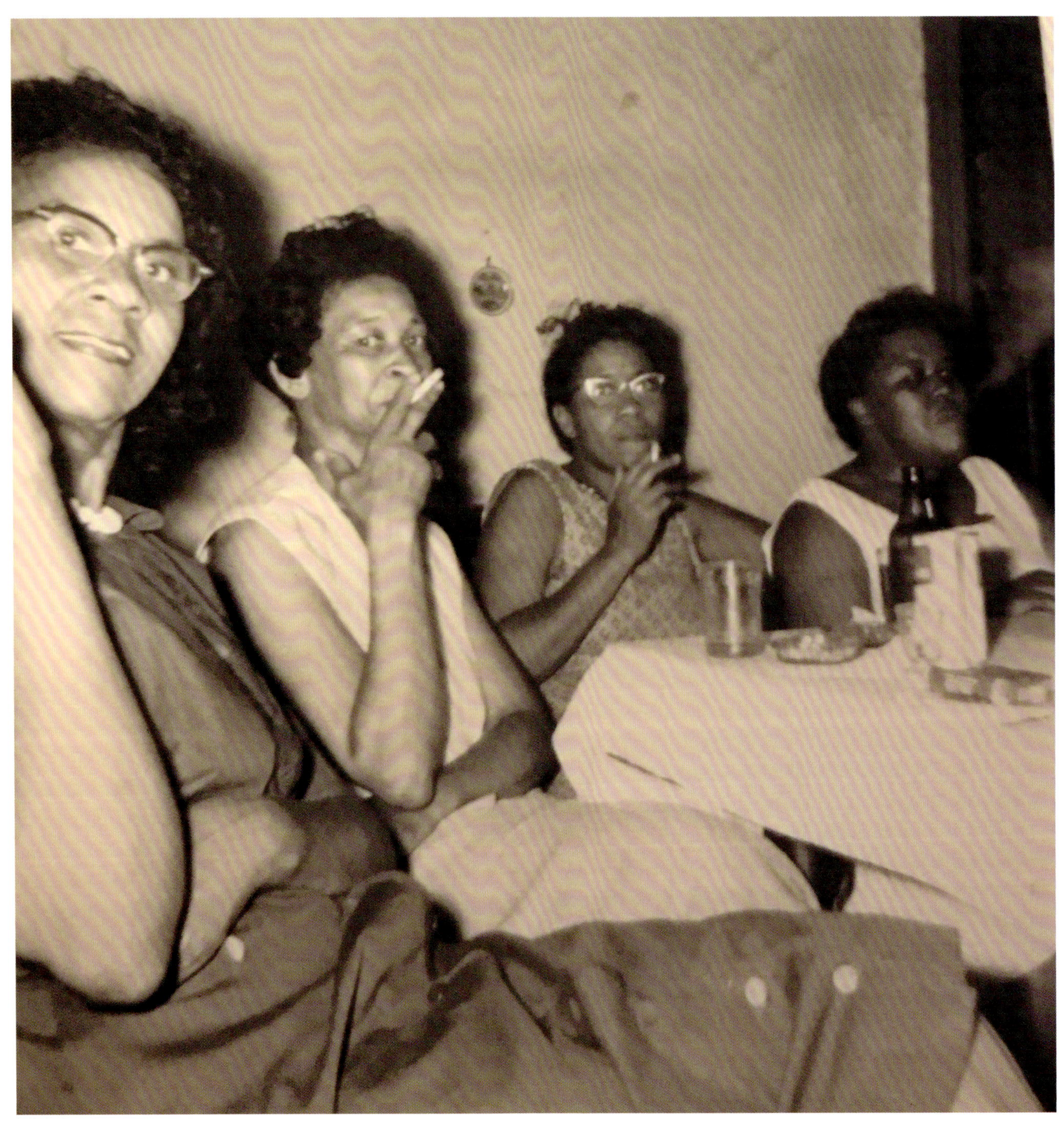

From left: Mertelia, Idelle, Frances, and Lucile
RICHMOND, VA
1962

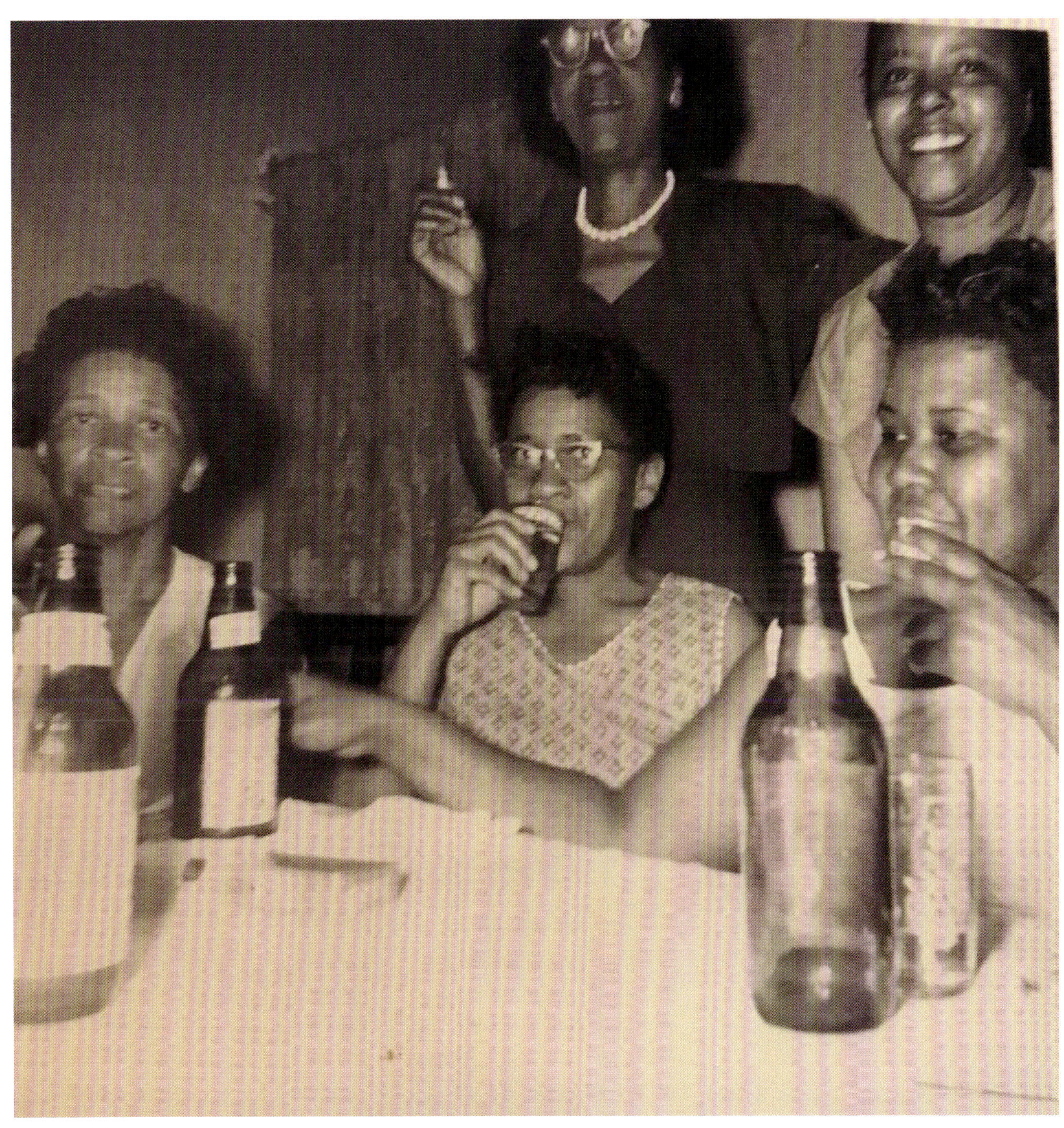

From left: (seated) Idelle, Frances, and Lucile; (standing) Mertelia and a family friend

RICHMOND, VA

1962

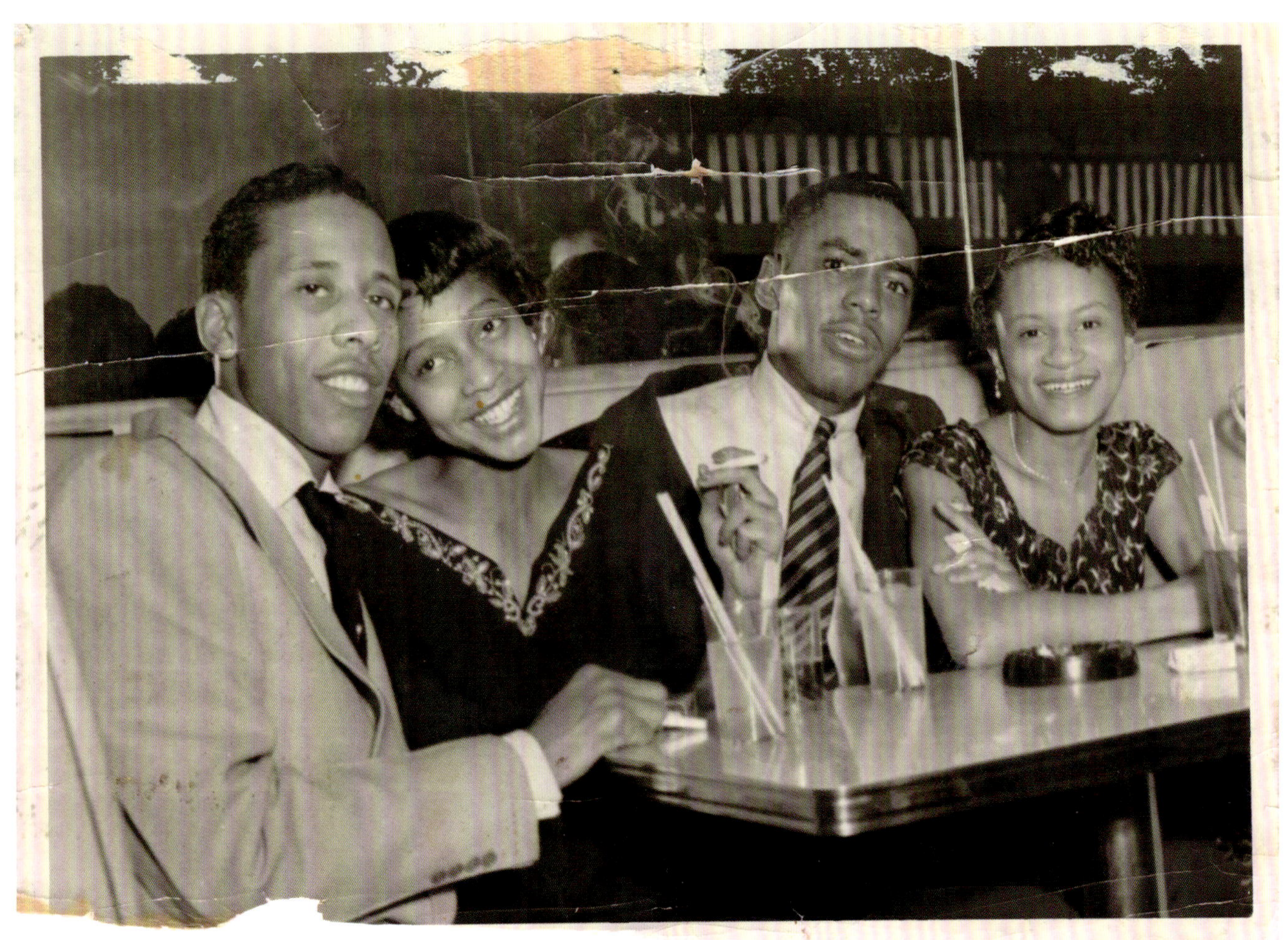

1950S

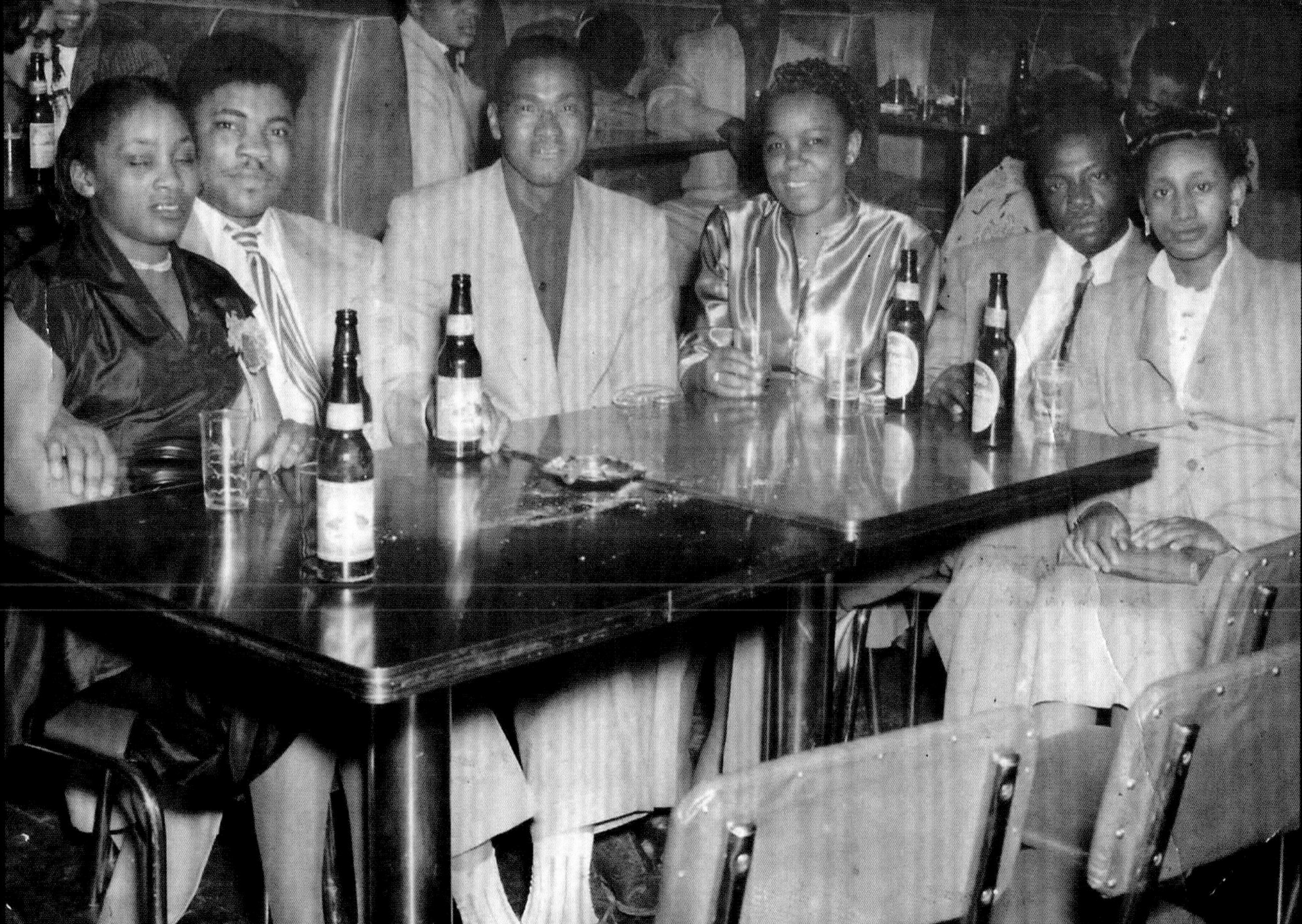

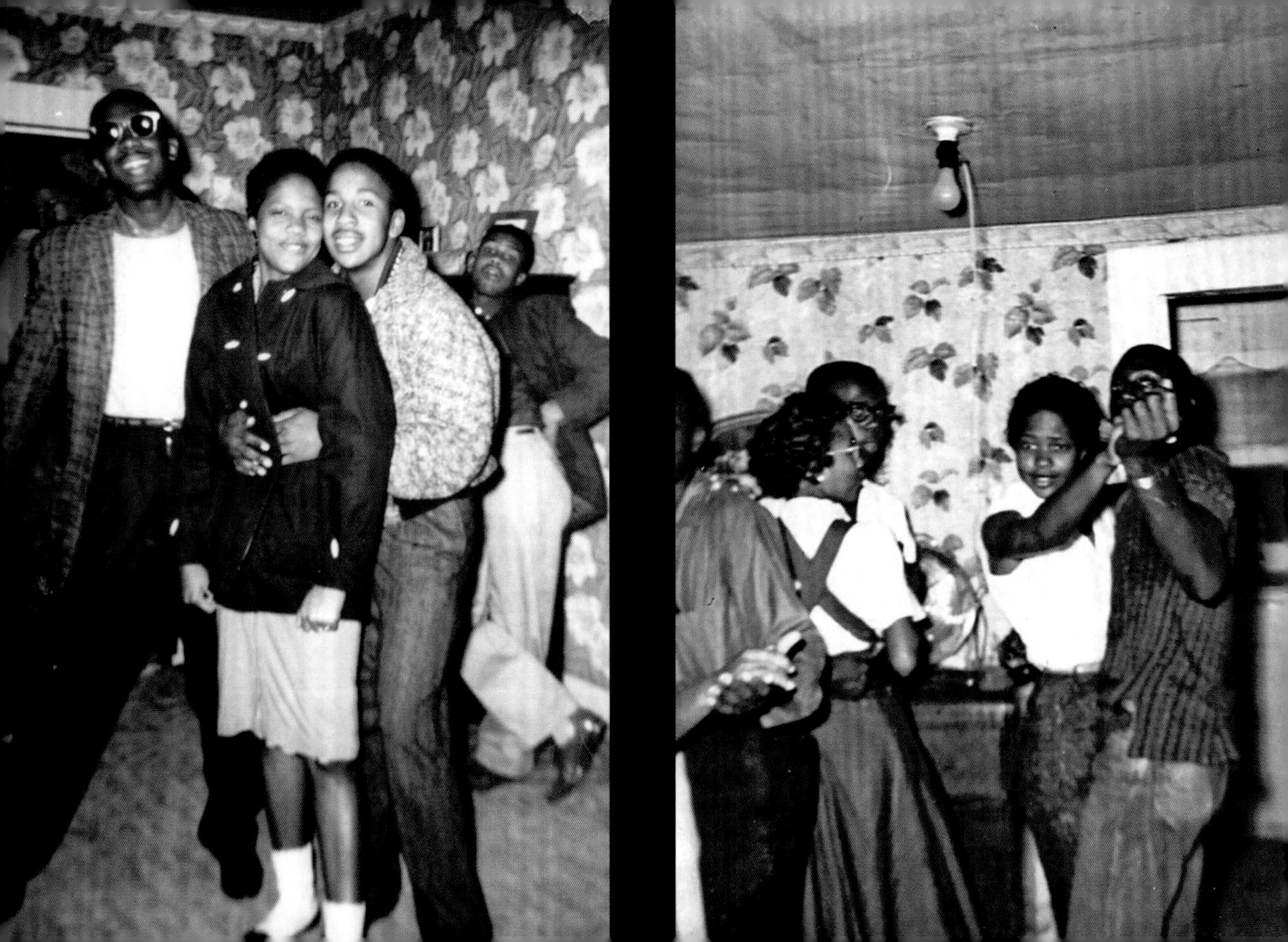

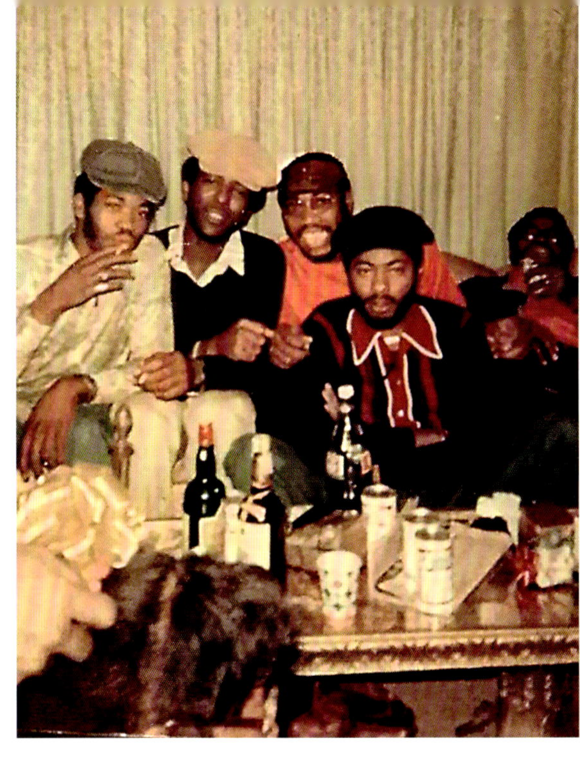

Gathering at the holidays
GASTON COUNTY, NC
CIRCA 1970

MEMPHIS, TN
1970S

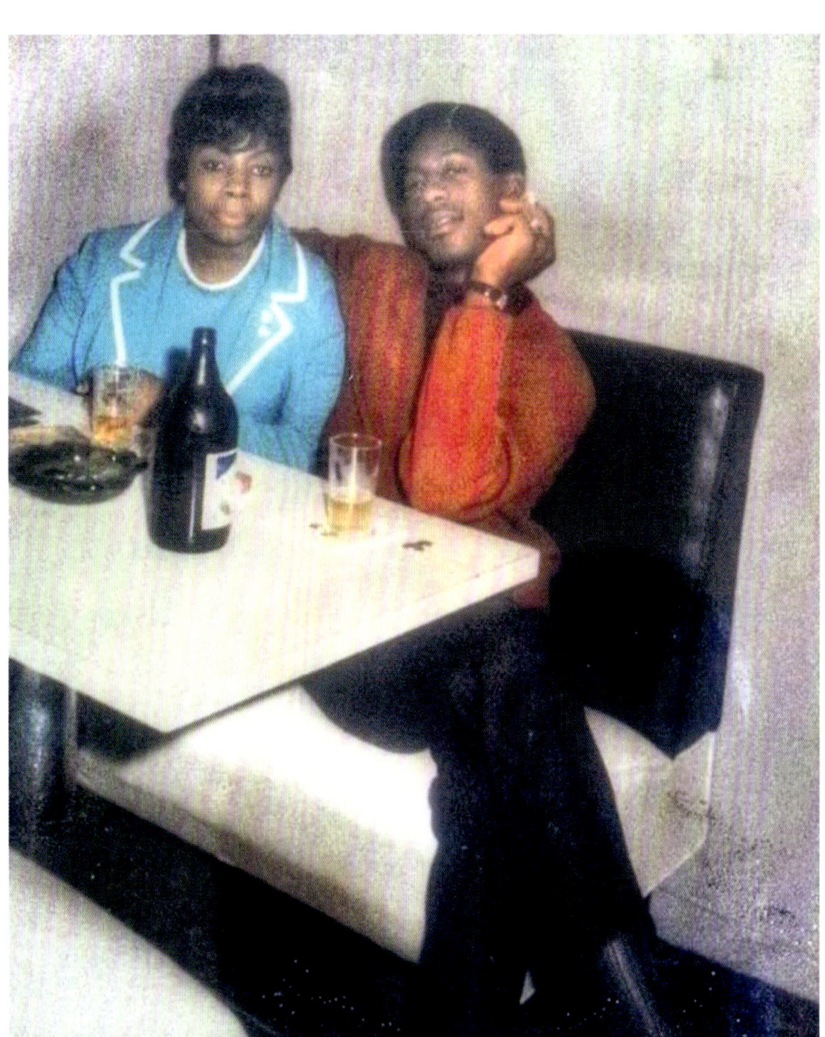

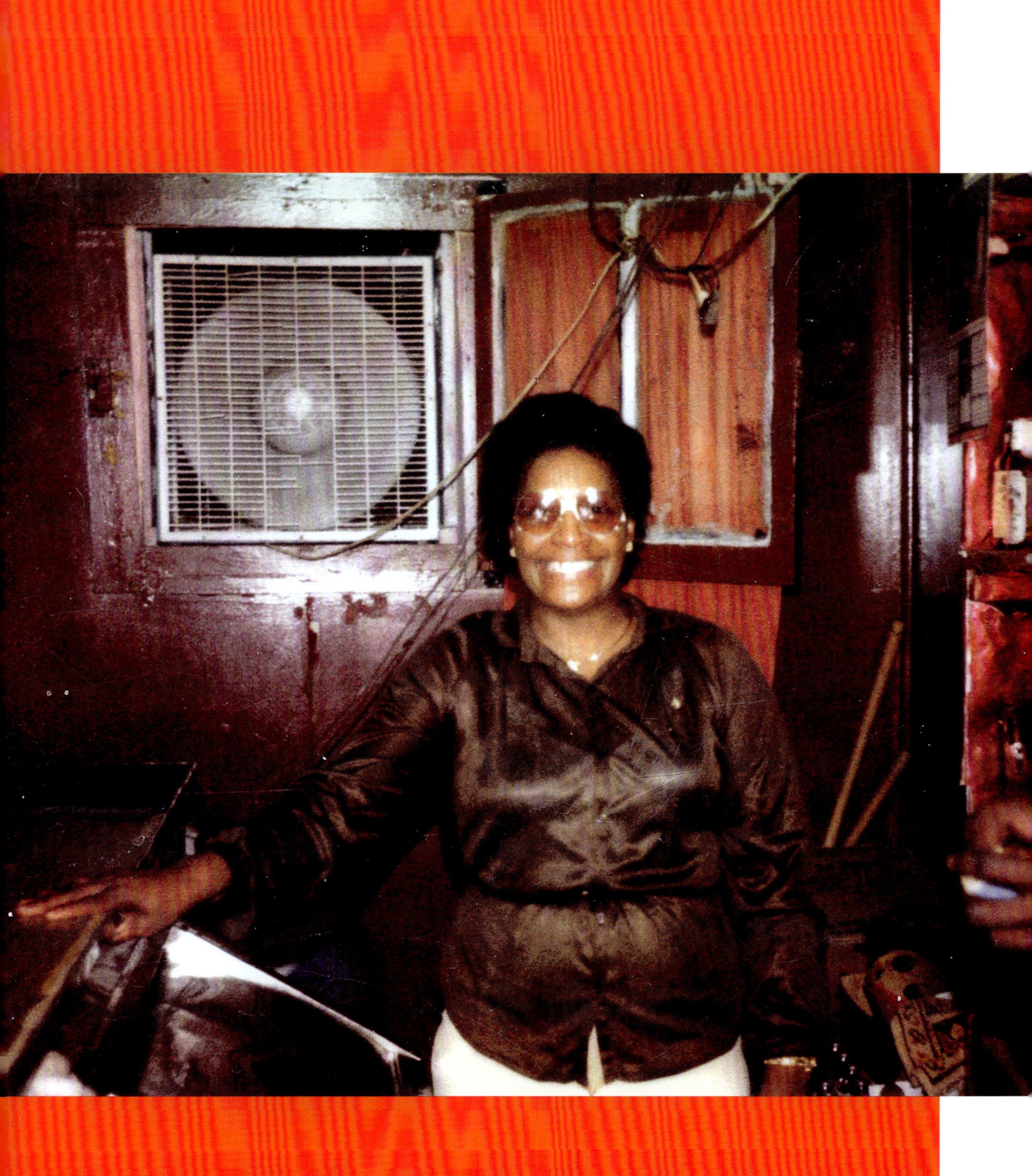

ATLANTA, GA

1972

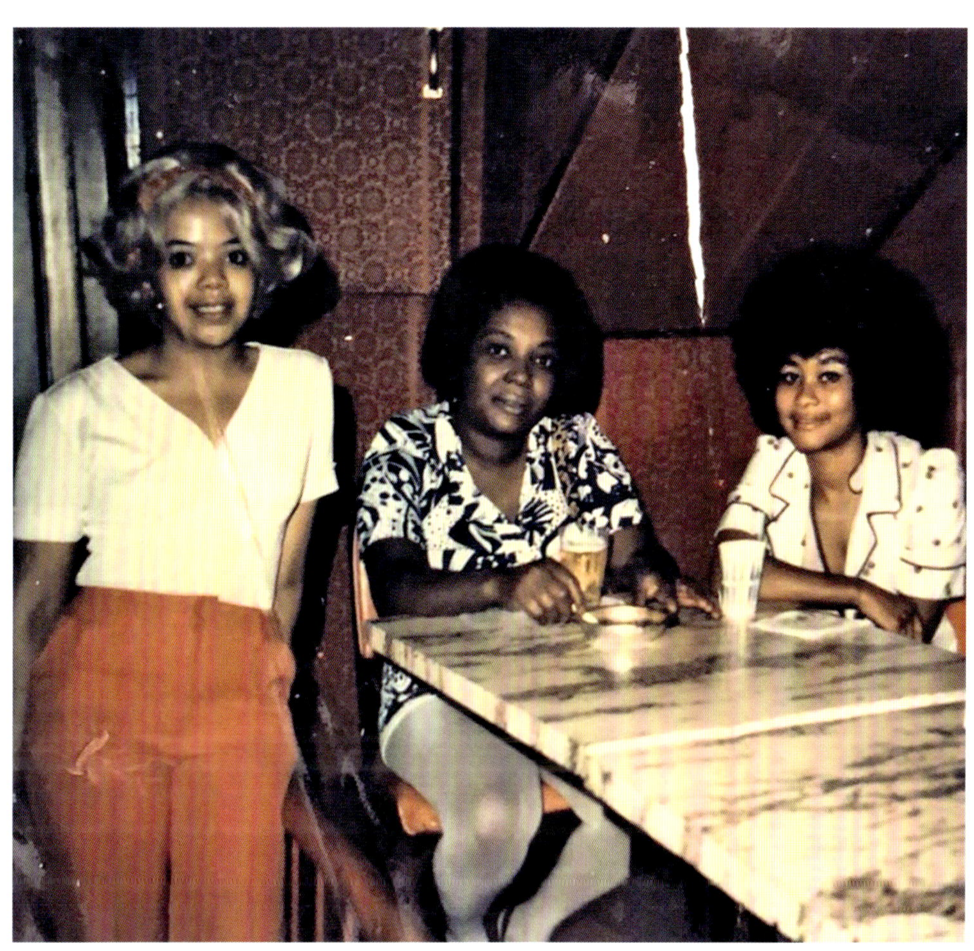

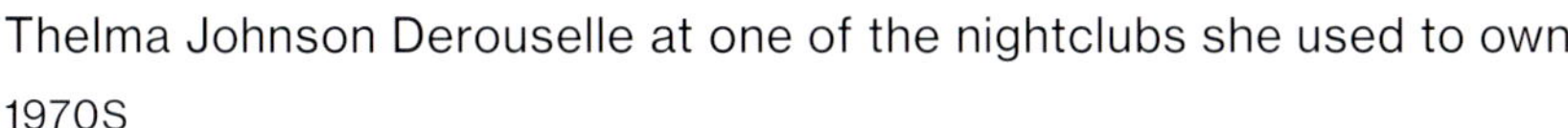

Thelma Johnson Derouselle at one of the nightclubs she used to own

1970S

PHOTO CREDITS

INSTITUTIONAL ARCHIVES

African American Museum & Library at Oakland, E. F. Joseph Photograph Collection page 180; Alabama Department of Archives and History pages 30 and 125; AUC Robert W. Woodruff Library Anna E. Hall Collection page 229; AUC Robert W. Woodruff Library Bishop Howard J. Dell Collection pages 140, 153, 154, 155, 156, 157, 159, 243, and 270; AUC Robert W. Woodruff Library Robert E. Penn Collection pages 100, 172, 174, 175, 199, and 200; The Barbara Brown Collection, Camden Archives and Museum pages 37, 198, and 256; Florida Memory State Library and Archives of Florida pages 53 and 98; From Plowshares to Diplomas: Digitizing Early Denton History, Courthouse-on-the-Square Museum pages 66, 67, and 216; Michael Francis Blake Photographs, Duke University Libraries pages 126, 127, and 134; R. W. Steen Library, Stephen F. Austin State University, Nacogdoches, Texas pages 169, 201, and 280; Rescuing Texas History, 2011 page 130; Rescuing Texas History, 2014, Austin History Center, Austin Public Library pages 132, 136, 181, 224, and 225; Rescuing Texas History, 2014, Dallas Municipal Archives page 33; Rescuing Texas History, 2016 page 152; Reverend Michael E. Haynes and the Lower Roxbury Black History Project at the Northeastern University Archives and Special Collections pages 36, 135, 137, 227, and 248; Stephen and David Hunter and the Lower Roxbury Black History Project at the Northeastern University Archives and Special Collections pages 35, 37, 50, 55, 61, 82, 88, 89, 105, 110, 111, 113, 136, 158, 160, 161, 162, 163, 165, 182, 183, 185, 203, 227, 228, 239, 251, 257, 264, and 273; Texas Cultures Online, San Antonio Public Library page 69; University of North Carolina at Asheville page 251; University of Southern California Digital Library page 24; The University of Texas at Arlington Library Special Collections pages 96, 97, 144, 149, 164, 208, 209, and 272.

FAMILY ARCHIVE SUBMISSIONS

Alesha Morgan pages 76 and 77; The Alexander Family (Brooklyn, NY, by way of St. Andrew, Grenada, WI) page 168; Alisha Henson page 271; Alkebuluan Merriweather page 278; Amber Aisha page 152; Amber George page 112; Angela Reagins page 133; Anny Marcela Pena Perea page 108; Ashley May pages 268 and 269; Ben DeSoto page 187; Bodeline Dautruche page 93; Briana Knox pages 51, 270, and 279; Brianna Jones page 30; Brianna Sancious page 148; Brooke Julien pages 230, 231, and 232; Brown/Cushnie Family page 94; Burrell Hall pages 44, 95, 121, 171, 207, and 217; Carsten Pennier page 139; Charyce LeClaire page 45; Courtney Edwin page 215; Courtney Smith page 147; Curtissa Green page 98; Cymelle Edwards page 43; Damien Rose page 106; Darius Smith page 242; Darryl Daley pages 112, 222, and 223; Deanna Martin page 68; Delia Gilliams' daughters, pages 87 and 99; Denise Greene page 202 and 255; Elbert Faust, Jr via his eldest daughter Kate Faust page 106; Eliane page 253; Gabriela Senises, pages 95 and 131; Gabrielle Brady page 80; Gioncarlo Valentine pages 131 and 170; The Gray family, from Jamaica, pages 211 and 267; Heather Butler pages 218 and 250; The Hinson/Hogg/Murray family page 196; Jakeelah White page 259; Jasmine Miah page 43; Jason Segarra page 241; Jemilah Jonesi page 186; Jennifer Danticat page 141; John Weatherall pages 85, 120, and 282; Ka'Jai Lewis page 197; Keath Day page 281; Kelli McKinney page 65; Khari Shiver pages 78 and 112; Khiyanna Jackson page 147; Kimberly Anderson pages 26, 68, 178, 179, 240, 276, and 277; Krow page 56; Kya Winbush pages 58 and 214; The Lewis family page 86; Marcus Kwame Anderson page 92; Matt Miller page 64; Mia Wyatt page 283; Michael Grant pages 27, 42, and 254; N'ya Evans page 210; Nia June pages 213 and 262; Nicole Counts pages 31, 102, 233, and 258; Peri (Ellis) pages 81 and 249; Producer Sango's great grandmother Arizona Frazier-Lisco and her brother J.V. Frazier page 223; Quinci Baker page 238; The Reagan family page 263; Robertson/Wilson Family page 86; Roderick Huntley Jr. pages 173 and 238; Rodney Cooper Jr. page 119; Sabriaya Shipley page 84; Sabrina Williams pages 236 and 237; Sadiyah Sabree page 114; Seren Sensei pages 28, 29, and 52; Shefon Taylor page 202; The Shepard and Phifer families page 114; Syreeta Gates/The Gates Preserve pages 54 and 133; Taja Sparks page 145; Taniya Williams page 146; Tara Hagins pages 79, 80, 176, 177, and 266; Tayah Young page 109; Taylor Anderson page 107; Taylor Dickinson page 115; Taylor Jones pages 25 and 53; Thessalonia Thomas page 103; Todd Sanders page 119; Tracey Davis pages 53 and 131; Travis Graham page 281; Tye Matthews Almonte page 252; William Marcellus Armstrong page 57.

ACKNOWLEDGMENTS

Thank you, God, for making a way.

Infinite gratitude to my maternal bloodline, those named and unnamed, including: Theresa, Corrine, Estellar, Cora, and Brenda. To my mom, Patricia, and my dad, Edwin, for lending their everlasting love and support through this realm and through the next. My partner, Gene, and our daughter, Geanna. Sylvia, Dominique, Dante, Ronsonet, Carla, Chauncey, Markale, Gilbert, Regene, Alexis, Malachi, Lauren, Mercy, Lisa, Myka, and Steven.

To my editors, Kaitlin Ketchum and Nicole Counts: your guidance and infinite wisdom have been lifesavers while embarking on one of the biggest projects of my life. Thank you for helping our family's legacy to live on. Thank you to designer Annie Marino, production manager Serena Sigona, production editors Ann Spradlin and Ashley Pierce, marketer Monica Stanton, and publicist Felix Cruz at Ten Speed Press.

Thank you to my village. Thank you to my community. Thank you to all who share my work and keep the work lifted in rooms and conversations.

Thanks also to Titus, Lutish, Eddie, Damion, Dominique, Randall, Damion II, Chauncey II, Chauncey III, Chaunacey, Leoniquia, Chelsey, Royce, Ta'Nyha, Yazmiyn, Braylen, Ziodonee, Deondre, Airyanna, Zayden, Kathy, Raymond, Wesley, Zoey, Nico, Theodore, Sadie, Juvada, Anita, Jakki, Kenneth, Timothy, Ms. Pamela, and Ms. Lorraine.

ABOUT THE AUTHOR

Renata Cherlise is a multidisciplinary, research-based visual artist and memory worker who uses various mediums to explore themes of identity and familial interiors within Black communities.

Born and raised in Jacksonville, Florida, Cherlise's projects bridge her southern upbringing with contemporary methodologies in digital spaces while reimagining themes in literature, history, and photography to render new perspectives of the Black experience. These ideas became the foundation for Black Archives, a multimedia platform founded by Cherlise in 2015 that spotlights the Black experience and incorporates archival imagery and histories through visual explorations of a Black past, present, and future. Going beyond the norm, Black Archives examines the nuance of Black life, from the alive and ever-vibrant to the everyday and iconic, providing insight and inspiration to those seeking to understand the legacies that preceded their own.

See more of Black Archives at www.blackarchives.co or @blackarchives.co on social media.

Published in the United States by Ten Speed Press, an imprint of Random House, a division of Penguin Random House LLC, New York.
TenSpeed.com
RandomHouseBooks.com

Ten Speed Press and the Ten Speed Press colophon are registered trademarks of Penguin Random House LLC.

Photo credits are listed on pages 284 and 285.

Typefaces: A2 Types's New Grotesk Square and Linotype's Neue Haas Grotesk

Library of Congress Control Number: 2022942084

Hardcover ISBN: 978-1-9848-5929-7
eBook ISBN: 978-1-9848-5930-3

Printed in China

Editors: Nicole Counts and Kaitlin Ketchum
Production editors: Ashley Pierce and Ann Spradlin
Designer: Annie Marino | Production designer: Claudia Sanchez
Production manager: Serena Sigona | Prepress color manager: Nick Patton
Copyeditor: Kaisha-Dyan McMillan | Proofreader: Bridgit Monroe Itkin
Publicist: Felix Cruz | Marketer: Monica Stanton

10 9 8 7 6 5 4 3 2

First Edition